MURDER
...by the grace of God

...to Avro Manhattan who struck on the plot

Lucien Gregoire
Friend-Biographer John Paul I

Did his struggle for basic human rights and dignity
for born-out-of-wedlock children, the handicapped, women,
the remarried, homosexuals and the poor
cost him his life?

authorHOUSE®

AuthorHouse™ LLC
1663 Liberty Drive
Bloomington, IN 47403
www.authorhouse.com
Phone: 1-800-839-8640

© 2013 by Lucien Gregoire. All rights reserved.

No part of this book may be reproduced, stored in a retrieval system, or transmitted by any means without the written permission of the author.

Published by AuthorHouse   09/17/2013

ISBN: 978-1-4772-9966-1 (sc)
ISBN: 978-1-4772-9965-4 (hc)

Library of Congress Control Number: 2012923728

The use of names, symbols or other references to the CIA or other organizations is solely to identify these organizations and should not be construed as endorsement by these organizations of any material in this book.

Any people depicted in stock imagery provided by Thinkstock or by any other licensor are models, and such images are being used for illustrative purposes only. Cover portrait by Roberto Macedo Alves is the exclusive property of the author and protected by copyright. See Appendix for specific sources of imagery in this book.

Because of the dynamic nature of the Internet, web addresses or links contained in this book may have changed since publication and may no longer be valid. The views expressed in this work are solely those of the author and do not necessarily reflect the views of the publisher; the publisher hereby disclaims any responsibility for them.

Actual words spoken by real people and biblical quotations in this book are in Estrangelo Edessa font. Some statements attributed to Albino Luciani have been condensed by the author but in no way do they take out of context what was actually said on specified occasions.

A few kind words

"Yes, I remember him. He was all you say he was, and much more. My hope for a more just church and a better world died with him."
Archbishop Bruce Simpson

"In revealing the dark secret that must have haunted him all his life, Gregoire forces the transformation of Christianity."
Toby Johnson, *White Crane Journal*

"One beautiful life explodes into a trail of death and destruction in the Roman Catholic Church."   Howard Jason Smith, *Boston Globe*

"Well reached exposé on how the United States controls the political destiny of other nations including the Vatican."   John Flynn, *The Guardian*

Table of Contents

Author		5
Introduction	Foreword to Murder	7
Chapter 1	The Murder of John Paul I	17
Chapter 2	The Worst of Children to the Best of Men	33
Chapter 3	The Minor Seminary at Feltre	48
Chapter 4	The Tyrant of Feltre	57
Chapter 5	The Seminary at Belluno	60
Chapter 6	The Politics of Albino Luciani	73
Chapter 7	His Ministry	81
Chapter 8	Murder in Fatima	105
Chapter 9	The Marxist Movement in the Church	117
Chapter 10	How a Pope is Elected	120
Chapter 11	The Murders of Cardinal Filipiak and Cardinal Gracias	138
Chapter 12	The Murder of Cardinal Yu Pin	139
Chapter 13	The Good Guys vs. the Bad Guys	140
Chapter 14	His Papacy	150
Chapter 15	The Murder of Metropolitan Nikodim	160
Chapter 16	Appointment in Milan	166
Chapter 17	Appointment in Vittorio Veneto	173
Chapter 18	Murder in the Veneto	181
Chapter 19	Albino Luciani and General Patton	187
Chapter 20	The Mud in the Street	194
Chapter 21	The Politics of Ghosts	198
Chapter 22	A Conspiracy of Popes	208
Chapter 23	Scene of the Crime	210
Chapter 24	Providential Coincidence	225
Chapter 25	'Operation Pigeon' to the 'Grace of God'	227
Chapter 26	I have some cards for you...wanna play?	232
Chapter 27	Motive and Opportunity	256
Chapter 28	The Innocence of Autocratic Crimes	274
Chapter 29	A Conspiracy Buff's Delight	278
Chapter 30	The Murder of Paul Marcinkus	288
Chapter 31	The Swiss Guard Murders	296
Chapter 32	The Murder of Aldo Moro	304
Chapter 33	The Murder of Paul VI	340
Chapter 34	The Murder of Cardinal Villot	347
Chapter 35	The Great Vatican Bank Scandal	351
Chapter 36	The Vatican-Contra Affair	356
Chapter 37	The Vatican Bank Murders	363
Chapter 38	Tittle-Tattle of the Ages	378
Chapter 39	The War in Central America	383
Chapter 40	Baby Pigeons	389
Chapter 41	Ides of March	393
Chapter 42	The Murder of Cardinal Suenens	403
Chapter 43	*"...by the grace of God."*	407

John Paul I Memorial
Baltimore Basilica, Baltimore Maryland

The plaque fronting this tree reads: '…planted in memory of the 34-day Pope.' As we will demonstrate herein, if he died before midnight as the Vatican claimed—33-day Pope—he could have died of natural causes. If he died in the early morning hours as the embalmers claimed—34-day Pope—the case for murder is practically certain. Though he was actually the 34-day Pope, he is referred to as the 33-dayPope in this book to avoid confusion.

Author

Born in New England, *George Lucien Gregoire* completed his undergraduate and graduate work in Massachusetts schools. In connection with his work in cooperative education and as founder of organizations affording education to impaired children, he has served on secondary school and university boards.

He spent his professional career as an officer of American and European corporations and was an American industrialist operating in Central America dealing with the same banks the Vatican was involved with when 'The Revolution of the Poor' and 'The Great Vatican Bank Scandal' he speaks of in this book took place.

He spent most of his military service as a Pentagon officer in the Arctic Circle in connection with espionage activities up over the top during the Cold War, and was a NATO (CIA) agent operating out of Milan when he first made the acquaintance of John Paul in the sixties, when the Pope—a little known bishop of a mountain province in northern Italy—was leading the 'Priest-worker Movement' which eventually gave rise to the Communist Party in the polls.

Scope

Some claim the Vatican Bank had to do with his murder. Others claim the threat he was to the capitalistic tenets upon which the United States had been founded rallied the CIA to action. Others claim his threat to change doctrine that unfairly penalized the lives of innocent people drove curial cardinals in the clandestine deed. Still others whisper his sexual orientation led to his untimely demise.

'Murder by the Grace of God' methodically examines each of these possibilities and reveals how each of them played a role in the murder of the youngest pope to die in four hundred years and the only pope in history whose death was unwitnessed.

"...We must rise up the courage that is within us, and set aside the preferences that have been built into us by our Christian forefathers, and together we will muster the strength to lift those restraints unfairly placed upon the everyday lives of so many innocent people by doctrine... for God-given human life is infinitely more precious than is man-made doctrine."[1]

[1] College of Cardinals 28 Aug 78

Introduction

Foreword to Murder

In 1988, Avro Manhattan—the world's foremost authority on the Vatican in world politics[1]—warned of the papal threat to force economic movement toward Marxism in the western world:

> "The lack of importance the United States gave to the election of a pope after the death of pro-American Pius XII through the election of John Paul II has become paramount in the thinking of subversive elements in the United States—the lingering evidence too striking to be ignored.
>
> The failure of the United States to influence the election of a pro-American Pope in 1963 was a lesson not to be repeated. The blatant adverse consequence of that blunder enormous, the price astronomical in terms of lost opportunity and the deployment of policies and billions spent by the United States counteracting the subversive actions of Paul VI.
>
> Paul disseminated his pernicious and anti-American principles via encyclicals condemning the basic capitalistic tenets upon which the United States had been founded. He condemned the imperialism of money and private property claiming to give wealth and land to the poor was to give them God's province...
>
> Paul's doctrine 'Liberation Theology'[2] took on horrendous roots where the poor were collectively dominant in Latin America, the stability of which was severely threatened. When they reached Central America, military and undercover operations had to be undertaken by the United States to halt his revolution of the poor.
>
> His doctrine 'Populorum Progressio'[3]—every man a fair share—fueled the movement toward communism in Europe forcing CIA intervention in Italy where Paul's devoted ally Aldo Moro's 'Historic Compromise'[4] threatened to bring about a communist state.

Murder by the Grace of God

In the spring of 1978, Moro was kidnapped while enroute to the House of Representatives on the morning he was scheduled to move communist ministers into control of Italian Parliament.

In the wake of the Moro murder, Paul's sudden and unexplained death was wrapped with subtle speculations and vague rumors. His deterioration had been so extremely unusual whispers concerning the acceleration of his demise circulated.

These suspicions were well justified when his death was met with delight in the headquarters of the CIA and the Pentagon which had labeled him the 'Pro-Communist Pope.'

Nevertheless, the providential death of Paul VI gave the CIA the opportunity to carry out its scheme to force election of a pro-American Pope. It joined factions inside the Church backing the Opus Dei anti-Communist candidate Polish Cardinal Karol Wojtyla...

When the avowed Marxist—Albino Luciani—was elected it struck a nerve of shattering proportions in the United States. In CIA headquarters the ball began to roll..."[5]

Baron Manhattan

The last days of Avro Manhattan

By mid-1990, courts investigating the wave of bombings in Italy in the 1970s, CIA terrorist activities in Central America in the 1980s, and the Great Vatican Bank Scandal, yielded great credence to what until then had been not much more than Manhattan's suspicions.[6]

Among other things, the courts proved *The Parallel SID*—a coalition of American and Italian Intelligence—had carried on vast bombings of civilian targets in Italy and wrongly framed communist youth groups to turn the mindset of the Italians against communism.

In early November 1990, a leak disclosed Avro Manhattan was writing a book proving: 'the conspiracy that masterminded the Great Vatican Bank Scandal was the same conspiracy that plotted the murder of John Paul I and other Marxist leaders in the Church.'[7]

This book—*Murder by the Grace of God*—is the book Avro Manhattan was writing when the Baroness Manhattan returned after a week in London to find him dead in their South Shields' home.[8]

Author's note: Baron Manhattan spent his life on the covers of world periodicals. To shroud the nature of his death, no obituary appeared in any newspaper in the world including Milan where he was born and London where he spent most of his celebrated life. A small post-burial notice appeared in the *South Shields Gazette*: 'A service held yesterday at St. Aidan's was followed by interment at Benfieldside cemetery ... " Whispers linger he shot or hung himself—not known; one has to assume he killed himself at the precise time he was in the process of bringing his lifelong work to fruition. Cause and date of death is unknown. Most biographies cite it as November 1990.

The last days of Albino Luciani

On **August 6, 1978**, Pope Paul VI died at Castel Gandolfo.

Cardinal Yu Pin, Archbishop of Taiwan and Marxist leader in the Eastern Hemisphere who controlled the eastern bloc of votes needed by Luciani to win the papal election, keeled over at Paul's funeral.[9]

Upon the election of Albino Luciani, who took the name *John Paul the First,* CIA affiliate Chicago Cardinal Cody accompanied a disgruntled Polish Cardinal Karol Wojtyla back to Krakow.[10]

On **September 1, 1978**, the new Pope called for a review of the Vatican bank including an accounting of the Church's worldwide assets in the interest of liquidating dead assets to support the *revolution of the poor* in Central America. The image of children literally starving to death gnawed at his everyday conscience.[11]

On September 3, 1978, in St. Peter's Square he hugged Rome's communist mayor in an embrace usually reserved for one's father.[12]

On **September 5, 1978**, he held an audience with Metropolitan Nikodim—youthful leader of the Russian Orthodox Church—at the time suspected to be—today known to have been—a KGB agent.

Enemies of ecumenism in the Vatican viewed the meeting as a step toward uniting the two branches of Catholicism now separated for a thousand years. The CIA viewed it as an attempt to seek Soviet arms support for revolutionaries struggling against American backed ruthless dictators in Central America. Nothing came of the meeting as Nikodim fell dead at John Paul's feet after sipping coffee.[13]

On **September 12, 1978**, Polish Cardinal Wojtyla flew back to Italy where he spent a week with two bishops who shared the papal palace with John Paul—Agostino Casaroli and Giuseppe Caprio; men he would soon promote past two hundred others that outranked them to the 2nd and 3rd most powerful positions in the Church.[14]

On **September 13, 1978**, Enrico Berlinguer—head of the Italian Communist Party—showed up at the Papal Palace; perceived by the CIA as an attempt to resurrect the 'Historic Compromise' designed to put communist ministers into control of Italian Parliament which mission had been sidelined by the recent murder of Aldo Moro.[15]

In early September it was no surprise appraisers showed up in the Vatican Museum as the new Pope had threatened the hypocrisy of the Vatican treasures for years. The surprise came when a real estate outfit showed up on **September 17, 1978** to survey the papal retreat at Castle Gandolfo—a resort of five sprawling palaces sitting on the Mediterranean among the most valuable real estate in the world.[16]

On **September 20, 1978**, came the most controversial statement of his brief papacy: "Ubi Lenin, ibi Jerusalem." "Where Lenin is, there is Jerusalem." 'Jerusalem' is synonymous with 'Paradise' in the Bible. The CIA quickly tabbed John Paul I the 'Bolshevik Pontiff.'[17]

On **September 22, 1978**, the 'Bolshevik Pontiff' changed the theme of the Puebla Conference in Mexico from 'Liberation Theology' to 'Liberation of the Poor' and announced he would preside over it.

The man who had once led the *priest-worker revolution* which had given rise to the Communist Party in the polls in Italy would now lead the *revolution of the poor* in Central America against the coalition of ruling juntas and the United States. In the United States *'revolution of the poor'* was then and still is today— *'communism.'*[18]

On **September 26, 1978**, John Paul scheduled an all-day private audience for October 24th with the Scheuer Group—an American group that supported the 'pill.' He would sanction the 'pill' to end the driving force behind poverty and starvation—overpopulation.[19]

On **September 27, 1978**, lifting a chalice to worldwide television cameras he threatened the Vatican treasures: "This chalice contains one hundred and twenty-two of the world's most pristine diamonds while children all over the world starve to death. Do you really think this is what Christ meant by His Church?"[20]

In each of his four public audiences he defined the scope of his papacy: "My job is not about this man or that man. It is about people who are hungry."[21]

John Paul's last words to Cardinal Colombo—his long time ally in his struggle to rid the world of poverty—demonstrates the supreme confidence he had in accomplishing his lifelong dream: "Sadly, Giovanni, when we have completed our work and everyone has enough; there will always be those who want too much."[22]

The threat of communism in Italy had resurfaced. The perils of a swell of mini-Cubas in America's backyard loomed on the horizon. The dangers to the security of the United States had become real.

Murder by the Grace of God – its sources

In 1984, David Yallop published *In God's Name* and, in 1989, John Cornwell published *A Thief in the Night*. These bestsellers still reign today as the premier books concerning John Paul's death.

Both these men are reputable world-renowned journalists. One can trust what they reported was the truth. One knows this for a more definitive reason. Most of their witnesses were alive after their books were released and the press confirmed the testimony they had published. However, neither Yallop nor Cornwell subjected their witnesses to the scrutiny of a court of law. That we will do now.

Moreover, we have a key witness for the prosecution not before heard from. Crucial testimony as to what happened to the money that disappeared in Central America in the *Great Vatican Bank Scandal* is my chat with Paul Marcinkus, President of the IOR depository.

Then one has my friend Jack. Some of what I speak of here is the record of our conversations and correspondence:

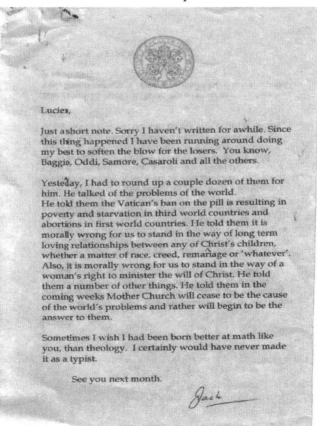

Lucien,

Just a short note. Sorry I haven't written for awhile. Since this thing happened I have been running around doing my best to soften the blow for the losers. You know, Baggio, Oddi, Samore, Casaroli and all the others.

Yesterday, I had to round up a couple dozen of them for him. He talked of the problems of the world. He told them the Vatican's ban on the pill is resulting in poverty and starvation in third world countries and abortions in first world countries. He told them it is morally wrong for us to stand in the way of long term loving relationships between any of Christ's children, whether a matter of race, creed, remarriage or 'whatever'. Also, it is morally wrong for us to stand in the way of a woman's right to minister the will of Christ. He told them a number of other things. He told them in the coming weeks Mother Church will cease to be the cause of the world's problems and rather will begin to be the answer to them.

Sometimes I wish I had been born better at math like you, than theology. I certainly would have never made it as a typist.

See you next month.

Jack

Even then, this sole surviving record of Jack doesn't tell us anything the newspapers don't tell us about the 33-day Pope.

Then there is my direct testimony of the man himself. I don't want to mislead the reader, I was a lifelong acquaintance of Albino Luciani. If you count the fingers on your hands and toes on your feet you will have the number of times I sat down in conversation with the man. So I can speak with some reliability of his childhood and young priesthood and of his fundamental ideology. Yet, that is all.

Luciani's ideology is not necessarily consistent with my own. For the most part we operated on opposite sides of the political arena.

When I first met him, he was a bishop leading the *priest-worker movement*—the revolution of the poor in northern Italy. Conversely, I was a NATO Intelligence officer charged with the mission to crush the *priest-worker movement* and the communist ideals it represented.

When as a pope he announced his support for the *revolution of the poor* in Central America, I was an officer of a corporate giant allied together with the coalition of ruling juntas and the CIA in crushing the *revolution of the poor* in Central America and returning the war-torn isthmus to the stability inherent in a capitalistic society.

Nevertheless, the mainstay of my testimony is not 'me.' Nor is it the witness of Yallop and Cornwell and others. It is the press.

From the time he became a bishop in 1958, the press recorded his every move up to the moment he was found dead in his bed in the fall of 1978. As one knows, it followed him well beyond death.

Alluding to the Marxist threads bonding them together and the sudden and unexplained deaths within Vatican walls of Cardinal Yu Pin, Metropolitan Nikodim and John Paul I in rapid consecutive order as if a machine gun had mowed them down—not one of them subjected to autopsy—Italy's largest newspaper *Corriere della Serra* posted the bold headline:

Why No Autopsies? A Chinese, a Russian and now the Bolshevik Pontiff, himself. [23]

If you want what the Vatican wants you to know, listen to what its pawns have to say. I give you what the newspapers have to say: more than five hundred indisputable witnesses to the revolutionary life and mysterious death of Albino Luciani.

Why the rush?

Why the urgency? Why only thirty-three days into his papacy?

Had he lived another week to attend the Puebla Conference in Mexico, the United States would have been looking at a half-dozen mini-Cubas sitting in its backyard.
Don't take my word for it. Take his word for it:

"It is the inalienable right of no man to accumulate wealth beyond his needs while other men starve to death because they have nothing." [24]

Had he lived another month to meet with the Scheuer Group, he would have made contraception the mainstay of Catholic family life.
Don't take my word for it. Take his word for it:

"In contraception one can understand why people do not believe they are sinning. It would be prudent not to disturb them... I recommend the anovulant pill developed by Professor Pincus be adopted as the Catholic birth-control pill." [25]

Had he lived long enough to complete his mission he would have destroyed the 'benevolent' capitalistic world we live in.
Don't take my word for it. Take his word for it:

"Charity is an excuse for individual compassion in a selfish world. It is the duty of society and should not be the option of its citizens." [26]

Note: Insofar as *Murder by the Grace of God* presents compelling evidence linking prominent American and Italian statesmen to the murders of Aldo Moro, Russian Orthodox leader Metropolitan Nikodim, Pope John Paul I and other leaders of the Marxist movement in the western world, the author reminds the reader it was the sworn duty of these men imposed upon them by the laws of their nations to head off what they viewed as a dangerous slide to the *left*.

Murder by the Grace of God

The strange set of circumstances that caused three men to sleep in the great bed in the Papal Apartment in the fall of 1978

CIA Director George Bush - Paul VI - John Paul I - John Paul II - Benedict XVI

1 Avro Manhattan wrote the all-time best selling 'Vatican' book *The Vatican in World Politics*
2 Paul's *Liberation Theology* in 1969 ignited a clergy-led *revolution of the poor* in Central America
3 Paul's *Populorum Progressio* in 1967 ignited the clergy led *priest-worker movement* in Italy which gave rise to the Communist and Socialist Parties in the Italian polls
4 Backed by Paul VI, Moro united his Christian Democratic Party (38.8%) with the Communist Party (34.4%) in the *Historic Compromise* positioning the coalition to control Italian Parliament.
5 Avro Manhattan's *The Dollar and the Vatican* 1988 pgs 130-142, summarized by the author; the central premise in Avro Manhattan's *Murder in the Vatican* (1985) and other of his books of the 1980s.
6 Prime Minister Andreotti confessed to Parliament the existence of *The Parallel SID* on October 24, 1990. The document was published in the December 1990 issue of *Panorama*. It confirmed Italian court findings that the CIA had conspired with Italian Intelligence in the bombings
7 *BBC News*, 7 Nov 90
8 Date of death is unknown; most sources list it as Dec or Nov 1990.
9 *L'Osservatore* 17 Aug 78
10 *Malopolska Silesia* 7 Sep 78 . Cody, a friend of CIA Director William Colby and a frequent visitor to CIA headquarters is claimed by most historians to have been a CIA subversive agent
11 *L Osservatore* 3 Sep 78
12 *La Repubblica* 4 Sep 78
13 *L Osservatore* 6 Sep 78
14 *Genova Secolo XIX* 13 Sep 78
15 *L'Unita* 14 Sep 78
16 *Il Tempo* 18 Sep 78
17 *La Repubblica* 21 Sep 78 Realizing his use of the word 'Lenin' might be misconstrued, he qualified what was going on in the Soviet Union was not paradise—it had never been a free communist society
18 *L'Osservatore* 23 Sep 78
19 *Washington Post* 27 Sep 78
20 *La Stampa* 28 Sep 78
21 *L Osservatore* 28 Sep 78; repeated this in each of his audiences. Sept 28 film clip is on You Tube.
22 *Corriere Della Sera* Milan 30 Sep 78. Via phone just before he retired for the last time.
23 *Corriere Della Serra* 6 Oct 78
24 *La Repubblica* 28 Sep 78; John Paul I last public audience televised. This film clip is on You Tube.
25 *Messaggero Mestre* 28 Jul 68
26 *Messaggero Mestre* 22 Jan 76. Paraphrased in his letter to St Therese in his book *Illustrissimi*

Important people in this book

Cardinal Benelli: Archbishop of Florence. He was in the midst of lining up opposition in the College of Cardinals to block the ratification of the Opus Dei Prelature when he met his sudden death.

George Bush: CIA Director. The author presents compelling evidence linking the future president to the Vatican bank scandal.

Roberto Calvi: President Banco Ambrosiano. Found hanging under Blackfriars Bridge—believed to have been lured to London by Opus Dei and P2 on the guise of a loan to get him out of his predicament.

Bishop Caprio: Treasurer of the Vatican bank. He handled the technicalities of the bank scandal transactions to Nicaragua. One of two bishops having access to John Paul the night he died; promoted to the 3rd most powerful position in the Church by John Paul II.

Bishop Casaroli: Vatican Foreign Minister. One of two bishops having access to John Paul the night he died; promoted to the 2nd most powerful position in the Church by John Paul II. As President of the Vatican bank directed the Vatican bank scandal transactions.

Cardinal Delargey: Archbishop of Wellington. Young friend of John Paul I died mysteriously shortly after John Paul II was elected.

Alois Estermann: Commander of the Swiss Guard. He, his wife and his alleged young lover Corporal Cedric Tornay were murdered in his Vatican apartment. Known to be the closest confidant of John Paul II, the author presents compelling evidence Estermann was the guard assigned to the post closest to John Paul I the night he died.

Cardinal Felici: Prefect Tribunal of the Apostolic Signatura. The Vatican's chief counsel was in the midst of investigating Opus Dei' involvement in the Vatican bank scandal when he dropped dead a few minutes after drinking wine in the consecration of the Mass.

Cardinal Filipiak: Archbishop of Gniezno. This archenemy of John Paul II died mysteriously the day before John Paul II's election.

Licio Gelli: Grandmaster of the Masonic Lodge P2. Of the Mafia and other killer organizations, P2 was the only one with a presence in the Vatican the night of John Paul's death.

Angelo Roncalli: John XXIII. Started the movement to transform the Church from what it had become—a symbol of wealth and ritual and preferences—back to the Church for all Christ had intended.

Murder by the Grace of God

Albino Luciani: John Paul I. That the Vatican was caught in a series of lies concerning his unwitnessed death gave rise to rumors of foul play. When elected, he was billed a 'liberal' by the Italian press.

Paul Marcinkus: President of the IOR. He got caught up in the Vatican bank scandal under John Paul II. Found dead a week after a court trying the Mafia for Calvi's murder attempted to extradite him.

Aldo Moro: Leader of the Christian Democratic Party during the reign of Paul VI. Kidnapped (subsequently murdered) on the day he was going to move communist members into control of Parliament.

Giovanni Montini: Paul VI. He stacked the College of Cardinals to elect Albino Luciani. Paul died under suspicious circumstances.

Metropolitan Nikodim: Archbishop of Leningrad and youthful Marxist leader of the Russian Church and KGB subversive agent code name 'Adamant' fell dead at John Paul I's feet after sipping coffee.

Carmine Pecorelli: Renowned journalist who was about to publish 'The Role of the CIA and Italian Intelligence in the Moro Murder' when assassinated. His office and the manuscript destroyed by fire.

Cardinal Ratzinger: Prefect of the Congregation of the Faith. After the assassination attempt of John Paul II, he was moved by Opus Dei to the Vatican to position him to replace the Pope if necessary.

Cardinal Suenens: Archbishop of Brussels. This liberal leader of the Church died under circumstances identical to those of John Paul I: 'Sitting up in bed reading a book clutched upright in his hands.'

Cardinal Vagnozzi: Prefect of Economic Affairs. Found dead in his apartment while conducting an audit of the Vatican bank.

Cardinal Villot: Secretary of State. His sudden death followed those of Paul VI and John Paul I. The bank scandal could not have taken place as long as he remained president of its central bank.

Cardinal Violardo: Paul VI's 'voice' in Italian Parliament and friend of Aldo Moro. He was found dead under a stairway in a darkened corner of the Vatican bank on the same day Moro was kidnapped.

Cardinal Wojtyla: Archbishop of Krakow & John Paul II. *Murder by the Grace of God* answers the question: How it is possible the same constituency of cardinals elected a liberal—Luciani—in one election and just a few weeks later elected a conservative—Wojtyla?

Cardinal Yu Pin: Archbishop of Taiwan controlled eastern votes needed by Luciani to be elected; he keeled over at Paul VI's funeral. Cardinal Delargey who insisted on autopsy died shortly afterwards.

Chapter 1

The Murder of John Paul I

"Never be afraid to stand up for what is right, whether your adversary be your parent, your peer, your teacher, your politician, your preacher, your constitution, or even your God." [1]

Albino Luciani

The day he became a cardinal he spoke to a youth group in Venice. He honors Susan B. Anthony and Abraham Lincoln for their courage to have set aside the tenth commandment of their God which held women as mere property of men and protected the right of one man to enslave another:

"Thou shalt not covet thy neighbor his property including his house, his wife, his slaves... "

Thirty-three days into his papacy, the youngest pope to die in four hundred years and the only pope in the two-thousand year history of the Church whose death was unwitnessed was found dead in his bed.

At seven-thirty on the morning of September 29, 1978, Vatican Radio broadcast the following bulletin:

> "Pope John Paul died before midnight last evening of myocardial infarction to the heart. He was discovered by his secretary Magee at six-thirty this morning who went to look for the Pope when he failed to show up for his morning chapel service... The bed lamp was on and he was sitting up in bed in his daytime clothes wearing his spectacles reading the 'Imitation of Christ' which book was held upright in his hands... " [2]

Contradictions and rumors

The medical community did not delay a day. The Italian Medical Society issued the statement: "It is irresponsible for a doctor to infer heart attack in an unwitnessed death without autopsy of a man who has had no history either himself or family of heart disease." [3]

There were a few contradictions in the release itself.

Murder by the Grace of God

The embalmers told Italy's most reliable wire service—ANSA—in his hands were notes written on the stationary of Vittorio Veneto.

They also said they were picked up by a Vatican van shortly after five-thirty, an hour before the release said the body was found.

In addition, they were told by Swiss Guards a nun had discovered the Pope. It was their opinion John Paul had not been dead for much more than an hour or two as it was a cold morning and the windows were wide open and the body was still warm.[4]

The nun who had discovered the body was interviewed.

The clock that should have rung and did not ring

Sister Vincenza told reporters she routinely delivered coffee at four-thirty each morning. When she first knocked there was no answer. She waited a minute or so and knocked again, this time a bit louder. It was obvious the Pope was still in the bathroom.

Though he normally woke at about four o'clock it was his custom to set his alarm clock for a few minutes before four-thirty in the event he overslept. If he was sleeping, the alarm would be ringing loud enough to wake the dead. At least, that is what she thought.

This meant he had risen at his usual time of about four o'clock and had completed his first task of each day—turned off the alarm.

She opened the door and entered the room intending to leave the tray on his nightstand.

The light was on. He was sitting up in bed in his daytime clothes reading papers held upright in his hands. She greeted him: "Good morning." He resembled a mime deeply engrossed in his reading.

It was not unusual for him once dressed for the day to be sitting up in bed reading when she delivered coffee. Vincenza, who had served him for twenty years, had come to know this man as a jovial one, always smiling, sometimes laughing and often joking.

At first she thought it was a joke. After all, he was smiling.

Actually, she knew it was a joke. He was wearing his glasses. Though nearsighted and required them to walk across the room, he did not require them to read. That is, to read in private.

Yet, someone not close to him would think he required them to read because he always wore them when reading from the pulpit to allow him to view his audience.

Nearsighted prescriptions provide for clear vision from twenty feet to infinity. At ten feet they begin to have a detrimental effect on vision. At normal reading length they can be as much as twenty times out of alignment. The practice is to read below the frame or use bifocals with a clear reading segment. John Paul wore bifocals.

Regardless, disturbed by the prank, Vincenza approached the bed: **"Please don't joke with me in this way, Albino."** As she placed the tray on the stand she realized something was wrong.[5]

Her testimony confirmed that of the embalmers: he was holding papers and not a book in his hands. More importantly, he had been discovered dead shortly after four-thirty and not at six-thirty.

That the clock should have rung and did not ring raised the eyebrows of the Agatha Christie buff. The Pope had turned it off or someone else who knew his practice had turned it off. Electric, it would have been ringing when the nun was at the door.

Any detective will tell you when one investigates murder, one must consider not only the evidence which is there, but also the evidence which should be there and is not there.

In the case of Hercule Poirot's *Hickory Dickory Dock*, we have the light bulb which should have been there and was not there. In the case of Sherlock Holmes' *Silver Blaze*, we have the dog which should have barked and did not bark. In the case of the 33-day Pope, we have the alarm clock which should have rung and did not ring.

Cardinals to be replaced

These contradictions of the embalmers and the nun gave birth to a rumor the notes held in the Pope's hands were listings of cardinals to be replaced; he was planning a shakeup of the Church's hierarchy—something that had been expected ever since he had been elected.

It was no secret Benelli would replace Villot as Secretary of State something both cardinals looked forward to. Benelli had been the architect of Luciani's election and was more than qualified to head up both the Church's banking and administration. Villot was looking forward to living in Rome and teaching in the Gregorian University.

But who were the others? Why was there such concern?

Other than this, there was concern about only one job. Except for the incumbent who would lose his job, the others didn't mean much.

The Prefect of the Doctrine of the Congregation of the Faith—the chief theologian of the Church—dictates the morals of the Catholic world. It was rumored the Archbishop of Utrecht Willebrands who had an open mind toward contraception, married priests, ordained women and an understanding of homosexuality would get the job.

This was sound as the Curial post Willebrands held—President of the Secretariat for Christian Unity—interfaced directly with the Prefect of the Doctrine of the Congregation of the Faith position and was viewed as a stepping stone to it. Yet, there was more than that.

In mid-September, John Paul had scheduled a symposium of opposing left-wing and right-wing bishops to examine these issues. He named Willebrands as its chair—the kind of assembly normally led by the Prefect of the Doctrine of the Congregation of the Faith.[6]

Poisoning

That the embalmers were roused from their sleep so early in the morning fired rumors of poisoning. It was the practice of the Mafia to embalm immediately after death to erase signs of arsenic and other poisons when they were the instrument of murder—the reason it was illegal in Italy to embalm until twenty-four hours after death.

Of course, Italian law did not apply in the Vatican. Yet, it had been the Vatican's practice to adhere to the law ever since it came into effect in 1946—embalming of popes had been delayed for twenty-four hours. This included Pius XII, John XXIII and Paul VI.

In the case of John Paul, ANSA News reported embalmers were roused at five in the morning, an hour and a half before the Vatican claimed the body had been found.[7]

A super sleuth reporter eventually verified the ANSA report by publishing a Vatican motor pool log proving a van was dispatched at 5:23AM on the morning John Paul's death to pick them up.[8]

There is the possibility one wanted to avoid a repetition of what had happened in the cases of Pius and Paul where skin discoloration and odor presented problems in the viewings. Yet, if this was true, why not summon the embalmers at a more reasonable time like eight o'clock which would have allowed more than ample time for the embalming before the first viewing in the St. Clementine Chapel at noon and would have avoided raising unnecessary suspicions.[9]

The bell cord

Most questionable of all was something killed him so suddenly he was unable to reach for the bell cord which hung a whisker from his right shoulder. This would have summoned in an instant the guard at the entrance to the corridor leading to the Pope's chambers. Also, he was not afforded time to press one of the service buttons on the intercom just to his left which would have brought to his side any one of five people who resided elsewhere in the palace that night.

John Paul also had the option of pressing an emergency button on the bedside console which would have activated a flashing light in the corridor just outside his quarters and buzzed the guard.

The Vatican newspaper reported an interesting coincidence.

On the previous morning maintenance workers happened to have tested the bell cord something that had not been done for years as Pope Paul always used the intercom. The bell rang so loud those in the palace thought it to be a fire alarm and headed for the stairs.[10]

The time of death

The time of death is critical to the supposition the Pope died of natural causes. It is also critical to the supposition he was murdered.

As we will demonstrate in what is to follow, if he died before midnight—as the Vatican claimed—he could have died of natural causes. Yet, if he died in the early morning hours—as the embalmers claimed—the case for murder is practically certain.

If he died before midnight his light would have been on all night. Both the nun and the Vatican release were explicit the light was on. This is consistent with he would not be reading in the dark.

The light was considered of very little importance by others. John Cornwell in *A Thief in the Night* does not mention it at all. David Yallop in his book *In God's Name* explains, **'The light had remained unnoticed all night by Vatican security guards.'** I don't think so.

Murder by the Grace of God

At the upper right hand corner of the palace building, the papal bedroom—the highest point in the outer perimeter of the Vatican—is in full open view of hundreds of hotels and apartment houses in the surrounding baroque district of Rome.

What's more, hundreds of tourists roam the vicinity into the wee hours of the night.

In addition, a small battalion of police guard the square round the clock.

Those, who hang their hat on the idea John Paul died before midnight, depend on the chance not a single person noticed the light was on all night.

papal bedroom top-right

That the light was not on all night was reported by a number of witnesses in the days following the Pope's death. We know the Pope's light was not on all night for more definitive reasons will we discuss later in this book.[11]

Too, if the Pope had died just before midnight the previous day, why would he be dressed in his daytime clothes? If one decides to read oneself to sleep one first dons one's bedtime clothes.

On October 10, 1978 Vatican Radio issued a corrected bulletin:

"While the death of John Paul came as a surprise, there was the fact the Pope suffered from a serious low blood pressure condition and was in very poor health and frail throughout his brief papacy. In his last days his legs were so swollen he could barely stand ...

John Paul did not have in mind to make revolutionary changes in the Vatican hierarchy...

We wish to correct our statement it was the Pope's secretary Magee who discovered the body. The Pope was first discovered by the nun who delivered his coffee at the usual time. When she sensed something wrong she summoned Magee...

We wish to correct our statement His Holiness was reading the 'Imitation of Christ.' This was a communications error. He was reviewing some notes. That he retained them upright in his hands in the midst of a massive heart attack is *by the grace of God...*

It is immaterial who found His Holiness. It is immaterial when he was found dead. It is immaterial when he died. All that is material is that he is dead..."[12]

Swollen legs vs. swollen ankles

Though it clung to its hypothesis of 'heart attack' which the medical world had all but demolished, the Vatican included 'swollen legs' in its 2nd release to set the stage for what would subsequently be its claim of 'pulmonary embolism.'

An embolism that results in near instant death—extremely rare—occurs when an enormous blood clot comes up from the legs and blocks the main artery leading to the lungs. A powerful pleuritic pain to the chest—different yet on a par with that of a heart attack—is followed by rapid beating of the heart ending in cardiac arrest.

David Yallop and John Cornwell conducted onsite investigations of the Pope's death. They interviewed medical and pharmaceutical personnel and established no Vatican doctor had treated him for any condition and no prescription was issued John Paul by the Vatican pharmacy during his brief papacy. Vatican doctors and pharmacists confirmed this to reporters after their books were published. [13]

Consequently, no Vatican doctor could be found to substantiate the Vatican's claims. Yet, one does have a competent witness.

Antonio Da Ros was the most qualified man in the world to write a book about the nature of John Paul's death and come up with a logical answer. He had not only been Luciani's person physician for twenty years, he had been one of his closest friends.

In his interview with Andrea Tornelli in 2003, Dr. Da Ros who had visited his friend John Paul three times during his brief papacy was asked about the swollen legs:

> "In the twenty years I knew him, he never spent a morning or an afternoon in bed. Luciani enjoyed extraordinary health, no heart, no dietary, no diabetic, no cholesterol problem...
>
> In the first week of his papacy there was slight swelling in the ankles; a long-standing condition with Luciani characteristic of mountain climbers who place undue pressure in vertical climbs.
>
> I advised him to walk more and from that time on he walked an hour or two each day in the roof garden. The condition was alleviated by the time of my third visit the week he died..." [14]

In his book *Illustrissimi* Albino Luciani, himself, speaks of this:

"He arrives at the cliff. He looks up, once, twice, many times. He makes his calculations. Here there must be a straight up climb, then a descent with double rope, then an ascent directly up over the ice.

He begins with a powerful respiratory system, a hardy heart and a driving ambition. He consults maps, makes notes, prepares a list of things he will need: backpack, rope, pulley, cord, pitons, wood wedge, axe, hammer, hooks, clips, shackles, spiked boots ... He chews gum and surveys the obstacles. He says, 'Maybe I'll make it.' Well, in the end, he really does make it. And what does he have for all this? Short-lived self-esteem and long-lived swollen ankles..." [15]

'Swollen legs' and 'swollen ankles' are very different conditions.

'Swollen legs' can be symptomatic of 'pulmonary embolism.' They are also consistent with 'high blood pressure.'[16]

Conversely, 'swollen ankles' are not consistent with 'pulmonary embolism.' Yet, they are consistent with 'low blood pressure.'[17]

At the time the Vatican issued its release of 'swollen legs and low blood pressure' it was thought by the medical community 'swollen legs' and 'embolisms' were consistent with 'low blood pressure.'[18]

But, today it is known low blood pressure has nothing to do with 'swollen legs' and 'embolisms'; 'high blood pressure' is the culprit. [19]

Herein we will present medical and criminology testimony in our examination of all of the possible ways the Pope could have died and heart attack and pulmonary embolism will not be among them.

As for now you will not find a cardiologist in the world who would testify in court, John Paul could have died of a heart attack or a massive embolus to the lungs and not have dropped his papers.

Low blood pressure

Reacting to the Vatican's claim of low blood pressure, a Venice newspaper published his physical exam of five months before his death which raised eyebrows concerning the alleged 'heart attack.'[20]

It showed him to be in extraordinary physical health. Yet, his blood pressure was normal—121 over 78.

This contradicted the Vatican's claim of 'low blood pressure' as at the time—1978—a count of 120 over 80 was considered optimal.

Giovanni Rama, the doctor who treated him for the condition, quickly corrected this misconception. He told reporters Luciani's blood pressure normally oscillated at about 100 over 60 and he had prescribed a small dosage of Effortil of five milliliters 3Xs a day which controlled Luciani's blood pressure at about 120 over 80.[21]

So Luciani's blood pressure did normally run on the low side.

You will not find a cardiologist in the world today who would not agree that low blood pressure is as surefire a prevention of heart attack and embolism that exists.[22]

The impracticality of death due to an arterial problem of any kind—given the position the body was found and his medical and family history—has been the subject of studies published in medical journals through the years.[23] That he did not succumb to either heart attack or embolism is the position of the medical community today.

The digitalis-Effortil rumor

Practically every author who has written about John Paul's death has plagiarized David Yallop's digitalis-Effortil theory—John Paul's Effortil was spiked with digitalis. Hence, being the strongest of rumors, we must put the digitalis-Effortil theory to 'sleep.'

Twelve drops—milliliters—of digitalis will kill in a few minutes.

Blurred vision and hallucinations are followed by abdominal pain and violent vomiting cumulating in congestive heart failure. In any event, one is certain to empty one's stomach.[24]

If digitalis was used to kill the Pope, it tells us something about the perpetrator(s). Only a novice would have employed the drug.

If nothing else the degree of vomiting it precipitates would ring a bell in the least suspicious doctor. Not a very wise choice when there are hundreds of lethal toxins which would have done the job with far less visible evidence. Vomiting is inconsistent with the position the body was found and none of those brought to the room mentioned it.

Hercule Poirot

One might wonder why so many authors ignored medical science and adopted the idea his Effortil had been spiked with digitalis?

Its creator—Agatha Christie—sold a lot of books.

Murder by the Grace of God

In the 1970s the 'Christie' market exploded on the heels of the box office buster motion pictures *Murder on the Orient Express* in 1974 and *Death on the Nile* in 1978—just before the Pope's death.

Adding digitalis to blood pressure medicine was first used by Agatha Christie in her mystery novel *The Secret of Chimneys* and subsequently in a number of her other works.

For example, consider the following dialogue from *Appointment with Death*, the most famous of Christie's plays starring the Belgium detective with the handlebar mustache—Hercule Poirot:

> Poirot *(scratching his temple):* "Digitoxin is a poison, is it not?"
> Dr. Gerard: "Yes, it is obtained from digitalis purpurea—the foxglove plant. There are four active elements: digitalin—digitonin—digitalein—and digitoxin which is the most deadly."
> Poirot *(with an inquisitive glare):* "And a dose of digitoxin?"
> Dr. Gerard *(gravely):* "A dozen drops of digitoxin thrown on the circulatory system would cause death by quick palsy of the heart."
> Poirot: "And, Mrs. Boynton had a heart condition?"
> Dr. Gerard: "Yes, she was taking a medicine containing digitalis to raise the blood pressure."
> Poirot: "Ah!" *(twisting his mustache)* "Quite interesting."
> Dr. Gerard: "You think digitoxin was added to her medicine?"
> Poirot: "Precisely. Digitalis is a cumulative drug. In a post mortem its presence would be owed to an overdose of her medicine..."
> Dr. Gerard: "Clever...clever. Most difficult to prove murder to a jury...The possibility of a mistake—or accident—overwhelming..."

The Belgium detective with the handlebar mustache is referring to one of those medicines grouped as 'digitalin' extracted from the foxglove plant to regulate the heart beat. For example: Lanoxin.

Whoever started the digitalis-Effortil rumor assumed Poirot was referring to Effortil because it was the most common medicine used to regulate the heart beat at the time of John Paul's death. Yet, whoever started the digitalis-Effortil rumor missed the boat.

Effortil is not extracted from the foxglove plant nor does it contain strains of digitalis. Effortil is Etilefrine Hydrochloride.[25] Nothing more, nothing less. Not of the digitalin' group, it would not have masked the presence of digitoxin in an autopsy. Too, unlike digitalin medicines one cannot overdose on Effortil. It is harmless.

With dozens of toxins that could have done the job effectively, digitalis would be a most foolish choice. Particularly when one considers there is no way the killer(s) could be certain an autopsy would not be performed. And that an autopsy would be performed was almost certain as John Paul's death was unwitnessed. Actually, in retrospect, it is mindboggling an autopsy was never performed.

I want the reader to stop and think about this for a moment.

When foul play is not suspected and one has no medical history of a life threatening illness, in the event of an unwitnessed death an autopsy is usually performed to determine cause of death.

Autopsy would be routine in the case of a head of state or any other person in the public eye. Yet, setting aside presidents and rock stars, consider one's own family. Why wouldn't one want to prevent the same thing happening to other family members?

That an autopsy was never performed is the most telling evidence Curial cardinals at the very least suspected foul play. Contrary to rumors there is no canon forbidding autopsy of a pope for cause.

Nevertheless, if the Pope had been taking Lanoxin it would make sense to spike it with digitalis as its presence in an autopsy would have been owed to the Pope's taking a medicine containing digitalis.

But, he was not taking Lanoxin. He was taking Effortil.

Too, John Paul's tiny dosage of Effortil diluted with digitalis might make him ill; it would have never killed him. It might make sense to spike his soup with digitalis, but not his medicine.

His Will

Concerning his Will, there are some things we know and other things we do not know. Among those things we know, Luciani willed he be interred in a plain pine box inscribed: 'Christ picked me up from the Mud in the Street and gave me to you.' The box was to be displayed behind a glass panel set into a side altar of the cathedral at Castlefranco in the Veneto country.[26]

The altar is dominated by Giorgione's Madonna framed by the soaring peaks of the Dolomites rising above the village of Canale d'Agordo where he was born and to the other side stand peasants in a meadow beneath the bishop's medieval castle at Vittorio Veneto. This would, of course, have exposed his corpse to autopsy.

We know from his Venice attorney he had willed his papers to the respective dioceses he had served. Yet, that his Will could not be found gave the Vatican sole authority to destroy records of anything he had said or done of a controversial nature. It prevented his family from demanding autopsy or anything construed as DNA today.

As we will explain later in this book, in the wake of his death teams showed up in Belluno, Vittorio Veneto and Venice destroying records of anything controversial he may have said or done.

Too, as a part of indoctrination an incoming pope is counseled by the papal attorney; in John Paul's case Pericle Felici. A pope's Will is a part of the process. At the very least, a rider is attached to the Will as the papacy dramatically changes one's legal position.

On becoming Pope one becomes a citizen of the Sovereign State of the Vatican and the Will must comply with its laws and not those of any other nation. Yet, there is much more than just that.

It is common for popes to include in their Wills their reflections on the direction the Church should take. In this respect, a pope's Will can—as it has on occasion in the past—be interpreted as doctrine. This is not usually a problem as popes normally conform to doctrine. Yet, in John Paul's case one has to consider he may have struck at the fundamental canon upon which the Church exists.

Certainly, he must have known he was in danger. The path his papacy had taken in the short term had not only alarmed many of those in his own ranks but his enemies across the pond as well.

He would have been a fool not to sense he might not live to attain the objectives he had worked all his life to achieve. He would have been a fool to have not set forth his intentions in his Will should he not live to bring them to fruition. Nevertheless, we have come to the suppositions regarding his Will—things we do not know.

Did his Will strike at the central doctrine of the Roman Catholic Church: **Some children are born better than others and are entitled to more?** Did he include in his Will the most prolific testimony of his ministry: **"We have made of sex the greatest of sins, whereas it is nothing more than human nature and not a sin at all?"**[27]

Did he strike at the integral core of canon law that invades the privacy of bedrooms? Did he change the definition of morality in the Church from what is acceptable in the bedroom in the minds of a bunch of old men in the Curia who have never been in the bedroom, to what is truly humanely right or wrong? One will never know.

What one does know, there existed at least nine copies of his Will: one hardcopy and one on microfilm in his attorney's office in Venice, a hardcopy in the diocese office in Venice, one hardcopy and another on microfilm in the Venice City Clerk's Office, one hardcopy and another on microfilm in the Vatican Office, one with his brother Edoardo, and a hardcopy held by his secretary Lorenzi. All of these disappeared simultaneously from the face of the earth.

Slipper socks, spectacles and a lock of hair

Some questions were raised by the Luciani family itself. His sister-in-law sought to recover a pair of slipper socks she had knitted for him. She knew, as a boy, he had often gone barefoot in the Italian Alps; she wanted to make sure he had something to keep his feet warm. They were white satin and had his coat of arms embroidered in gold on them. They may have been used to wipe a tinge of blood a needle or even a creature might leave. Regardless, they vanished.[28]

Then there were his spectacles. Though they were found on the body, they disappeared. It could be someone close to him who knew he did not require them to read—not involved in the deed itself—had been a part of a conspiracy; realizing a mistake had been made placing them on him, pocketed them. If they survived they would assay of foul play. Perhaps, they were just broken in the shuffle.[29]

A friend, in response to a request for a lock of hair, received a clump of jet black hair which she claimed was not his as his hair was graying. A strand of hair can assay of poison centuries afterwards.[30]

According to John Cornwell's *A Thief in the Night* which was commissioned by the Vatican, John Paul's niece spent a half-hour in the room alone with her uncle's corpse the morning of his death:

> "...he seemed to be smiling at me. His face showed no sign of suffering...There was something very strange. He was wearing his daytime clothes. Why would he not be wearing his pajamas if

reading in bed? ...The sleeves were all torn. Why should they be torn like that? I wondered..."[31]

One can trust the accuracy of her testimony. A devoted disciple of the Vatican, why else unnecessarily add fuel to the fire?

This was the first thing reporters went after when Cornwell's book was published. She never denied: "...both sleeves were badly torn."[32]

It is certainly ironic in death that he was smiling.

Of hundreds of photographs of his brief papacy, not one has survived in which he is not grinning from ear to ear—the reason he is remembered as the 'smiling pope.' For those who claim he broke under the weight of the papacy, he was having the time of his life.

The watch that ticked the time of death

We know from the testimony of those who shared his last dinner—a side from his usual conversation, laughing and joking—the Pope had been preoccupied with his new watch. He kept fumbling with it to determine if it was waterproof as it was his custom not to remove it for sleeping or even in the shower. It was of such an unusual design Vincenza remarked: "It looked like it had come out of 'Dr No.'"[33]

We also know from her testimony it had been Pasquale Macchi who delivered the watch to the Pope. It likely arrived in the mail as Macchi—serving in transition—handled the mail. It would have come from someone he would have accepted it from. We have the possibility a third person could have used the name of someone close to the Pope who they knew to be out of touch for a few days.

Like the slipper socks and the glasses, the watch vanished. Popes are prone to sainthood and potential relics are not normally returned to kin. Yet, Vatican Radio reported the Vatican archives never received them. Regardless, I will leave this with you to ponder with all the other baffling circumstances of this man's untimely death.

Scorpions

Finally, we have the scorpions for those who wish to nibble on them. Whereas a pale yellow scorpion allows the victim time to seek help, the giant golden mutation injects enough venom to kill a dozen men on the spot. The miniature desert in the gardens at the papal retreat Castel Gandolfo was home to this creature at the time.

Because its sting would have left the Pope in the position he was found and the coincidence the scorpions disappeared from the Castel Gandolfo after the Pope's death, it has found its way into books.

To employ a scorpion in the murder of a pope is surely a remote option. Yet, to get to the truth we must examine all the possibilities.

Nevertheless, we are left with some questions.

Who placed the spectacles on the nose of the man who did not need them to read? Who turned the light on which was not on all night? Who turned the alarm clock off which did not ring? Who dressed him up in his daytime clothes? Who tore his sleeves? Who gave him the watch that ticked the time of death? Was the watch set for the time of death? Who took the spectacles, the slipper socks and the watch? Who took the time to methodically destroy all nine copies of his Will and why? Who bred the scorpions at the Castel Gandolfo? Where did they go after John Paul's death?

There is only one absolute fact on which to build our case: the only circumstance of his death agreed to by all witnesses including the corrected Vatican release, his secretaries, the nun who found him, the embalmers and all others brought to his room:

'The bed lamp was on and he was sitting up in his daytime clothes wearing his glasses reading papers held upright in his hands.'

This leaves us with the glaring inconsistency the Pope could have remained in a sitting-up position with notes still clutched upright in his hands if he had suffered a massive heart attack. Only the most gullible accepted the Vatican's explanation *"...by the grace of God."*

Yet, it is from these few bits and pieces we must begin our work. From these few observations, employing the analysis and deduction techniques which lifted Sherlock Holmes to the top of his game, we will prove this good man was murdered. Yet, unlike our nineteenth century predecessor, we will not be dealing with the make-believe world of yesterday. We will be dealing with the real world of today.

We will prove beyond a shadow of doubt when he was murdered, how he was murdered, why he was murdered, who pulled the 'trigger,' and, most important of all, who ordered the dreadful deed.

Here, is the proof—the absolute proof—how John Paul and those around him fell victim to twentieth century capitalism as it was jointly embraced by the Vatican and the United States.

Murder by the Grace of God

Nevertheless, unless one first understands the mystery of his life, one will never be able to solve the mystery of his death.

So now let us step back to that time the little boy Albino Luciani would begin to mold his destiny. Let us walk with him through those years he would build his dream which would guide him to his fate— of two hundred and sixty-five popes and ten thousand cardinals the only one whose remains are triple-sealed in a lead-lined vault today.

Now, come. Let us talk with him. Let us walk with him in the woods together with his good friend Pinocchio and the Cat and the Fox and the Poodle Medoro. Let us bear witness as...

"One Beautiful Life explodes into a trail of death and destruction in the Roman Catholic Church."

Howard Jason Smith, Boston Globe

1 *Messaggero Mestre* 7 Mar 73; 10th commandment as it appears in all Bibles predating 1881
2 *Radio Vaticana* 29 Sep 78. *L'Osservatore Romano* posted a Curia edited synopsis
3 *La Repubblica* 1 Oct 78.
4 Mario di Francesco of the *ANSA News Agency, Italy's most reputable wire service* 29 Sep 78
5 *ANSA News,* 29 Sep 78   *La Repubblica* 1 Oct 78 and other newspapers reported variations. There is a rumor Vincenza told French reporters she had found the body in the bathroom; 'French reporters' who have never been identified or found. This, of course, would contradict her own testimony and the testimony of John Paul's secretaries Lorenzi and Magee and that of the official Vatican releases.
6 *Utrecht Socialist* 19 Sep 78
7 *ANSA News Agency* 29 Aug 78
8 *La Stampa* 12 Dec 89
9 *Associated Press* 5 Apr 05 Massimo Signoracci confirmed John Paul was embalmed at 11AM
10 *L'Osservatore Romano* 28 Sep 78
11 *La Repubblica* 3 Oct 78
12 *Radio Vaticana* 10 Oct 78 *L'Osservatore Romano* 11 Oct 78 posted excerpts
13 *La Repubblica* 3 Jul 84 – *La Stampa* 17 Dec 89
14 *Il Giornale* 27 Sep 03 Andrea Tornelli interview with Dr. Antonio Da Ros
15 *Messaggero di S Antonio* May 73 Albino Luciani's letter to Hippocrates
16 post-2000 medical dictionaries; search: swollen legs high blood pressure
17 post-2000 medical dictionaries; search: swollen ankles low blood pressure
18 pre-1985 medical dictionaries; search: swollen legs embolism low blood pressure
19 post-2000 medical dictionaries; search: swollen legs embolism high blood pressure
20 *Messaggero Mestre* 14 Oct 78
21 *Il Messaggero Romano* 16 Oct 78.
22 post-2000 medical dictionaries; search: low blood pressure heart attack embolism
23 *JAMA* Oct 79 - British Medical Journal 216
24 *Deadly Doses* Serita Stevens; search: digitalis symptoms
25 any medical dictionary; search: Effortil
26 *Nostro Veneto* 24 Jul 67. Also, direct witness author.
27 *Messaggero Mestre* 14 Nov 71 *La Repubblica* 18 Mar 77 He repeated this many times
28 *La Repubblica* 17 Oct 78
29 *Radio Vaticana* 22 Oct 78 '*Missing Spectacles?*' Vatican archive claims it never got the spectacles Popes are prone to canonization. Potential relics and are not returned to the family. He had two pair.
30 *La Repubblica* 2 Nov 78
31 *A Thief in the Night* John Cornwell
32 *Messaggero Mestre* 3 Nov 89 Lina Petri (Pia Luciani when she viewed the Pope's corpse)
33 *L'Osservatore Romano* 28 Sep 78. Vincenza refers to Ian Fleming the creator of *James Bond*

Chapter 2

The Worst of Children to the Best of Men

"I say to those who kneel mumbling before plaster dolls of 'Our Lady of the Mind.' May I suggest you should have devotion to the true lady 'Our Lady of the Pots and Pans,' the simple housewife, preparing the soup, peeling the potatoes, baking the bread..."[1]

Albino Luciani, Bishop Vittorio Veneto

Albino Luciani was born into dire poverty in a small village in the Italian Alps to a scullery maid and a migrant worker.

His mother was a devout Catholic who prayed before crucifixes made of bits of wood. She told him the only path to heaven was on his knees in prayer.

His father was a social activist atheist who burned his mother's crucifixes in the stove. He told him the only path to heaven was on his feet helping others.

When he was six years old, his grandfather told him, "Albino, today, you believe in Jesus and Santa Claus. Well," he apologized, "there is no Santa Claus. We've been kidding you."

He cried himself to sleep that night. How could they take Santa away from him? In his dreams he waved adieu to Santa, but he still had his Jesus. He pleaded, "Please don't take my Jesus from me."

The next day he trudged along the railroad tracks in the knee-deep snow. His shoes were tattered and worn and they did not match and his feet were frozen and they tormented him with each step. Yet he continued on, pausing here and there, filling his pail with scraps which had fallen from the rumbling coal cars.

A day earlier he had gazed through the store window at the golden crucifix. At three hundred lire a pail he needed three more pails full and he would have enough to buy this treasure for the best mamma in the world. A leer tinged his lips as he imagined his papa's frustration when he would try to burn this one. It broadened into a smile when he thought of the surprise and wonderment his mamma would have when she would open the gift on Christmas morn. He imagined her puzzled expression when she would read the card:

Murder by the Grace of God

> You gave him life; I gave him hope.
> Together for a time; we gave him paradise.
> Now my quest must end; but for you the work goes on.
> The struggle must endure; for the challenge remains.
> The hope is still there; for his dream must never die.
>
> Santa

The worst of children

The icicles poured like waterfalls from the rooftops all the way down to the walkways beneath them. In the summertime, each house had its own identity—its own personality - red - green - blue - orange. Each had been a tiny splinter in a magnificent rainbow. But, now in the wintertime, each was just one of an endless row of crystal figures in an enormous glass menagerie.

The parade of weather-beaten wooden carts moved through the tiny hamlet of Forno di Canale in the Italian Alps as they had every other morning. The snow was heaped so high on each side of the road for the most part they passed unseen.

Yet, the shouts of the barkers broke the stillness of the morning air: "milk - milk - milk," "cheese - cheese - cheese," "lamb - lamb - lamb," "bread - bread - bread," "eggs - eggs – eggs." Their voices echoing through the whitecapped rocky mountain gorge.

Yet, one had made its way before them—no wares—no barker—no echo. A silent one…a ghostly one…a hopeless one…

The cart rumbled along the dimly-lit snow-covered cobblestone streets in the wee hours of the morning; its chauffeurs, pausing, here and there, gathering their ghoulish haul—those of Italy's two million street orphans who hadn't survived the wintry night.

Only the creaking of the wheels and an occasional thud of a frozen tot broke the quiet of the dawn.

They were orphans because they were the worst of children—BASTARDS. They called them BASTARDS because they were children who had been born out of wedlock. No one wanted them. That is, no one in their right mind wanted them.

Everyone hated them. That is, everyone who went to church. In those days everyone went to church. Every priest, every nun, every monk, every devout parent, every brainwashed child, despised them.

Each time their frozen bodies would pass by in the cart, they all thought it to be right. The only hint of compassion now and then, "...they are better off dead." Everyone thought there was something holy about it. After all, it had been written in their Holy Bible. These were the worst of children—BASTARDS.

That is, everyone except Piccolo—the little boy Albino Luciani. He thought it was wrong. He didn't care if it was written in a book. In fact, he knew it was wrong. He knew it was wrong because his revolutionary socialist atheist father had told him it was wrong.[2]

His first mortal sin

Luciani told me of the first time he had missed Sunday Mass:

> "I had just turned eleven and was as poor as a church mouse and often went hungry myself. Yet, I did have a mamma and papa to take care of me and love me.
>
> They were away visiting a sick friend on that subzero Sunday morning when I made my way to church with my fellow Catholics.
>
> We passed a dozen orphans who were begging in the street. They were orphans because they had been born out of wedlock, the reason why they were barred from church. It had been God the Father's sacred testimony in Deuteronomy 23: 'A bastard child shall not enter into the congregation of the lord.'
>
> It was this that first made me realize what a monster Moses was, that first made me realize the Old Testament was not the word of God. As a matter-of-fact, it was not even inspired by God; it was obviously inspired by the hatred and greed of evil men.
>
> It may have been the intense cold that inspired me, but, nevertheless, I turned around and hurried back to my house and quickly cooked up a cauldron of soup with all the vegetables and lentils I could find and, although it meant we would go without them ourselves for days, I took it to the orphans and placed it in the snow in the midst of them.
>
> For the first time in my life, I realized what Christ had meant when He said, 'Where two or three are gathered together in my name, there am I in the midst of them.'
>
> By that time church was over. I had missed Sunday Mass—a mortal sin in those days. I decided to go into the church to ask

forgiveness. But, I forgot they locked the doors outside of service hours to keep the orphans from coming in to get warm.

It was then—at that moment when those doors would not open—I realized what Christ had meant by His word 'Church.'

It was then—at that moment when those doors would not open—I decided to become a priest.

It was then—at that moment when those doors would not open—I decided I would change the Church back to what Christ had intended.

It was then—at that moment when those doors would not open—I realized my devout mamma was a sheep and my atheist papa was a lion.

It was then—at that moment when those doors would not open—I began to shed my wool and groom my mane.

I hoped the scolding I would get when my parents returned would not be too harsh. I underestimated the wrath of my mamma. She took me into the bedroom and left me on my knees pleading for God's forgiveness for having broken His sacred law.

Later, when my papa returned, he pulled me up off my knees and hugged me. He told me what I had done was wonderful.

He told me to ask Christ to forgive my mamma. I should not think ill of her as she was caught up in Christianity—something he often called the 'Opium of the Masses.' Drugged with belief, she is unable to judge what is truly right or what is truly wrong.

Though my mamma taught me the idolatry of Christ, it was my papa who taught me the reality of Christ; it was he who taught me right from wrong. While I loved her dearly, my mamma was too caught up in the Opium of the Masses to know right from wrong."[3]

The best of men

Many years later on a chilly autumn evening I sat by the fireplace in an overstuffed armchair. I reached for the newspaper and read:

Associated Press, September 21 1978, Vatican City: As he has on other occasions, after an audience, yesterday, John Paul called for assistance from his listeners. A teenage youth stepped forward.

The Pope asked, "What is your name and how old are you?"
"Anthony." With a touch of pride, "I am sixteen."

"Good. Tell me Anthony, what is the greatest of sins?"

The boy looked sheepishly around the hall, nervously twitched his lips, hesitated, and finally stammered, "I suppose sex?"

The Pope smiled, "Sorry, to have put you on the spot. Yes, we have made of sex the greatest of sins, whereas in itself it is nothing more than human nature and not a sin at all.

"I will give you another chance. Now, Anthony, think, what is really the greatest of sins?"

The boy thought a moment. "I guess murder?"

"Well, you are getting warmer. But, what I am looking for is the cause. Not the result."

The boy was lost for words.

The Pope told him, "Anthony, the greatest sin of all is hatred—hatred of other kinds of people who live their lives differently. Hatred usually goes hand in hand with its partner greed."

The boy agreed, "Now that I think of it, you're right. Hatred and greed have been at the root of all the grief of mankind: countless wars of ethnic cleansing, murdering and destruction of individuals, and, at times, entire populations."

"Why do you suppose you didn't think of it when I first asked you?" the Pope asked.

The boy didn't blink an eyelash, "That's easy. The catechism tells us sex is the greatest of sins."

"And why do you suppose doctrine holds the greatest of sins to be sex?" The Pope waited.

The boy cast a dumbfounded look at the Pope.

John Paul told the youngster, "Anthony, doctrine was made by men who thought there was something wrong with sex. Too, by abstaining from sex, they placed themselves above everyone else...more than half of the saints were canonized for not much more than their purity... It is that Mother Church confuses sex with morality that blinds her vision to know right from wrong..."[4]

Contraception

A week or so later I picked up another newspaper.

Murder by the Grace of God

Associated Press, September 28, 1978, Vatican City: In a general audience yesterday, the Pope talked of the Church's responsibility to help control the world's population:

> "...I have been discussing birth control for forty-five minutes. If the information I have been given—the mixture of statistics—if that information is accurate, then during these few moments over one thousand children under the age of five have died of malnutrition. During the next few hours while you and I look forward with anticipation to our next meal, another five thousand children under the age of five will die of malnutrition. By this time tomorrow, thirty thousand children under the age of five, who at this moment are alive, will be dead of malnutrition. God does not always provide. It is our sacred responsibility to provide," his voice took on a demanding tone, "and we will provide now."[5]

Superstition

A dedicated disciple of John XXIII when it comes to ridding the Church of myth, as he had on many occasions as a bishop and a cardinal, he struck at what John had labeled: 'The Fatima Cult'

Fatima crown contains 24 pounds of gold and 1,700 diamonds

> "It is beautiful to see people showing thanks to Our Lady for graces received. Yet, it is sad to see crowns of immense value placed on plaster idols as objects of superstition.
>
> It is equally as depressing to see people in a stupor running fingers along rows of crystal beads mumbling vain repetitions, likewise in a superstitious way.
>
> Isn't our Lady too the Mother of the Indians, of the Chinese, of the Africans, of the Guatemalans? Indeed she is.
>
> The most beautiful tiara on the Virgin's head is a row of hospital beds in Bombay, a row of water wells in Mongolia, a row of schoolrooms in Burundi, a row of starving children being fed in Central America...
>
> I want you to scratch your brow and think for a moment.

If Jesus wanted us to fall down on our knees and worship plaster idols of Him, He would be everything He told us not to be.

I will say that again, in case you missed it the first time.

If Jesus wanted us to fall down on our knees and worship plaster idols of Him, He would be everything he told us not to be.

This is also true of His Mother.

We practice these superstitions because we know we are not doing what Jesus told us to do.

We refuse to shed our desire for wealth and our hatred of people who live their lives differently. We wrongly think if we butter Jesus up, we will fool Him into letting us into His house. Believe me, Jesus is not the fool we make Him out to be..."[6]

His last public audience

"...This morning, I flushed my toilet with a solid gold lever. At this moment, bishops and cardinals are using the Raphael Bathroom on the second floor of the Papal Palace which trappings, I am told, would draw tens of millions of dollars at auction..."

Believe me, one day, we who live in opulence while so many are dying because they have nothing, will have to answer to Jesus why we have not carried out His order: 'Love thy neighbor as thyself.'

We, the clergy, together with our congregations, who foolishly substitute gold and pomp and ceremony in place of Christ's instruction, who judge our masquerade of singing His praises to be more precious than human life, will have the most to explain...

Embrace the words of Paul VI in the Populorum Progressio:

> 'It is the inalienable right of no man to accumulate wealth beyond the necessary while other men starve to death because they have nothing.'"[7]

Faith

He asked, "Can one of the children come up to help the Pope?"

A young boy stepped forward. "What is your name and what grade are you in?"

The boy stammered, "Daniele. I am in the fifth grade."

The Pope put his hand on the boy's shoulder. "Now, Daniele, do you want to stay in the fifth grade or would you rather go on to the sixth grade next year?"

Daniele startled the Pope, "I want to stay in the fifth grade. If I go on to the sixth grade I will lose my teacher."

John Paul smiled to the crowd. "Well, this boy is different than was the little boy Luciani, for when I was in the fifth grade, I would say to myself, 'Oh, if only I were in the sixth.' And, when I was in the sixth, I would say to myself, 'Oh, if only I were in the seventh...'"

Turning to the boy, "Daniele, we have within us a need to make progress—to move forward. Only with progress can we find the truth. We started out living in caves and then progressed to huts and now we live in homes with modern kitchens and bathrooms.

First we went by foot, then by horse, then by cart, then by train, then by automobile and, today, by airplane. Always advancing—never looking back. This is the law progress...

More importantly, has been our progress in accepting our fellow human beings as we do ourselves. Our enemy is what has gone before us. We wrongly assume our ancestors were smarter than we are. We wrongly accept what they wrote in their books is the truth. We assume that what they had to say was right and this misconception pulls us backward, instead of forward.

In truth, we are much smarter than were our ancestors. As each generation comes forward it benefits from all the knowledge that has been accumulated by all those which have gone before it. Tell me, Daniele, what did God do on the first day of creation?"

The boy looked up at the Pope with a puzzled frown, "Why, He divided the waters that were there to create Heaven."

John Paul followed, "And, on the second day?"

Daniele, "He gathered the waters together to allow the dry land to appear and He grew grass, trees and flowers."

Nodding agreement, the Pope continued to probe the boy, "Now, how about, the third day?"

Daniele, "God hung the sun and the moon and the stars in the heavens to give light."

The Pope smiled, "You have a good teacher. No wonder you don't want to leave her. Nevertheless, when Moses told us the story of creation, he was not aware that the earth was round and rotating on its axis and controlled by its sun. So he told us God had told him the earth was flat and God hung the sun and the stars in the heavens the day after He created the earth and its vegetation.

He told us this because he didn't know at his time it is the sun that is the center of our solar system and controls all life on our planet. It is because he didn't know the facts—the truth—Moses told his followers God had told him God had created vegetation the day before He hung the sun in the heavens.

Yet, today we know the truth—no vegetation can exist without the process of photosynthesis which is a product of the sun. In fact, the earth, itself, could not exist without its sun."

Daniele, with a triumphal smirk, "But, God would have told the story of creation as people at the time believed the world to be."

"Daniele, think. Would God have had reason to have lied?"

The boy remained silent.

"God had no reason to have lied. Actually, God had great motive to have told the truth. For had He told Moses the truth— had God revealed the true organization of the universe—it would have proved He was the true God.

It would have explained a great mystery of that time how it was possible for the sun to rise in the east each morning and set in the west each evening? How did it ever return to the east?

So God had great motive to have told the truth.

Yet, Moses, in convincing his people he had talked to God, inspired them to take the Promised Land so future generations would think God gave that land to the Jews. So Moses would have had great motive to have lied.

Now listen very carefully to what I am about to say to you. I want you to keep it with you always."

As his eyes roamed around the hall the Pope raised his voice so that all would hear what he had to say. "Daniele, I do not believe the same God who has endowed us with reason and intellect has intended us to forego their use; we would believe a God—who had great motive to have told the truth—lied, and a man—who had great motive to have lied—told the truth.

Moses thought he was telling the truth. But, today we know he was not telling the truth because, at his time, he did not know the truth. Daniele, if we are ever to know the truth, we cannot start with falsehoods. We must start with what we have determined to be the truth to a given point in time and go forward.

As each generation comes and goes we grow closer and closer

to the truth. Daniele, the truth does not lie in the past; it lies in the future. It is your job to help society in its struggle to find it."

The Pope's eyes held the boy, "Daniele. Let me tell you a story.

In America, Negroes were once taken from their children and placed in bondage and the white church-going Christians thought it was right because their 'faith' told them it was right.

They thought this way because they wanted to stay in the fifth grade because they could not give up their teacher.

Their fifth grade teacher was the God of the Old Testament. He could not have been more explicit in His Commandment, *'Thou shalt not covet—desire to take from—thy neighbor his property, including his house, his wife, his slaves, his ox, his ass.'*[8]

Their God felt so strongly slavery was right, He protected the right of one man to enslave another in His only written law.

Then one day, a man named Lincoln and others like him came along and scratched their heads, 'There is something wrong here? Let us go onto the sixth grade.' There they found a new teacher, His name was Christ and Christ told them slavery was wrong.

In *Matthew 9*, when asked, 'Which commandments must I keep that I shall have eternal life?' Christ expressly excludes the Tenth Commandment. Christ makes it clear Moses' intent to protect the right of one man to enslave another was wrong."

The boy whispered, "I never thought of it in this way."

John Paul continued, "Through the centuries, Mother Church has had the same problem the American Christians had back before Lincoln's day.

In Moses' time the Israelites slaughtered thousands of their peaceful Canaanite neighbors including all of their children and thought it was right because their 'faith' told them it was right. Back in Christ's time they would stone unwed mothers to death and thought it was right because their 'faith' told them it was right. In medieval times the Crusaders slaughtered millions of Muslims and Jews and thought it was right because their 'faith' told them it was right. In the World War our country sided with Germany in its quest for the superiority of the white race and the annihilation of other races because our 'faith' told us it was right.

Daniele, not too long ago when I was your age, every village in Italy had a cart that went about the streets each morning picking up the frozen bodies of orphans who had not made it through the winter nights. At the time, all we good Christians thought it was right because our 'faith' told us it was right. Now, a few generations later, we know it was wrong. It was an atrocity.

Just a few weeks ago, the first artificially inseminated child was born. Catholics condemn the child. The reason they condemn the child is because their 'faith' condemns the child. So even today, faith does not know right from wrong. Today, we persecute many kinds of people who live their lives differently and continue to think it is right because of what someone once wrote in a book.

Daniele, you too must make progress or you will never be able to help society in its search for the truth.

You will never be able to make your mark toward making this a better world to live in for those who come after you."

Daniele, "Now I know why I must go on to the sixth grade."

"Yes, Daniele, you have your sacred commission. You must go on to the sixth grade, then on to the seventh, and then on to the eighth. You must go forward, always advancing, never looking back. Progress must be your guiding ambition. So that someday the whole world will come to know the truth. So that the day will come about when all men and women will treat each other equally as Christ commanded: 'Love thy neighbor as thyself.' Not as they have in the past because someone wrote something in a book."

He cautioned, "Daniel, 'faith' is what someone once wrote in a book to take advantage of others who didn't know what we know today. It is not the truth. It does not know right from wrong…"

Daniele, "But, how else would we know right from wrong?"

The Pope pointed to his temple.[9]

Women ordination

On CBS News the following day:

This morning in an audience with Philippine bishops, John Paul was challenged about rumors a woman might soon be ordained.

In his Sunday Angeles on September 10th he had declared, "God is the Father, more so, the Mother."

Asked by a bishop what he had meant by his declaration, John Paul told the assembly: "According to tales told by ancient men, God is the Father. According to all we know, God is the Mother."[10]

The next day, I woke up to the news:

Just thirty-three days into his pontificate, Pope John Paul died last evening... Vibrant and on the job to the end, he was sixty-five... the only Pope whose death was unwitnessed... On hearing the news, Cardinal Benelli of Florence called for an autopsy... Born of a social revolutionary atheist father who had placed him in a seminary at the age of eleven with the commission to bring change to the Church... What would have been John Paul's papacy is perhaps best defined by his compassion for born-out-of-wedlock children, women, homosexuals, the poor and others oppressed by scripture as expressed in the underlying message of his acceptance speech in the Sistine Chapel on August 27, 1978: "...We must rise up the courage to set aside the preferences that have been built into us by our Christian forefathers...Together we will muster the strength to lift those restraints unfairly placed upon the everyday lives of so many innocent people by doctrine... for God-given human life is infinitely more precious than is man-made doctrine."[11]

'Acceptance speech' as used above is a misnomenclature.

John Paul chatted with the cardinals for hours in a closed session. Its message is limited to what various right-wing and left-wing cardinals told various right-wing and left-wing blocs of the press—the reason newspapers reported variations of what was said. Yet, from what is known, he made a partisan effort to appeal to all.

His 'greetings to all' message particularly to the oppressed, won the hearts of those on the left. Cardinals Benelli and Felici were pleased with the high priority given 'revision of canon law' the reason the Florence newspaper *La Nazione* focused on this point.

Progressives who took 'ecumenism' to include all religions were happy he committed himself to it. Conservatives were content as they took 'ecumenism' to be religious unity within Catholicism thus the Vatican paper *L' Osservatore Romano* focused on this point.

Third world prelates were pleased with his overly compassion for the poor and his emphasis on 'human rights and international justice.' Thus Latin American media focused on this part of what he said.

He made friendly tones toward the 'Synod of Bishops' which was taken by Brussels' Cardinal Suenens that future bishops including popes be elected by the Episcopate to avoid polarization of the hierarchy of the Church as reported in *L Europeenne de Bruxelles*.

The most widely published words: 'The Church exists not to be served by the world but instead to serve the world,' mirrored Jack's letter to me: 'Mother Church will cease to be the cause of many of the world's problem and instead will begin to be the answer to them.'

Cardinal Willebrands, the most outspoken cardinal for women ordination and married priests who had just recently defended the rights of homosexuals in a fatal gay-bashing incident:

> "When faith incites hatred, suffering and death, the thread which weaves its moral fabric is flawed..."[12]

...told reporters:

> "It is a disaster. I cannot put into words how happy we were on that day we had chosen John Paul. We had such high hopes. It was such a wonderful feeling, one that comes once in a lifetime, a feeling that fresh air was about to flow into our Church."[13]

Five days later, *Associated Press,* October 4, 1978, Vatican City:

> "...The coffin, a pine box as reserved for paupers, was hemmed in by the princes of the Church in their rich and elegant attire...

Cardinal Leon Joseph Suenens, leader of liberalism in the Roman Catholic Church, gave the final tribute for his dear friend:

'Like a shimmering white light he rose up from the mud in the street and left no one untouched.

For those of us at the top, from heads of churches, to leaders of nations, to those of great scientific achievement; he was the Enlightener—the Imitation of the Holy Ghost.

For those of us at the bottom, from the poor, to the homeless, to the handicapped, to the oppressed; he was the Redeemer—the Imitation of Christ.

Above all, he was the best of men.'" [14]

Thus was the beginning and the end of Albino Luciani. Now, witness the whole of him. This is the Testament of Pope John Paul I.

VATICAN CENSORSHIP

Italian media

In sourcing Italian newspapers, one must caution against *L'Osservatore Romano, El Gazzettino, Prospettive nel Mondo* and a host of other journals owned by the Vatican. These papers published Vatican censored versions of what was said by Albino Luciani on particular occasions concerning controversial issues. More often—than not—they took what was actually said completely out of context.

Wikipedia

The reader is also cautioned against *Wikipedia* insofar as it references these same Vatican controlled sources. *Wikipedia* is a reliable source for date of birth, date of death and positions held by the men in this book; not much more.
It allows those who never met him— self-appointed right-wing and left-wing 'scholars' on Luciani's life—to blog on its site; unreliable to his true testament.

Vatican transcripts

Vatican transcripts available on the Internet and in libraries of what a pope said on a specific occasion are rarely representative of what was actually said and are often contradictory of what was said. This is particularly true of his September 13th audience on 'faith.' If one takes the time to view the clip of John Paul's September 27th audience on *You Tube* one will find a simple man speaking in everyday conversation: **"This is not about this man or that man. It is about people who are hungry."** Conversely, the Vatican transcript of this audience—available in libraries and on the Internet—portrays a great orator addressing a group of Noble laureates—it will drive the most astute scholar to the dictionary.

John Paul's public audiences ran two to four hours. The Vatican transcripts can be read in less than a minute or two—in most cases not remotely representative of what actually took place. His central message repeated in each of his audiences: **"My papacy is not about this or that man. It is about people who are hungry,"** does not appear in any of the transcripts. Yet, it has survived in all four film clips.

During his audiences he interviewed seventeen people including twelve children—the meat of what he had to say. All of these ended up on the Vatican's cutting-room floor.

The Daniele conversation exceeded a half-hour. The Vatican Transcript of his audience of September 27, 1978 does not mention it at all. Only a few briefs reached most newspapers:

> ...himself lowering the microphone to the boy's height.
> "Do you always want to be in the 5th grade?" the pope asked Daniele Bravo. "Yes," the boy replied. "So that I don't have to change teachers."
>
> Flustered, the pope roared with laughter and said, "Well, you are different from the pope. When I was in 4th grade, I worried about making it to the 5th and when in the 5th, about passing to the 6th. You must move on."
>
> **Philadelphia Evening Bulletin, Sept 28, 1978**

1 *Veneto Nostro* 12 May 65 republished: *La Nazione* 18 Sep 65
2 The introductory comments are Albino Luciani's testimony to the author as dramatized by the author. *Deuteronomy 23 'A bastard child shall not enter the congregation of the Lord.'* Moses condemnation of born-out-of-wedlock children is why the word 'bastard' continues to have a terrible connotation today despite the stigma is now dead. In 1973, Paul VI motioned to make Luciani a cardinal. Luciani sent a message unless Paul reversed canon's condemnation of bastards, he would refuse the *red hat*. Paul complied. Yet, even today an illegitimate child cannot be a priest, a Swiss Guard, etc.
3 Albino Luciani's testimony to the author dramatized by the author.
4 *Associated Press* 20 Sep 78 also carried in its entirety by ANSA, Italy's premier wire service. Excerpts of the Anthony interview were reported in world newspapers sourcing the *Associated Press*
5 John Paul originally said this to Cardinal Villot on September 19th. He repeated it in his 4th audience.
6 *L Osservatore Romano* 28 Sep 78. His criticism of Fatima escaped Curial censors and has been inadvertently published in Vatican and other right-wing publications
7 John Paul 27 Sep 78 - 4th audience spanned three hours. A Vatican edited five minute film clip that survives on You Tube includes the quote, *"...It is the inalienable right..."*
8 The Tenth Commandment as it appears in the oldest surviving texts and in eastern Bibles including the Jewish *Torah* today: *"Thou shalt not covet (desire to take from) thy neighbor his property, including his house, his wife, his slaves, his ox, his ass."* In the twentieth century, most Bibles changed its context: *"Thou shalt not covet thy neighbor his...servants or employees..."* Moses held women like animals as mere property of men and protected the right of one man to enslave another.
9 This relatively substantial text of the boy Daniele interview is a composite of excerpts published in *La Repubblica, La Stampa, El Mondo, Corriere della Serra, Corriere del Alpi, The Times*, the *Washington Post*, the *Boston Globe*, the *Philadelphia Bulletin and other world newspapers.*
10 *La Stampa* 12 Sep 78. Other newspapers reported variations of what was said reflecting various political positions. John Paul originally said this on Sunday September 10, 1978.
11 *Associated Press* 29 Sep 78
12 *De Groene Amsterdammer* 21 Sep 78; the most famous quote attributed to the Ditch cardinal
13 *De Groene Amsterdammer* 2 Oct 78
14 *L Europeenne de Bruxelles* 5 Oct 78

Chapter 3

The Minor Seminary at Feltre

"The most fundamental weapon of war is not guns and bombs. It is propaganda which conditions children of nations to hate children of other nations so that when they grow up they will kill each other for the few at the top."[1]

Albino Luciani

It was a dark dismal afternoon in the month of October of nineteen hundred twenty-three when eleven year old Albino Luciani climbed into the carriage that would take him to the seminary at Feltre—his first stop on a long journey which would eventually lead to Rome.

His father, who had spent a lifetime trying to change the Church from the outside, decided it could only be changed from the inside. He committed his son to the task.

In those days, prep schools—particularly minor seminaries—were reserved for the very rich; priests came only from wealthy families. One of the reasons priests do not take a vow of poverty.

The best a poor boy could look forward to was a monk's robe. His father, Giovanni Luciani—a leader in the Socialist Party—made a deal. It would contribute the money; he would contribute Albino.[2]

In his farewell, the revolutionary outcast of the Veneto country commissioned his son, "Albino, unlike those hypocrites who prance about the Vatican palaces in magnificent robes of silk and satin with jeweled chalices and rings of diamonds and rubies and gold, you must promise me you will live your life in imitation of Christ."

Emulating Albino's fondness for chess, he gave the boy his game plan, "Play your game carefully and work hard until that day when at the helm of their ranks you will establish the common dignity of all Christ's children in the Church." He left him with one last word of caution: **"Never risk your king to save a pawn."**[3]

So it was, his Papa, together with his little brother Edoardo, with tears in their eyes, waved goodbye, on that chilly dark dismal drizzling autumn afternoon, to this **Pauper who would be Pope.**

A sacred pledge

The road to Feltre had been a difficult one for the little boy.

In the impoverished town of Canale d'Agordo his family had been the poorest of the poor. His father was not only an atheist, he was a militant socialist activist—a thorn in the side of the Church.

So much so, he had to migrate hundreds of miles away where he was unknown to earn enough to support his family. Too, he spent much of his earnings feeding and building sheds for the orphans.

Nevertheless, Feltre was a big step up for the boy Luciani.

To begin with the buildings had indoor plumbing. In the poor mountain village where he had grown up none of the houses had indoor plumbing. Going to the bathroom in the wintertime was the worst of times. That is, it was the worst of times for everyone except the born-out-of-wedlock orphans. They would often sneak into them to keep warm. For them, it was the best of times.

For this reason most people kept padlocks on them to keep the orphans out. Nevertheless, going to the bathroom would never again be the worst of times for Albino Luciani. Actually, the worst of times for this little boy were not over. They were yet to come.

Luciani told me of the time he knelt in the chapel at Feltre:

"It was at the age of eleven I began my ministry.

The haunting memory of the hopeless struggle of the orphans would trouble me all my days. These unfortunate children would become the central focus of all my energy. It was then, in the solitude of that tiny chapel, I made my sacred pledge to Christ:

'I offer you no great cathedral, no chant, no offering of gold.

All I have to give is my promise that I will do what you have told me to do. I know not where this path leads. All I know is that you have told me to take it, and that is all I need know.

If at its end there is nothing there, it is enough for me that you have allowed me the opportunity to have walked this way; that you have placed on my shoulders this sacred burden.

I care not if it takes me over the highest mountains, or across the widest seas, or against the armaments of all the armies of the earth, or even through fire. I intend to do this thing with all the strength, vigor and courage that is in me as if the very existence of each and every one of your children depends on me, alone.'"[4]

Murder by the Grace of God

"...only the thud of an occasional tot broke the quiet of the dawn."

The bell tower

When he had first arrived at Feltre, he had gazed up in wonderment at the bell tower which annexed the school. It was the first time he had seen a building so tall—easily twice the height of the next tallest building in town. In total mass, it was every bit as big as was the school itself. It made no sense to him one would build such an immense structure at monumental cost just to house a bell.

It was when he gazed up at the bell tower, he realized how far the Church had strayed from what Christ had intended. It would use an immense amount of money it collected for the poor, which could be used to build housing for a hundred orphans, to house a bell.

He noticed something very strange about the tower. There was no lock on its door. Why no lock on the door to the bell tower? He was soon to find out there was another purpose of the tower.

The strange little boy in the schoolyard

Luciani told me of his first brush with homosexuality:

"I was twelve when I found there was another kind of BASTARD.

He was a delicate little boy who spoke with a lisp and waved his hands in a funny little way. All the kids laughed at him in the schoolyard. Then one day he died. No Mass was said for him. He was put in a burlap sack and buried in the village dump.

Gaio explained to the class Giovanni had been born bad so the Devil had taken him back. But, I knew the priest was wrong. I knew Giovanni, like all Christ's children, had been born good.

I knew why he had jumped from the bell tower. He couldn't take it any longer. That afternoon as I stood over my friend's grave, I vowed I would never let anyone laugh at him again."[5]

As he crept into his teens, Albino came to realize many of his classmates were gay despite few of them displayed effeminate traits as had Giovanni. He knew why. A teenager who contemplated the priesthood had to make the great sacrifice of celibacy.

Under canon law, all sex outside of marriage is mortal sin. A straight youth had the option of marriage and could look forward to a life of sex free of sin. For him celibacy was a great sacrifice.

But a gay teen could never marry and for that reason if he was devout—in those days everyone was devout—he was condemned to a life of celibacy anyway. So in choosing the celibate life of a priest, a homosexual teen wasn't giving up anything.

Some others were girls in boy's bodies. The priesthood allowed them to dress up in beautiful gowns and live their lives as objects of admiration otherwise reserved for the fair sex.

In the five years he would be at Feltre, a dozen of his classmates leaped from the bell tower. Some were homosexual or transsexual teens whose identity was uncovered by their 'holy' keepers. A few were discovered to have been born-out-of-wedlock and went off the tower on the eve of their excommunication. Others developed deformities. One was crippled in an accident and another stopped growing and was determined to be a midget. Each one, with his dream of becoming a priest shattered, went off the tower on the eve of expulsion—the remains splattered across the cobblestones below.

No Mass was said for any of them. Each of them, one by one, was put into a burlap sack and taken to the town dump. It had been Moses' sacred words in *Leviticus:* "The lord spoke to Moses saying, whosoever should he be that hath a blemish, whether he be a blind child, or a lame child, or a child with a flat nose (Negro), or a child broken-footed, or broken-handed, or a hunch-backed, or a dwarfed child, or a child of disease is not to approach the altar of the Lord."

His rise to the world stage

Albino Luciani's rise to the world stage did not begin when he became a cardinal in 1973. It began in 1926 when he was just thirteen years old. He had wiggled himself into the job of assistant editor of the school paper and his first commentary through his father's influence was republished in  a socialist literary journal and eventually reached all of Europe:

> "...The problems of the world will come to an end when nations in accordance with their copyright laws, require the Old Testament be prefaced: 'This is a work of fiction. Keep away from children.'
>
> A function of copyright laws is to protect the public from what might not be true. The state is derelict in its duty in failing to place a warning on this book as many people are using it to guide the way they live their lives and this is costing many others their lives.
>
> There is not a word in this book that has been proven true. On the contrary all of its major claims have been proven false.
>
> Everyone knows the earth is round. Let us not be so foolish as to believe a man who talked to a God who thought it was flat.
>
> It is obvious to any man or woman of good conscience this book was not inspired by God; rather it was inspired by the greed and hatred of evil men..."[6]

Most laughed, they took it to be a joke. Some were critical of the boy's audacity, some called for his expulsion, others going so far as to call for his excommunication. On the other hand, one of them—Albert Einstein—called the boy prodigy's article, "**The first bit of common sense to ever come out of the Roman Catholic Church.**"[7]

Just a few months later, when it seemed the smoke had cleared, Albino struck again. He wrote his first editorial and, again, through the influence of his father, though it did not attain the notoriety of the first article, it showed up in periodicals throughout Europe:

> "I cannot accept Moses was the holy man the Church and the motion pictures make him out to be. Moses introduced fascism to

the western world, the concept some kinds of people are better than others and are entitled to more. That ideology which fosters hatred of certain kinds of people and a rich and poor society, one in which some children are born into immense wealth and other children are born into dire poverty.

Moses embraces God the Father's dream in which the white male rules at His side with woman held in man's servitude and all others who are different are to be subordinated, annihilated or cast into slavery. Among these are those with *'flat noses'* (Negroes) and *'those of physical blemish'* (the handicapped).

In all my life I have never seen a black person as black people are not allowed in Italy. We are an entirely white Catholic country because the minds of the voters are controlled by a Vatican that wants to preserve the purity of our superior race...

On the other side, Christ introduces communism to the world, the ideology based on the premise all God's children are created equal and are entitled to share equally in God's province.

Christ dictates a world in which every child has an equal opportunity at a good and healthy life, a far different world than we live in today. Christ gives us only two commandments: 'Love thy neighbor as thyself' and 'Sell all thou hast and give to the poor.'

These are the pillars of society: Equality and Christ on the *left* and Fascism and the tales of ancient men on the *right*...

Despite Christ's overwhelming testimony two thousand years ago, Christianity remains deeply steeped in fascism today.

Mother Church in her support of a fascist state has chosen the tales of ancient men over the word of Jesus Christ, Himself."[8]

Albino's editorial was in response to an order by Pius XI a week earlier requiring all children be enrolled in the new *Fascist Scout Organization* that served as the kindling wood for World War II.

Conditioning children for war

While at the Feltre seminary he had his first look at a big city. Since early childhood he had excelled in chess and was permitted to go to Milan—his anonymous benefactors financing the trips.

Albino made the acquaintance of Russian teens his own age.

He found it was propaganda which conditioned Catholic children to hate children of communist countries and vice versa. It was this strategy that enabled a few at the pinnacles of churches and nations to cause the mindless masses at the bottom to sacrifice their lives in war to the benefit of those at the top.

He found Russian children were every bit as good as he was. On the other hand, the Russian children found their western counterparts were not as good as they were. They had heard stories about how Catholic countries treated born-out-of-wedlock children. Yet, they believed it to be Russian propaganda. When they found out it was true they thought less of their western friends. In their homeland all children were seen to be equal. There were no orphans in the streets.

His Russian roommate Alexander Rotov was a bit older than he was. Made possible by the Russian's fluency in Italian they struck up a relationship which would endure until Rotov's death in 1959.

The Russian would sire a son—Boris Rotov who would rise as Luciani's counterpart in the east—the Russian Orthodox Church.

On his return to Feltre another editorial *'The Shroud of War'* posted in a socialist journal again reached a level of notoriety:

"The most fundamental weapon of war is not bullets and bombs. It is propaganda which conditions children of nations to hate children of other nations and vice versa so that when they grow up they will kill each other for the few at the top."[9]

He tastes of the forbidden fruit

In addition to the required studies of Feltre designed to brainwash students in fascism, Albino got a glimpse of the other side of the coin. Through his father he obtained a parade of forbidden books.

Among them were Darwin's *Origin of the Species* and Mendel's *Experiments in Plant Hybrids*. He took a particular interest in these pioneers of modern day genetics believing they would eventually pave the way to a time when all children would be born healthy.

He found Albert Einstein's works most fascinating, particularly as they defined the infinite unit of creation—the atom—from which all life and matter evolved. He would refer to *'Einstein's Theory of Evolution'* and be corrected by his teachers that he was confusing Einstein with Darwin. Only he knew what he was talking about.

There were books on astronomy, anthropology, archeology,

chemistry, physics, history, and psychology—how the mind works.

Then there were those banned from Catholic seminaries—the 'Bibles' of other religions including Mohammed's *Koran,* the Hindu scripture the *Vedas,* the *Sutras* and the *Tripitaka* of the Buddhist culture. There was an endless array of others.

He became fascinated with Laozi—Taoism—who like Einstein centuries after him defined man as a microcosm of nature. In all, he spent months scouring through the worlds of the other Gods.

Above all, the Church banned any book that mentioned sex, even scientific journals. That he was exposed to books which discussed sex at an early age made possible the most prolific testimony of his ministry: **"We have made of sex the greatest of sins, whereas in itself it is nothing more than human nature and not a sin at all."**[10]

Most instrumental to the man he became were those on socialism.

Among these were the works of a nineteenth century monumental progressive Antonio Rosmini. Rosmini—a homosexual—believed the purpose of society was to protect the rights of the individual and not the other way around; chagrin to the Vatican which limited human rights and dignity to those who conformed to its doctrines.

Rosmini's propositions for change in the Church were roundly condemned by the Vatican. Albino Luciani adopted Rosmini as his philosophical mentor at an early age.

Specifically he embraced Rosmini's criticism of the Church as set forth in the theologian's thesis *The Five Wounds of the Church:*

1. **Priest education limited to doctrine isolated from the emerging social revolution.**
2. **Social distancing of the clergy from the congregation**
3. **Autocracy: appointment of bishops by a Pope who elect a Pope.**
4. **Clergy are clever politicians who use tales told by ancient men to attain their political objectives.**
5. **Church is a cult caught up in blood rituals and idol worship and immersed in ownership of property and immense wealth.**

He studied at length Marx' *Das Kapital* and Lenin's *The State and Revolution* and *The Rise of Capitalism in Russia* and countless others. He swallowed up Marx and Engels' *Communist Manifesto.*

Murder by the Grace of God

He quickly put two and two together:

Marx' Ideology	Christ's teaching
All God's children are equal	Love thy neighbor as thyself
Redistribution of wealth society	Sell all thou hast give to the poor

Marx had tried to bring Christ's teachings into a selfish world.

He reasoned Christ was crucified because He threatened to bring about a redistribution-of-wealth society. The Romans, like we do today, lived in a rich and poor society controlled by a few at the top.

Nevertheless, it was these books and his father's guidance which molded him into the social revolutionary he would become.

They would also provide him with the ammunition he needed to have some fun—to play with the minds of his captors at Feltre.

1 *Povera Tigre Belluno* 22 Jul 28
2 The grant was anonymous. It is reasonable to believe it came from the party his father belonged to
3 Luciani conveyed to author Mar 68 - dramatized by author to the best of his recollection
4 Luciani conveyed to author Mar 69 - dramatized by author to the best of his recollection
5 Luciani conveyed to author Mar 69 - dramatized by author to the best of his recollection
6 *Parish Bulletin Feltre* 10 May 26   *Povera Tigre Belluno* 22 Jun 26
7 *Leidsch Dagblad* 25 Jun 26
8 *Povera Tigre Belluno* 12 Dec 26
9 *Povera Tigre Belluno* 22 Jul 28
10 *Messaggero Mestre* 14 Nov 71 *La Repubblica* 18 Mar 77 He repeated this many times

Author's note: stories of Albino Luciani's days as a seminarian and as a young priest—not included in this book—are in its sequel:

The Reincarnation of Albino Luciani*

In Search of the Human Soul

*based on Albino Luciani's thesis 'The Origin of the Human Soul according to Rosmini.'

Chapter 4

The Tyrant of Feltre

"God is the Father, more so, the mother."[1]   John Paul I

Today, visitors to Feltre can view a display of old notes, the only surviving record the boy Luciani had ever been there: a dozen or so reprimands; some not much more than a slap on the wrist while others threatened expulsion and even excommunication.

As he had been in grade school he was a rascal and a tyrant at the minor seminary in Feltre. The Church's biographical briefs will tell you this. They will not tell you why. Here, I will tell you why.

Origin of ghosts

To the little boy of Feltre it was more a matter of fun than it was one of sarcasm when he attacked the primitive nature of ritual.

One day he drew a comparison between the Christian dancing around his statues at festival time and the American Indian dancing around his totem poles—the ritual was the same, just the ideology differed. He compared them to their common ancestor the Cro-Magnon which archeology had recently discovered had once danced around an altar of bear skulls tens of thousands of years ago.

He reasoned man's tendency to believe in 'ghosts' began with the Neanderthals. Excavations testify Neanderthals began to bury their dead about two hundred thousand years ago. The bigger the man, the more dangerous the spirit, the deeper buried—up to depths of ten feet. This was also the beginning of man's tendency to believe he could somehow beat the rap of mortality and live forever.

It also marked the beginning of 'faith' from which emerged the Cro-Magnon altar of bear skulls whose gods lived in the deepest darkest of caves, the sly witchdoctor of Africa whose gods lived in the jungle, the cunning Aborigine wise man whose gods of the South Pacific lived in the sea, the clever Celtic who dreamt up the Banshee who lived in the forest, and the devious Eskimo angakok who created the god Agloolik who lived under the ice. This continues all the way down to today's gods who live somewhere up there.

These god-makers of the past were in common—all unscrupulous men who capitalized on man's mortality to attain political ambitions.

He would often play with the minds of his keepers. He was well positioned to do this. They had read one book. He had read them all.

"How about the Bonobo?" Albino looked up at his teacher.

"The what?" Don Filippo had obviously never heard the word.

The boy went on, "Of the fifteen species of the higher primates including man only the bonobo recognizes the parity of woman.

As a matter-of-fact, in the world of the pigmy chimpanzee, woman is dominant, man is subservient. In the world of the pigmy chimpanzee," he told the class what he would tell the world fifty years later, 'God is more our Mother than She is our Father.'"

Don Filippo could not contain himself, "Blasphemy! Only man can be of divinity. We know this as a matter-of-fact."

"...as a matter-of-fact?" Albino looked up at his teacher.

Filippo spoke down to the boy, "Yes, it is the fundamental truth on which Christianity is built. Christ was a man. What's more, God—His Father—was a man. His mother was a mere animal."

"Let's see," mumbled the boy reaching for his copy of the New Testament. "Here in Matthew. I guess this is what you are talking about: 'When Mary was espoused to Joseph, before they came together, she was found to be with child. Joseph was minded to put away her privily and not make her a public example...'"[2]

He paused anticipating all the possible ways his teacher might counter his next move. He let him have it, "It is a matter-of-fact Mary cheated on Joseph. Jesus was conceived out-of-wedlock. He was a Bastard—born-out-of-wedlock. According to canon law Jesus could never be a priest, let alone a God."[3]

Foolishly, Don Filippo took the bait, "You are taking it out of context. Read the rest of the verse."

Albino read, "'Behold the angel of the Lord appeared in Joseph's dream, saying, Joseph, Mary is conceived of the Holy Ghost...'"

Don Filippo locked up his case, "It is a matter-of-fact the Holy Ghost was the Father of Christ."

The class turned and looked at Albino as if he had been the last one in line when the brains had been passed out.

The boy agreed, "Yes, it was a Ghost who had sex with Mary. But it is not a matter-of-fact. It is a matter-of-faith.

"The matter-of-fact is Mary cheated on Joseph. We don't know who Jesus' real father was. Christ was a Bastard. Not only born-out-of-wedlock, He was born of adultery—a product of sin. This is a matter-of-fact. What you are talking about is a matter-of-faith.

"Yet, suppose we say you are right, all that counts is a matter-of-faith." Don Filippo could not hold back a triumphal grin.

"No man can claim to be Jesus' father. Yet, a woman was His mother." The boy's eyes roamed about the room as if something was wrong. "This room should be filled with girls, not with boys!"

The image of the bell tower towering up over the splattered remains of Albino Luciani struck into Don Filippo's brain.[4]

So it went on for four years, the teenager literally torturing his masters. Each one of them wanted him out of the school as quickly as possible in order that they could survive with their sanity.

In that everything he had to say was wrong to them, none of them could rightfully give him passing grades. Yet, it was the only way they could get rid of him for the grant from the boy's anonymous donor was far too much for the diocese to give up.

So it was on a sunny afternoon in the early summer of nineteen hundred twenty-seven, Albino Luciani graduated at the bottom of his class in the courtyard at the foot of the bell tower in Feltre.

The class valedictorian gave his promise to serve God and the wreaths were passed out—catechism, theology, liturgy and so forth. One by one, his classmates strolled to the platform to pick them up.

Had there been wreaths for history, anthropology, archeology, astronomy, biology, chemistry, genetics, mathematics, physics, compassion, courage and change; he would have taken them all.

Yet, he did take one—perfect attendance. While at Feltre, he had not missed a class. They couldn't take that one away from him.

Nevertheless, the following day the boy Luciani was gone. The masters of Feltre would celebrate. But, they would never forget him. No matter how hard they tried, they would never forget him.

Authors' note: He published the ideology of this story in his 1973 letter to Lemuel (see '4' below). More of his seminary days not in this book are in its sequel 'The Reincarnation of Albino Luciani'

1 He said this on Sept.10, 1978 in his Sunday Angelus and repeated it again on Sept. 28, 1978
2 *Matthew 1*.If made public, Mary would have been stoned to death as required by Moses' Law.
3 According to canon law a boy born out-of-wedlock cannot be ordained a priest even today
4 *Messaggero di S Antonio* Feb 73 – his letter to Lemuel *Illustrissimi* is based on identical ideology. Direct testimony of Albino Luciani to author dramatized by the author

Chapter 5

The Seminary at Belluno

"Like the snail who crawled up the Obelisk leaving its slimy trail behind it, he (hatred) has left his mark on History."

Albino Luciani in his letter to Mark Twain[1]

In the following autumn a grant surfaced from the anonymous donor and the youth Luciani showed up at the seminary in Belluno.

There was no easy way out here for those who found themselves in violation of Moses' laws. No bell tower. One had to resort to a bottle of pills, a straight razor or a combination of a rope and a chair.

Unlike the villages of Canale d'Agordo and Feltre which had an occasional spot of color, Belluno was a sprawling city of sameness. Every house, every building including the seminary was of the same shade of beige stucco blanketed with a sea of orange tiled roofs.

The seminary here in Belluno was as large as the one at Feltre had been small. There were as many teachers here in Belluno as there had been students at Feltre where he had groomed his mane.

He was determined not to repeat the record he had at Feltre which had brought him poor grades. Here he would give them what they wanted. He took the early lead and the others would never catch up.

Though deeply immersed in his studies, he could not ignore what was going on in the outside world around him.

The Axis Powers

One might ask why Italy was Germany's ally in the war.

In Hitler's case, one must consider why he went after the Jews, Slavs, atheists, homosexuals and other outcasts of Christianity.

These dissidents had for the most part evaded enlistment in the German military in World War I. They would have been fighting against an enemy which had far less discriminatory policies than the country they would be fighting to defend.[2]

What's more, a number of them had been caught operating as

spies for Russia during the war. If Christian Germany were to win the war they were destined to live their lives in perpetual oppression.

Hitler intended to wage his war against the Slavs—Russia and its eastern allies who had a tolerance of Jews, atheists, homosexuals and other outcasts of Christianity.

Hitler knew if he were to win the war he must first remove these 'silent enemies' from his own ranks to prevent the undercover tactics which—in his mind—had cost his Fatherland the First World War.

In Italy's case, uppermost was the black-white issue.

As devout Catholics, the Italians believed in the superiority of the white race. It was for this reason blacks were not allowed in Italy and other predominately Roman Catholic countries of Europe—the reason why few of them died in concentration camps.[3]

In 1935, Italy invaded Ethiopia, a country of fifty million blacks. Realizing soldiers stationed in Ethiopia might integrate themselves with the natives Mussolini imposed heavy penalties for interracial copulation. The minimum penalty for an Italian was five years and that for an Ethiopian could range all the way up to death.

In any event pregnancies were aborted and offsprings—if any— disappeared. Although it was mostly kept under the table, Italy's occupation of Ethiopia surpassed the Holocaust in infanticide.[4]

Though the United States was no angel itself concerning the treatment of blacks, the atrocities were so great in Ethiopia that it joined together with its allies and placed sanctions on Italy. These sanctions which remained in place at the start of the war together with its fascist convictions made Italy the great ally of Germany.

Yet, there was a more intrinsic reason Italy was Germany's ally.

The Tri-Axis Powers

When the war began—by a whisker over Italy—Germany was the most Christian nation in the world split evenly between Catholics and Protestants. Ninety-nine percent of its population was Christian and the others—Jews and atheists—were destined for the camps.

Likewise the Italian army was entirely Christian. The mind of every single soldier was controlled by the sitting Pontiff. Every one of them would do whatever Pius told them to do.

Unlike the allied armies which spanned many religions, the Axis

Murder by the Grace of God

army was entirely Christian. There was not a Jew, a black, a Muslim or for that matter an atheist in the German and Italian armies. What's more—true of all Christians of the time—these soldiers were devout Christians who thought it a mortal sin not to attend services on Sunday and fell on their knees and prayed to Christ each night.

The Nazi uniform had a small zippered pocket. In the standard issue, if the recruit was Catholic it contained a pair of rosary beads. If one was Protestant it contained a small book containing passages from the Bible including the 23rd Psalm: "...Though I shall walk through the shadow of death...the Lord is my Shepherd..." the reason battlefield photographs of fallen German soldiers usually show either rosary beads or a prayer book in the hands.

Nazi battlefield graves

The Axis powers had the largest chaplain corps of any army in world history. If a soldier was caught not attending services he ran the risk of being tabbed an atheist and sent to a death camp.

The British hymn *Onward Christian Soldiers* could be heard in German and Italian for miles in and about battlefields.

Motion pictures and books portraying German troops shooting up churches in Poland and other occupied countries could not be further from the truth. This may have been somewhat true of the Russians, but not of the Germans. This was Vatican propaganda put in place after the war designed to separate modern day *Catholicism* from what it was then and continues to be today—*Fascism.*

Hitler's Guard at Mass
Lodz Poland
Sept 23, 1941

Brown Guard
Brussels Belgium
June 6, 1940

Hitler leaving Mass
Berliner Dom
March 16, 1943

It was this more than anything else which made the Vatican the great ally of the Axis powers. They shared a common ideology—*fascism:* some people are better than others and are entitled to more. This gave them a common enemy—*communism:* all children are created equal and are entitled to share equally in God's province.

Embers of war

Fascism had been implanted in Italy and Germany years earlier. When one plans to take over the world in the future one starts with the young who will carry out the plan in the future.

In preparation for World War II the Vatican used the *Catholic Scouts of Italy* to indoctrinate Italy's youth into fascism. In 1925, Pius XI and Mussolini began graduating children from the *Catholic Scouts*—a social group—to the *Fascist Scouts*—a military troop. [5]

In December 1926, Pius issued an order to elementary schools in Italy requiring enrollment of all children in the *Fascist Youth Organization*. As already discussed, this action prompted thirteen year old Albino Luciani to make his debut onto the public stage.

That Mussolini and Pius were grooming these children for war was apparent in that they dispensed with the angelic dress of the *Catholic Scouts* in favor of military uniforms for the newly formed *Fascist Scouts* and trained them in military tactics. As early as the age of eight, boys were trained in the use of firearms and, more importantly, they were brainwashed in fascism in an intense Vatican propaganda program to hate children growing up in Slavic countries.

By 1933, the process had been completed and Italy's youth had been indoctrinated into its *Fascist Youth Organization*. Yet, less than fifty thousand had been enrolled in its counterpart in Germany—the *Hitler Youth*. As Mussolini had before him, Hitler appealed to Pius. Overnight Germany's youth were enrolled in the *Hitler Youth*. [6]

By 1938, the scouts of the Axis powers were ready for war.

Fascism   **The Vatican**

In February 1929, Pius XI and Mussolini entered into the '*Lateran Treaty*' formally uniting the Roman Catholic Church with the fascist

Murder by the Grace of God

movement in Italy. There began a campaign to preach fascism—some kinds of people are better than others—openly from the pulpit. An election referendum was held which invited the populace to vote its support of the new fascist government.[7]

Pius issued a letter to Catholics in Italy. It was read from every pulpit in the country and published in every newspaper instructing the congregation to vote 'Yes.' The voters went to the polling stations on March 24, 1929. The vote was 8,519,539 'Yes' and 155,761 'No.' Mussolini became the recognized dictator of Italy.[8]

This demonstrates the immense power the Pope had upon the Italian people at the time. Although Mussolini would never waiver from the mission his people had given him, the Italians would string him up in Milan just fifteen years later.

Nazism The Vatican

On January 30, 1933, Hitler became Chancellor of Germany and established his *New World Order:* "The Federal Government must preserve and defend those Christian principles upon which our nation has been built and which define our morality and values"[9]

He drafted the *Enabling Act* intended to make himself dictator of Germany. On March 12, 1933, he established the *Coalition of the National Socialist (NAZI) Party and the Nationalist People's Party.*[10]

The coalition's first action was to open the first concentration camp—a converted factory just south of Berlin at Oranienburg. Members of the *Communist Party* and *Social Democratic Party* who otherwise would have voted against him were its first inmates.[11]

Yet, the measure required a two-thirds majority of the Federal Assembly and his new Nazi coalition controlled only 340 of its 647 seats. The balance of power rested in the *Catholic Centre Party*. Ludwig Kaas—a priest and pawn of Pius XI—headed the *Centre Party*. As Mussolini had before him, Hitler appealed to the Pope.[12]

On March 23, 1933, Kaas gave the order and the *Catholic Centre Party* cast the decisive block of votes passing the *Enabling Act.*

In an act of ironic symbolism, Kaas, himself, cast the specific vote which made Hitler dictator of Germany.[13] Kaas' vote changed Germany from a democracy to an autocracy. A day later the Vatican became the first foreign state to recognize the new government.[14]

A few months afterwards on July 20, 1933, Pius XI and Hitler entered into the *German Concordat*—the union of the Vatican with the Nazi Party of Germany. This together with the *Italian Concordat* of 1929 completed the fusion of the Tri-Axis Powers—Germany, Italy and the Vatican. The table had been set for World War II.[15]

Yet, there was an enormous difference between the *Italian Concordat*—the *Lateran Treaty*—and the *German Concordat*.

In the *Italian Concordat* the Vatican had among other things, gained its sovereignty and title to the property which makes up the Vatican State today in exchange for its allegiance to Mussolini.

In the case of the *German Concordat* the situation was much different. Pius formalized his allegiance with Hitler solely because he shared the dictator's philosophies as set forth in *Mein Kampf*—**some kinds of people are better than others**—which remains the central canon of the Roman Catholic Church today.

As a part of the strategy Pius dissolved the *Catholic Centre Party* merging its members into the *Nazi Party*. With the completion of this union Pius, Hitler and Mussolini were on their way to war.

On August 24, 1933, Hitler held a huge rally in Neukolln Stadium in Berlin to celebrate the *German Concordat*. Secretary of State Eugenio Pacelli (Pius XII) and Papal Nuncio Orsenigo joined him on the podium. Three hundred priests and bishops lined the wall of the stadium.[16]

One is on solid ground when one says the success of the fascist movement in Europe rested entirely upon papal decisions. Neither the Italian nor German referendums would have passed without sanction of the Pope. Mussolini would have never become dictator of Italy and Hitler would have never become dictator of Germany.

It was clearly the Pontiff who was the puppeteer who held the strings which played the marionettes which would eventually act and dance their way into World War II and snuff out fifty million lives.

The concentration camps

Murder by the Grace of God

The day before he became dictator, Hitler opened the camp at Dachau—a base model for the vast network of death camps that would eventually follow. Because he was tied up with the *Enabling Act*, Hitler did not attend opening ceremonies. Vice Chancellor Franz von Papen and the German Apostolic Delegate Cesare Orsenigo did the honors. As they entered the gates of the prison they were saluted by a group of bishops and Nazi officers gathered there.[17]

The early inmates included social revolutionary activists, union leaders, Jews, gypsies and gay youths who had been rounded up in gay meeting places. Initially, Hitler went after those who opposed the *Enabling Act* and those who were suspected of having spied for the Russians in the First World War.

Inmates were branded with serial numbers and forced to wear patches which identified them by color: red for political dissidents - violet for anti-Christians - black for social revolutionary activists - pink for homosexuals - yellow for Jews - brown for atheists and gypsies. Gypsies were Slav-atheists who wandered in Germany.

Cesare Orsenigo, Pius XII and the death camps

Orsenigo eventually became the fall guy for the Vatican. After the war he was blamed for failing to convey to Pius XII what was going on in the death camps during the war. Some claim he went so far as to block this information flowing from others to the Vatican. His ideology mimicked that of Hitler. He told a German reporter a week after Germany invaded Poland: "The Jew will not fight in behalf of the Fatherland because he is selfish to his own end. He will undermine our struggle to bring about a worldwide Christian society."[18]

It is inconceivable Pius XII was unaware of the Holocaust. Orsenigo had for many years been his closest confidant. In 1930, when Pius XII (Cardinal Eugenio Pacelli) vacated the Nuncio post in Germany, he appointed his closest friend Orsenigo to fill the job.

To see things clearly as they happened one has to put events in the chronological order in which they occurred.

On September 1, 1939, Germany invaded Poland.

In late September, Warsaw and Krakow fell to the Germans.

On October 6th, German occupation of Poland was completed.

On October 14th, groundbreaking of Auschwitz took place outside Krakow. It would evolve into a network of forty-eight death camps within Poland which would murder upwards of five million.

On November 9th, Pius XII removed Filippo Cortesi as the Polish Nuncio and appointed Orsenigo the additional duty of Pro-Nuncio to Poland. That Pius did this at the exact time it was decided the death camps would be concentrated in Poland is powerful evidence he not only knew of the horrific plan, he had conspired with Hitler to bring it about. Yet, one always has coincidence. One will never know. [19]

Orsenigo was permitted to travel freely to Poland including his publicized trips to Auschwitz at Krakow and Treblinka at Warsaw. [20]

Orsenigo served as the clandestine contact between what was going on in the death camps and Pius XII. His close friendship with Hitler is documented by hundreds of surviving photos of himself with the Fuhrer. So much so, if Hitler was not so recognizable, one would think him Orsenigo's bodyguard.

The Boxer Rebellion

The young seminarian Luciani at Belluno watched and waited.

He knew it had been these same dictates of Christianity that had inspired the Boxer Rebellion in China at the turn of the twentieth century which had driven the Christians out of China. He was about to see it happen all over again in World War II and he would live to see it happen, once more, in the Vietnam War.

Until Christian preachers started to preach hatred of people who live their lives differently, the Chinese never knew what the word 'bigotry' meant as all people were children of the same God.

Murder by the Grace of God

"Love thy neighbor as thyself" is not original to Christ. It was the primary thesis of Taoism and had been the way of life in China for five hundred years before Christ's time. It is also the fundamental thesis of communism. As one knows, it has never become the way of life in much of the western world which claims Christ as its God.

The Boxers knew the United States, a Christian nation, held other than whites as inferior peoples. Blacks, Asians, Native Americans, Hispanics and other ethnic peoples were made to live as outcasts. They were not permitted in white neighborhoods and were confined to live under unbearable conditions in impoverished ghettos. They were not provided equal opportunity in jobs and education. [21]

Blacks were imprisoned if caught using 'white' toilets or riding in the fronts of buses or sitting in the ground-floor pews of churches. They were often taunted, tortured and even killed in hate crimes.

Unlike the Bible, there is no censure of homosexuality in either the Vedas—Hinduism—or in the teachings of Laozi—Taoism.

It follows, in China, homosexuals—though considered ill by most sects—were accepted in society and provided basic human rights.

In the United States they were imprisoned for long terms and victims of the most heinous of hate crimes. In the south thousands of gay teens were taunted into suicide by deranged Christian parents.

Perhaps, most heartless of all, though mostly kept under the table, born-out-of-wedlock children were shunned in America—the stigma so powerful that disclosure left only one way out—suicide.

The Boxers knew it was the white Christian preacher who was the driving force behind this kind of hatred. They didn't want this influence in the east. Western wars had been ethnic cleansing wars.

Though China had wars of aggression, it had never thought there to be differences among peoples and this extended to all people who lived their lives differently regardless of creed, atheism, race, ethnic origin and even homosexuals.[22]

On the other hand, religious persecution through the years has been widespread in China; true of all communist nations which view western religions as the central source of prejudice and hatred.

Vietnam...why did we go?

Luciani would live to see the Boxers eventually progress into the Vietnam War. After the Boxers threw the Christians out of China, the Vatican continued to maintain a presence in French Indo-China which encompassed Laos, Cambodia and Vietnam—countries which bordered China to the south. Other than this, Catholicism had been restricted to the Philippines and other island nations in the east.

In 1954, the French pulled out of Vietnam and by 1955 the Vatican had lost its foothold in mainland Asia which blocked its strategy to annihilate atheism and convert China into its fold.

In September 1955, Pius claimed an apparition. He told Italy's largest newspaper *Corriere Della Sera:* **"I saw the Lord close to me in all His majesty...I heard the true and distinct voice of Christ."**[23]

Cardinal Roncalli (later John XXIII) of Venice was caught off guard by a reporter as claiming the Pope was making up stories to lead the world into a third world war: **'...If we are to have a true church it must be built on truth, not built on myth."** [24]

Roncalli reasoned the Pope had claimed to have seen Christ to facilitate his paving the way for World War III.

The French had recently pulled out of Vietnam and the Church had lost its foothold in mainland Asia—a stronghold of communism.

Communism holds the relationship between a man and his God to be a personal and sacred one and should not be a business by which men take advantage of man's fear of his mortality to accomplish political objectives. This made communism Pius' greatest enemy.

Nevertheless, Pius was about to entice the United States to fight his war. What better way than if Christ had given the order.

Cardinal Spellman of New York arranged a 3-day audience for U.S. Secretary of State John Foster Dulles and his son Avery Dulles with Pius XII. Avery was a Jesuit priest in Spellman's diocese.[25]

Despite the French half-century presence in Vietnam it remained overwhelmingly Buddhist—atheist. Unlike one might be led to believe it was in the hallowed halls of the Vatican—not in the hallowed halls of Washington DC—the Vietnam War began.

The Vatican's strategy was to force conversion of Vietnam, Cambodia and Laos through civil war. Once Catholicism regained a foothold in mainland Asia it would spread northward into China annihilating atheism—Buddhism—in its wake.

Avery Dulles' single achievement in life is that he influenced his father to involve America in Vietnam which cost upwards of eight million lives. Avery would in time become the only American not a bishop ever made a cardinal in recognition of this 'holy' attainment.

An important part of the Pius/Dulles/Spellman strategy was to place into power Ngo Dinh Diem—a devout Catholic and a long time personal friend of Spellman. Diem, together with his brothers—one the archbishop and the other the chief of police—rose to power on October 26, 1955 less than a week after the Vatican meeting. [26]

The Diems would rule Vietnam with an iron fist closing temples and ostracizing Buddhist priests; many burning themselves to death in protest of American backed religious persecution.

Three weeks after the summit with Pius XII, John Foster Dulles announced American intervention in Vietnam. [27]

The Kennedy Assassination

One of the most credible theories surrounding the assassination of President John Kennedy grew up out of his intention to pull out of Vietnam. The theory pointed to a conspiracy of right-wing elements in the Vatican and factions in the CIA to continue the war.

Kennedy found that though South Vietnam was overwhelmingly Buddhist, there was not a Buddhist in the South Vietnam army. It was entirely Catholic. This told him the war was not between South Vietnam and North Vietnam, but between the South Vietnam Catholic army and the North Vietnam Atheist army.

When he realized America was fighting a religious war intended to annihilate atheism, Kennedy started to pull troops out of Vietnam just three weeks before his assassination. An American pull-out would end the Vatican's plan. CIA-Vatican intrigue went to work. [28]

There has been no war more fundamentally based on religion than the Vietnam War which pitted organized religion—the Vatican, against organized atheism—Buddhism. So much so, the war gave birth to the misconception communism is synonymous with atheism.

Spellman took on such an active role in organizing the Vietnam War it is rightly remembered today as **'Spelly's War.'**

Years earlier in the Korean War, *Radio Hanoi* capitalized on America's discriminatory policies against blacks driven by Christian preachers. So much so, black soldiers were reassigned to non-combat duty away from Korea—the reason very few of them died in Korea. It didn't take long for the American Negro to realize he was fighting for a country that considered him a subordinate human being and against the Chinese who considered him an equal.

The American Civil War

Back in Belluno—widely read in world history—Luciani knew the American Civil War also had its roots in what Moses had to say.

In 1841, the Baptist Church split into the southern church and the northern church, the former believing in the 10th Commandment which protected the right of one man to enslave another: 'Thou shalt not covet (desire to take from) thy neighbor...his slaves,' and the latter no longer accepting slavery as the word of God. It was this division in the Baptist Church that set the stage for the Civil War.

Luciani saw this happening all over again as he witnessed the glowing embers of war—the fascist scouts, the concentration camps, the growing hatred of non-Christians and the fusion of the Tri-Axis Powers marching toward World War II and fifty million lives.

During this trying period, though often tempted to do so, he never approached the press. He knew to act would demolish his ability to carry out the commission his father had given him—to change the Church back to what Christ had intended.

"...faith and the conviction with which we speak."

Luciani spoke at length of humility at his graduation ceremony. He reminded his classmates to never forget they are mere men.

> "The preacher is unique among entrepreneurs.
>
> All businessmen know immensely more about their products and services than do their customers—the reason they are able to sell their wares.
>
> Yet, we as preachers know no more about the existence of a God, or which God is the true God, than do our customers.
>
> As a matter-of-fact, we will know nothing about the afterlife until after we are dead. Then, perhaps, we may never know.
>
> All we have is our faith and the conviction with which we speak. We came here with one of these. The good fathers gave us the other.
>
> Let us take them with us. Let us feed them - nourish them - train them - cherish them - protect them. For these are the horses

Murder by the Grace of God

of the carriage that will one day take us to our destiny.

Let us never use them—our faith and the conviction with which we speak—to spread hatred of any of God's children no matter how different they may appear to be or how different they choose to live their lives.

Rather, let us use them to help bring about a day when all men and women—no matter how scorned by doctrine—will be accepted with equal human dignity under the laws of nations..."[29]

On July 7, 1935, in a city of beige stucco topped off with orange terra cotta roofs, Don Albino Luciani was ordained a priest.

He had learned to heed his father's words: "Play the game carefully...never risk your king to save a pawn."

Author's note: Vietnam War casualties: South Vietnamese Army 184,000 100% Christian mostly Catholic; North Vietnamese Army 1.1 million 100% Buddhist and Hindu; up to 7 million civilians mostly Buddhist some Hindu. 58, 913 American soldiers never knew they died for Pius XII. For those who think the Soviet Union had something to do with the war, Russian casualties = zero.

1 *Messaggero di S Antonio* Nov 73 - *Illustrissimi* letter to Mark Twain.
2 Over 2 million Christian crosses mark the World War I dead in military cemeteries in Germany. The *Star of David* marks less than twenty of them. Search: German cemetery photos
3 The short story *'The Red Faced Captain'* in the author's book *'The Reincarnation of Albino Luciani'* recounts an incident in which General Patton defied Pius XII by marching his black battalion into Italy
4 Search: Italian history – *Occupation of Ethiopia*.
5 Search: Italian history – *Fascist Scout Organization*
6 Search any German history book – *Hitler Scouts*
7 *La Repubblica* 12 Feb 29 -   the Lateran Treaty was ratified by Italian Parliament Jun 7, 1929
8 *La Repubblica* 25 Mar 29 -   though Mussolini had assumed some dictatorial powers before this time, he had not been previously been recognized by the people as dictator
9 *Berliner Zeitung* 2 Feb 33
10 *Berliner Zeitung* 13 Mar33 *'Nazi Party Coalition'*
11 *Berliner Zeitung* 15 Apr 33 *'Oranienburg'*
12 *L Osservatore Romano* 19 Mar 33
13 *Washington Post* 24 Mar 33 *'Enabling Act, Berlin'*
14 *L Osservatore Romano* 29 Mar 33
15 *Berliner Zeitung* 22 Jul 33 *L Osservatore Romano* 22 Jul 33
16 *Berliner Morgenpost* 25 Aug 33
17 *Berliner Zeitung* 24 Mar 33
18 *Berliner Morgenpost* 10 Sep 39 - *Phayer* 2000 - search: Cesare Orsenigo
19 *L Osservatore Romano* 9 Nov 39 *Berliner Morgenpost* 10 Nov 39
20 *L Osservatore Romano* 1 May 40 *Zycie Warszawy* 15 Jul 42
21 True today. In the United States blacks comprise 12% of the population and 40% of the prison pop.
22 In the 20th century, as parts of China became westernized (Christians and Muslims) racial, ethnic and sexual orientation prejudices surfaced in some provinces.
23 *Corriere Della Sera* 16 Sep 55
24 *Messaggero Mestre* 29 Sep 55.
25 *L Osservatore Romano* 23 Oct 55   John Foster & Avery Dulles three day audience with Pius XII
26 *Washington Post* 27 Oct 55
27 *Washington Post* 7 Nov 55
28 *New York Times* 6 Nov 63
29 *Il Corriere Delle Alpi* 12 Jun 35

Chapter 6

The Politics of Albino Luciani

"...chastity is a repression, a remnant of fascism, an out-of-date medieval practice. It is time to bring about the sexual revolution."

Albino Luciani letter to Aldus Manutius *Illustrissimi* [1]

In 1984, David Yallop did something much more important than prove the case for murder. He revived the liberal identity of Albino Luciani which the Vatican had all but annihilated after his death.

From the standpoint of murder there is a big difference between what I have to say in this book and Yallop's book *In God's Name*.

From the standpoint of the life of the 33-day Pope, the complete biography presented in this book is entirely consistent with the biographical brief presented in Yallop's book *In God's Name*.

Burying the evidence

In the aftermath of John Paul's death, I visited my friend Antonio Cunial—bishop of Vittorio Veneto—hoping to secure some of Luciani's records that I might one day put them to writing. He told me agents from the Vatican Foreign Minister's office had taken them to Rome. I asked him why he had surrendered the records.

Bishop's Castle Vitorrio Veneto

When confronted, Cunial called Luciani's lawyer in Venice and was told his Will had provided records pertaining to his ministries as a priest and as a bishop be left to relevant dioceses he had served. Yet, as Luciani's Will could not be found, Cunial had no legal grounds to resist and surrendered the records.

He told me something else. There had been a break-in at the local newspaper and some of its archives stolen. This did not mean much to me as when he was a bishop most of the important things he did reached notoriety and were recorded in many newspapers.

Yet, as a common priest, the record was in Belluno. I arrived too late. Bishop Ducoli had given up Luciani's documents on demand.

Still one could depend on the Belluno newspaper *Corriere delle Alpi* for the twenty years he spoke out on humane issues as a priest?

Unfortunately, this is not the case.

A P2-Opus Dei coalition bought out the newspaper in the early seventies to seal archives of articles it had published of John XXIII.

As Patriarch of Venice, John XXIII had been critical of the visionary saints. It was he who coined the phrase 'The Fatima Cult.'[2]

He had been equally critical of Lourdes, La Salette and other forerunners of Fatima. He reasoned each of these visionaries had obviously plagiarized those that had come before them.[3]

This was at the core of Pope John XXIII's ministry—to change the Church from one built on myth and a make-believe world to one based on truth and the real world we live in. As we will demonstrate, this was also at the core of Albino Luciani's existence.

In the 2003 edition of 'Murder in the Vatican' (not recommended) I wrote: 'In the Veneto, I picked up a box of his original sermons.'[4]

Drafted on what I recognized as diocese stationary and thinking them real, I incorporated what they had to say in that book.

An astute reader—a renowned paleographer—exposed them a fraud. Forensic testing resolved them, indeed, a fraud. So well executed, they had obviously been planted by Vatican censors in their efforts to annihilate the true record of Luciani after his death.

If you take the time to visit the Veneto country as I have many times, you, too, can pick up 'original' drafts of his work; phony diocese letterheads carefully bathe in tea to give them a tinge of age—easy bait for the everyday sucker. Beware of authors who take to the Veneto country and publish 'original' copies of his work.

'The Origin of the Human Soul according to Rosmini'

Perhaps the most widely publicized manipulation of the political remains of Albino Luciani involved his doctoral thesis.

As we have said, at an early age Albino Luciani adopted Antonio Rosmini as his philosophical mentor. One might wonder why his ministry mirrors that of Rosmini whereas surviving 'originals' of his thesis 'The Origin of the Human Soul according to Rosmini' entirely refute what his nineteenth century mentor had proposed.

After his death, Albino Luciani's 'doctoral thesis' was displayed in the Vatican Museum. A tourist—a typewriter manufacturer—recognized it as being typed on a typewriter he had developed in 1958, more than a decade after Luciani had executed the work.

The Vatican explained the discrepancy citing the 'Imprimatur' which prefaced the document. 'Imprimatur' is not about what is in a book. It is a declaration of what is 'not' in a book. It certifies that its contents have been purged of anything contrary to Catholic doctrine.

Regardless, soon afterwards another 'original thesis' surfaced in the Apostolic Library and was distributed to all Catholic university libraries in Europe. This one typed on a 1940s vintage typewriter.

This **'Vatican Deception'** belittles Luciani suggesting he wasted his doctoral days examining the possibility of genetic orientation of the human soul. A worthless task as everyone knows if the soul was of genetic origin it would decay at death. It doesn't take a PhD to tell one that. Also, cleverly deleted from the Vatican fraud is Luciani's endorsement of Rosmini's thesis **'The Five Wounds of the Church.'**[5]

Author's note: Albino Luciani typed his doctoral thesis on a Remington portable typewriter that had been given him in 1929 which typed only in uppercase letters.

The press

Even the surviving press for which I rely on for much of what I have to say has to be evaluated with caution.

In the spring of 1974, questioned concerning the psychological community's declaration homosexuality is a God-given birthright, a Vatican-owned newspaper reported him as saying: **"It would seem sex natural of a man is a part of love for one of the opposite sex."**[6]

This is what he did say. Yet, is it is not all that he said.

An independent paper reported: **"It would seem sex natural of a man is a part of love for a person of the opposite sex. Yet, God makes exceptions and society must accommodate God's exceptions..."**[7]

The right-wing paper reported only part of what was said.

On the anniversary of the medical declaration he spoke of the difficult road ahead to unravel the stigma that had wrongly been associated with homosexuality: **"As long as one can be accused of being a homosexual, we have not put this one behind us."**[8]

Murder by the Grace of God

Curia censorship

As we have said, as a rule the Curia censors what a pope actually said before it gets into print. Many authors have written of this.

One has Roger Crane's play *The Last Confession* starring David Suchet:

SCENE: Papal Apartment ten days into John Paul's papacy

JOHN PAUL: *(reading a newspaper - disturbed)* "The Vatican press has changed my speech again...This isn't what I said at all. Just official statements cleverly redrafted by the Curia. They even have me celebrating the tenth anniversary of the encyclical against birth control. Everyone knows I intend to revise it."

LORENZI: *(agreeable nod)* "There is also an article of your condemnation of the birth of the recent test-tube baby."

JOHN PAUL: "They know of and are ignoring the letter I wrote congratulating her parents." *(Raising his voice in anger)* Damn them!"

LORENZI: *(gasps)* "Holy Father!"

JOHN PAUL: "Forgive me." *(smiling)* "Just a figure of speech..."

Then there is the play *Torn Lace, Shattered Dreams:*

SCENE: Papal Apartment on the evening before John Paul's last public audience

MAGEE: *(reading a newspaper)* "It says here, 'The Anti-communist Pontiff refused to join the priest-worker movement.' They have it in all the newspapers."

JOHN PAUL: *(laughing)* "They've got it partly right. I never joined it. I led it."

MAGEE: *(dumbfounded look)*

John Paul: "Paul VI drafted *Populorum Progressio*—the inalienable right of all men to an equal share of God's province. Read my book *Illustrissimi*. I make clear my support for the *priest-worker movement* in my letter to Dickens in which I compare the capitalist to a camel crossing the desert: As his hooves pound the grains of sand the camel cries out in triumph, 'I am crushing you.' The grains allowed themselves to be crushed. Then the wind spoke, 'come little ones...together we will rise up in a storm and bury him under a mountain of sand.' Paul was the wind. I am the storm."

MAGEE: *(a look of surprise)*

John Paul: *(agitated)* "And this name-tab, 'Anti-communist?' They are confused by what is going on in Russia. The Soviet Union is an autocracy. It was never a true communist society. Tomorrow, I will tell the world what communism really means. Tomorrow, I will tell the world what Christ really means."

MAGEE: *(casts another dumbfounded look)*

JOHN PAUL: "It is the inalienable right of no man to accumulate wealth beyond his needs while other men starve to death because they have nothing."

The uncontested political record of Albino Luciani

Luciani's best seller *Illustrissimi* is a collection of letters he wrote to historical and fictitious people. Interspersed between the lines of its relatively heavy theology is the political ideology of Albino Luciani.

Even here one must dig up the 1973 Italian edition as the Vatican went to work on 'original editions' published after his death.

The English translation was published after he died in December 1978 under the scrutiny of ultraconservative Cardinal Wright who edited out much of what Luciani stood for particularly as it pertains to his compassion for women, homosexuals and the poor.

In some cases no more than a word is added or deleted to change the context of what Luciani actually wrote. In other cases, letters are entirely deleted like those that address his widely known support for the 'pill' and Planned Parenthood.

In all, Luciani published fifty-six letters in the Italian paper *Messaggero di S Antonio* between 1972 and 1975 of which only forty survive in the English translation and those censored.

A few of Albino Luciani's letters did survive in *Illustrissimi* with relatively minor modifications vs. those originally published. The following letters are as originally published by the Italian magazine.

"Dear Pinocchio:

I was seven years old when I first read your adventures. I can't tell you how much I liked them. In you, I recognized myself as a boy, and in your surroundings I saw my own...

My dear Pinocchio, there are two famous remarks about the young. I commend the first by Lacordaire, to your attention: 'Have an opinion and assert it!' This is one of reason. It is the lion. It will win for you.

The second is by Clemenceau, and I do not recommend it to you at all, 'He has no ideas of his own, but he defends them with ardor!' This is one of belief. It is the sheep. It will lose for you...

Think of this, as you go through life, as you run through the woods with the Cat and the Fox and the Poodle Medoro,

Your magical friend, Albino"[9]

Murder by the Grace of God

Luciani contrasts the progressive democrat Lacordaire on the *left* and the conservative republican Clemenceau on the *right*. One need not go further than his letter to his dear friend Pinocchio, one of his most famous, to determine on which side of the aisle he stood.

His letter to Pinocchio is consistent with the papal video clip of a televised audience on September 27, 1978: "Look, Daniele, the Lord has put in us a desire to progress, to go forward..."[10]

Again, in his *Illustrissimi,* he points to the socialist and away from the self-serving republican in his expedition beyond the wall:

"Dear Casella:

I have had the good fortune to have visited those places which, as we all know, lie beyond the wall.

For each of us, I have found that we will live beyond the wall as we have chosen to live on this side of the wall.

First, I was granted the privilege of seeing Hell. As I peered in through the gates, I saw an immense room with many long tables.

On these were so many bowls of cooked rice and gourmet delicacies as one could imagine, properly spiced, inviting.

The diners were all seated there, filled with hunger, two at each bowl, one facing the other. Then what?

To carry the food to their mouths they had, in oriental fashion, chopsticks affixed to their hands, but so long that no matter how great their efforts, not a single grain of delicacy could reach their mouths. Although starving, they could not take of these things.

Then, I was able to peer into Heaven.

Here again, I saw a great room with the same tables, same gourmet delicacies, same long chopsticks affixed to their hands. But here the people were happy, smiling and quite satisfied. Why?

Each, having picked up the food with the chopsticks, raised it to the mouth of the companion that sat opposite, and all was right.

So my dear Casella, we must learn here, as we make our way toward the great wall, how to use the chopsticks, else we will not know how to use them when we are on the other side of the wall.

Your magical friend, Albino"[11]

Once more, from his pen in *Illustrissimi:*

"My Dear Figaro:

Well then, who and what are you my dear Figaro?
A variety of dress? A mixture of feminine and masculine?
Poor Figaro, against all these nobles with their coats of arms, these bewigged bourgeois, who themselves do every trespass.
They are no better, perhaps, worse than you.
Barber, marriage broker, adviser of pseudo diplomats, yes, ladies and gentlemen, whatever you like.
They demand that you alone be honest in this world of cheats and rogues.
Do not accept what they say, my dear Figaro. You, too, are a citizen.
Sadly, perhaps, your only solution is in revolution!

Your magical friend, Albino"[12]

Luciani refers to scant condemnation of homosexuality in the Bible. Less than a half dozen ambiguous mentions of it as compared to more than eighty condemnations of heterosexual sexual activities calling for the death penalty and permanent exclusion from heaven.

Doctrinal position

For those who are lucky enough to stumble across a 1949 edition of *Catechism in Crumbs,* one will find the formation of his doctrinal position: '…as long as doctrine did not treat people unfairly he conformed to it. Yet, whenever doctrine placed undue hardship on the lives of innocent people, he stepped in.'

The day he became a cardinal Luciani paid homage to Lincoln for having had the great courage to have defied the written word of his God: "Thou shalt not covet (desire to take from) thy neighbor his property, including his house, his wife, his slaves, his ox, his ass."

He told a youth group in Venice:

"Never be afraid to stand up for what is right, whether your adversary be your parent, your teacher, your peer, your politician, your preacher, your constitution, or even your God!"[13]

Murder by the Grace of God

His letters to Carlo Goldoni in his book *Humbly Yours* prove him an ardent feminist. For those who can't accept his written word, we have the papal film clip: **"God is our Father, more so, our Mother."**[14]

His central mission

From his struggle as a young boy with the orphans, to his letter to Charles Dickens in *Illustrissimi* in which he refers to capitalism as a **'wicked system,'** to the path his papacy had taken in its brief tenure, this man's mission was no secret. So much so, he was universally recognized by both those on the *right* and those on the *left* as a monumental Marxist—an enemy of the capitalistic world he lived in.

One day in Venice he was bombarded by activists on a range of issues from the 'pill,' women ordination, homosexuality, remarriage, priest celibacy and so forth; issues of the emerging social revolution he had from time to time championed. He stopped them:

> **"As long as there is a single child anywhere on earth who is starving to death because he or she does not have enough to eat, there exists no other problem in the world."**[15]

How can one possibly wiggle one's way around it?

> **"It is the inalienable right of no man to accumulate wealth beyond his needs while other men starve to death because they have nothing."**[16]

Doesn't sound like much of a republican to me!

1 *Messaggero di S Antonio* May 71 - *Illustrissimi* letter to Aldus Manutius
2 *La Stampa* 17 Aug 54
3 *Messaggero Mestre* 22 Aug 56
4 *Murder in the Vatican* 2003 (not recommended)
5 Search Antonio Rosmini on the Internet and libraries
6 *Il Gazzettino* 12 Feb 74. The Vatican had a controlling interest in *Il Gazzettino*
7 *Nostro Privilegio* 13 Feb 74
8 *Messaggero Mestre* 17 Dec 74
9 *Messaggero di S Antonio* Jun 72
10 *Associated Press* 27 Sep 78 and most world newspapers. Search You Tube film clip Albino Luciani
11 *Messaggero di S Antonio* Sep 73 - *Illustrissimi*
12 *Messaggero di S Antonio* Apr 72 - *Illustrissimi*
13 *La Nuova Venezia* 6 Mar 73 Basilica San Marco
14 *L Osservatore & Associated Press* Sunday Angelus 10 Sep 78
15 *La Nuova Venezia* 17 Dec 77
16 John Paul saying this in his September 27, 1978 audience can be viewed on You Tube

Chapter 7

His Ministry

"Democracy which finds its strength in rule by the people can only find its sacred duty to society in preserving the basic human rights and dignity of its loneliest individual."[1]

Albino Luciani

Albino Luciani's first post was in the small village in which he had grown up. He had been on the job for less than a week when he was summoned to the rector's office for his first commission:

"My sister is gravely ill. She will not make it another month.
That is not the bad news, for we must all meet our maker.
The bad news is she will not see Him for long. She remarried outside the Church and has been living in a state of mortal sin."

The old man reached across the desk grasping the young priest's hand with a frightened look as if he were hanging from the edge of a cliff, "You must rescue her from Satan. It is your sacred duty to convince her to renounce her husband or she will surely be buried in unholy ground and burn in the everlasting fires of hell."

When Albino arrived at the hospital he was given another task. The woman's doctor met him outside her room and told him she had only a few hours to live and asked if he would tell her this.

Rosary beads ran like a miniature freight train through her fingers to rumbling repetitions. Though dealing with a woman who had remarried, he was, nevertheless, dealing with a devout one.

Taking up her hand he told her the bad news—she had only a few hours to live. He followed it up with the real bad news: "Unless you renounce your husband, you will surely go to hell."

To his astonishment she answered with a question: "What do you think I should do?"

The young priest struggled between his duty and his heart. He answered her question with another question: "Do you love him?"

A tear ran down her cheek: "With all my heart."

Her hand still in his, Albino fell silent wondering what he should do. During his seminary days he had excelled at soccer, so much so, his team had never lost a game. Yet, now the clock was running out and he was about to lose this one.

His eye caught the tiny crucifix hanging from the beads. He had his answer: "I wonder what Jesus would do in this case?"

Holding a tear in the corner of his eye, he cuffed her hand tightly: "Then cling to it, your love for your husband. Don't ever give it up. Not for me, not for your brother, not even for the Pope, not for all the popes who have ever reigned.

Your love for your husband was not given to you by men. It was given to you by God. He would not be happy if you were to give it back to Him to satisfy the whims of mortal men.

I promise you, if you have the courage to do this for me, there will be reserved for both you and your husband a place in heaven. Believe me, if it takes me all the remaining days of my life, I will make this possible for you."

Unwinding the beads from her fingers, he reached for a photo of her husband on the bedside table and placed it in her hands. She died still clutching the picture three hours later.[2]

Thus began the ministry of John Paul I.

Checkmate!

Of all the persecutions imposed by the Church on innocent people, it was its position on remarriage that tormented him the most. He could not accept the Church could take it upon itself to refuse sanctification of the union of two people who—having had made a mistake in choosing a mate at twenty—had fallen truly in love at thirty. It troubled him deeply the Church condemned millions of people to have lived out their lives in loneliness and despair who otherwise would have lived out their lives in loving relationships.

In 1950, he wrote a letter to Rome recommending Hitler and Mussolini be excommunicated posthumously.[3]

Ignored, he followed it up with another letter demanding the authority to grant annulments be moved to the local bishop level:

"I am greatly tormented Mother Church would see it as her duty to close the Gates of Heaven to so many young innocent people who have at last found true love and, yet, see it as its duty to leave the Gates of Heaven open to the likes of monsters."[4]

A leading Italian tabloid capitalized on his expertise in chess. Its headline read: 'SCACCO MATTO'— 'CHECKMATE!'[5]

Pius moved for excommunication but his undersecretary of state, Montini, stopped him warning it would cause an uproar in the press.

Montini recalled the young priest from Belluno. During the war, Luciani had approached him to use his influence to gain asylum in the Vatican for five hundred Jews who had shown up on a boat in Naples. Montini struggled with Pius for a compassionate decision. Instead, the Pope ordered the boat to Germany to death camps.[6]

These encounters marked a turning point in Luciani's life; they won him the favor of Giovanni Montini who eventually rose to the papacy—Paul VI, which would eventually lead to his own papacy.

"...sex is good and beautiful..."

Luciani was convinced removing the stigma associated with out-of-wedlock pregnancies would eliminate what was at the time the leading cause of abortions—family embarrassment.

He relived his childhood in his memoirs:

> "I could hear my mamma and aunt and sister talking in low tones. Every time I entered the room there was a hush-hush. Then one day my sister took a holiday. I was told she had gone to a nearby village to rest for awhile, but they didn't fool me at all. I knew exactly what was going on. As I fell on my knees that night I vowed I would someday bring an end to it all. Believe me, I will."[7]

A pioneer of the sexual revolution, he was the first in either the public or private forum to introduce sexual education into schools. He wanted to bring about a day when sex would be discussed openly between parents and children. Until his time, sex—being sinful—was not to be talked about in either the family or schools.

He looked forward to a time when sex would be seen as good and beautiful rather than being condemned as shameful and sinful.

He knew the Church's position that sex was evil caused many children to grow up in a state of trauma resulting in guilt complexes which led to less than healthy sex lives and, at times, even suicide:

> "My part in this thing is to bring about a day when the young girl would no longer think she has gotten herself into trouble as the preacher might lead her to believe. Rather she would realize that she had gotten herself into paradise."

Today few abortions are owed to embarrassment. It is much to the credit of Albino Luciani millions of children—who might otherwise have been aborted—now see the light of day.

Orphanages

As a cardinal he often spoke of Italy's enormous homeless orphan population. One day looking up at the immense dome of the Basilica di San Marco in Venice, he told his congregation: "We must learn to lower our ceiling height to make room for all of Christ's children."[8]

In his twenty years as a bishop and as a cardinal, Albino Luciani never built a single church. Yet, he built forty-four orphanages, many of them equipped with schools and clinics.

A monk, one of an army of monks and nuns who had spent most of their lives in prayer, spoke of him:

> "He literally pulled us up off our knees pleading to plaster idols and put us to work; we brothers building and maintaining orphanages and serving as youth counselors and the nuns teaching class and others caring for those children too ill to come to class."[9]

Whenever faced with the question as to whether to use money raised from the faithful for a church or an orphanage, he would ask himself: "Now, what would Jesus do in this case?"

Strange parents

Faced by an orphan population of two million in Italy, it was his lobbying in Italian Parliament that made it legal for single persons to adopt children in Italy. An opposition member challenged:

> "But, that would make it legal for homosexuals to adopt children."

Luciani responded:

"The desire to parent children is a basic human need...Until we can guarantee basic human rights to the tiniest minority we cannot truthfully call ourselves a democracy."

His adversary didn't give up:

"Homosexuals have a record of splitting up after the 'honeymoon' is over causing children to lose one or both of their parents."

Luciani closed the gap on his attacker:

"There are two major forces involved in making for long term loving relationships and regardless of what Rome might believe sex is not one of them.
 Sex is more often than not a declining force in relationships. It has little to do with the long term survival of a union.
 The longevity of a relationship of those who parent children that is so instrumental to protecting the stability of children until they reach adulthood depends not on sex, but on those forces that create long term relationships—love and companionship.
 In companionship, the homosexual has the edge. Two people of the same sex who fall in love make much better companions of each other because they are likely to share common interests. Children parented by homosexual couples are less likely to undergo the ordeal of arguments and the trauma of divorce..."

Still his attacker didn't give up:

"But, homosexuals are pedophiles..."

The bishop from the remote mountain province cut him off:

"Homosexuality is a God-given instinct. Pedophilia is a Satan-driven perversion. Yet, we should address the question.
 If our objective is to prevent pedophilia in adoption then the only logical action is to permit only homosexuals to adopt children only of the opposite sex. This would reduce incest in adoptions to zero as the sex of the victim is determined by the sexual orientation of the predator.

Murder by the Grace of God

Conversely, if we permit heterosexual couples to adopt children, children of both sexes would be at risk. Regardless, on average, homosexual adoptions reduce the risk in half."[10]

The measure passed. Overnight, thousands of orphans were provided loving and economic support by single parents. Some were gay couples of which one of the parents adopted the child, as it remained illegal for parents of the same sex to adopt the same child.

Little is known of Luciani's involvement with gay parents other than a few notes written in connection with his orphanages:

"We have found homosexual couples will take handicapped and born-out-of wedlock children which make up most our orphan population today. Heterosexual couples go for the cutest and healthiest children as if shopping for a puppy in a pet shop."[11]

There is another note written in diary format:

"Dear Mamma,

I have for years counseled a young couple. They have great sexual attraction for each other, yet, beyond that they have nothing in common. I have yet to be in their presence when they have not been arguing or yelling at each other.

What's more, they both suffer from an ongoing drug and alcohol addiction problem for which they have not sought counsel. Both children, having been bombarded for years by the incompatibility of their parents, are now confined to institutions. In that I sanctioned this marriage, I must live out my days with this on my conscience.

Last week, this couple came to me on a matter of such great urgency I had to cancel another appointment. They told me of a neighbor—one of the new single parents in Italy—a homosexual. Another man has been living with him for many years.

I have known of this queer couple for some time. Both men are contributing members of the community and spend much time helping out in the orphanage. Their two beautiful children, a boy and girl, are the envy of all who are privileged to experience them.

One night, as they were leaving, tears formed in their eyes.

They told me, it grieves them they cannot take all the children home with them.

Mamma, it is this experience, more than any other that has caused me to understand the qualifications of a good parent.

There is something terribly wrong with a society that thinks that one's sex is what makes one a good parent...

Your loving son, Albino"[12]

'Strategy of a Strange War'

Years before the psychiatric world came to the same conclusion Luciani realized sexual orientation could not be changed by therapy.

As a seminarian, he wrote a paper which brought him bad marks.

Yet, he found that unlike sexual orientation, sexual behavior can be conditioned by therapy. He reasoned either of two forces drives a sexual act—*love* or *lust*. When people are in love, *love* tends to drive the act. When people are not in love, *lust* tends to drive the act.

He reasoned a homosexual male can be conditioned to engage in sex with a woman only by changing the motivating force from *love* to *lust*. "...Yet, he will never be able to truly fall in love with her. He might grow to like her, develop affection for her, parent children with her, but, he will never be able to truly fall in love with her..."

Conversely, he had ministered in prisons and found heterosexual men who engaged in homosexual acts. Yet, no matter how long it went on, when a heterosexual male had an intimate relationship with another male he could never fall in love with him.

He concluded one's God-given instincts cannot be changed. He speaks of this in his paper *Strategy of a Strange War:*

> "Like all animals, we are born with two basic instincts: the instinct of survival, and its adversary, the instinct of compassion.
>
> It is the instinct of survival which moves the newborn puppy out of the womb to the teat. It is his instinct of compassion which causes him to move aside and let his little sister have some too.
>
> These instincts are with us all the days of our lives.
>
> They determine everything we do as everything we do is either done for ourselves or for others.

> Though we are scarcely aware of it, an inner struggle goes on within each of us every day of our lives. Each time the fork in the road comes up—often only minutes apart—our instinct of survival tells us: 'Now what is in this for me?' Our instinct of compassion tells us something else: 'Now, what is in this for others?'
>
> Many of our actions are reflections of these basic instincts.
>
> We don't teach babies what to laugh at or what to cry about. They are born with this instinct. All babies will laugh at the same things and cry about the same things and they will laugh and cry about these same things for all the remaining days of their lives.
>
> The tendency to fall-in-love is a manifestation of the basic instinct of compassion.
>
> The kind of person one falls-in-love with cannot be changed. It would be like trying to condition a child to laugh when something terrible happens and cry when something hilarious happens.
>
> These instincts are the fabric of the human soul. Although they cannot be changed in this life, it is within our power to weave them into the next life..."[13]

When doctrine unfairly penalized innocent people he stepped in.

It was in Italy the Vatican first limited hospital visitation rights to family members. The intent was to keep partners of homosexuals out to facilitate the priest demanding the dying partner renounce his or her loved one: "Otherwise, you will certainly go to hell!"

As a bishop, in defiance of the papal decree, he ordered hospitals within his jurisdiction to admit longtime partners of homosexuals into intensive-care units on at least six occasions reported in the press and many more not reported in the press.[14]

Across the pond

When civil rights laws were passed in the United States in 1964 the Christian-right—having lost its quest to keep the black in a corner—turned its hatred toward homosexuals. By the end of the decade millions of homosexuals had been incarcerated—those in northern states for short sentences and those in southern states for long terms. Alabama came within one legislative vote of requiring the death penalty for a single homosexual act in private.

In the wee hours of the morning in the spring of 1967, acting on a tip from a neighbor, police broke into the home of Robert Wise and Timothy Wilson, both 22, outside Augusta Georgia.

Caught in the act, they were tried and sentenced to twenty years. Timothy Wilson served only four days of his term. He cut his wrists and bled to death in his cell on his twenty-third birthday.[15]

Timothy Wilson did not stand alone in his demise.

During the ensuing quarter-century homosexuality surfaced as the leading cause of suicide in Bible-belt states. Upwards a quarter million gay children and teens—born to parents whose minds were deranged by the hatred of Christian preachers—took their lives.[16]

In the spring of 1969, the local newspaper boy delivered a copy of the *New York Times* to the bishop of Vittorio Veneto. Bishop Luciani's eye caught the headline: **'Police Murder Young Gay.'**

In an accompanying photo impaled facedown atop a heavy iron picket fence surrounding a police station was a small-framed boy; a half dozen spikes had penetrated his body from his neck to his thigh. The tips were wet with blood.

As he read the article he saw the caption was wrong. The boy, though in critical condition, was still alive. The fence was cut with blowtorches and the boy was removed to St. Agnes Hospital with the spikes embedded in his body.

The Hispanic teenager had been arrested by an undercover cop in Washington Square and brought to the station for booking.

Fearing disclosure to his parents, the youth pleaded for the police to let him go. When he went to use the restroom two officers were overheard threatening to force themselves on the youngster and the boy was either thrown from or leaped out of a window into the dark of the night and landed atop the fence.

The officers were suspended pending an investigation and were eventually returned to active duty when a witness who occupied a booth testified he had not seen anything; he had only overheard the confrontation and the most he could come up with is that one of the officers used the term: **"little faggot."** [17]

Approached by a reporter, Luciani was asked for his assessment: **"When religion sanctifies hostility, it erases its morality."**[18]

A week later the boy died. Infuriated by his death, homosexuals for the first time stood their ground and fought off police in what is remembered today as **'Stonewall.'**[19] The gay revolution had begun; the prediction he had made in his letter to Figaro had come about.

Four years later, in December 1973, the American Psychiatric Association adopted the resolution homosexuality is a matter of instinct and not a matter of illness. It ordered its members to begin the work of removing the stigma long been associated with it.[20]

Luciani, referring to the declaration of the psychiatric community homosexuality is God's will, got himself into trouble with his congregation when he made the remark: "**I wonder how long it will take for the sheep to get this one.**"[21]

Even after Galileo proved via his *Falling Bodies Law* the earth was round and rotating on its axis, Christians continued to believe it was flat because the Bible told them it was flat until years later when Magellan sailed off to the west and returned from the east. Even then, half of them refused to believe the earth was round.

Despite medical science proved its claim, most of the population influenced by preachers continued to believe sexual orientation was a matter of choice. Luciani would often taunt clergy who chose to ignore what the medical community had to say: "**Psychology, the science of human theology, excuses homosexuals. Does the fault lie with parents who didn't discipline their children or does the fault lie with the God who made them?**" For the most part he was ignored.

"...stamp out what Hitler stood for..."

In July 1976, the French physician-priest Marc Oraison made public his homosexuality. Backed by the psychiatric world's declaration he declared homosexual love was God's will.

Luciani warned Oraison in a public release: "**If a priest preaches as he does, everything is ruined.**"[22]

Of the things he said of homosexuality, this is the most widely known because it was included in the Vatican's original biographical brief of the 33-day Pope published shortly after his death. The Vatican included this tidbit as it was the only thing he ever said that might be taken as a condemnation of homosexuality.

It is clearly a criticism of the priest and not of homosexuality. Luciani warns that the priest should have kept his identity private—one can best help oppressed people by appearing to be an outsider. One is far less effective if one appears to be trying to help oneself.

Suggesting he was concealing his own sexual identity, a few days after the Oraison incident, he was asked by a reporter why he helped "those kinds of people?"

Alluding to the quarter of a million homosexuals murdered in concentration camps, he replied: "If we are ever to be truly free, we must stamp out what Hitler stood for once and for all."[23]

"...their liberty oppressed..."

In 1978, Paul VI permitted him to address Vatican cardinals on the possibility the Church encourage homosexuals to enter into long term loving relationships as they were the only group large enough to provide loving and economic support to children who otherwise would be aborted by women too young or too poor to afford them.

Luciani argued the Church's position exiled them from society, forcing them into loneliness and despair. He reasoned the Church's position was one of prejudice as science had proved the condition cannot be changed and the Bible's condemnation of homosexual acts was scant compared to its vast condemnation of heterosexual acts.

Yet, he was able to convince no more than a handful of his audience the matter should even be discussed. He thanked Paul for having given him the opportunity. Turning to the cardinals who had rejected his proposal his voice took on a rare tone of bitterness:

> "'The day is not far off when we will have to answer to these people who through the years have been humiliated, whose rights have been ignored, whose human dignity has been offended, their identity denied and their liberty oppressed.' What is more, we will have to answer to the God who created them."[24]

The innocence of sex

Concerning what he considered to be a more fundamental issue, he became outspoken about the population explosion. He argued the Church's ban on contraception was creating massive poverty and starvation in the poor countries of Asia, Latin America and Africa.

Its position on birth control was resulting in untimely pregnancies forcing abortions in the United States and Europe. "The Church's policy on birth control is in direct conflict with its policy on abortion. The Church, itself, is the underlying cause of the lion's share of abortions... Mother Church must cease to be the cause the world's problems and rather become the answer to them."[25]

What changes he would have made had he lived will never be known. What one does know is that he died on the eve of the time he would have lifted the Church's ban on contraception. One knows this for he could have never rid the world of poverty—his number one objective—unless he first eliminated the driving force behind it.

On April 11, 1970, Luciani told his priests:

"It is easy to find persons who use the pill and other contraceptives and do not believe they are sinning. If this were to happen it would be best not to disturb them... There has rarely been such a difficult question for the Church, particularly, in its intrinsic implications as it affects other doctrinal issues..."[26]

'...other doctrinal issues' strikes at the heart of papal power. According to canon law only a pope can determine 'who can have sex without committing sin and who cannot.' This defines morality in the Catholic world. According to doctrine, all sex outside what a sitting pope defines as marriage is mortal sin including masturbation, remarriage, homosexuality and even impure thoughts.

A Catholic is defined as one who believes only a pope can decide who can have sex without committing sin and who cannot—the reason, today, hundreds of millions of good Catholics—having made a slip in choosing a mate at age twenty—at thirty have fallen truly in love, are living out their lives in loneliness and despair. Take this unique power away from a pope and a pope is just another man.

Christ did not give this authority to the Pope. A group of early century men who thought there was something wrong with sex made it up. So much so, they elevated themselves above everyone else by abstaining from this natural biological function of the human body.

The *Council of Trent* which today defines morality in the Roman Catholic Church rises and falls on the premise all sex is evil. So much so, it explicitly subordinates marriage to celibacy:

'If one saith that the marriage state is to be placed above the state of virginity, or of celibacy, and that it is not more blessed to remain in virginity or celibacy, than to be in matrimony, let him be excommunicated.'[27]

Whereas quite understanding of homosexuals, Luciani was no more compassionate of them than he was of heterosexuals who engaged in sex outside of marriage and those who had not reached the age of marriage—equally condemned by the central moral doctrine of the Roman Catholic Church: **all sex outside of marriage is mortal sin.**

In his mind, homosexuals were not a minority as they claimed—together with their heterosexual allies they were in the majority.

His secretary in Venice Mario Senigaglia recalls:

"He was an understanding man. He would say to teenagers: 'We have made of sex the greatest of sins whereas in itself it is human nature and not a sin at all. Think of sex as being good and beautiful. Also keep in mind, as with all other gifts from God, it comes with responsibility, both to yourself and your loved ones.'

He would counsel couples contemplating marriage that it is irresponsible not to engage in sex before marriage: 'Unlike Mother Church might pretend it is not the whole of marriage. Yet, being incidental to marriage, it is prudent to test the waters before one drowns...'"[28]

David Yallop describes Cardinal Villot discussing contraception with John Paul I. He tells the cardinal: **"Eminence, what can we old celibates really know of the sexual desires of the married?"**

In general, Luciani could not understand how a group of old men in Rome, who had never been in the bedroom, could take it upon themselves to tell others what they can or cannot do in the bedroom.

Marriage

Traditionally, marriage had been a contract between a man and a man—a barter in which the merchandise was a maiden. *Falling in love* had little to do with it. It was common for a man to trade his daughter for a cow and think he got the better part of the deal.

Marriage was a one-way street to satisfy the lust of the man and grow his property—children. Marriage vows before 1853—the year in which women became human beings in the United States—were a woman's one way pledge to serve her master, "I promise to obey..."

In the mid-nineteenth century woman gained recognition as a human being and was no longer the mere property Moses had made her out to be. The definition of marriage began to change from being a business transaction between two men to what is emerging today as being a union of any two people who are mutually in love.

We are speaking here of society and not of the Church.

The definition of marriage within the Church remains today as it was first written into canon law in the seventh century: **permission of a sitting pontiff to have sex without committing sin.** According to canon law, the sole purpose of the Sacrament of Matrimony is to satisfy the body—*lust*. It has nothing to do with the mind—*love*.

Its dogma condemning transsexuals demonstrates marriage in the Catholic world is a union of bodies and not of minds. A woman defined by the psychological world to be a woman born into a man's body cannot marry a man; she can only marry another woman.

That marriage in the Church serves only to satisfy the body (*lust*) and has nothing to do with the mind (*love*) is cast in concrete in that no priest will marry a paraplegic or other person handicapped in such a way they cannot consummate sex.[29]

That satisfaction of body's *lust* and not *procreation* is the purpose of marriage in the Church is most clearly demonstrated in that every Catholic priest will marry a man and a woman well beyond their childbearing years into their nineties and beyond.

Nevertheless, in the nineteenth century *falling in love* began to define marriage in society. Yet, it still had to negotiate the hurdles society placed upon it: creed, race, social status, and so forth. A Jewish girl who fell in love with a Christian man could not marry him. Nationalities were involved. A Pole could not marry a Russian and so forth. Too, age was a factor. The man had to be older than the woman. If the woman was older it was frowned upon.

Even if the engagement passed all the tests of society, it still had to pass the will of the family or the two could not marry. One had to choose between one's family and one's happiness. This was true of everyone, those at the top and those at the bottom.

Then there occurred an event that would ignite a revolution which eventually would change the definition of marriage once and for all. Marriage would no longer be the decision of others or for that matter the state. It would be solely the decision of two people who fall in love. It would be an individual decision and not the decision of the majority. It would be the duty of the state to sanction the individual commitment of two people who are in love, no matter who those two people happen to be.

On December 10, 1936, Edward VIII, King of England, told the world: "**I abdicate my throne for the woman I love.**"

Edward had been engaged to Wallis Simpson, a divorcee who was not of royal blood. He had sought the approval of his family, the Church of England and the political establishment to no avail.

Albino was twenty-four when Edward abdicated. In Edward he saw courage, the same kind of courage his mother had shown when she had married his socialist-atheist father a quarter of a century earlier. In marrying a renegade, she too had given up her family.

At commencement services of his seminary in Vittorio Veneto in the summer of 1960 he spoke of love:

> "...Though the Bible's only account of falling in love involves two men: *'It came to pass...the soul of Jonathan was knit with the soul of David. Then Jonathan made a covenant with David, because he loved him as his own soul,'* it applies to everyone..."[30]
>
> Therefore we must hold in sanctified trust this most hallowed personification of God's creation—this perfect balance of mental energy that exists between any two people when they fall in love—whether it exists between man and woman, or black and white, or Christian and Jew, or believer and atheist, or German and Russian, or royalty and commoner, or virgin and divorcee, or man and man, or woman and woman, or paraplegic and paraplegic, or hermaphrodite and eunuch, or what have you...
>
> The rest of this thing one calls 'love' is nothing more than the animal in us. To think differently—it somehow pertains to physical parts of the body—is to say the Holy Sacrament of Matrimony pertains equally to the apes in the wild as it does to human beings.
>
> When Christ said: *'Let no man put asunder what God has joined together,'* He was speaking of that beautiful state of mind that exists when any two of God's children fall in love no matter who they happen to be—a union made by God. He was not speaking of ancient rituals performed by mortal men dressed up in long robes muttering vain repetitions—a union made by man."[31]

When he said this, the motion picture '**Guess Who's Coming to Dinner**' had not yet previewed and most of the unions he spoke of were condemned by preachers as being against God's will.

Interracial marriage

In the ensuing months, civil rights advocates in the United States—faced by polls overwhelmingly against integration—continued their struggle state-by-state to make interracial marriage legal.

As keynote speaker at the Christian Democratic Party Convention in Milan in 1963, Luciani criticized the American process:

> "The sacred duty of society is to protect certain inalienable rights for all of its citizens. It is not the option of any of its tributaries to abuse those rights. The right to fall in love with whomever God deems one fall in love with is the most precious of these rights...
>
> Democracy, which finds its strength in rule by the people, can only find its sacred duty to society in preserving the basic human rights of its loneliest individual."[32]

In 1967, an interracial case *Loving vs. Virginia* reached the United States Supreme Court. The Lovings had been convicted of interracial marriage and sentenced to a year in the state prison for having married. Chief Justice Earl Warren, read the high court's decision:

> "The freedom to marry has long been recognized as one of the vital personal rights essential to the orderly pursuit of happiness by free men. Marriage is one of the basic civil rights of man, basic to ones existence and survival...Under the Constitution of the United States, the freedom to marry...resides with the individual and cannot be infringed upon by the state, or by the majority."[33]

On the fortieth anniversary of the court's ruling, June 12, 2007, Mildred Loving, a plaintiff in the case told reporters:

> "Surrounded as I am with wonderful children, not a day goes by I don't think of Richard and our love, our right to marry, and how much it meant to me to have the freedom to marry that person who is most precious to me, even if others thought it to be the wrong kind of person for me to marry.
>
> Government has no business imposing some people's religious beliefs on others; especially if it denies people civil rights.

I am proud that Richard's and my name are on a court case that reinforces the love, commitment and fairness, that all people, black or white, young or old, straight or gay, seek in life..."[34]

The Catholic marriage ceremony ending 'until death do us part" defines the Sacrament of Matrimony as being between two mortal animals which is consistent with the description of heaven in the Old Testament: 'The Lord came to me saying: Thou shalt not take thee a wife into this place, neither shalt thou bring sons or daughters...'[35] And, in the New Testament: 'In this place one shall be as the bride of Christ...all of your love will be for Christ alone...'[36]

'Il Pedophilia Del Clero'[37]

In another of the young seminarian's works that drew low marks he addressed the question why the rate of pedophilia among priests was so much higher than that of the general population and why it appeared to be primarily homosexual in nature whereas in the general population pedophilia was overwhelmingly heterosexual.

Homosexuals in the priesthood

He recalled his time at Feltre:

> "All sex outside of marriage is mortal sin. A heterosexual has the option of marriage and can look forward to a life of sex free of sin. For him, celibacy is a great sacrifice. But, a homosexual can never marry and therefore he is condemned to a life of celibacy anyway. In choosing a celibate life, a homosexual isn't giving up anything. ...this yields a high ratio of homosexuals in the priesthood..."

Transsexuals in the priesthood

He addressed the inconsistency, priests versus nuns and monks:

> "I am puzzled there is a relatively low incidence of homosexual pedophilia among nuns and monks who outnumber priests four to one. Certainly, all three professions would attract the same mix as they offer one a life of celibacy, one dedicated to God. I wonder what could be the difference between a priest and a monk or a nun that drives such a high rate of pedophilia among priests."

He looked at those who had gone before him. One researcher determined the vestments were attractive to transsexuals.

A monk's brown robe would not suffice, as everyone would be wearing the same 'dress.' Conversely, the male counterpart—men born into women's bodies—would have no interest in the convent. At the time, convents required they spend their lives in a black dress. These 'men' wanted to wear pants, not dresses.

The researcher concluded the vestments themselves resulted in a significant transsexual population among priests and practically no transsexual population among monks and nuns. Yet, Albino already knew this as many of his classmates had exhibited feminine traits—the priesthood allowed them to dress up in beautiful gowns and live out their lives as objects of awe otherwise reserved for the fair sex.

Like a homosexual, a transsexual contemplating the priesthood didn't have to give up anything in celibacy; unable to marry, she was otherwise condemned to a life of sin.

This is best demonstrated by Benedict XVI. At the age of five, he was among boys who bestowed flowers at the feet of the Archbishop of Munich. He fell in love with the cardinal's elaborate gown and announced that evening he was going to be a cardinal.[38]

For the most part, Benedict set aside the white smock of his predecessors for the more lavish dress of the pre-John XXIII era—magnificent robes of regal attire and added much of his own. Film director Franco Zeffirelli called Benedict's wear: **'too sumptuous for modern times.'** Though there is no reliable foundation for it, Queen Elizabeth is said to have said of his wardrobe: **'too effeminate for my everyday tastes and far too elegant and overdone for royal affairs.'**

Here, Benedict steps out for the evening in a velvet cape lined in white ermine in a gown layered in white satin and fine lace over beige chiffon. He is particularly fond of lace and has a meticulous fetish for gold insofar as it promotes his majestic image. Famous for his vast collection of Prada shoes, here he wears Giorgio Brutini slippers. His wardrobe—the most lavish of any monarch living or dead—boasts hundreds of pairs of slippers from leading fashion houses.

From 1981 to 2005, Benedict XVI—Joseph Ratzinger—served as *Prefect of the Doctrine of the Congregation of the Faith*—supreme dictator of morality in the Catholic world.

In 2003, he enacted the doctrine transsexual surgery cannot alter gender and barred those who undergo sex-change surgery from marriage, ordination and religious life.[39]

Christ never damned homosexuals, transsexuals or transvestites. Yet, He did, many times, condemn the Hypocrite.

Regardless, Albino Luciani's conclusion makes sense today.

Though the transgender population is small, it is relatively large compared to the priest population. There are upwards of ten million transgenders in the United States and only fifty thousand diocesan priests. It is reasonable to conclude that driven by their fetish for beautiful gowns there is a relatively large percentage of transgenders among priests, the reason why sacristies boast a full length mirror.

Author's note: Transgenders includes homosexuals whose sexual orientation drives a preference for apparel and/or mannerisms of the opposite sex—i.e. butch females / effeminate males. Also included are transsexuals whose preference for apparel and/or mannerisms of the opposite sex is driven by sexual identity, i.e. born with the mind of the opposite sex—i.e. a 'woman' born into a man's body or a 'man' born into a woman's body. A 'woman' born into a man's body will instinctively pass up the toy truck and reach for the doll in infancy whereas a 'man' born into a woman's body will instinctively pass up the doll and reach for the truck—i.e. Tom boy - Sissy. Transsexuality, being a function of the frontal lobes, cannot be changed by therapy. Unable to change the mind, the only alternative is hormonal treatments and/or surgery to adjust the body to match the mind. Consistent with the general population, most transsexuals are heterosexual but having a body of the opposite sex lead a homosexual lifestyle. Also included in transgenders are transvestites who acquire a fetish for apparel of the opposite sex for reasons other than orientation. See *the story' The Enchanting Stenographer' in 'The Reincarnation of Albino Luciani.'*

As 'Prefect of Morality' Ratzinger covered up the 'Scandal of the Maltese Altar Boys' in 1993 among other pedophile scandals.[40]

Author's note: At the time of the scandal the altar boys who serve the Pope were under Ratzinger, Prefect of the Congregation of the Faith. Allegations were boys attending St. Joseph Boy's School on Malta were molested while serving in the Vatican. Ratzinger enacted a rule which sealed off communications of the boys with their homes during their tenure and required them to take an oath under penalty of self-excommunication, 'What happens in the Vatican stays in the Vatican.'

Heterosexuals in the priesthood

One might wonder why a straight male who had the option of marriage and a life of sex free of sin would enter the priesthood.

The answer is obvious. They think there is something wrong with sex. Otherwise it would make no rational sense at all to give it up.

He sums up his case

In his study—'Il Pedophilia del Clero'—Albino Luciani concludes the priesthood is made up of three groups:

- ✓ homosexuals
- ✓ transsexuals
- ✓ heterosexuals who think something wrong with sex

Luciani's conclusions are consistent with priest pedophilia cases tried in world courts. According to the best records available, about forty percent of predators have been determined to be transsexuals and another forty percent have been determined to be homosexuals. This leaves twenty percent who think there is something wrong with sex—Genophobia or adversity to sex is a serious mental illness.

The youth Luciani often wrote in humor. *Il Pedophilia del Clero* was no exception. Frustrated why priests were required to take a vow of celibacy and not one of poverty, he ended his paper:

> "Giving up one's money can help a lot of people.
>
> On the other hand, struggling against one's God-given inclinations doesn't help anyone. It makes no contribution to society. It is without purpose. Most perilous, being unnatural it may seriously disturb the mind and endanger others; particularly the young.
>
> Christ said: 'If thou wilt be perfect, sell all thou hast and give to the poor.' He didn't say: 'If thou wilt be perfect, keep it in your pants!'"

In the spring of 1978, he criticized an American bishop for paying off the alleged victim of a pedophile priest:

> "It would be better that we try our accused fellow servants in a court of law so they can be cleared of any wrong doing and if found guilty they should pay their debt to society.
>
> It is not Mother Church's business to pay their debt in cash, particularly to pay it with money intended for the poor. Besides, if we take no action to get at the truth, we may very well be endangering countless children in the future."[41]

The Prince and the Princess

Albino Luciani had been the first bishop installed by John XXIII.

At the conclusion of the ceremony his stepsister who headed up the congratulatory reception line approached him and motioned to bow to kiss his newly acquired bishop's ring.

So horrified was he that this woman—who had been such great support to him—would bow to him, rather than extending his hand, he grasped her in his arms and held her for a time. The congregation was moved to tears. A group of Vatican cardinals appalled at what they had witnessed stood off to one side frozen in hostile stares.

On releasing her, this newest prince of the Church—realizing he had broken Church protocol—turned toward the Pope.

Rather than apologizing, he told John XXIII: "**A prince must never forget his sister is the Princess and his mother is the Queen!**"[42]

Archbishop by Popular Demand

In September 1969, the Archbishop of Venice died. Thinking a Vatican cardinal would be chosen to fill the post, thousands of protestors marched through the streets of Venice demanding the bishop of the remote mountain diocese of Vittorio Veneto be named.

When Luciani was elevated to the post, the press billed it as **'the vote of the people.'** But, as we shall see in what is yet to come, Paul VI had already chosen Albino Luciani for the job. As a matter-of-fact he had already chosen him to one day fill his own job.

Under Arrest

It might interest the reader to know during his tenure as Patriarch of Venice Albino Luciani lived as a common man rather than as the crown prince of the Church he was.

He would often go incognito through villages dressed in clothes befitting a bum. He would learn firsthand the needs of his people.

This together with that he came across as a regular guy rather than a man of great stature occasionally got him into trouble.

In one case he was apprehended by police in a park frequented by homosexuals in an impoverished section of a town and asked for identification. When he failed to produce his papers they placed him under arrest. When he claimed to be the Patriarch of Venice they didn't believe him and took him to an asylum.[43]

Shoes of the Fisherman

On another occasion, he escaped to the Lido for a few days.

His shorts were so fringed and worn and his shoes so tattered and torn, a tourist handed him a fifty lire note. It was time for a change.

Peering in a store window, he evaluated a pair of sandals.

The workmanship was of such fine quality as if made for a god. He went in the shop and tried them on. A perfect fit but the price too high. He would make do with the old ones a few more years.

Going out of the shop he took a bench along the lagoon.

A youth in ragged clothes came along. He had no shoes.

Getting up, he beckoned the boy to follow him into the shop, intending to buy the sandals and give the boy his old shoes.

When he put them on, the youngster's eyes beamed in awe at the magnificent splendor of the sandals.

Together they went out of the shop, the boy in the sandals and he in his old shoes, still tattered and torn.

He bid the youth goodbye.

He returned to his bench. A tourist tucked a coin into his hand.[44]

"...a bit of red would help"

Again, in shorts and sandals, on still another occasion, he arrived at a village church and was told the church had closed for the day.

Returning to his car he told his aide to drive on. Ignoring his instruction, the young priest disappeared into the church.

A few minutes later, the church's rector came out to the car. Apologizing, he told the cardinal: **"Your eminence. Perhaps, a bit of red would help."**[45]

The Janitor of the Patriarch's Palace

On another occasion he entered into a conversation with a group of students in a pub and invited them to come to see him at home on the morrow: **"I live next to the Basilica di San Marco."**

"You mean the Patriarch's Palace?"

"Yes," he nodded.

"For whom should we ask?" they queried.

"Just ask for Piccolo," he smiled.

The next day they arrived at the palace and asked for Piccolo. They were taken to an elevator flanked by Swiss Guards. Exiting the elevator they were led to an office flanked by more Swiss Guards.

They were astonished to find Piccolo sitting by the window chatting with Pope Paul who happened to be visiting him that day.[46]

The Confessor

A fifteen year old boy told of his confession with the priest Luciani in which he ranted on and on for twenty minutes about his sexual exploits and awaited his penance. "Good, you have told me of your God-given nature; now tell me of your man-made sins. Tell me of malice in your heart for any of God's children whether they be black, bastard, gypsy, queer, atheist, communist, Russian, Jew ..."[47]

The Hypocrite

Luciani despised wearing vestments. Besides being effeminate, he thought there to be something hypocritical about them.

One day, in shorts and sandals, in the plaza fronting his Venice palace, he was asked by a retarded boy to pose with him for a photo.

He motioned to kneel down beside the boy. The boy stopped him: "Could you put on your beautiful clothes?"

Luciani disappeared into the palace. Shortly, he returned wearing his cardinal's robe, miter and golden staff.

"There are times," he told the boy's father: "we must shed our humility and put on our hypocrisy. This is one of them."[48]

The Paper Cup

The most widely published incident while he was bishop of Vittorio Veneto occurred when he ordered his priests to melt down their golden crucifixes, chalices and other implements of idol worship to build a halfway-house for handicapped children.

The press reported one pastor complaining to his congregation: "He would have us serve the Eucharist out of a paper cup."

The next day a parcel arrived from the bishop's castle. The pastor eagerly ripped open the box. There to his surprise was a paper cup.[49]

Murder by the Grace of God

Note: In 1959, when he ordered his 270 priests to sell their golden crucifixes and other idols of worship to build a halfway house for the handicapped was the first time he reaped world headlines.

1 *Christian Democratic Party Convention* minutes Aug 63: *Albino Luciani Bishop Vittorio Veneto*
2 direct testimony Albino Luciani to the author
3 *Corriere delle Alpi* 7 Jun 50
4 *Corriere delle Alpi* 15 Jul 50
5 *L'Epresso* 19 Jul 50
6 *Princeton Packet* 2 Apr 49
7 direct testimony Albino Luciani to the author
8 *Messaggero Mestre* 17 Mar 73
9 *Treviso Notizie* 1 Jun 68
10 *Parlamento Italiano ABA35868* 16 Jan 61 *'La Singolo Condizione di Genitore Albino Luciani'* The law was reversed in 1966 after Prime Minster Aldo Moro left office
11 *Treviso Notizie* 12 Jan 59
12 direct testimony Albino Luciani to the author
13 Gregorian University Rome, *'Strategia di Una Guerra Sconosciuto, Don Albino Luciani 1943'*
14 *Veneto Nostro* 14 Apr 63   22 Aug 66   27 Dec 67
15 *Augusta Chronicle* 12 Apr 67
16 *Statistical Abstracts of the United States* 1960-1979
17 *New York Times*   May 69
18 *Veneto Nostro* 12 Jun 69
19 *N Y Times* 29 Jun 78 See *'Reincarnated Courage'* in *'The Reincarnation of Albino Luciani'*
20 *Washington Post* 16 Dec 73
21 *Messaggero Mestre* 17 Dec 73
22 *Messaggero Mestre* 17 Jul 76; *Il Gazzettino Venezia* 19 Jul 76 reported a right-wing version
23 *Il Gazzettino Venezia* 23 Jul 76
24 *L'Osservatore Romano* 29 Mar 78   Luciani paraphrased Luis Cernuda's poem, *'The Family'* adding the phrase *"... What is more, we will have to answer to the God who made them!"*
25 *Messaggero Mestre* 11 Mar 70
26 *Messaggero Mestre* 12 Apr 70
27 *Canon of Trent 1565* .Canon law is explicit : *all sex outside marriage is mortal sin.*
28 *Messaggero Mestre* 22 Jun 70
29 *Catholic Encyclopedia. Search:* 'paraplegic marriage,' e. g, Brazil De Brito 22 May 05
30 *Samuel 18*. Jonathan falls in love with David
31 *Veneto Nostro* 26 Jun 60
32 *Christian Democratic Party* minutes 22 Aug 63
33 *Loving vs. Virginia* United States Supreme Court 12 Jun 67
34 *Washington Post* 13 Jun 07
35 *Jeremiah 16*
36 *The Book of Re*velations 3-9 paraphrased by the author
37 *Il Pedophilia del Clero* Gregorian University in Rome. *Biblioteca Apostolica Vaticana*
38 search: Benedict XVI biography
39 *Catholic Catechisms* dated after 2003
40 *Kullhadd* 13 Jul 93.
41 *Messaggero Mestre* 17 Mar 78
42 *La Stampa* 28 Dec 58 He sold his bishop and cardinal rings to help build orphanages
43 *Treviso Notizie* 12 Jan 71
44 direct testimony Albino Luciani to the author
45 *Messaggero Mestre* 11 Jul 74
46 *Messaggero Mestre* 14 Aug 76
47 *L'Unita* 15 Sep 55
48 The author recreates this incident in the short story *'The Cardinal's Bench'* in the sequel to this book: *The Reincarnation of Albino Luciani: In Search of the Human Soul.*
49 *Veneto Nostro* 16 Jun 59

Chapter 8

Murder in Fatima

"Visions are harmful to true religion. They are particularly dangerous when used to promote political ends."[1]

Angelo Roncalli

In July of 1975, Luciani launched the most vigorous attack of his ministry. He criticized a South American bishop for capitalizing on a comatose twelve year old girl who was alleged to have the Stigmata.

The girl had been injured and had never regained her faculties. The bishop and her parents put her on display through a one way window set in the wall of her bedroom. In a circus-like atmosphere they paraded thousands of pilgrims past her room for a fee.

"I can understand why Mother Church might turn her head the other way when greedy people capitalize on defenseless children in this way. After all, she is at the source of this kind of satanic ritual. What bothers me most is that men and women of good conscience of the state stand aside and do nothing about it."[2]

Stigmata and the Shroud

Stigmata had been a money-making scheme ever since the 13th century when St. Francis had been the first to display wounds in the palms of the hands. Most popes since his time have capitalized on this sideshow of the Roman Catholic Church.

_{Author's note: First century crucifixion involved the driving of spikes into wooden planks placed over the arms beneath the bone-line into the cross. Spikes were driven crisscross through the ankles into the cross. Hanging impaired one's ability to breathe causing one to put pressure on the heels resulting in immense pain. The victim struggled for hours eventually dying of asphyxiation.}

_{The early icons placed the spikes in the palms as it was more artistic and all artists since have followed this practice. It would not take a PhD in structural engineering of the anatomy to tell one that razor-sharp first century nails in the palms would not support the weight of a human body.}

_{Angelo Roncalli—John XXIII—once said: "Saints are political appointees of a sitting pope." He would eventually become one. On September 3, 2000 John Paul II beatified Pius IX who in the eyes of those fighting for equality in the Church was a rogue of monstrous proportions. To pacify those on the *left*, he beatified John XXIII, something he would have otherwise never done.}

Murder by the Grace of God

The official position of the Church is the shroud is a fake. When it first appeared in France in 1353AD, Pope Innocent VI ordered an investigation. A year later Bishop Pierre d'Arcis of Paris decreed:

"After diligent inquiry and examination, it is the work of human skill and not miraculously bestowed... it is clearly an imprint of an image in the façade of Angouleme Cathedral ... Bishop Henri de Peituers falsely and deceitfully created the hoax...'[3]

Innocent declared it a hoax and ordered it removed from display. After he died it resurfaced. His successor Pope Urban V allowed the charade to go on. Yet, no pope has ever reversed the official decree.

Luciani once told me, "Take a peek at Jewish custom as to how they buried their dead. The body was wrapped as told in the Gospel of John: 'Then they took the body and wound it in linen clothes, as the manner of the Jews to bury...Then cometh Simon Peter into the sepulcher, and seeing the linen clothes lie, And the napkin that was wrapped about his face, not lying with the linen clothes, but wrapped together in one place by itself.' "[4]

If an image of Jesus' face survived, it would be on the napkin, not on the shroud.

Nevertheless, if Stigmata were an act of God, the Church should have been granting sainthood to those afflicted in the arms.

The vast majority of Stigmata including those of St. Francis have been self-inflicted. In the case of the comatose girl in Latin America it was torture. Yet, millions of people do develop cancerous and bleeding sores, sometimes in the legs, toes, genitalia, buttocks and so forth. When they appear in the hands, one claims Stigmata.

In independent examinations by laboratories in Arizona (1969), Oxford (1973), and in Zurich (1978), the Shroud was dated with 99.93% accuracy to the 14th century—the time it first appeared.

The Angouleme Cathedral was competed in 1128AD two hundred years before the Shroud first appeared in a neighboring village.

In 2003, a computer module proved the Shroud was executed by applying a mixture of resin and human blood over the Angouleme relief. The image of the Shroud itself differs slightly because of aging and a crack that occurred in the sixteenth century and the way the cloth was placed to secure the image. The hair pattern on either side of the image under a microscope is an exact match, strand for strand.

| Shroud 1353AD | Relief 1119AD | Copy 2003AD |

Above: The centerpiece of the façade of the Angouleme Cathedral completed in 1128AD two hundred years before the Shroud first appeared. Lower center: Christ's face in the relief. Lower-right: image retrieved in 2003 by applying powdered resin to the sculpture and placing a cloth over it. Lower-left: the Shroud of Turin.

Lourdes

In 1964, Luciani visited Lourdes on the guise of pilgrimage. Two 'miracles' had made the case for Bernadette.

A spring had sprung forth in the grotto. The original newspaper reports described the first apparition: **"Bernadette went into the grotto to fetch 'water' for the day."** Transcripts published after 1936 read: **"Bernadette went into the grotto to fetch 'wood' for the day."**[5]

The second issue, the more critical one, was that the 'girl' told Bernadette she was the Immaculate Conception. At the time, the Doctrine of the Immaculate Conception—Mary had been born without original sin—was not known to the general congregation.

Like other progressive doctrines, this was politically motivated to bring the Church into sync with social changes. The Christian world had traditionally viewed women as property. Following Europe's lead, in 1853 laws were passed in the United States elevating women from 'property' to 'human beings. This brought pressure on Rome to elevate the concept of women in the Church.

In late 1854, Pius IX drafted the doctrine of the Immaculate Conception.[6] His discovery after all these years that Mary had been born free of original sin was kept under the table while he searched for an opportunity to convince the public of its authenticity.

It was that Bernadette spoke of this doctrine that made her a saint. Luciani was convinced the spring had always been there. Yet, he was puzzled as to how she could have learned of the doctrine.

In 1971, he returned to Lourdes to investigate this event.

The first apparition occurred in February 1858. The apparitions which followed were witnessed by crowds. She told them: "I have seen a girl of my age silent as to who she was. She would reveal her identity in six months."[7] At the time Bernadette was fourteen.

In early March, two days before the apparition in which the 'girl' would reveal her identity, Bernadette was interviewed by a bishop from the Vatican. The vision was witnessed by ten thousand people. All they saw was Bernadette talking to the air. Afterwards, she told the crowd: 'The girl told me: "I am the Immaculate Conception."[8]

The next day, dozens of crutches appeared lined up against a wall, suggesting crippled pilgrims had walked away. Townsfolk told Luciani they had been placed there by villagers seeking to capitalize on the visions. Within days, the poverty stricken town was booming.

There was no greater feminist activist in the history of the world than Albino Luciani. One could ask why he would destroy the myth of the Immaculate Conception when it would contribute to one of his lifelong objectives: to bring about equality of women in the Church.

He would not take part in deception to fool people into thinking women equal. He would remove obstacles the Church and society had placed in her path. Woman, herself, would prove she was equal.

Fatima

In 1916, Lucia Santos, age 9, and her cousins Francisco Marto, age 7, and Jacinta Marto, age 6, were tending sheep outside of Aljustrel Portugal. The specter in the first vision was the 'Angel of Peace.'

The second vision, a few weeks later, featured the '**Angel of Portugal.**' In the third vision, still another angel gives Lucia Holy Communion and Francisco and Jacinta a drink from a gold chalice.

So convincing was she that even though her mother told reporters Lucia was a pathological liar— **"Lucia wants to become a saint. She knows many have been made saints for no other reason than they convinced the Church of visions."**—they capitalized on Lucia's tale.[9]

A reporter questioned the younger children Francisco and Jacinta. Their recollections of what the angel said not only contradicted Lucia but contradicted each other. Lucia refuted her cousins as being too young to understand what they witnessed.

'Short Mission'

In December of the same year, a Portuguese writer—Jose Santos Silva—in his book *Short Mission* told of the appearance of a '**Lady**' to two children tending sheep. To the extent his story included secrets told to children by the '**Lady**' he plagiarized the *La Salette* visions of September 1846 in southern France which alleged a '**Lady**' appeared to two children herding cows and told them secrets.[10]

Yet, the timing of his book suggests he was motivated by the events of 1916. Regardless, he wrote of a 'ghost' appearing to more than one person at a time—a rare occurrence in saintly visions.

The visions of Fatima in 1917 were quite different from those of Aljustrel in 1916. Like '**Short Mission**' they involved a '**Lady**' rather than angels. Also, Lucia arranged the younger children would only see the '**Lady**' but not hear or participate in the conversations to avoid contradictions which had been a problem for her at Aljustrel.

The first apparition of the '**Lady**' took place on May 13, 1917 at Cova da Iria near Fatima and was witnessed by a small crowd and a pair of reporters. A comparison of the 1858 Lourdes transcript and the 1917 Fatima newspaper reports demonstrate Lucia plagiarized Bernadette in describing the '**Lady**.' Both have identical wording: **"The Lady was clothed in light wearing a white mantel edged in gold. A star was caught in the folds of her dress. She herself was as if made of light...I saw a girl of fourteen who was silent as to whom she was. She would reveal her identity in six months."**[11] In both transcripts is the wording: "I want you to build a chapel here in my honor."[12]

Bernadette had, herself, plagiarized Juan Diego in his testimony of the apparition of the 'Lady' of Guadalupe in 1531: "...The light around her formed a dress edged in gold; a gold star in its hem. She told me 'Tell Bishop Juan to build a chapel here for me.'"[13]

When confronted, Cardinal Antonio Belo of Lisbon explained: "The timing and descriptions of the visions and the request for a chapel would be identical as they involved the same Lady."[14]

Although the younger children were excluded from conversing with the 'Lady' there were contradictions as to what they saw. For example, in her testimony to the reporters Lucia claimed: '...the Lady was wearing huge magnificent dazzling earrings.'[15]

When questioned independently, the younger children had never mentioned the earrings. When pressed for an answer, Jacinta did not remember much of the earrings other than 'they were beautiful.'[16]

Francisco thinking it a trick told reporters: 'the Lady was wearing a veil which covered her ears. I could not see her ears.'[17]

Realizing her younger cousins were becoming dangerous to her deception, Lucia decided they not witness future visions.

The next vision was on June 13, 1917, the feast of St. Anthony.

Lucia spoke of her conversation with the 'Lady.'

"Will you take us to heaven?" asked Lucia.

The Lady said: "I will take Jacinta and Francisco soon. You will remain. Jesus wishes you to make me known and loved on earth..."

When questioned why the younger children had not witnessed the vision, Lucia said: "Only I was brave enough to see the Lady."[18]

The miracle of the sun

According to newspapers, despite heavy rains, drawn by the Lady's promise they would see Jesus, Himself, a crowd of eighty thousand witnessed the last vision at Fatima on October 13, 1917.

The next day, no newspaper in the world mentioned the miracle of the sun. Not one of them mentioned anything unusual other than: "after a morning of rain the sun broke through the clouds at noon..."[19]

On October 22, 1917, a Spanish tabloid started the ball rolling.

It reported, four people had seen the sun do more than come out: 'In a fiery ball it had crashed down upon them.' 'Tabloid' is used here as a rag that pays witnesses for tales of the occult and smut.[20]

The tabloid *Ilustracao Portuguesa* picked up the story on October 29, 1917. Plastered across its front page were pictures of the crowd looking up to the sky. One can only surmise they were responding to Lucia's pointing to the sky and shouting: "There she comes." [21]

The New York Times and *The Times* (London) sent investigative reporters to Portugal. Other than a few witnesses with hands out for fees in exchange for what they 'saw,' they interviewed a huge number of credible witnesses who had seen nothing unusual at all.

From 1917 through 1929 when the Vatican picked up the ruse again, you will not find mention of Fatima in *The New York Times* or *The Times;* reputable journals ignoring Fatima as: 'irresponsible journalism intended to put Portugal on the paranormal map.'

A turn of events

With science and the legitimate press destroying the myth of the 'miracle of the sun' the credibility of the visions rested solely on the Lady's prediction: "I shall take Jacinta and Francisco soon..."

A year later on October 19, 1918, *Jornal de Leiria* posted an article that the Lady's prophesy had failed. Francisco and Jacinta were not only still alive; they were in the best of health. Word spread rapidly through all of Portugal the visions had been a hoax.[22]

The following week both Francisco and Jacinta fell ill.

Six months later Francisco was dead.

His illness is relatively unknown as he was deprived of medical attention. His beatification record cites: 'severe dehydration, painful breathing and chest rash.' Death certificate: 'respiratory failure.'[23]

It was that he refused medical treatment and chose to suffer that he was beatified explicit in his beautification certificate:

> "In refusing medical treatment Francisco satisfied the Lady's will, 'Are you willing to bear all the sufferings our Lord wants to send you for the conversion of sinners?' Francisco accepted his fate." [24]

One can only surmise the good fathers in Rome wanted to set an example for other children that they might conceal their maladies from their parents and doctors that they too might suffer for the conversion of sinners. Kind of gives credence to those who label the Roman Catholic Church 'the most dangerous cult in the world.'

Murder by the Grace of God

In the event poison was involved—not a known fact—Jacinta was removed from access by the predator for the rest of her life.

When her brother died, authorities recognizing the severity of her illness transferred her to St. Augustine Hospital at Ourem where she was treated for pleurisy often mistaken for edema. A few months later she was transferred to St. Stephen Hospital in Lisbon.

After months, unable to diagnose a wide range of problems from painful breathing, unexplained odor and psoriasis in the chest area, surgeons performed exploratory surgery opening the chest cavity. She died ten days later. Death certificate: **'pulmonary edema.'**[25]

<blockquote>
Author note: The Vatican rumors these children died of the 1918 Flu—inconsistent with both the beautification investigation of both deaths and hospital records and the 1918 Flu epidemic.

Symptoms of the 1918 Flu were not what one thinks of as those of a seasonal flu today.

The 1918 Flu was readily diagnosed—coughing up of blood and/or bleeding from the ears and darkening of the stool to the extent one swallowed blood ending in pneumonia. Death normally occurred in a few days. If one survived more than a week, one built up immunity and lived.

We know this for a more definitive reason. If either child had exhibited symptoms remotely akin to the Flu he or she would have been required by law to be quarantined in an infirmary.

The facts: We don't know what Francisco died of as he was never hospitalized. We do know Jacinta was hospitalized for months and doctors were unable to determine her illness other than it was consistent with—not necessarily—arsenic poisoning. We also know both children fell ill at the same time in the same house. It is reasonable both suffered of the same illness.

Arsenic poisoning is not limited to mystery writers; it is a favorite of real killers. Available in many household chemicals, it is easily administered. Tasteless and odorless, it is easily concealed in food or drink. All one need do is go to a library and read a book.

More murders go undetected when slow arsenic poisoning is the instrument of murder than any other method. It results in symptoms characteristic of a wide range of natural illnesses and unless a doctor specifically suspects foul play it will go undetected.

For example, in 1970, a jaundiced-skin man was admitted to a Chicago hospital complaining of tiredness, thirst, dehydration, sore throat, painful breathing and chest psoriasis.

Test after test was done; the physicians were at a loss as to what was wrong with him.

At a nursing station, one physician overheard students discussing the case. One, a mystery buff, joked: "Maybe his wife is poisoning him." The physician tested for arsenic. The results were positive. His wife had been doctoring his coffee.[26]

Initially there is jaundice, esophagus soreness and coughing up of blood. It progresses slowly to a deteriorating condition accompanied by severe dehydration, flaking skin in the chest area, painful breathing, bloody urinary discharge most often culminating in pulmonary edema.[27]
</blockquote>

Regardless, accompanied by reporters, the diocese bishop visited Fatima and told Lucia Santos the sad news. The last of her co-visionaries was dead. Lucia broke into ecstasy and jubilance.

The Lady's prediction **"I will take Francisco and Jacinta soon..."** had come true. Lucia was on her way to becoming a saint.[28]

When questioned by the reporters why she was not saddened by Jacinta's death, Lucia told them she knew Jacinta was in heaven.[29]

The Church recognizes this as a miracle. Any criminologist will tell you it is grounds for premeditated murder.

"She didn't see it dance"

On July 5, 1977, Luciani visited the village where Francisco had died and Saint Stephen Hospital in Lisbon where Jacinta had died.[30]

The next day, he visited Lucia at Coimbra. Scores of reporters swarmed the cardinal as he left the convent. They looked for the familiar smile. All they got was a look of anguish. When asked why Lucia had not discussed the 'miracle of the sun' with reporters the day of the miracle, Luciani told them: "She didn't see it dance."[31]

It could be Lucia was the pathological liar her mother claimed her to be. It could be she was a paranormal schizophrenic who really believed the things she imagined she saw. It could be she had actually seen a ghost. These things explain Fatima.

But, they do not explain why Lucia predicted the deaths of her co-visionaries. Countless books portray the 'loving' Lucia taking a bowl of soup on her daily visits to her sick and dying cousins. One will never know.

<small>Author note: There is no better example of how the Vatican manipulates the Internet than in the case of Francisco and Jacinta Marto. Vatican controlled Wikipedia reports the children died of the 1918 Flu and the details of their lives and deaths are posted on Wikipedia by the Vatican. A year after 'Murder in Fatima' first appeared in this book, the Vatican posted a multi-million dollar film on You Tube demonstrating Albino Luciani's devotion to Fatima. Not what the press has to say.</small>

After the spark of enthusiasm which followed Jacinta's death—the 'Lady's' prophecy had come true—only the most devout clung to Fatima. In the darkened corners of pubs and in schoolyards were whispers of 'murder' in the coincidental deaths of the children.

Nevertheless, the coincidental publication of 'Short Mission' prior to the first vision and the testimony of the overwhelming consensus of witnesses who saw nothing unusual on October 13, 1917 nailed the case shut for doubters. Scientific journals which had demolished the authenticity of the 'miracle of the sun' and the lack of mention of it in the Sunday editions the day after it allegedly took place nailed the case shut for those who accept the real world they live in.

Unlike Lourdes which had exploded overnight into prosperity, Fatima remained in relative poverty. The Vatican not only failed to encourage the hoax, it did much to discourage it. Benedict XV disclaimed it. The presiding bishop never visited Fatima again.

Murder by the Grace of God

For the next decade, Fatima remained not much more than one of hundreds of dots on the make-believe paranormal map of Europe.
In 1929, events occurred that made Fatima into what it is today.

On June 7, 1929, Pius XI entered into the *Lateran Treaty*—a union between the Vatican and *fascist* Italy. The treaty caused an uproar of leftist factions both within and outside the Church.

Concerning distribution of wealth—though at His time never having heard of socialism, He relies on charity to bring it about—Christ obviously stands firmly on the left: 'all children are equal and are entitled to an equal share of God's province.'

Fascism— 'some of God's children are created better than others and are entitled to more'—is clearly Christ's enemy. It was obvious to anyone who had awareness of the gospels that the Church had separated itself from Christ whom it claimed to represent.

Pius had to convince the faithful Christ had changed His mind. He sought to convince them that socialism and communism was evil and fascism was sacred. He had invoked his infallibility to no avail. He decided only a ghost could change the gospels.

The French and Russian Revolutions

To best understand what transpired here, a bit of history.

The Romanovs were the last of a long line of Tsarist autocracies which had imposed poverty and suffering on the people of Russia. Yet, the Russian Revolution was as much an attack on the ally of the Romanovs—the Russian Orthodox Church—which likewise was immersed in vast wealth while Russian children starved to death.

Socialism—everyone an equal opportunity—emerged from the French Revolution (1789-1799). Communism—everyone an equal share—emerged from Marx/Engels' 'Communist Manifesto' (1848).

Socialism and communism quickly rose up as the archenemy of the Russian Orthodox Church and of the Roman Catholic Empire—cults of idol worship immersed in vast wealth preying on a populace of poor scrabbling in the mud of the streets.

The Bolsheviks intended to change the Church from the idolatry of Christ it had become, to the ideology of Christ He had intended.

The Fatima Conspiracy

Through the years thousands of children have claimed to have had visions of Our Lady. For the most part they had been ignored.

What separated *Fatima* from the others was the same thing that separated *Lourdes* from the others. It happened to come along at the right time. It happened to come along when a sitting pontiff was searching for a 'supernatural ghost' to authenticate a 'political goal.'

Fatima occurred at the precise time the Russian Revolution took place. The visions began shortly after the provisional government removed the Tsar from power in the spring of 1917 and they ended on October 13, 1917—the day the Bolsheviks came to power.

Pius plotted to use *Fatima* to convert Russia back from a society in which all children are seen as equal—Christ's ideology—to one in which some children are better than others—fascism.

Pius selected some of what Lucia had actually told newspapers at the time and added much of his own. His main embellishment would eventually become the central message of Fatima—**'conversion of communist Russia.'** What's more, he got Lucia to conspire with him. Lucia had not mentioned 'Russia' at all to reporters in 1917.

It was not unusual for Lucia to add to or change her stories as historical events like the *Lateran Treaty* materialized.

At one point she revealed the **'Lady'** had predicted World War II in what is today the *Second Secret of Fatima*. The faithful were astounded the **'Lady'** could have know this in 1917—a miracle. Lucia revealed the secret in 1941 after World War II was in full swing.

Pius XI used *Fatima* to justify the Vatican's union with fascist Italy in the *Lateran Treaty* and used it again in 1934 in winning over the votes Hitler needed to pass the *Enabling Act* which made him dictator of Germany which eventually cost fifty million lives.

On October 13 1930, Pius through his appointed bishop declared *Fatima* **'worthy of belief'** and released the central message of Fatima **'conversion of communist Russia.'** A message that reporters who had covered the events of 1917 in great detail had by an act of divine providence missed. [32]

There had been five apparitions witnessed by crowds reported in newspapers. When she was questioned as to why she had not mentioned Russia, Lucia explained that there had been a sixth apparition on August 19, 1917 not witnessed by others in which the 'Lady' had told her: **'Pray the Rosary for the conversion of Russia...If Russia is free to scatter her errors through the world, the Holy Father will have much to suffer and many nations will be annihilated...'** [33]

The wave of pilgrims headed for Lourdes and La Salette suddenly detoured toward Fatima. Overnight, Lucia became much more than just another nun on her knees in a secluded convent.

Pius had removed Christ from his path.

He was on his way to World War II and fifty million lives.

As Cardinal Angelo Roncalli of Venice had warned:

"Visions are harmful to true religion...particularly dangerous when used to promote political ends." [34]

1 *Messaggero Mestre* 29 Sep 55
2 *Messaggero Mestre* 12 Jul 75
3 *Biblioteca Apostolica: Vaticana.* Independent DNA analysis date the Shroud between 1250-1350AD
4 *Gospel of John* 20
5 *Biblioteca Apostolica: Vaticana, Notre-Dame de la Grotte a Lourdes* pg v.
6 *Biblioteca Apostolica: La Dottrina della Concezione Immacolata*
7 *Biblioteca Apostolica,* Notre-Dame de la Grotte a Lourdes pg x
8 *Biblioteca Apostolica:* Notre-Dame de la Grotte a Lourdes pg xii
9 *O'Seculo* 31 Aug 16
10 *Short Mission,* Silva 1917. The book is available in some large city libraries.
11 *Jornal de Leiria* 20 May vs. *Calendario de Nossa Senhora da Fatima* p iii
12 *La Dottrina Della Concezione & Immacolata Calendario de Nossa da Fatima O'Seculo* 29 May 17
13 *Biblioteca Apostolica, El registro de Nuestra Dama de Guadalupe* p v
14 *O'Seculo* 29 May 17
15 *Ordem* 14 May 17   -   *Calendario de Nossa Senhora da Fatima* p x
16 *Ordem* 16 May 17   -   *Calendario de Nossa Senhora da Fatima* p xii
17 *Ordem* 16 May 17   -   *Calendario de Nossa Senhora da Fatima* p xi
18 *O'Seculo* 14 Jun 17   -   *Calendario de Nossa Senhora da Fatima* p xx
19 *O'Seculo* 14 Oct 17
20 *El Tiempo* 22 Oct 17
21 *Ilustracao Portuguesa* 29 Oct 17
22 *Jornal de Leiria* 19 Oct 18
23 *La a Tempo di Record di Beatificazione Francisco Marto* p vi
24 *La a Tempo di Record di Beatificazione Francisco Marto* p xii
25 *O'Seculo* 21 Feb 20   - *La a Tempo di Record di Beatificazione Jacinta Marto* p vi. The Vatican record agrees with St. Stephen Hospital Jacinta died of pulmonary edema and not the 1918 Flu.
26 *Deadly Doses* Serita Stevens   *Chicago Tribune* 17 Jul 70
27 *Mosby's Dictionary of Medicine* 7th *Edition* or other medical dictionary approved by the AMA
28 On February 13, 2008, Benedict XVI opened the beautification process for Lucia Santos
29 *O'Seculo* 21 Feb 20
30 O'Seculo 5 Jul 77
31 *O Dia* 9 Jul 77
32 *The New York Times* 14 Oct 30   -   *The Times* 14 Oct 30
33 *L Osservatore* 14 Oct 30; 'Lady' reappeared to Lucia repeating this message on Jun 13, 1929
34 *Messaggero Mestre* 29 Sep 55

Chapter 9

The Marxist Movement in the Church

> Angelo Roncalli = John XXIII
> Giovanni Montini = Paul VI
> Albino Luciani = John Paul I

"If we are to have a true church, our faith must be built on truth, not on myth."[1]

Angelo Roncalli

The Marxist movement in the Roman Catholic world began with the election of John XXIII in the Sistine Chapel on October 28, 1958.

It ended with the death of John Paul I in the great bed of the papal apartment on the morning of September 29, 1978.

What brought these two men together in a common cause?

Unlike the overwhelming majority of popes who have been born into immense wealth, these men had been born into poverty.

They knew as children what it was to wonder where their next meal was coming from. It is no surprise they joined together to bring about a society which affords every child an equal share of God's province—Marxism.

Yet, the bulk of the Marxist movement in the Roman Catholic Church was driven by the man who came between them—Paul VI. What could this man—born into wealth and nobility—have possibly had in common with the other two?

Like the man who would succeed him, Paul had been born to a socialist atheist father. Like the man who would succeed him, by the time of his thirteenth birthday he had lost his faith—that is, his faith in what the Church had become. It was not until late in his teens he, too, realized the Church could only be changed from the inside.

Yet, what was it that all three of these men had in common?

They wanted to change the Church back to what Christ had intended—'a church for all people' more specifically 'a church for the poor.' They wanted to move the Church away from the idolatry of Christ it had become: 'men dressed up in women clothes prancing about altars of marble of gold and entranced fools lining up in the cannibalistic ritual of devouring their God,' back to the ideology of Christ He had demanded: 'Sell all thou hast and give to the poor.'

They intended to move the Church away from ghosts of the past it had been built on lest it self-destruct in the meantime: the 'Burning Bush' that spoke to Moses in the desert, the two dozen other Ghosts that had appeared to the prophets, to the angel-ghost that appeared in Joseph's dream telling him that his wife had had sexual intercourse with still another ghost—the Holy Ghost—which established Jesus Christ as being one more Ghost—this one, too, with a capital 'G.' What's more, they did not believe in the ghosts of more recent times.

This is, perhaps, best demonstrated by John XXIII.

On August 17, 1959, the day on which the *Third Secret of Fatima* according to the Lady's instruction was to be revealed—John XXIII returned the letter to the archives unopened as not to promulgate the hoax. During his papacy John canonized six saints. Every single one of these had spent their lives working with the sick and the poor. Not one of them had claimed to have talked to a ghost.

In 1985, Avro Manhattan wrote:

> "Roncalli did not approve of visions or miracles. He prided himself on having—besides large hands—equally large feet, planted firmly on the ground. 'Visions,' Roncalli warned: 'are harmful to true religion... particularly dangerous when they are used as a means of promoting political ends.'"[2]

Roncalli reasoned miracles contradicted the premise of salvation:

> "It makes no sense to pray for the recovery of a young boy who is suffering from cancer when if he dies one knows he goes to heaven. Christ said: *'Blessed are little children for theirs is the Kingdom of Heaven.'* If the boy survives to adulthood his chances are immensely diminished: *'Many are called, few are chosen.'* We pray for his recovery because we know he is not going anywhere."[3]

Roncalli, Montini and Luciani saw lack of education as the driving force behind the populace's tendency to believe in ghosts.

The visions of Guadalupe, Lourdes and Fatima are unquestioned in third world countries. These men realized if they failed to free the Church from the world of myth it had been built on, third world countries would eventually become first world countries and the tendency to believe in ghosts on which the Church depended for its existence would dissolve. As Roncalli so profoundly put it:

"His Church is not of buildings of wood and stone, nor is it of myth and fancy. It is in your heart. It is in your compassion for others."[4]

A mythical church of idol worship

A real church of compassion

This triad of men—Roncalli, Montini and Luciani—would destroy the mythical foundation the Church is built on and return it to the sacred ideology of Christ which Matthew, Mark, Luke, John and Marx wrote of. They would pull them up off their knees mumbling vain repetitions to plaster idols and put them to work helping others.

1 *Messaggero Mestre* 17 Dec 56
2 *The Dollar and the Vatican* 1988 Avro Manhattan
3 *Corriere Della Sera* 12 Mar 55
4 *Messaggero Mestre* 25 Dec 57 Basilica di San Marco Roncalli paraphrases Christ

Chapter 10

How a Pope is Elected

"When the political infighting that goes on when a pope is elected turns to murder."

Todd Hamilton *Los Angeles Times*

According to canon law the decision as to who becomes Pope must be Christ's decision and not that of a group of men politicking and collaborating among each other.

The public perceives the electors as being a group of old men cloistered together in the Sistine Chapel in prayer. It is led to believe the only guidance a cardinal has in making his choice is prayer. As a matter-of-fact, prayer has little to do with the election of a pope.

Like any other election, the election of the Supreme Pontiff of the Roman Catholic Church is a political process. A cardinal does not cast his vote for another cardinal because he thinks he will look pretty in a white satin gown. Likewise, he does not cast his vote for a man because Christ appears to him and tells him who to vote for.

Like any other progressive or conservative, the voting cardinal casts his vote for the candidate who most closely shares his own ecclesiastical convictions. As in any other election he trades off a part of his own convictions in order in return to get a piece of the action. The political infighting that goes on when a pope is elected is often fierce and there have been times it has turned to murder.

In modern times, with the exception of Pius XII and John Paul I, popes have handpicked their successors. Historically the reigning pontiff would move his choice into either the secretary of state position or the pastoral Italian archdioceses of Milan and Venice.

With the exception of John Paul II, all twentieth century popes have come out of these jobs. This includes Pius X, Benedict XV, Pius XI, Pius XII, John XXIII, Paul VI and John Paul I.

The 1958 conclave

As Pius XII aged, he realized Giovanni Montini would get the vote.

Montini had gained popularity with field cardinals in that he had often embarrassed Pius on humane issues. Despite his progressive views, his relative youthfulness had gained the alliance of many of the Curia hardliners during his ten years as pro-secretary of state.

At the same time, the papal nuncio to France, Angelo Roncalli had also gained a level of popularity with field cardinals, particularly in his work to sever the Vatican from its lingering fascist's roots which union with Hitler and Mussolini had led to World War II.

Under Roncalli's leadership, France was at the forefront of the anti-clerical movement which rose up after the war and was fed up with the fascist policies the Vatican continued to cling to. Yet, not a cardinal and lacking Montini's visibility as pro-secretary of state, he was not widely considered as a viable candidate for the papacy.

In 1953, Pius moved Roncalli to the coveted post of Patriarch of Venice and at the same time made him a cardinal.[1] There were now two liberals—Roncalli and Montini—in the race for the gold.

When Montini, who had acted as secretary of state for ten years, was not included in the 1953 consistory, it sparked rumors he had refused the 'red hat.' The secretary of state position had not only traditionally been occupied by a cardinal it had been occupied by the ranking cardinal. Had Pius had any intention Montini succeed him, he surely would have formalized Montini's appointment as Cardinal Secretary of State and put him in direct succession to the throne.

One might conclude Montini was not included in this consistory because of his relatively young age—still in his fifties at a time men were typically made cardinals in their sixties and seventies. Yet, in the same consistory, Pius awarded the red hat to his favorite son the Archbishop of Genoa, Giuseppe Siri—only forty-seven at the time.[2]

Nevertheless, despite Montini's and Pius' denials in the press the rumor Montini refused the red hat persists even today.[3] Yet, what we know of him tells us he did not refuse the red hat.

Most cardinals—though they may pretend otherwise—yearn to succeed to the papacy. Men are not—as one might think—dragged yelping, howling, squealing and kicking against their will to the papal balcony. This was particularly true of Montini and Wojtyla who openly voiced their papal ambitions throughout their ministries.

Yet, unlike Wojtyla, it was expected Montini would succeed to the papacy. Unlike his colleagues Roncalli and Luciani who feigned humility in accepting the post, Montini accepted it as his legacy.

In 1954, Pius moved Montini from the Vatican to Milan to lessen his grasp on the Curia votes. Again, he withheld the red hat.

Yet, when Pius died Montini still controlled a substantial block of cardinals; they would vote only for him or his choice. Newspapers listed Siri and Montini in a dead heat for the papacy as the conclave opened on October 25, 1958 despite Montini—not a cardinal—was excluded from the conclave. In retrospect, neither Siri nor Montini won the election. How could this have come about?

The leading candidates in the election were Montini followed by Roncalli on the liberal side of the aisle and Siri unchallenged on the conservative side. The war had been a wake-up call as to the dangers of frozen conservatism. The trend was away from fascism.

At that time a liberal was not what a liberal is today. Though he had his roots in doctrine, the liberal sensed something wrong with it particularly where it unfairly penalized the lives of innocent people.

Conversely, the conservative remained frozen in doctrine—he didn't care how much suffering it imposed upon innocent people.

In 1958, a conservative was a dedicated fascist limited only to what had been lost to him by Hitler and Mussolini in the war.

In retrospect today, one can only surmise Pius' strategy—faced by a growing open-minded majority—was to split the liberal vote between Roncalli and Montini and pave the way for his favorite son—the youthful conservative archbishop of Genoa, Giuseppe Siri.

In that Roncalli won the election, it follows Montini yielded his votes to the aging cardinal. What's more, we know he did this before the conclave went into session as Montini was not in the conclave. How do we know this? Post-election events tell us this.

Shortly after his election—December 15, 1958—John XXIII elevated Montini and twenty-two of Montini's loyal supporters to the College of Cardinals. Should John have died the following day, Montini would have won a successive election in a landslide.[3]

John's intention is obvious in the consistory listing. Montini is listed first. Never before in the history of the Church or since has a pope held a consistory in the year of his election.

His intent was to guarantee Montini's succession should anything happen to him in the short term. It is obvious to all but the most gullible, a deal had been struck between the aging Roncalli and the youthful Montini in the days leading up to the 1958 conclave.

The practice of listing their choice of succession first has been true of many popes. Albino Luciani led the list of thirty cardinals in Paul's consistory of March 5, 1973.[4]

On the same day he made Montini a cardinal, John made Albino Luciani a bishop—the only bishop in history ever appointed on the same day as a consistory.[5] One can only surmise this was to position Luciani to succeed Montini should the latter fall victim to foul play.

When Roncalli became archbishop of Venice he had adopted the young priest from Belluno as his aide. The bond between Montini and Luciani dated back much further. During the war Luciani had intervened many times on behalf of the oppressed and often enlisted Montini's sway with Pius to bring about compassionate decisions.

Nevertheless, a covenant had been struck between Roncalli and Montini before the conclave began. What's more, those cardinals Montini had persuaded to vote for Roncalli in 1958 knew they were actually voting to place Montini in direct succession to the throne.

Setting all this aside, there is the possibility strategy, politicking and collaborating among men has nothing to do with electing a pope. It may be Christ did speak to those cardinals committed to Montini in the conclave and told them to vote for Roncalli.

Although the choice of Pius XII remains vague, and the choice of John XXIII could not have been more obvious, there was no case more certain than was Paul VI's intent Albino Luciani succeed him.

Shoes of a Fisherman

Of all the demands Albino Luciani had made upon the Vatican through the years, none was more widely publicized than was his ongoing demand it liquidate its treasures to annihilate poverty and starvation in the world. In his early years he didn't have to look further than his own village to see children starving to death.

As a bishop he saw much more. He became a close friend of Pericle Felici when the latter was serving as papal nuncio to Africa. Through Felici's intercession he established a mission at Burundi, manning it with his own priests, monks and nuns.

When he first arrived in Vittorio Veneto and pressured his priests to sell their gold to build a halfway house for the handicapped, he gained worldwide attention. In the coming years—in an ongoing assault—Luciani brought public pressure on Rome to sell treasures held in warehouses and not on display to help finance his African venture to no avail. Nevertheless, of all the things Luciani had gained notice for, none had gained more press than his ongoing condemnation of the hypocrisy of the Vatican treasures.

In 1968, the Anthony Quinn movie *Shoes of the Fisherman* premiered. The film depicted the rise of a Russian to the papacy that resembled the real life Luciani to a tee. It told of a bishop who strolled in shorts and sandals incognito through the darkened ghettos of his diocese under assumed names. Most striking of all, it exploited Luciani's most widely known threat to Rome—liquidation of the Vatican treasures to annihilate poverty in the world.

In the film, Anthony Quinn—a newly appointed pontiff—shocks the world by announcing his intent to sell off the Vatican treasures to annihilate poverty and starvation in communist China.

That the Pontiff in the film so closely resembled Luciani and ignored the character Morris West had built into his novel brought Luciani much notoriety. There is no mention at all of the liquidation of Vatican treasures in the *book* which is the focal point of the *film*. Regardless, the movie was a godsend for Luciani and the fame it brought him financed many of his third world ventures.

In the following year 1969, Paul VI raised Luciani to Archbishop of Venice. The Pope sent a public message to the bishop of the remote mountain province: **"The gods of Hollywood have spoken. The time has come for you to begin your journey to Rome."**[6]

Everyone knew exactly what Paul was talking about.

The papal buzzer

Whenever cardinals gathered in Rome and Luciani was among them, though only a common bishop he sat next to Paul. In one well publicized instance in a public audience, Paul could not locate the little buzzer on his chair that would summon an attendant.

Luciani reached for Paul's hand and guided it to the button. Paul looked back at him. Not aware the microphone would pick up his comment: **"So, you already know where the papal buzzer is."**[7]

The papal stole

In 1967, at Christmas service in Vittorio Veneto, Paul removed his stole and placed it upon Albino Luciani's shoulders. Through the years Paul had often repeated this gesture. Yet, it usually went unnoticed until he did it in 1972 in the Piazza San Marco in Venice before twenty-five thousand people and an international television audience. Now the whole world knew Luciani was the choice.[8]

Stacking the College of Cardinals

In the early 1970s, Paul began stacking the College of Cardinals to the *left*.

He raised the number of voting cardinals from eighty to one hundred and twenty and filled most of the vacancies with liberals. Of the last fifty-six cardinals Paul appointed, all but three were known to have liberal tendencies.

In the consistory of 1973, Paul not only made Luciani a cardinal and listed him first, but of the other twenty-nine appointed that day there was not one who would not vote for him.

The voting conclave had remained at seventy for five hundred years. John XXIII—in order to guarantee his successor would be Montini—raised the number to eighty and made it clear he would not be restricted to it; when he died there were eighty-two.

A cardinal has only two responsibilities: 1) he elects a pope, and 2) he advises a pope. Yet, popes have many closer advisers than cardinals from heads of state to common laymen, priests and nuns. It makes no difference whether he has fifty or a thousand cardinals. The only unique function of a cardinal is his role in electing a pope.

Paul's only possible motive in increasing the number of voting cardinals was the same as that of John.

To guarantee Luciani succeed him, Paul had two choices: 1) he could refuse to reconfirm existing conservatives when their terms lapsed, or 2) increase the authorized number of cardinals and fill the vacancies with liberals. Something we know he did do.

Most significant, Paul eliminated cardinals over the age of eighty from voting reasoning senility. At the time all eighteen over eighty were ultraconservatives who would have voted against Luciani.

As a follow-up to eliminating those over eighty, he raised the authorized number of cardinals to one hundred thirty-eight in order to hold the voting conclave at one hundred twenty. This created eighteen voting vacancies, most of which had—in rapid consecutive order—been filled by Paul with liberals before his death. Had Paul

Murder by the Grace of God

not made this change his successor would not have been Luciani.

That this was his intent is demonstrated in that no other voting process in any nation excludes the aging. Even more demonstrative, in the 2005 and 2013 elections the cardinals elected aging men to the papacy who would obviously reign well into their eighties—not bright enough to elect a pope, yet, bright enough to be a pope.

As he lay on his death bed, Paul could be reasonably confident through the process of addition that Luciani had about seventy-five votes—a marginal victory—the two-thirds plus one vote required to win. Yet, he could not be certain his choice would succeed him.

Barely conscious—falling in and out of a coma the night before he died—Paul promoted Cardinal Yu Pin of Taiwan to the position of *Grand Chancellor of Eastern Affairs*—the most powerful position in eastern Catholicism. The intent was to give Yu Pin the influence he needed in the upcoming conclave to add the dozen or so eastern cardinal' votes to Luciani's list. When Paul went to rest, he knew his choice would succeed him. That is, if nothing happened to Yu Pin.

On the campaign trail

Philadelphia 1969
Cardinal Krol and Cardinal Wojtyla

In that most modern popes have succeeded to the papacy through the sway of their predecessors one might wonder how Karol Wojtyla—practically unknown in the media—wiggled his way into the papacy.

Being a fixed conservative, Karol knew he would never get the nod from Paul. He would go to the voters themselves.

We remember him as the most widely traveled pope in history. He was also the most widely traveled cardinal in history.

In the ten years he was a cardinal Karol visited more than two hundred cities. He visited just about every field cardinal including his well publicized six-week trips to the United States in 1969 and 1977 in which he visited every city where a cardinal resided.

In all, seventy-two trips to foreign countries. One might wonder what reason could he have had to have spent so much money from the poor box for so many expensive vacations. What could these trips possibly have had to do with his responsibilities as archbishop of Krakow? The only logical answer is he was lining up the votes.

In the 1978 conclaves, Wojtyla was the only cardinal who had a personal relationship with each of the others. He had slept in each of their mansions, had tasted wine with each of them at dinner and enjoyed morning breakfast with each of them on their verandahs.

In truth Karol did not rob the poor box to pay for his trips.

Like Albino Luciani, Karol Wojtyla had a benefactor who would pave his way to the top. The Polish cardinal's ten year 'campaign' was funded by his good friend Josemaria Escriva, founder of Opus Dei. Wojtyla and Escriva had met in 1965 at the Vatican II Council in Rome. The following year Karol made his first 'campaign' trip.

Opus Dei is a commune; it requires members to contribute most of their income to the cult. Though a secret society, it is no secret it uses its resources for political purposes and it is no secret, today, it financed the Polish cardinal to the pinnacle of the Catholic world.

Opus Dei is an order of extremists. It believes salvation can be obtained only through adoration. It does not believe helping others has anything to do with it. Although Opus Dei is per capita one of the richest organizations in the world, it does little to help others.

Its sole brush with charity is its *Harambee* mission in Africa which it uses as a lure to indoctrinate youth into its fascist fold.[9]

Opus Dei was founded in 1928 to counter movements within and outside the Church that were escaping doctrinal captivity.

Women gained the right to vote and were threatening to leave the kitchen. Jews were permitted to practice their religion in Catholic countries. Homosexuality was gaining a level of tolerance.

Murder by the Grace of God

On the world stage, the Soviet Union—archenemy of fascism—was coming into power. In his own homeland of Spain, democracy was raising its ugly brow. All these things horrified Escriva.

Escriva's thesis, *The Way,* dictates the path to salvation: "**Blessed be pain... Sanctified be pain. Glorified be pain.**" It so closely mirrored Hitler's *Mein Kampf* Escriva was accused of plagiarism.[10]

In the late thirties, Licio Gelli—an officer in Mussolini's *black shirts* who had once served as an intelligence officer under Hitler—was sent to Spain to support Franco's insurrection of the Spanish people. Escriva and Gelli quickly struck up an enduring relationship.

Escriva and Gelli were at his side when Franco came to power in 1939. Opus Dei quickly infiltrated Franco's cabinet and brought about ruthless oppression of the Spanish people—the clandestine cult providing the ideology and Franco providing the executioners. Together they murdered more than a million innocent people.

In March 1941, Escriva praised their great ally: "**Hitler will take care of the Jews. Hitler will take care of the Slavs.**"[11] After the war, he would minimize the damage. Escriva told a reporter: "**History is unfair to Hitler. It claims he murdered more than six million in his death camps, whereas, less than four million actually died.**"[12]

Gelli's Rat Line funneled Nazis to South America. Though Gelli gets the historical credit because he headed it up, the *Rat Line* was an Opus Dei scheme of which Gelli was an operations officer.

In 1946, Escriva and Gelli enlisted Carlos Fuldner into the ranks of Opus Dei. Fuldner had been an officer in Hitler's SS Guard and an old friend of Escriva, the reason why Escriva was able to make his remark in 1941: '**Hitler will take care of the Jews...**" Only the SS Guard knew what was going on in the death camps at that time.

Gelli and Fuldner ran rescue efforts from Madrid to Argentina for Nazi war criminals seeking refuge. Among those rescued were Adolph Eichmann and Josef Mengele though there are conflicting reports the latter may have escaped through the *Pius XII Rat Line*—a network of monasteries from Poland to Naples to South America.[13]

Knowing Luciani controlled a block of votes, Alvaro Portillo—Primate of Opus Dei—invited him to address its convention. In his invitation he cited the commonality of Luciani and Escriva in their '**Imitation of Christ.**' The strategy was to win his support for Wojtyla.

Luciani refused: "**True. Msgr. Escriva and I are in common. We** both believe the Imitation of Christ is the path to holiness. Yet, Escriva's teachings are materialistic. He believes salvation can be had solely through the Imitation of Christ's death, self-flagellation and the chanting of vain repetitions. I believe salvation can only be had through the Imitation of Christ's life, helping others..."[14]

When Opus Dei met in Milan the next month, Portillo introduced its candidate as "Papa Stanislao." The crowd broke into frenzy for forty-five minutes before Wojtyla was able to begin his speech. 'Stanislao' was Karol's chosen name should he ever rise to the top.[15]

When Karol Wojtyla rose to the papacy, like Franco before him, his cabinet was infiltrated by Opus Dei members from Agostino Casaroli at the top, down to his valet Angelo Gugel at the bottom.

His personal secretary—Stanislaw Dziwisz—was a flagellation practitioner of the cult. As if to hint His Holiness, himself, required an occasional flogging of the rump while he prayed the rosary.

When in 1982, John Paul II raised Opus Dei to *Prelature of the Holy See,* he did it in the face of an uproar, not only among Jews, Slavs, homosexuals and others Escriva had persecuted through the years, but among men and women of good conscience all over the world. Twenty years later, when he canonized Escriva a saint, it confirmed to all—except the most gullible—a tit-for-tat deal had been made between Josemaria Escriva and Karol Wojtyla in 1965.

The mystic of conclaves

Unlike what one might think, popes are not elected in conclaves. Consider the rules as they apply before, during and after a conclave.

If a cardinal relates in any way anything relative to a conclave's voting process, he self-excommunicates himself. For this reason, no cardinal has ever revealed anything relative to the voting process.

Yes, after a cardinal dies, an author of deception might claim the cardinal had confided with him before his death and write a book to capitalize on the suckers. Yet, no media has ever published what a cardinal said concerning the voting process while he was still alive.

During the weeks between a pope's funeral/resignation and the ensuing conclave, the cardinals are sequestered together in Rome.

Unlike what the public might believe, this time is not spent in prayer. It is spent electing the next pope. Cardinals can often be

Murder by the Grace of God

spotted in the red hat-frequented haunts in the city chatting away.

Although cardinals are forbidden to allow personal relationships to influence their vote, there is nothing in the rules prohibiting lobbying, nominating, negotiating, politicking or even tallying of votes before a conclave begins, provided it is done privately.

In that popes in recent history have been elected on either the first or second day, it is obvious the cardinals have already known the choice when the conclaves began. Otherwise, in a secret election, as required by conclave rules, it would take years before anyone would by chance come up with two-thirds of the votes.

Once a conclave convenes, however, the rules tighten up. Unlike what the media, fiction writers and Hollywood might portray, no lobbying, nominating or politicking is permitted—only silent prayer.

Yet, rules have changed from time to time. At one time, cardinals were permitted to be accompanied by aides and medical personnel.

In 1976, Paul tightened up the rules, making the 1978 conclaves the most covert in history. He restricted attendance to the voters.

The day before the first day

The press reported John Paul I was elected in a one-day conclave. Technically a conclave begins the day before it begins. Thus, though elected in one day, he was elected in the August 25-26 conclave.

On the day before the first day the cardinals attend Mass in St. Peter's Basilica followed by the ceremonial procession and chanting of *'Veni Creator Spiritus'* on their way to the Apostolic Palace.

A few hours afterwards the cardinals attend a prayer service in the Pauline Chapel after which they proceed to the Sistine Chapel.

> Two by two, the cardinals passed in splendid procession, past eager nuns, tourists and journalists. The prelates arrayed themselves in front of Bernini's Throne of St. Peter in the apse of the Basilica, a marvel of four Baroque statues of outsized saints who lead the eye to a dazzling bronze sunburst that all but explodes through the cupola.
>
> Four at a time, the cardinals came to the altar table to eat the wafer and sip the wine that symbolizes the body and blood of Christ in Catholic doctrine. The nuns below flocked to the railings to receive the same communion from priests in white surplices.
>
> After the mass, the cardinals walked back through St. Peter's to the Vatican Palace, and several exchanged greetings with friends behind the railings. Cardinal Reginald Delargey of New Zealand was heard telling one man, "I'll see you Monday."
>
> Italian television interrupted its coverage of an amateur baseball game yesterday to record the opening of the conclave. The cardinals, again in scarlet robes, wearing pectoral crosses and scarlet miters over scarlet skull caps, were seen sitting in the overly hot Pauline Chapel. They were reading what appeared to be hymn or prayer books. Behind them was Michelangelo's "Conversion of St. Paul," a masterpiece the public does not get to see.
>
> Then Cardinal Jean Villot, administrator of the church until a new pope is elected, signaled to the Sistine Chapel's choir, men and boys in white

Los Angeles Times August 26, 1978

In 1978, the doors to Sistine Chapel were sealed at about 5PM the afternoon before the first day of each of the conclaves.

The Camerlengo renders a lecture on the importance of secrecy.

Each of the cardinals walks to the front of the chapel and takes an oath of secrecy. He vows under penalty of self-excommunication he will not take the tiniest note from the conclave and he will whisper nothing of what transpired in a conclave for the rest of his life.

With one hundred eleven cardinals this takes about two hours.

The cardinals then draw cell lots and retire for the evening.

The seating arrangement

Prior to the election of Benedict XVI in 2005, intermittent counts were not announced to the participating conclave cardinals.

Yet, there is a supposition based on innocent Vatican releases that have reported that the winner has been consistently seated in the center chair of the first table on the St. Peter's side of the Sistine Chapel, and the most likely runner-up was seated in the center chair of the first table on the opposite side of the Chapel.

This would suggest that at the end of each ballot, the scrutinizers place the leading vote-getters in a pre-arranged seating arrangement.

For example, in the election of 1963, *The Times* reported: "**...The Camerlengo approached the Milan cardinal seated in the center of the first row and opposite him was Cardinal Siri of Genoa...**" and in Luciani's election in 1978: "**...Cardinal Villot came to the cardinal bishop in the center seat and opposite him was Karol Wojtyla of Poland...**" and in Wojtyla's election: "**... Villot placed his hand on the shoulder of the Polish cardinal who was seated in the center chair...**"[16]

Media mayhem

There is no other major world event in which the public is more vulnerable to fiction writers and tabloids than is a papal election.

The reason is that no one other than the participating cardinals knows what goes on in a conclave. This affords the opportunity to sensationalize events beyond one's wildest imagination.

Despite Paul had many times publicly pointed to his choice as Albino Luciani and had made a series of elector changes to that end; the press did not consider the Venice cardinal a candidate at all.

Murder by the Grace of God

Despite the press knew the Polish cardinal Karol Wojtyla had campaigned around the globe and had reported he had been seated in the 'runner-up chair' in the Luciani election, it did not consider him to be a candidate in the second conclave of 1978 at all. It published a list of candidates led by the liberal Benelli and the conservative Siri.

On the day Karol Wojtyla was elected a tabloid reported: "...Benelli fell five votes short on the first ballot...The conclave turned to Colombo who took himself out of the race... Unable to decide on an Italian cardinal on the first day, the College decided to look elsewhere and elected the Polish cardinal on the second day."[17]

How did this tabloid possibly know this? No one has ever found out the name of the cardinal who leaked this to the rag.

In reality, no cardinal leaked it to the tabloid. It made it up.

Yet, everyone believes this to this day, despite that no one other than the cardinals know what took place. Everyone believes this to this day, despite that the media had demonstrated in its predictions it knows nothing about what goes on when a pope is elected.

This not only fails to explain the question why the same cardinals elected a liberal in one election and elected a conservative a few weeks later; it makes it even more absurd. In one ballot, almost two-thirds of the conclave voted for a liberal—Benelli—and a few hours later, more than two-thirds of them elected a conservative—Wojtyla.

Benelli was even further to the *left* than was Luciani.

For example, concerning matters like sanctification of remarriage, Luciani would have moved authority to the bishop level; Benelli would have left it up to the individuals themselves.

The press would have one believe the Polish cardinal had not been considered at all on the first day, yet, on the second day—despite cardinals are not permitted to lobby, nominate or politick under the conclave rules—made a complete about-face and switched from a liberal to a conservative on the spur of the moment.

This is not to say—despite the rules—some chatting does go on between ballots and this chatting can gain a few votes for candidates, but surely never a gain of two-thirds of the votes in a single windfall.

Yet, this is how fiction books and motion pictures have described the election of John Paul II ever since: "...Unable to decide upon an Italian cardinal on the first day, the College decided to look elsewhere and elected the Polish cardinal on the second day."

This is just not how the real world works.

To understand how it does work, we must clear up the public's misconception of the number of ballots in modern elections.

'Luciani was elected on the fourth ballot on the first day'

John Paul I's election in 1978—involving 111 voting cardinals—could not have possibly involved more than two ballots—most likely one ballot—on the first day.

Despite the obvious, there is the widely publicized misconception **'Luciani was elected on the fourth ballot on the first day.'** This leads one to the more crucial misconception: **'Wojtyla was elected on the eighth ballot on the second day.'** We will address this momentarily.

As for now, it seemed Luciani's election had been prearranged. He had been elected in the days leading up to the conclave. [18]

The reason for a very limited number of ballots on the first day is the lengthy procedural requirements of the first day: [19]

> Invocation prayer – Cardinal Secretary of State
> The reading of the rules of election – Camerlengo
> The cardinals repeat the oath of secrecy
> The election of the scrutinizers
> The oaths of the scrutinizers
> Sermon by the senior Cardinal Deacon
> Sermon by the senior Cardinal Priest
> Sermon by the senior Cardinal Bishop
> Keynote sermon Camerlengo
> Distribution of ballots to cardinals
> Lunch including restroom privileges

According to the rules governing the 1978 conclaves:

> A round of voting is to begin each day at 9.30 A.M. and 4.30 P.M.
> But Vatican spokesmen admitted they did not know whether ballots can be taken morning and evening under the lengthy procedures to be used. Each cardinal must walk to the altar in the chapel, say a brief prayer, vote and return. Then the votes must be counted and recounted.

The Times London October 15, 1978

The 1978 conclave rules called for two rounds of voting each day.

Arithmetic confirms Luciani was elected on the first ballot and possibly confirmed on a second ballot on the first day.

A 111 cardinal conclave at two minutes each yields 222 minutes upwards of four hours per ballot. To this one has to add scrutinizing, counting, burning of ballots—a minimum of five hours per ballot.

Each slip had the name of the voting cardinal (preprinted) and the name of the cardinal he voted for (handwritten). The scrutinizers check each slip to be certain a cardinal has not voted for himself.

If the number of slips does not agree with the number of voting cardinals or if the count fails, the ballots together with tally slips and any notes taken by any cardinal are burned together with a chemical which produces a puff of black smoke from the Sistine Chapel.

If a candidate gains two-thirds-plus-one-vote, the ballots are recounted and then scrutinized again to be sure the winner did not vote for himself and final checks and balances are made. The count is then verified by the Camerlengo.

A follow-up vote is taken in an attempt to get a unanimous decision—Christ has spoken so to speak. The ballots are burned with straw emitting a puff of white smoke—a new pope has been elected.

Given the lengthy morning events and an unprecedented number of voters, Luciani was elected on the first ballot.

As the cardinals entered the conclave, they already knew who they were going to vote for—and why.

Post-1996 Conclave Rules

In 1996, John Paul II made changes to conclave voting procedures confirming the number of ballots possible on the first day of a 100+ cardinal conclave. He changed the conclave rules:

1. One ballot on the first day and four ballots on succeeding days. Except for the first ballot on the first day, he eliminated the lengthy procedure of each cardinal walking to the altar and saying a prayer on each vote.

2. The scrutineer is to call out the name of each cardinal voted for when he transfers the name from the voting slip to the tally list. The electors no longer depend entirely on the seating arrangement to know how the voting is proceeding. [20]

The elections of John Paul II and Benedict XVI

In the election of 2005, Joseph Ratzinger was the overwhelming favorite as he had been elected by the same cardinals to be the ranking cardinal—Dean of the College of Cardinals—in 2002. That they had elected him to the second ranking job in the Catholic world it made sense they would elect him to the top job a few years later.

Consistent with the rules—'**one ballot on the first day**'—a puff of smoke bellowed at 6:51PM on the first day—one ballot. A puff of white smoke bellowed at 5:01PM on the second day—three ballots.

The press reasoned correctly that he won the election on the first ballot and reconfirmation was made on the second day.

Like Albino Luciani, Joseph Ratzinger won on the first ballot on the first day. The cardinals already knew who they were going to vote for before they entered the conclave—and why.

Yet, let us go back to the more crucial election—John Paul II.

Though deliberations leading up to the conclave that elected Albino Luciani were widely reported in the press, those leading up to Karol Wojtyla's election were mostly kept under the table to avoid the rumors which surfaced concerning Luciani's election.

The media correctly attributed Luciani's 'quick' election to lobbying and tallying of votes before the conclave opened.

One journalist gave a convincing report that the election of Luciani had actually taken place over beer and wine at *L'Eau Vive*. He published photographs of key cardinals from both sides enjoying festivities at the quaint French restaurant behind the Pantheon for eight hours just two days before Luciani was elected.[21]

Then there is the famous comment of Cardinal Delargey to a reporter as he entered the conclave: "**I'll see you Monday.**"[22]

This was confirmed by Luciani, himself, in his first pontifical words to his newly acquired congregation: "**A funny thing happened on the way to the conclave...**" implying the cardinals had already decided on the winner before the conclave opened.[23]

To prevent a recurrence of what had happened in his case, actions were taken to restrict gatherings of cardinals in Rome. No cardinals showed up at *L'Eau Vive* or other traditional haunts of the red hats in Rome in the days leading up to the second conclave of 1978.

Murder by the Grace of God

The most one could come up with was that a group of cardinals attended a private Mass and gathered for the afternoon in the Church of Saint Andrew's at Quirinal on October 8, 1978, the Sunday before the conclave that elected John Paul II convened.

The group—representative of moderates and conservatives in the conclave—included Wojtyla of Poland, Siri of Genoa, Cody and Krol of the United States, Arns of Brazil, Gantin of Africa and curia cardinals Hume, Baggio and Poletti. Among those not cardinals, were Wojtyla's seminary roommate Deskur and the Polish bishop Rubin—Secretary of the Synod of Bishops—Casaroli and Caprio who had met with Wojtyla midway through Luciani's papacy.[24]

It is its St. Stanislaus Kostka Chapel that makes this church on Quirinal Hill a tourist attraction. Stanislaus—Stanislao in Italian—a 16th century Polish Jesuit novice was Wojtyla's patron saint.

The Holy Spirit works in strange and mysterious ways. Perhaps, 'He' had already picked Karol for the top job? One will never know.

Newspapers did report events customary of all papal elections,

> The last of 10 preconclave meetings was held yesterday by the College of Cardinals as workmen put finishing touches on the Sistine Chapel for the world's oldest and one of its most secret and important elections.
>
> The cardinals drew lots for the cells

Washington Post October 17, 1978

In announcing Karol Wojtyla's election, the press assumed **'John Paul II was elected on the eighth ballot on the second day.'**[25]

For starters, one knows there could have only been one ballot—certainly not more than two ballots—on the first day.

The tabloid reporting of John Paul II's election **"The cardinals, unable to agree on an Italian cardinal on the first day, decided to look elsewhere on the second day..."** rests entirely on the misconception there had been four ballots on the first day.

One or two ballots is certainly not nearly enough to conclude, **'...unable to agree on an Italian cardinal on the first day...'**

That Karol Wojtyla was elected on the first ballot is central to our understanding the solution to the most puzzling circumstance of all:

How is it possible the same constituency of cardinals elected a liberal in one election and just a few weeks later elected a conservative?

We will answer this question before we wrap up our investigation.

As for now, John Paul II was elected on the first day of the conclave that elected him. It was extended to a second day to obscure the corroboration and politicking that goes on before the conclave opened. [26] In all probability to obscure **'when the political infighting that goes on when a pope is elected turns to murder.'** [27]

Wojtyla celebrates three weeks after Luciani's death

1 *L'Osservatore Romano* 13 Jan 53
2 *L'Osservatore Romano* 13 Jan 53
3 *La Repubblica* 16 Dec 58   -   search: cardinal consistories 1958
4 *La Repubblica* 6 Mar 73   -   search: cardinal consistories 1973
5 *La Repubblica* 16 Dec 58
6 *La Repubblica* 16 Dec 69
7 *L'Osservatore Romano* 6 Aug 67
8 *Veneto Nostro* 26 Dec 67 - *La Repubblica* 2 Apr 72
9 *Harambee* charter
10 *The Way* Escriva   -   *Mein Kampf* Adolph Hitler
11 *Metro Madrid* 2 Mar 41
12 *IL Mondo* 7 May 47 Camp records = 4 million. Total count is estimated at 6 million plus.
13 *Odessa File* Frederick Forsyth
14 *Messaggero Mestre* 3 Feb 78
15 *Corriere Della Sera* 2 Mar 78
16 *The Times,* London: 22 Jun 63 – 27 Aug 78 – 17 Oct 78
17 *Fatti Duri* 18 Oct 78
18 *La Repubblica* 28 Aug 78
19 *Catholic Encyclopedia* and canon 1978 conclave rules
20 *Catholic Encyclopedia* and canon 1996 conclave rules
21 *La Stampa* 28 Aug 78
22 *La Mondo* 27 Aug 78   Monday = tomorrow
23 *La Repubblica* 4 Sep 78
24 *La Stampa* 16 Oct 78
25 *La Repubblica* 18 Oct 78
26 electing before the conclave opens will continue to be the practice of all future papal elections. The candidate will be elected on the first day. The elections will be announced on the second day to obscure the politicking, corroborating, negotiating and tallying of votes that go on before the conclaves open.
27 *Los Angeles Times* Todd Hamilton review of *Murder by the Grace of God*

Chapter 11

The Murders of Cardinal Filipiak and Cardinal Gracias

Two days before the funeral of Pope Paul, the Interim Pope received similar telegrams from opposite sides of the globe:

"Jean Cardinal Villot, Sovereign State of the Vatican

Most Holy Eminence,

    Today, on the way to the airport, His Eminence was stricken with severe abdominal pain. We had to return to Gniezno.
    I will keep you advised. I expect he will attend the upcoming conclave.

Kolab Mizenski, Secretary Boleshaw Filipiak, Archbishop of Gniezno."

"Jean Cardinal Villot, Sovereign State of the Vatican

Most Holy Eminence,

    As we started to go to the airport, Cardinal Gracias suffered a terrible stomach ache. We have returned to Bombay.
    I will keep you posted on his recovery that he will attend the conclave.

Raj Sharma, Secretary Valerian Gracias, Primate of India."

    Boleshaw Filipiak died on the day before his lifelong archenemy Karol Wojtyla was elected to the papacy.[1]
    Valerian Gracias died midway through John Paul I's papacy in a Bombay Catholic hospital of '...an ailment doctors were unable to diagnose and could not treat.'
    A similar diagnosis was reported for two other cardinals—Reginald Delargey and Trinh Nhu Khue—stricken at the same time.
    All four death certificates of these eastern cardinals issued by Catholic hospitals cite: 'inoperable adenocarcinoma.'[2]

---

[1] *Parkiet* 15 Oct 78   see also *Catholic Encyclopedia*
[2] *Maharashtra Times* 16 Sep 78   Tap Chi Cong San 28 Nov 78   Dominion Post 29 Jan 79

Chapter 12

The Murder of Cardinal Yu Pin

There were some events that surrounded the funeral of Paul VI that may have been related to the first conclave of 1978.

The day before Paul's funeral, Belgium radio announced Leon Joseph Cardinal Suenens—Primate of Belgium—had been killed by a falling section of an aging building façade in Brussels. The radio report based on eyewitnesses of the event was premature.[1]

It had been a visiting French bishop that had been killed. It had been that the incident occurred near the cardinal's palace and the bishop was wearing black garb topped off with a red zucchetto that caused witnesses to mistake him for the cardinal.

Of course, if this was true—witnesses on the ground made such a misjudgment—it was likely anyone on the roof would have made the same mistake. Suenens—leader of change in the Catholic world— was one of the most influential members in the upcoming conclave. Yet, the incident was a mere foretelling of what was about to come.

Cardinal Yu Pin keeled over at Paul's funeral. The Vatican cited 'heart attack.' Cardinal Delargey, closest friend of Yu Pin who had shared rooms with him the night before, called for an autopsy. He insisted Yu Pin had no history at all of heart disease. Newspapers demanded autopsy. The body was quickly embalmed and returned in a sealed coffin to Taipei for interment.[2] Delargey—the youngest cardinal in the conclave—was unaware of his own impending doom.

A week later, came another strange happening. Cardinals Benelli and Suenens narrowly escaped death when a small section of a frieze fell from the Torre Borgia missing them by inches. Though Vatican buildings are aging, this is rare as the facades are routinely checked for defects to protect the tourists who roam Vatican City.

A notice in the Vatican paper called for increased inspection.

In Brussels, because the incident resembled that which had killed the bishop two weeks earlier, the press pointed fingers.[3] In time, the incidents were discarded as having been coincidence.

1 *Le Soir Brussels* 10 Aug 78
2 *London Times* 9 Aug 78 details of Yu Pin's death is covered on the Internet
3 *L'Osservatore Romano* 22 Aug 78 *Le Soir Brussels* 25 Aug 78

Chapter 13

The Good Guys vs. the Bad Guys

"Some kinds of people are born better than others and are entitled to more... little boys are better than little girls...." Roman Catholic Church

Albino Luciani = John Paul I
Karol Wojtyla = John Paul II
Joseph Ratzinger = Benedict XVI

John Paul I and his successors John Paul II and Benedict XVI were very different kinds of men, the latter doctrinal conservatives and the former a monumental progressive. Just how far apart were these men in their ideologies and why did they think so very differently?

To begin with, one must consider their upbringing.

Both Karol Wojtyla and Joseph Ratzinger were born into well-to-do families. Unlike Albino Luciani they never knew what it was to wonder where their next meal was coming from.

This made them less compassionate of the poor; they were able to champion a ban on contraception and dine on fine wines and rest their heads on pillows of down in lavish palaces and think it right.

Conversely, Luciani supported the pill. Conscious that the ban on contraception was the driving force behind the spread of disease, poverty and starvation in third world countries, he thought it wrong.

More fundamental to the men they would become, Albino had been born to a mishmash of parents—an atheist father and a devout mother—while Karol and Joseph had been born to devout parents of the conviction that whatever the men in Rome had to say was right.

Karol Wojtyla

From the age of six Karol was educated in the Wadowice Military Academy which brainwashed its students in fascism.

Non-Christians in Poland were made to live in ghettos and were not provided opportunity, particularly higher education. To preserve the purity of the white race, blacks were not allowed in Poland.

Karol has been unfairly criticized because he refused to join the **Resistance** and instead worked for the Nazis. In Poland, everyone went to work for the Nazis. What's more, they went to work for the Nazis eagerly except for Jews, Slavs, homosexuals and supporters who escaped to the sewers. It was in Krakow the 'Resistance' picked up the nickname **'The Underground'** where it was literally confined to the city's sewers.

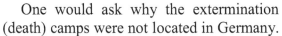
8 year old Karol with mother

One would ask why the extermination (death) camps were not located in Germany. After all, Poland bordered Russia which was the most imminent threat. The German people would not have supported them.

It was that the Poles were so intensely fascists—anti-Semitic, homophobic, atheist-haters and anti-socialists—the extermination camps were built in Poland and the overwhelming number of those who lost their lives in the Holocaust—including a million children— died in Poland.[1] This doesn't mean the Poles were bad people; just that they were good Catholics—haters of other kinds of people.

This is seen clearly in that the Nazis never tried to hide the atrocity from the Poles. The largest and most dreadful camps were located in the largest metropolitan areas—Treblinka at Warsaw and Auschwitz at Krakow—to draw on the Polish workforce.

The Auschwitz extermination system alone included forty-eight camps and there were scores or others—Sobibor, Belzec, Chelmno, you name them. It took millions of men to build and maintain them with their ovens and gas chambers in such a short time. Though the Nazis oversaw their construction, Hitler did not divert millions of soldiers from his front lines to build them. The Poles built them. What's more, they provided technical, maintenance and other specialty services to the death camps on an ongoing basis.

The heaviest toll of all was at Auschwitz. The first inmates came from the sewers and ghettos of Krakow.

Karol—like other Polish youths—shared the common ideologies of Hitler and Pius XII: white superiority, segregation of blacks, persecution of homosexuals, Jews, Muslims and certain other ethnic peoples. Karol—like everyone else—was caught up in the *Opium of the Masses—Catholicism—Fascism.*

At the time this was the way the mainstream thought. Even those oppressed thought it was God's intention they be subordinated.

We see this even today where seven hundred million members of the so-called fair sex pay a man in Rome for their salvation—a man who conditions their children from an early age little boys are better than little girls—the pivotal canon of the Roman Catholic Church. We see this today where millions of homosexuals pay this same man for their salvation, among the most homophobic men who ever lived. We see this even today where…

One would wonder why Poland fell in a few days.

The Poles and the Nazis shared the same ideals. Their common enemy was **communism**, not **fascism**. In Poland, Karol was just one of an army of Polish **fascists** who went to work eagerly building camps and supply factories for Hitler's **fascist** regime.

The Poles built much of the infrastructure Hitler needed to fight his war. They broke ground on Auschwitz a week after Germany's occupation and had it up and running in the space of a few months. They built hundreds of supply plants including the IG Farben and Solvay chemical plants which annexed the main Auschwitz camps.[2]

Karol progressed rapidly from a quarry laborer to a supervisory position in the Solvay chemical plant which produced the pesticide Zyklon B used to gas prisoners in death camps.[3]

In his job as distribution supervisor, Karol traveled to Treblinka and other camps in the Nazi extermination system. The film **'Pope John Paul II'** staring John Voight depicts Karol as quartermaster of the Solvay depot. A **Resistance** leader—Boleshaw Filipiak—solicits Karol to divert supplies to the **Resistance**; Karol refuses.[4]

While at Solvay, Karol joined a theater group. The love of his life was the theater. He wanted to be an actor. The record shows he was quite an actor, often commanding the leading role. Twenty-two year old Karol is shown here in the  leading role of a romantic satire of Hitler's youth performed before Nazi officers. One could ask, if he wanted to be an actor and had no interest in the priesthood, why he entered a seminary?[5]

As the war progressed and an allied victory became imminent, Polish youth who had shown loyalty and were rising in the Nazi civilian ranks were being forced into the German Army.

To escape enlistment, Karol entered a seminary. During the war no adult male was exempt from the draft including fathers of young children. Even advancing age was no excuse. If a man was able-bodied, he was inducted. The exception was seminary enrollment owed to the immense demand for chaplains in the German army.

Seminary deferment gave Karol a window of two years in which time he gambled the war would be over. While in the seminary, Karol realized he could use his acting abilities in the Church. There was a great similarity between the two professions. Both preachers and actors deal with the world of make-believe.

Eagle's Nest

Unlike Karol Wojtyla, Joseph Ratzinger wanted to be a priest from the start. As already discussed, when he was five years old Joseph fell in love with the Cardinal of Munich's elaborate gown and announced at dinner that evening he was going to be a cardinal.[6]

Obersalzberg[7] is a sprawling mountainside resort area tucked in between the village of Berchtesgaden and the district of Traunstein in southeastern Germany. In 1933, Hitler built his residence here—The Berghof. Most other Nazis including Adolf Eichmann, Herman Goring, Heinrich Himmler and Martin Bormann, had homes here.

Hitler headquartered his SS Guard—the Leibstandarte—in nearby Traunstein.[8] Hitler's pride and joy was the *Traunstein Scouts*, a composite of the *Jungvolk*—ages 10-14, and the *Hitler Youth*—ages 14-16. Both operated under the auspices of the SS Guard. To put it bluntly, the Traunstein-Berchtesgaden area was crawling with Nazis.

In the spring of 1937, Martin Bormann broke ground on Eagle's Nest—a mountaintop retreat—a gift from the Third Reich to the Fuhrer in honor of his fiftieth birthday.[9]

A strange happening

In the spring of 1937, Joseph's father, a police officer in western Bavaria, did a strange thing. At a time retirement was not a part of a common man's life and Hitler needed every man either on the front lines or in factories, Joseph's father took 'early' retirement.

Yet, even more bizarre, at a time when most people died in the same village in which they had been born, he moved his family from what had been for centuries their ancestral home in Marktl am Inn in western Bavaria, all the way across the country to Traunstein.

In his biographies Joseph Ratzinger claims: **"My father hated the Nazis and what they stood for..."** As we know today, they stood for the same thing both the Vatican and Hitler stood for at that time.

One can wonder why he pulled his family up from their ancestral roots and moved them across the country to the heart of Nazism in the western world and took a house a few kilometers from Kehlstein Mountain at the exact time Eagle's Nest was being woven at its top.

The only logical answer is he was either employed as a security officer at the Hitler compound or was a member of the SS Guard headquartered in Traunstein. One will never know. [10]

Yet, what one does know is that his father hated the Nazis so much he moved his family to Traunstein which was crawling with Nazis forcing Joseph into Hitler's personal scout troop.

It is reasonable to surmise Joseph had the privilege to have been reviewed by the Fuhrer as the Traunstein troops were often invited to Eagle's Nest. Yet, the extent of their relationship is not known. We do know he was a poster boy in 1942.

Joseph Ratzinger age 14

Joseph at Eagle's Nest

In 1984, when photos surfaced of John Paul II's fascist activities in the war, he ordered incriminating photos of prominent cardinals destroyed; the reason few wartime photos of Benedict have survived. Nevertheless, what does the man have to say for himself?

> "...It was on my tenth birthday we arrived in Traunstein...at first, inducted into the Jungvolk...on my fourteenth birthday I was promoted to the Hitler Scout troop as required by law. Yet, I did not participate in the scouts and refused to attend meetings. Before reaching draft age I intended to get an exemption by entering a seminary. But as the tide began to turn against the Axis powers in 1943 the draft age was lowered to sixteen. I was drafted into the army and assigned to an anti-aircraft battery protecting a depot herding Jews in Hungary. Still I refused to fire a shot. A year later I became a part of the *Austrian Legion*...When the end of the war became imminent in 1945, I deserted..." *Benedict XVI* [11]

"...refused to attend meetings? ...refused to fire a shot?"

I can't say for sure, but I don't think this is how armies are run.

It is not unusual for those who were the 'good guys' who fought to maintain the status quo of yesterday, when the 'bad guys' of yesterday won the race and became the 'good guys' of today, to claim to be the 'bad guys' of yesterday and the 'good guys' of today.

Nevertheless, neither of these men—Karol Wojtyla nor Joseph Ratzinger—has come clean of his past. What's more, they have been unable to break free of what the little boy Albino Luciani's father once called the *Opium of the Masses—Christianity*—**some kinds of people are born better than others.** The reason, Benedict conditions children at an early age that little boys are better than little girls. In a world in which women serve as presidents of nations, a little girl cannot look forward to the lowest rung of 'holy' progression.

Coincidence

Today, by sheer coincidence, in a few minutes it is possible to take a tour bus from the stately home in which Karol Wojtyla grew up in Wadowice, to the Military Academy where he was schooled, to the

Murder by the Grace of God

Auschwitz concentration camp he would pass each day on his the way to the Solvay chemical plant where he worked for the Nazis. It is possible in the same few minutes to take a bus from the house Joseph Ratzinger lived as a teen, up the mountain to Eagle's Nest, and even less time to visit the SS Guard headquarters in Traunstein.

On the one hand, one has Karol Wojtyla who during his formidable years wore the military uniform of a fascist school and once furnished cyanide pellets to death camps used to murdered three million men, women and children.[12] On the other hand, one has Joseph Ratzinger who during his formidable years wore the military uniforms of the Jungvolk and Hitler Scouts and once guarded a depot herding Jews to the Auschwitz extermination network.

Both of these men were well qualified to head up the Roman Catholic Church—the largest fascist organization in the world. Fascism = some kinds of people are better than others: unless they are born-out-of-wedlock or homosexuals little boys are better than little girls... celibates are better than the married... the remarried are second class Catholics unfit to receive the Eucharist... etc. etc. etc.

Albino Luciani

Well, just where was Albino Luciani during the war?

Like Karol Wojtyla, as a seminarian he was exempt from military service. Yet, unlike Wojtyla who opposed the Resistance, he became a part of it.

It was when he was a student at the Gregorian University in Rome that he sought asylum in the Vatican for five hundred Jews docked at Naples.

In the north, his knack for mountain climbing facilitated his ministering Resistance members hiding in difficult to get at places in the Italian Alps. Here, he wears the soft cap of the Italian Resistance.

He told me of the most difficult moment of his life:

> "I felt the pulse of a thirteen year old boy run out between my fingers. Shot while blowing up a railroad trestle to cut off military supplies coming from Poland."

The end of a dream

Regardless, if Hitler had won the war, all that Karol Wojtyla and Joseph Ratzinger had ever dreamed of would have become a reality.

We would, today, be living in a world of white male superiority rather than in this world in which we find ourselves, this world of equal rights and dignity for everyone, this anti-*Christian,* anti-*Fascist* world of social justice for all, which, as we speak, threatens to be extended even to homosexuals, transsexuals and perhaps worst of all atheists—people who bring their children up in the real world of today rather than the make-believe world of yesterday.

World War II broke the backbone of fascism which had been the way of life in the western world for thirty-five hundred years. Unlike previous wars, it did much more than to decide the superiority of one nation over another. From its embers would rise the social evolution, beginning with integration and eventually expanding into feminism, planned parenthood, sexual education, divorce and remarriage, single parenthood, the right to believe or not to believe, and most decent of all: the right to marry that constituency of human life most precious to one's being no matter who that person happens to be.

After the war, Wojtyla and Ratzinger rose up as leaders in the effort to preserve segregation of blacks. Conversely, Luciani rose up as an anti-segregationist, not only in the Church but in society.

As feminism, remarriage, contraception, homosexuality and other splinters of the social revolution raised their 'ugly' heads, Wojtyla and Ratzinger raised their voices and held up their hands to stop them, while Luciani became the driving force behind them.

In truth, back in those days, Wojtyla and Ratzinger were the 'good guys.' Luciani was the 'bad guy;' polls being overwhelmingly against each of these offerings as they came onto the table.

After the war, referring to the dangers of the gullibility of men, Luciani told a reporter: "It was not so much Hitler and Mussolini who were the culprits in this thing, as it was the ignorance and the weakness of the minds of the masses that believed in them"[13]

Two different Gods

Perhaps the greatest difference between these men was their relative doctrinal convictions. Whenever doctrine placed undue hardship on the lives of innocent people, Luciani stepped in. On the other hand, Wojtyla and Ratzinger, as doctrinal conservatives, didn't care how much suffering doctrine unfairly placed on the everyday lives innocent people. In their minds, what pre-medieval self-serving men had once written was etched permanently into their souls.

Nothing better demonstrates the difference between Wojtyla and Luciani than their treatment of born-out-of-wedlock children.

During the twenty years Wojtyla and Luciani served as bishops, each of their countries—driven by the Vatican's condemnation of out-of-wedlock children—suffered from a vast orphan population of over two million in each country. During that time Wojtyla built and dedicated fifty-three churches and not a single orphanage. Luciani built and dedicated forty-four orphanages and not a single church.

Each time the fork in the road would come up, Albino Luciani would ask himself: **"Now, what would Jesus do in this case?"**

Karol Wojtyla thought of Jesus as not much more than a **'golden crucifix on a wall and a piece of bread in a cup.'**

Nevertheless, these were two very different kinds of men, driven by two very different kinds of Gods.

Wojtyla and Ratzinger—the 'good guys' of yesterday—striving to preserve the last bits of fascism Hitler had left behind, and Albino Luciani—the 'bad guy' of yesterday—like Marx before him striving to bring the reality of Jesus Christ into a modern world...striving to stamp out what Hitler stood for, once and for all.

---

1 It is estimated 6 million died in the Holocaust. Of this only 4.0 million have been identified by records of which 3.1 million died in Poland: Auschwitz 1,300,000 – Belzec 435,000 – Chelmno 152,000 – Sobibor 200,000 – Treblinka 870,000 – Warsaw 200,000 – other Poland 209,000. Overall, about 85% or 5 million of these in Poland. See list of concentration camps on Internet or in libraries.
2 Nuremburg trials 1947-1946: *IG Farben Solvay Trial*
3 Nuremburg trials 1947-1946: *IG Farben Solvay Trial*
4 Film *'John Paul II'* staring John Voight 2005
5 Biographies of John Paul II claim he was part of an underground theater which promoted anti-Hitler plays as if that were possible during the war; a claim contradicted by photos that show Nazi officers in the audience. It is also inconsistent with the known fact he worked for the Nazis at Solvay.
6 Benedict's biographies recount five year old Joseph's reaction to the Archbishop's elaborate gown
7 Search: *Obersalzberg Berghof* on Internet or in libraries
8 Search: *Leibstandarte* or *Obersalzberg* on Internet or in libraries
9 Search: *Kehlsteinhaus* on Internet or in libraries
10 The supposition Joseph Ratzinger's father was either a SS Guard or employed as a security officer at Eagle's Nest, is based solely on the known facts reported in this dissertation.
11 *The Austrian Legion* was a Nazi terrorist organization which brutalized dissidents in the years leading up to the war. It was integrated into the German Army as a branch of the SS Guard in 1939 and used in espionage activities and rounding up dissidents for the concentration camps.
12 That Karol Wojtyla distributed cyanide to camps is a known fact. It is not known if he knew its use.
13 *Messaggero Mestre* 1 Apr 46

The ecclesiastical record of two popes

Doctrine	Luciani Moderate	Wojtyla Conservative
Liberation Theology	yes	no
Contraception and Planned Parenthood	yes	no*
Contraception to prevent disease	yes	no*
Redistribution of wealth society	yes	no
Charity in a capitalistic society	no	yes
Vow of poverty (all clergy)	yes	no
Vow of celibacy (all clergy)	no	yes
Abortion embryonic development*	yes	no
Abortion viable fetus	no	no
Genetic Research	yes	no
Ecumenism	yes	no
Election of the Pope by bishops	yes	no
Ordination of women	yes	no
Ordination born-out-of-wedlock children	yes	no
Homosexuality is God's will	yes	yes
Love and commitment define marriage	yes	no
Sanctification of remarriage	yes	no
Mysticism & visionary saints	no	yes
Little boys are superior to little girls	no	yes

*Luciani supported the 'pill' to prevent untimely conception and condoms to prevent disease. Though he encouraged destruction of diseased and impaired fetuses, the orphanages he built to permit children to be born which otherwise would have been aborted testify he condemned abortion of a healthy viable fetus.

Sequence of creation/*prevention*: sperm → egg ← *pill/condom* → fertilized egg ← *morning after pill* → embryo → tissue ← *1st term abortion* → heart beat → brain wave ← *2nd term abortion* → viable fetus ← *3rd term abortion* → birth.

Benedict XVI positions are similar to John Paul II except for homosexuality. Driven by intense hatred of homosexuals, Benedict used his political influence to deprive them of basic human rights under the laws of nations. He decreed it an 'objective disorder.' The psychiatric world holds homosexuality one's birthright whereas Genophobia —adversity to sex—is a recognized 'mental illness.'

Francis I positions are similar to those of John Paul II except that he would permit condoms to prevent disease under restricted circumstances. Like John Paul II he would permit gay priests provided they are celibate. His policy is the same as John Paul II: It's okay to be gay as long as one does not engage in homosexual acts.

Chapter 14

His Papacy

"What is important is not how many children are born. What is important is that every child that is born has an equal opportunity at a good and healthy life.[1]

Albino Luciani

Joannes Paulus I

The six mounds in the foreground represent Italian peaks for which he held the speed record when he became a bishop in 1958. The three stars stand for the attributes his father had built into him: compassion, courage and change. The lion represents his father Giovanni Paolo Luciani.

Author's note: Within a year of his ordination he was taken to a sanatorium with suspected TB which turned out to be a life threatening bout with High Altitude Pulmonary Edema brought on by hi-altitude activities. He speaks of this in his letter to St. Therese: "Thinking I had Tuberculosis at a time TB antibiotics had not been developed, they took me to a sanatorium to die. They found out I had spent too much time high up in the mountains..." [2] He would have a second bout with HAPE after the war. Authors who have not researched hospital records refer to these bouts with HAPE as 'bronchitis' or 'pneumonia' plagiarizing 'pseudo biographers' who came before them.

In late summer 1978, Paul VI died. As the conclave approached, *The Times* of London published the leading candidates for succession. In order of their promise, were listed cardinals: **'Benelli, Siri, Hume, Pignedoli, Baggio, Suenens, Poletti, Lorscheider...'** [3]

The Patriarch of Venice was not on the list. It was no secret Paul had stacked the College of Cardinals heavily to the *left* toward his favorite son. Yet, this would have moved the vote toward most any other liberal, the most visible being Benelli and Suenens.

Yet, Paul had not openly endorsed either of these; he had placed the papal stole solely upon the shoulders of Albino Luciani.

How was it possible it had missed the boat? A week earlier:

They Have no Souls

The knocker knocked. It was the nun Vincenza. She handed him the morning newspaper. She uttered in anguish, "They say they have no souls." She scuttled out of the room.

He read the headline: 'First Test-tube Baby Born in England.'

He read it again, this time aloud, as if he had to hear it to believe it: "'First Test-tube Baby Born in England.'"

His eyes caught another headline: Vatican City. The Dean of the College of Cardinals, Carlo Confalonieri, condemned the English child born of artificial means. The aging cardinal cited the decree of Pius XII prohibiting genetic experimentation. Rapid fire from palaces of cardinals from around the world, from Italy to Germany to Poland to Latin America to the United States, backed him up; some suggesting such children have no souls and others stopping just short of labeling the infant 'a child of the devil.'[4]

It was no secret he was the favorite son of Paul VI. Paul had made him Patriarch of Venice the most coveted pastoral spot in the Catholic world and stepping stone to the papacy. It was also no secret Paul had stacked the voting conclave heavily in his favor.

Paul was eighty and not well. If Paul were to die now the vote would be close. Surely if he spoke out in defense of this child he would enrage those cardinals who had come out so strongly against her. He would risk losing those votes. He would risk all his father had done, and all he had done, and all John had done, and all Paul had done, to make possible his succession to the papacy.

He thought back to that day he had climbed into the carriage that had taken him to Feltre. How could he get around what his papa had told him? "...never risk your king to save a pawn."

Yet, his papa had also made him pledge: "...you must promise me you will live your life in imitation of Christ..."

"Hmmm?" the man in the red cap murmured to himself: "I wonder what Jesus would do in this case?"

He pressed the intercom. It buzzed twice, "Vincenza, here."

"Have you seen Lorenzi?"

"He's here with me now," the nun replied.

"Good. Send him in."

Lorenzi strolled into the study.

He was an angelic priest to say the least, as devout as they come. Being the cardinal's secretary, he knew his manager's mission; something that could only be accomplished if he were to rise to the papacy. He knew the vote for the papacy would be close. It had been one of his hobbies to keep track of it—those voting cardinals in the field and those in the Vatican.

The man in the red cap did not look up. He was busy scribbling a note on a scrap of stationary. He handed it to his visitor.

"My dear Lorenzi, I want you to post this to the parents of the newborn child in England."

Lorenzi read the note:

"My Dearest Lesley and John Brown

My very personal congratulations to you on the birth of your little girl. I want you to be assured there is reserved for you and your child a high place in heaven.

Albino Luciani, Patriarch of Venice"[5]

The young priest smiled at his mentor, "Good, a private note. I was wondering how you would handle this one."

The Patriarch of Venice picked up another piece of stationary and scribbled again. "Here, my dear Lorenzi. I want you to issue this release to the world press. I want it to go out today. We have not a moment to lose."

Lorenzi read the wire:

"I have sent my most heartfelt congratulations to the English baby girl. As far as her parents are concerned, I (the Church) have no right to condemn them. If they acted with honest intentions and in good faith, they will be deserving of merit before God for what they wanted and asked the doctors to carry out. Albino Luciani, Patriarch of Venice."[6]

Lorenzi looked at his boss as if he were about to jump off a tall building, "But, Paul is ill. He might not make it another day, let alone another week. A private message to the parents might make some sense. But this message to the world will enrage those in the conclave who have come out against her. It will cost you the pa..."

The man behind the desk cut him off.

"A private message to this little girl's parents will not end the rumor these children have no souls. When prejudice rears its head, one must nip it in the bud. If it costs me the papacy in this world so be it. If it costs me my soul in the next world so be it. We have not a moment to lose. Carry it to the ends of the earth. Do it now!"

Lorenzi shot the cardinal one last look of appeal, but to no avail. He carefully stuffed the papers into his shirt pocket and hurried reluctantly out of the room.[7]

Aftermath

Pope Paul was in seclusion at Castel Gandolfo. A reporter asked him for his response to Luciani's press release challenging the papal decree prohibiting artificial insemination, going so far as to reserve a place in heaven for both the make-believe child and her parents.

Paul told the reporter: "The cardinal could not have been more right. There is reserved for these courageous parents and their little girl a high place in heaven. Unfortunately, I cannot say the same for many of us who hold high places here on earth."[8]

Luciani was challenged by the press that test-tube babies would aggravate the orphan problem he had worked so hard to alleviate. It would make it possible for sterile and homosexual couples to have children, robbing Italy of those who could parent orphans.

He told the reporter:

> "My good friend Einstein once told me he could not accept the existence of God because he could not accept God would play dice with His children. There is something horrific about how God goes about making children.
>
> Millions of fertilized eggs are drowned in the sewer in everyday intercourse. Others are born physically and mentally impaired to live unbearable lives and die unspeakable deaths.
>
> Here, on the realization of this great event, it makes no sense for man to allow God to continue to have His way in this thing. Artificial insemination will eventually lead to man's greatest achievement, the creation of a perfectly healthy child every time.
>
> What is important is not how many children are born, but that every child that is born has an equal opportunity at a good and healthy life. Genetic research will eventually take us there."[9]

Einstein, himself, had once said of him: "Luciani thinks of things today, as the rest of us will think of them in centuries to come."[10]

Regardless, his message to the parents of Louise Brown was viewed as the most defiant rebuttal of a papal decree by a ranking prelate of the Church since Martin Luther. In upstaging cardinals who otherwise would have voted for him, he had not only removed himself as a candidate for the papacy; rumors surfaced when his reconfirmation came due that year, it would not be forthcoming.

Many believe a cardinal once appointed is forever a cardinal. Not so. Cardinals are appointed for five-year terms and require reconfirmation of the reigning pontiff when their terms lapse.

Nevertheless, Paul died in the ensuing week.

John Paul the First

Astonishingly, when the white smoke rose from the Sistine Chapel on August 26, 1978, it bore Albino Luciani's name. On the first ballot the count was at least seventy-five for Luciani; the minimum, of two-thirds plus one vote required to elect him.[11]

Within Italy, right-wing newspapers tabbed him: 'a reckless liberal' whereas most papers tabbed him: 'a progressive with an open mind to changing doctrine in those cases it is unfair to innocent people.'[12]

Not much was known of him outside of Italy.

He had been tabbed 'a moderate' outside Italy on the few bits that had reached the world press. Like the time he ordered his priests to sell their gold chalices and other implements of idol worship to build an orphanage, to the times he had been caught baptizing born-out-of-wedlock children, to the times he had been caught distributing the Eucharist to members of the Communist Party, to the times he ordered hospitals to admit partners of homosexuals into intensive care units, to the time he had defended their right to adopt children, to the times he had been caught officiating at funerals of the remarried, to the times he challenged the ban on contraception, to his courageous defense of the first artificially inseminated child in England just a month before his election ...

The Philadelphia Inquirer reported: "Cardinal Luciani's election is a signal to the world that the Church is steering a course from the traditionalists who say the Church is changing too fast toward the progressives who say it is advancing too slowly."[13]

> There have been signs—in his church work, his speeches and his temperament—that Pope John Paul is not a'hard-line conservative unwilling to change on various issues. "History is history," he said when elevated to cardinal five years ago. "We must look to the future with fresh hopes and new ideas."
>
> *Baltimore Sun*

> The new Pope is regarded as a moderate who is concerned with maintaining traditional Catholic values while at the same time lending Church support to issues of social justice.
>
> *The Times*

> clear. The Church in Italy has made something of an uneasy peace with the powerful Communist and Socialist parties, and under Paul VI it has made bold diplomatic overtures to communist countries. The new Pope
>
> *Philadelphia Evening Bulletin*

> "The choice indicates that the cardinals want to face the complex problems of modern times with prudence and with a moderate like Luciani rather than a conservative," said Kronos, a major Italian news agency.
>
> *Philadelphia Inquirer*

The campaign manager

It is no secret Cardinal Benelli orchestrated Luciani's election.

It is likely, in rounding up the votes, Benelli encountered cardinals demanding a clean bill of health—not unusual in elections.

At the time Louise Brown was born, it was apparent Paul was in his last days. Albino Luciani spent the week before the death of Paul VI at the Stella Maris Institute on the Lido.

Dr. Da Ros, when asked if Luciani had gone for treatment told Tornelli: **"No. Luciani had gone on holiday to read, to walk, to rest."** [14]

This makes sense because Luciani always stayed at the Stella Maris convent on the Lido when holidaying on the resort island.

Msgr. Senigaglia agrees Luciani did not go for treatment but does attest: **"...he had a full medical checkup just before the conclave."** [15]

This also makes sense because 'checkup' is a business the clinic is in. Yet, the results of this physical exam have never been found.

Murder by the Grace of God

It is reasonable to believe Benelli took the exam certificate into the conclave should the matter arise. The document like all papers in a conclave would have been required by conclave rules to be burned.

Then it might be that the Vatican destroyed the document because it attested to a man of impeccable health. One will never know.

Just another man

From what was known of him change was definitely on the horizon.

In accepting his pontificate Luciani took the name John Paul I. History recorded he named himself in honor of his patrons—John XXIII who had made him a bishop and Paul VI who had made him a cardinal and had paved his way to the top. Yet, one can surmise, he also had in mind his beloved father Giovanni Paolo Luciani—John Paul Luciani—who had sheared his wool and groomed his mane.

His installation took place before a makeshift altar in St. Peter's Square. He refused to be crowned with the jeweled encrusted tiara which in the past had been the focal point of papal coronations.[16] Instead he allowed a pastoral stole—the symbol of a common priest—placed upon his shoulders. He did not intend to rule from the throne. He intended to walk among his people.

Whereas both the rank-and-file and the hierarchy of the Church viewed the crown as a symbol of royalty, John Paul saw something else. He saw in it the right to a good and healthy life for a thousand children who would otherwise starve to death.

His refusal of the tiara hinted at what would become more and more apparent in the coming days; he would liquidate much of the Vatican treasures to annihilate poverty. His peers, the crown princes of the Church, felt much of their own regency endangered.

In order to calm the fears of those who had refused to vote for him, he did something no other pope before him had ever done. He immediately confirmed appointments of all existing cardinals.

Yet, he reduced in half the substantial bonus cardinals receive upon the election of a new pope—a forewarning to his eventually reducing salaries of Vatican cardinals which at the time was the equivalent of what is today one hundred thousand after-tax dollars.

He refused to order the Fisherman's Ring cast, the symbol of the majesty of the papacy. [17] Nor did he ever extend his hand for the ceremonial kiss. He would have no one bow to him. Rather he would embrace his visitor, not in a ceremonial way, but in a real way.

Luciani had never been a man of formalities. As a bishop, he had refused to be addressed as 'Your Excellency.' As a cardinal he had refused to be addressed as 'Your Eminence.' As a pope, he refused to be addressed as 'Your Holiness.' He asked everyone, from heads of state to little children to address him by his birth-given name.

As a bishop, he said Mass every Wednesday morning. He would have newly ordained priests say Mass on Sundays and dressed in a smock he would serve as the priest's acolyte. He carried this practice into the Vatican. He would have seminary graduates say Mass in his private chapel and serve as their acolyte.

He had a knack for explaining complex issues in a simple way. On one occasion, he took a microphone out of a cardinal's hand and gave it to a six-year old boy as if to suggest what the child had to say was more important than what his prince of the Church had to say.

When he shook hands with the communist mayor of Rome, Vatican cardinals shot vicious glances. When he hugged him in a way one reserves for one's parents, they shrugged in despair.

On one occasion, he was reported in the tabloids as being seen in the square walking among the people wearing shorts and sandals.

On another day he disappeared. No one could find him. Cardinal Villot sounded the alarm. After hours of searching, the Pope showed up at the Papal Palace dressed in a smock befitting a common monk.

> Villot challenged him: "Where have you been?"
>
> "I have been to see who is where and who is doing what. I have been to the Vatican Bank or, as you prefer to call it, the Patrimony. I stopped in and had words with Peter but I could not find Paul."
>
> Villot warned: "You are not to go anywhere without being escorted by guards. Do you understand? It is too dangerous."
>
> "Guards?" as if reminded of something he had put on hold for the moment, the Supreme Pontiff of the Roman Catholic Church told his Secretary of State: "Your eminence, I want you to issue an order the Swiss Guards are not to kneel when I approach them. I am not a God. I am a man. I am just another man."[18]

> "God is the Father, more so, the Mother."

In his Sunday Angelus September 10, 1978 he declared: "...God is the Father, more so, the Mother."[18]

Some inquired if a fourth person might soon be added to the Holy Trinity? Others inquired if a woman would soon be ordained? Still others were confused if Christ was a man; how could He also be a 'Mother?' Then there were those who thought he had gone too far.

Regardless of what conclusions various constituents made of his declaration; one thing is clear.

In defiance of the most universal doctrine of not only the Roman Catholic Church but of all world religions—'little boys are better than little girls'—he raised woman above man. [19]

The scope of his papacy

He asked, he listened, he learned. He talked, he told, he taught. He grinned, he smiled, he laughed. Above all, he hugged. Best of all, they learned to hug him back.

He made few friends among leaders of churches and nations, yet, he quickly won the friendship of the common man.

His positions concerning those that practice Planned Parenthood, out-of-wedlock children, the remarried, homosexuals and others oppressed by doctrine, were made clear in his first homily:

> "A particular greeting to all who are now suffering throughout the world; to the sick, to prisoners, to exiles, to the persecuted, and particularly, to those upon whom restraints are unfairly placed by doctrine in their everyday lives.
>
> Let our differences mold into one and together we shall rise to bring the world to one of greater justice. We call upon all of you, from the humblest underpinnings of nations, to heads of state.
>
> We encourage you to build an efficacious and responsible structure for a new order, this one more just and honest... together we will muster the strength to lift those restraints that have been unfairly placed upon the everyday lives of so many innocent people by our doctrinal convictions... for God-given human life is infinitely more precious than is man-made doctrine."[21]

Yet, the lion's share of his papacy was headed for the poor. From his opening embrace of the communist mayor of Rome, to the audit of the Vatican Bank, to the appraisals of the Vatican treasures, to his meeting with the KGB mediator Metropolitan Nikodim, to his covert meeting with the head of the Communist Party, to the time he said **'Ubi Lenin, ibi Jerusalem,'** to his intent to lead the Puebla Conference and liberation of the poor, to the time he told the capitalistic world: **"It is the inalienable right of no man to accumulate wealth beyond his needs, while others starve to death because they have nothing."**[22]

In each of his public audiences he specifically defined the scope of his papacy as to leave no doubt about it: **"This is not about this man or that man. It is about people who are hungry."** [23]

Finally, there are his last words to Cardinal Colombo before he retired in the papal apartment on the evening of September 28, 1978: **"Sadly, Giovanni, when we have completed our work, and everyone has enough, there will always be those who want too much."**[24]

NOTE: See Chapter 2 for excerpts from papal audiences

1 *La Repubblica* 2 Aug 78. Luciani's response to a reporter on artificial insemination. On average, an artificially conceived child is healthier than a naturally conceived child. This difference is becoming greater as genetic science progresses. If the job is done right, an artificially inseminated child cannot be born of known genetically transmitted impairments or disease. When all genes that cause birth defects are identified, artificially inseminated children will be born free of genetically transmitted impairments and disease. Responsible parents will resort to contraception and artificial insemination. Irresponsible parents will risk children born of genetic impairments and disease that would otherwise be prevented.
2 *Messaggero di S Antonio* Jun 73 – Albino Luciani letter to St. Therese
3 *The Times* London 14 Aug 78. Other newspapers published similar lists without Luciani's name
4 *L'Osservatore Romano* 26 Jul 78
5 The private message was never published. The nature of the message is in Luciani's press release
6 *Messaggero Mestre* 27 Jul 78; *Associated Press* 28 Jul 78
7 *Messaggero Mestre* 26 Jul 78; dramatized by the author
8 *L'Osservatore Romano* 30 Jul 78
9 *La Repubblica* 2 Aug 78 Cardinal Luciani responds to a reporter on artificial insemination
10 *Princeton Packet* 2 Apr 49
11 conclave rules of 1978
12 *La Stampa* 28 Aug 78
13 Philadelphia Evening News 27 Aug 78
14 *Il Giornale* 27 Sep 03 Andrea Tornelli interview with Dr. Antonio Da Ros
15 *Messaggero Mestre* 10 Oct 78 Msgr. Mario Senigaglia
16 The twenty-two papal tiaras are encrusted with over 1,700 diamonds and other precious gems
17 John Paul did wear a ring given participants in the Second Vatican Council
18 *Associated Press* 14 Sep 78   also see Roger Crane's play *The Last Confession*
19 *L'Osservatore Romano* 11 Sep 78
20 All world religions recognize God as 'He.' The reason for the spellcheck 'error' when one refers to God as 'She.' All religions were founded by men. God is a Man!
21 *Associated Press* 27 Aug 78 Sistine Chapel   various newspapers reported various excerpts
22 Associated Press 27 Sep 78 public audience. See You Tube filmclip *Last Days of Johannes Paulus*
23 Associated Press 27 Sep 78 public audience. See You Tube film clip *Last Days of Johannes Paulus*
23 *Corriere Della Sera* Milan 30 Sep 78. John Paul's last words to Cardinal Colombo via phone

Chapter 15

The Murder of Metropolitan Nikodim

"There is no inner conflict for me. It is told me by both my patron saint of state—Marx; and my patron saint of faith—Christ."[1]

Metropolitan Nikodim

Boris G. Rotov, better known as Metropolitan Nikodim—youthful leader of the Russian Orthodox Church—had been the chief negotiator in which the Eastern Church agreed to participate in the Second Vatican Council provided there would be no condemnation of communism or atheism during the conciliar assemblies.

It may not have been coincidence, he happened to be John Paul's first foreign visitor. Boris would have never become Metropolitan of Leningrad at the early age of 32, had it not been for Albino Luciani. As we have said, his father and Albino had met the year before Boris was born, and had kept up a relationship through the years.

Boris' father was an atheist. What's more, Boris' mother was also an atheist. Both dedicated enemies of Catholicism.

One could understand how Albino Luciani born of a mixed-bag of an atheist father and a devout mother could grow up to be a priest. Yet, it staggers the imagination to think Boris G. Rotov—reared entirely by atheist parents—could grow up to be a priest.

It was no coincidence, both were charged with the job to change Catholicism from what it had become—a labyrinth of myth, pomp, ritual, scandal and prejudice, back to the church of the poor Christ had intended; Albino working the western front, Boris working the eastern front. Too, it was no coincidence they would die twenty-two days apart, just twenty-two feet apart.

Albino had told the elder Rotov of his father's strategy: 'that the Church could only be changed from the inside, he had committed his son to the task.' It follows, Boris' father had given his son the same commission: 'change the Church back to what Christ had intended.'

Nikodim called for the redemption of the American Christian:

"Here in my part of the world, I must take orders from my Kremlin bosses, certainly, if not at least, I am at no necessity to pretend they and I pursue the same end. For me, it is that which is told me by both my patron saint of state—Marx; and my patron saint of faith—Christ. So there is no inner conflict there for me.

There is no originality in Marx. His word was to bring Christ's cause into a changing world. Yet, on the other side of the world, the American part of the world, the situation is poles apart...

In America, freedom of religion means the right to force Christian beliefs through its Christian majority on others. In Russia, we look at it differently. Here, freedom of religion is the right to believe or not to believe. Yes, it has restrictions, as we are limited to practice religion within the privacy of our homes and churches.

Here, Christian bells and Muslim loudspeakers—the booming billboards of organized religion—are banned. In America, church bells ring out at will advertising the Christian majority. Yet, prayers over loudspeakers in Muslim neighborhoods are banned.

There, tax laws exempt churches, imposing higher taxes on the nonbelievers. The nonbeliever pays for the believer to believe. The believer uses his tax-free advantage to spend billions—collected under the guise to help the poor—radio and television time, to spread hatred of Jews, blacks, atheists, homosexuals and others who don't conform to his rules. Gestapo squads invade pubs and bedrooms and cart offenders off to prison.[2]

Here, preachers are imprisoned for preaching hatred of others, and we don't invade bedrooms in the middle of the night.

Yet, what demonstrates, most of all, America is not what it pretends to be, is its closed borders to its poor neighbors to its south. It calls itself a Christian nation, as if to say Christ would slam the door on these poor children. Most brutal of all, it is Christian money and military power supplied to ruthless dictators that keeps these children who live south of its borders starving to death.

Free? America has not the least conception of what the word means. Though we, here, don't pretend to have it, we at least know what we are striving for: free, to be so free, to that point at which one's freedom imposes on the freedom of others..."[3]

Two cups of coffee and a few almond cookies

Murder by the Grace of God

On September 6, 1978 *L Osservatore Romano* reported:

> "...Cardinal Willebrands led the Metropolitan into the Pope's private study...A delegation of Orthodox clergy waited outside for an audience ...The Pope poured two cups of coffee, placing one in front the Russian. Nikodim added a teaspoon of sugar. Bringing the cup to his lips he found it too hot. As he set it down, he fell back into his chair grasping his throat. John Paul felt briefly for signs of life, then opened the door which brought a Swiss Guard and others into the room...The archbishop had previously had heart attacks..."[4]

The Washington Post reported: "Nikodim repeatedly denied being a communist. Yet, he has on an ongoing basis befriended the Soviet regime which has restricted religion..."[5]

> Metropolitan Nikodim was born Boris Gheorghevich Rotov at Rozan, near Moscow, October 14, 1929. He was ordained a deacon at the age of 17 years, and priest at 20. He served as bishop of Yaroslav and Minsk before becoming metropolitan of the ancient See of Novgorod and at the same time of Leningrad.
> He was widely traveled and spoke several languages. During his stay here, he lived in institutions of the Jesuit order in the Roman hills southeast of the city He

The Times, London, September 7, 1978

His fluency in many languages erased a rumor an interpreter had been in the room. It was partly that he was an accomplished linguist he was the Orthodox 'president' on the World Council of Churches.

He was particularly fluent in English and Italian. He had picked the latter up from his father as a boy. While at the Vatican II Council (1962-64), he had adopted Rome as his second home, the reason he had spent a month in Rome before meeting with John Paul.

John Paul—true of most modern popes—was fluent in French, Italian, English and Spanish in addition to Latin.

The report confirmed John Paul was alone with the body: 'felt briefly for signs of life before opening the door.' If there had been anyone else in the room they surely would have opened the door.

Yet, whether or not the Pope was alone with the Metropolitan is immaterial to murder, unless the toxin was in the sugar and not in the coffee. If cyanide crystals been involved, they were not in the pot, as it would have killed the Pope when he poured the coffee.[6]

Anyone close to them would know the Pope did not take sugar and the Metropolitan had a sweet tooth. Of course, this would mean Nikodim—not the Pope as rumored—was the intended victim.

That the Vatican claimed he had not tasted the coffee could have been its intent to head off rumors. Yet, if he had tasted the coffee, though there are many toxins which incite heart attack, there is not one that would kill one so quickly if ingested. Conversely, cyanide in a gaseous form attacks membranes resulting in instant death.

That the Metropolitan grasped his throat would be consistent with cyanide. The heart is a muscle and a massive heart attack strikes as a 'charley horse' to the chest; one grasps one's chest, not one's throat.

The speed with which he died is demonstrated that no newspaper reported that any effort was made at resuscitation. The first person to respond to the Pope's call was the guard not more than a couple of minutes after the seizure. Swiss Guards—in addition to being human fighting machines—are trained paramedics and schooled in CPR.[7]

The press reported 'heart attack.' Yet, unlike the Pope who had no record of heart problems, Nikodim—though never hospitalized—had suffered as many as a half dozen mini-attacks earlier in life.

Nikodim had been a competition swimmer in his youth and his doctor had recommended a few laps each morning—the reason he stayed at the Jesuit compound outside Rome which had an Olympic pool. It had been his powerful physical and mental stamina which had been a big part of his rapid rise in the Orthodox hierarchy.

La Repubblica reported: **'The pool boy had watched the Russian taking vigorous laps for a half-hour that morning as he had every morning without resting, but noticed nothing unusual.'**[8]

La Stampa was less respectful: **'The pool boy described Nikodim with his immense physique covered front and back with hair down to his hands resembled a water buffalo splashing through the water.'**[9]

Motive

Yet, in Nikodim's case, if one considers murder, one must determine motive. Could there have been a motive in his case?

We have already speculated the CIA may have suspected the Pope sought Soviet arms assistance for the *revolution of the poor* he

Murder by the Grace of God

was about to lead in Central America. Today it is known, Nikodim was a KGB agent working under the code name **'Adamant.'**

The Metropolitan's alliance with the left-wing Soviets had won him bitter enemies in the Orthodox Church. The Orthodox Curia was even further to the *right* than was the Vatican Curia. Nikodim represented the **'John Paul the First'** of the Russian Orthodox world.

There were those who reasoned the meeting behind closed doors in the Pope's private study—rather than in his public office where he normally met with dignitaries—was part of a plot to reunite the two churches. This made Nikodim the enemy of both those within the Orthodox and Roman churches who opposed ecumenism.

One can understand why the Vatican would not opt for autopsy as it never does. Yet, why didn't the Orthodox Church order autopsy to dispel widespread rumors of the time? It wanted him out of the way.

Nikodim was even more dangerous to the conservative-right in the Orthodox Church as the Pope was to the conservative-right in Rome.

Because there was no autopsy one will never know if murder was involved. Yet, if one assumes he died of a natural heart attack; one must consider the mathematical odds.

One must consider a few seconds in the span of a man's life.

The chance he had suffered up to five trivial attacks years before, and the one that killed him occurred at the precise moment he met John Paul behind closed doors. It occurred at the precise second he lifted the cup to his lips, and finding it steaming succumbed to death. So sudden, resuscitation was not considered by the Swiss Guard swiftly on the scene. So sudden, he grasped his throat instead of his chest. So sudden, the crowd who wanted him dead did not have the chance to roar as the ball went into the net!

Pauper who would be Pope

Albino Luciani had come onto the world's stage together with his secretary Lorenzi in an outdated *Lancia 2000*. Had the automobile been brand new, and it was not, it would have been unbecoming a common priest much less a prince of the Church. Its fenders had been scorched by time and for the most part it had lost its color. So much so, Swiss Guards stopped it at the Vatican gates and demanded identification. It was a tin box, designed and built for paupers. Forty days later he left in a pine box, designed and built for paupers.

He had made the rounds, pauper, then altar boy, then seminarian, then priest, then bishop, then cardinal, then pope, then pauper, once more. He left a few personal items including his exercise equipment and two cockatiels. There was a pair of cut glass cruets which had been given to him by his mother the day of his ordination.[10] There were a few other gifts, plaques and medals he had received through the years. Yet, not as much as a single lira in a checking account. He had given all he had to the needy, this **Pauper who would be Pope.**

Baby Pigeons

Nevertheless, I have some answers for you here. Among them are the baby pigeons. Yes, why there are no baby pigeons?

One knows dogs come from puppies and cats come from kittens and cows come from calves. But, just where do pigeons come from?

Perhaps you have never noticed? You never wondered why, in all of your life, you have never seen a baby pigeon? Go to Saint Peter's Square in Rome, or for that matter any of the grand piazzas of Europe, or the great parks of America, and you will see tens of thousands of pigeons and not a baby pigeon among them.

What's that? You believe they must be somewhere else? Well, go and try and find them and you will find they are not there. For pigeons, among all of God's creation, come from somewhere else.

So, I have some answers for you here. Among them is the answer to the greatest mystery of all. Something that, like the baby pigeons, from day to day you could not see, yet, always assumed was there. As in the case of baby pigeons, I will prove it is not there.

Now, let us go back to that time, so very long ago, when I first visited the remote mountain province of Vittorio Veneto. Back to that time, when I first met this man called 'Piccolo.'

1 *'Leningrad kava Veteran* 17 Oct 76
2 At the time Nikodim said this one in four police in the United States were in vice or moral squads invading bars and other establishments and even bedrooms
3 *Leningrad kava Veteran* 17 Oct 76
4 *L Osservatore Romano* 6 Sep 78
5 *Washington Post* 6 Sep 78
6 *Deadly Doses* Serita Stevens - white cyanide crystals are easily concealed in sugar.
7 *Swiss Guard Code*
8 *La Repubblica* 6 Sep 78   9 *Kommersant* 6 Sep 78
9 *La Stampa* 6 Sep 78
10 in the author's collection

Chapter 16

Appointment in Milan

"Freedom without equality is not what it pretends to be. The diamond would be made of paste."[1]

General George Patton

Spring

It was an exact point in time, the first day of spring, that day on which the sun rests directly over the equator; that day on which all over creation, the sun rises due east and sets due west and day and night end in a dead heat in time.

The Boeing 707 rose slowly out of Kennedy over New York harbor before banking to the left headed in its intended direction. As it made its turn, I looked down at that grand lady who lifts her lamp by the golden door. I wondered how she ever came about.

After all, we were a Christian nation. Our forefathers, every one of them was a Christian. Of those who signed the Declaration of Independence, there wasn't a single black, not a single Jew, not a single gay, not even a woman among them. At least I didn't think so.

It seemed to me, a towering figure of Christ would be more appropriate at these gates to what was, indeed, the Promised Land.

In all of Europe I knew only one person. Problem was I didn't know he was in Europe at the time. A rival back in high school in my run for the roses, one of those people I just had to beat out in life.

His name was Jack. He was much smarter than I was. Problem was he didn't know it. He thought I was much smarter than he was. He had gathered this from how well I had done in school; I could keep pace with him down the stretch only to lose him at the wire. He had no idea how much harder I had to work for what I got than he did. For him winning the race was like Sinatra singing 'My Way.'

And he won the race going away. I was just another student in the crowd of several thousand when I watched him take the stand on graduation day. On this day, many years later, I couldn't remember a single thing he said. Vainly, I thought, "If it had been me, everyone, privileged to have listened, would remember everything, every single word, I said." As the plane started to take down the time zones, I thought back to graduation day:

> ...that day they were all wearing blue blazers. Usually it was only me. Day after day, year after year, it had only been me. The others in sweaters, blue jeans, sneakers, whatever they laid their hands on when they got up in the morning. They used to call me 'pretty boy' - 'momma's boy.' Then one day one of them called me a 'pansy.' That's the day they found out my small fists could hit and my feet could kick. Sooner or later they learned my help with their homework made the difference between honors and failure. So, although I had made a run for it, I didn't come in first or even second, but, nevertheless, when the wreaths were passed out, I took home with me the ones labeled Catechism, Mathematics and History. What's more, the yearbook caption alongside my picture read: 'Most likely to become a cardinal of the Church.'

Well, I was never to become a cardinal of the Church. When the fork in the road came up, Jack took the path that said 'Christ,' and I took the one that said 'Money.'

He went on to attend Holy Cross where he, once again, took the honors and then began to work toward becoming a very special kind of priest. He took his doctorate in psychiatry at Johns Hopkins and registered as a licensed psychiatrist. His objective was to become a member of the Vatican's Commission on Spiritual Occurrences—its investigative panel for miracles, apparitions, exorcisms and other spiritual claims. As for me, I went on to Massachusetts schools of higher education, majoring in international finance and banking in pursuit of the pot of gold at the end of the rainbow.

Though our chosen vocations had caused us to lose touch, it was the providential entrance of another kind of business into our lives that brought us together for one last time: politics—world politics.

'Populorum Progressio' vs. 'Lateran Treaty'

On March 27, 1967, occurred an event that would threaten the capitalistic world we live in. Paul VI issued his edict *Populorum Progressio:* 'The economy of the world should serve all of mankind and not few at the top... every man an equal share...'

Murder by the Grace of God

"It is the inalienable right of no man to accumulate wealth beyond his needs while other men starve to death because they have nothing' is most often attributed to John Paul I because it was his last public declaration before 'waking up' dead in his bed. Yet, in truth, it was the central thesis of Paul's edict *Populorum Progressio.*

It was also the central thesis of Karl Marx' *Das Kapital* published long before either Paul VI or John Paul I had been born.

Paul intended his edict for the whole world. Yet, just outside the Vatican walls, his doctrine ignited the *priest-worker movement* which in due course would give rise to the Communist Party in Italy.

This presented Paul with a crisis as the *Lateran Treaty* which had established Vatican sovereignty in 1929 included a provision of separation of church and state. In exchange for its independence, the Holy See would abstain from political intervention in Italy.

For this reason, though many priests were active in the *priest-worker movement*—thus its name—the papacy took strict measures that no bishop or other direct appointee of the Vatican be associated with the movement despite that it had been driven by a papal bull.

It follows, in any encouragement a bishop might give the *priest-worker movement*—communism, he would distance himself from the movement as to avoid violating the *Lateran Treaty.*

For example, in Luciani's letter to St. Therese in *Illustrissimi:*

"A justified strike is in progress...to feel solidarity in progress of men fighting for their rights, is Christian charity... It may cause me discomfort because I am not directly concerned with the dispute."[2]

Here again, Luciani defines 'charity' as an involuntary function of the state—*Populorum Progressio*: 'every man an equal share.'

One might wonder why he praises a movement on the one hand, and denies he had anything to do with it on the other hand. He tells a white lie to protect the sovereignty of the Vatican. In truth, Albino Luciani had a lot to do with the *priest-worker movement* in Italy.

Today, in retrospect, we know many bishops had a hand in directing the *priest-worker movement.* We also know they worked through ghost lieutenants, more often than not supplied by foreign dioceses to prevent the government from tracing priests involved in the movement back to their ecclesiastical roots. Most of these were sent by European dioceses. Yet, a few came from the United States.

As for Jack

Richard James Cushing's father—an immigrant from Ireland—had labored as a blacksmith in the trolley repair pits of Boston's elevated railway system. Richard's young life had been engulfed in labor unions and he had planned to go into government to achieve a redistribution of wealth society in the United States.

A cousin—a priest—convinced him he could more effectively accomplish his political objectives in another branch of politics—the ministry. He would be particularly effective if he were to use his political acumen to rise to high places; much as Albino Luciani's father had counseled him to follow the same strategy.

Yet, even when he rose to the pinnacle of the Church in Boston, Richard found his hands tied. He could do little more than preach compassion for the poor; poor, whose existence was driven by the basic capitalistic tenets upon which his country had been founded.

When Paul issued *Populorum Progressio,* Cushing envisioned a redistribution of wealth society spreading from Italy to Spain, then to all of Europe, and eventually back to the United States.

He sent a wave of 'lieutenants' to support Paul's war on poverty in Italy. Jack having been born into an Italian family was fluent in Italian—a natural for the job.

As for me

NATO—North Atlantic Treaty Organization—was established in the postwar with the mission to keep communism out of Europe.

At the time of Paul's edict, I was a Pentagon intelligence officer stationed in the Arctic Circle involved in propaganda activities and recognizance missions up over the top.

When disturbances flared up in Italy, I was reassigned to a NATO detachment in Milan—thus my first trip to Europe.

The mission of the unit was to crush the *priest-worker uprising* in Italy which threatened to spread communism to all of Europe.

So it was by providential coincidence, Jack and I, once again, became rivals: I struggling to defend the basic capitalistic tenets upon which my country had been founded, and Jack foolishly trying to bring about a Christ-like society, one knows will never work.

Nevertheless—having decided to pair a few days leave with the free trip—my plane set down in London.

During that time, I witnessed the splendor of Christianity.

As I made my way across Europe, I must have set the world record for visiting churches including most of Europe's largest.

Because it was too far out of my way, I had to skip Seville. But the others, all the others, from the majestic dome of St. Paul's, the great stone claws grasping at Notre Dame, the magnificent azure leaded glass windows of Chartres, the ashen wedding-cake towers of Cologne, and now, finally, the immense Duomo di Milano with its threatening weather-beaten gargoyles oxidized by time guarding the great plaza spreading out before it—Milan's playground of princes and paupers. I marveled them all. I relished them all.

Yet, it wasn't these great edifices that impressed me the most. It was something else. Something I would find in Milan. Something I would stumble onto quite by accident. Something I would carry with me all of the remaining days of my life.

Besides its great cathedral and its great square and its crystal galleria, Milan has a fourth great treasure—something most tourists never witness—the city's great park of the dead. There you can see it all, every bit of yesterday, every bit of days gone by.

The land of the dead

As I entered the cemetery, I became a part of it all. The only sound was my footsteps and the breath of a slight breeze. The sky was foreboding as if it were a good day for a funeral. Had there been a lake, and there was none, it would have held dark waters as there was not a thing in the sky to give it life. It seemed all of the living, had forgotten all of the dead. I was alone—alone as one could be.

I found myself wandering in the world's greatest metropolis of the departed—endless rows of mansions of stone. Some even with windows as to provide their silent tenants a view of their neighbors' palatial abodes. There seemed to be more marble and granite houses in this land of the dead, than there were houses outside in the land of the living—each one different—each one commanding the attention of its own artist, its own architect, its own engineer.

Interspersed, here and there, were sculptures, mostly of marble and granite, yet, a few of precious metals, some even studded with jewels—each one frozen in common death, echoing its individual message of life—each one befitting a prince—no, a king—no, a god. Collectively they echoed of immense wealth. No wonder they lost the war, they had all their money tied up in monuments.

woman morns two male figures

...each one frozen in common death echoing its individual message of life...

Nowhere could a single flower be found. As if to ensure the beauty of God's creation not overpower these great works of man. There was only the green grass, working its way in a maze in and about these magnificent monuments and dwellings of the dead.

I proceeded down the main boulevard of this great city of death. Flanked on either side by mausoleums of superlative grandeur, some sealed up like the tombs they were, and still others showing off their merchandise. Through heavy ornate iron grates, I could glimpse the sarcophagi themselves—of marble, of bronze, of gold, of glass.

I listened. Silence, silence all about me, as not to wake those who were sleeping there. As I came to the end of the avenue, I turned the corner and suddenly stopped dead in my tracks. Not dead-dead, but dead in my tracks. There, to just my left, a half dozen small white granite stones sat in a row on a blanket of green grass which lay before a matching manicured hedge of green shrubbery. The power of their simplicity eclipsed the grandeur of all that was about them.

On each stone was carved a heart. Within each heart an image of Washington. "The Purple Heart," I thought to myself. I thought something else, "Here is the real reason why they had lost the war."

Approaching with all the solemnity the moment commanded, in

Murder by the Grace of God

my mind echoed the faint sound of the bugle - the hallowed roll of the drums - the distant roar of the cannon.

A spot of light peeked down through the overcast sky to mark this precious moment in time. As to give one light to read:

Frank Phillips, 1st Lt. 1921-1944, 7th Army, Distinguished Service Cross

Richard Edwards, PFC 1925-1944, 7th Army, Bronze Star

Jerome Rose, 2nd Lt. 1919-1944, 7th Army, Silver Star

Brian Pickering, Pvt. 1924-1944, 7th Army, Bronze Star

Anthony Jackson, Pvt. 1922-1944, 7th Army, Bronze Star

Patricia Wilde, 1st Lt. 1919-1944, Army Medical Corps, Bronze Star [3]

It didn't say it. Yet, I clearly heard it: "That they shall not have died in vain." One of those things one calls 'tears' crept up out of my heart and ran from the corner of my eye, and moved toward its lid. I looked first to the right, and then to the left, and then, again, to the right, and finally to the left, once more.

Holding the tear on the edge of the lid, I spoke as if I were a great orator on a world stage: "Not Thomas Paine with his pen, nor Patrick Henry with his eloquence, nor Paul Revere with his horse, nor Washington with all his courage, not even Lincoln at Gettysburg, have spoken louder. For you have made more noise for freedom than all the others who have gone before you or have come after you. I pledge to you this day, to each and every one of you, that each and every one of you will not have died in vain."

I have carried that pledge, that duty with me all of my life. I have carried it every day, every hour, every moment of my life. I have carried it in my mind, and in my heart, and in my very soul.

Now it is time to carry out that solemn promise, to answer that fervent prayer. To carry it out for each and every one of them; that what they dreamed of, those things they fought for, those things they willed to be; will come to be, for each of them, and for me, and for you, and for all humanity.

1 *Affria Italiani* 28 Sep 44. General Patton at the grave of gay soldier Sept 25, 1944
2 *Messaggero di S Antonio* Jun 73 – Albino Luciani letter to St. Therese
3 by the end of the century all American solders interred in private cemeteries in Europe were relocated to private cemeteries in the United States, Arlington Cemetery or the American Cemetery at Maastricht. Pseudo names are used for soldiers other than Jack's uncle; the author did not note them at the time. Yet, they are representative of those that were there.

Chapter 17

Appointment in Vittorio Veneto

"...to the betterment of others, no matter how small..."   Aldo Moro

the bishop's castle at Vittorio Veneto

It was not long before the gods of good fortune smiled upon me.

My mother, a union leader in the electronics industry, spent her professional life struggling against the exportation of American jobs and expertise to Asia. For the most part, her notoriety was confined to newspaper headlines she shared with the Massachusetts senator Ted Kennedy who at the time supported free trade.

In the end, only a tiny handful of jobs remained in her electronics corporation which at one time had employed tens of thousands of Americans. In her loss, she took her troupe to Washington and established the first retraining legislation for those who had lost their jobs. She spent her remaining days administering the program.

Regardless, Jack's mother happened to attend one her rallies.

She told my mother that Jack had been transferred to Italy. He, too, was working as "some kind of a union leader."

Knowing Jack was a priest in the Boston diocese, I talked the colonel into sending me to the Veneto, that I might link Archbishop Cushing to the *priest-worker uprising* in Italy.

Murder by the Grace of God

A few weeks later I took the train to Venice. It was from there, I took the train to Mestre and from there to Vittorio Veneto.

Enroute, protestors—mostly in their teens and twenties—lined the platforms as the train passed through the stations. The tone of their demands sounded more like a revolution than the '**Equal Pay for Equal Work**' their signs demanded.

I—a young man in a tee shirt and jeans—could easily be mistaken for one of them. One of the benefits of an intelligence officer was one usually dispensed with a uniform.

Exiting at Vittorio Veneto, I pushed my way through an angry mob. I took the first right, then the first left, and, again, the first right, and finally, the first left, once more.

author on his first trip to Vittorio Veneto

I stood in front of what appeared to be an old southern hotel—a southern hotel in the most northern part of Italy. It was surrounded by an aging wall eight or nine feet high. It was of the same shade of amber stucco as was the rest of the town. It was topped off by one of those orange terracotta roofs that sprawl over all Italian villages.

I pounded with both fists as loud on the great wooden door as I could. I heard footsteps on wooden steps. They reached firmness for a time, then, again, on wooden steps, then firmness, once more.

Then there was the juggling and clattering of the unlocking of the door. Standing before me was a little old lady who looked as if she had just stepped out of an Italian motion picture.

I followed her into a garden reception area where I scratched out a registration card and surrendered my passport. I asked her for directions to the bishop's castle as she led me to my room which overlooked a canal that ran behind the hotel. I freshened up a bit and headed back out onto the street.

I passed over an ancient stone bridge which channeled down a narrow street hemmed in on both sides by row houses, each one of amber stucco and each one in a general state of disrepair.

It was as if I was to see a green house, or a blue house, or a yellow house, I would remember it all of my days.

On the town's edge I entered a tunnel that had been carved into an ancient wall. At its end I stepped into medieval times, a twelfth century plaza. I sensed Romeo and Juliet might be sleeping nearby.

Unlike the village, where stucco had been the tradesman's craft, the buildings here were entirely built of stone and the tatter and torn of the ages had survived unrepaired. The cathedral overpowered the plaza which lay before it. Partway up a mountain was what I rightly presumed to be the bishop's castle—a medieval group of turret-topped towers, only the tallest of which had survived intact.

I passed an old stone trough with lions and gargoyles strewing water in a pool. There were statues set into arched niches in the ancient walls, a few of which had lost their original inhabitants.

As I looked up, jagged white-tipped darkened cliffs of the towering Dolomite Mountain chain surrounded the realm, like a giant horseshoe—a bit of the medieval ages trapped in a rocky gorge.

Suddenly, a man came running toward me wearing a 'Minnie Mouse' tank top. He smiled and waved as he passed. I judged he must have been about fifty. I was surprised the recent jogging fad in the states had reached this remote part of the world.

At the same instant, great bells rang out. Not in a rhythmic sort of way, but in a clanging sort of way, as if they did not want anyone to know what they had to say. The old church was of the identical washed-out color of its surroundings. Its nave was out of balance with its tower, as if they had run out of money in the middle ages, when I guessed the building had been built.

I started my ascent up a narrow cobblestone road hemmed in by ten-foot walls which wound up the side of the mountain to the castle.

Exhausted, I entered through the ancient arched gates into a courtyard. It centered on a fountain, not unlike others I had passed on the way. Water was splashing out over its edges onto the courtyard floor and was running down around me out of the castle arches. A gardener was trimming hedges off to one side. Off to the other side was a beat up car of forties vintage.

The house was of beige stucco and was set within the castle ruins. Its focal point was a grand symmetrical staircase. One set of stairs led up to a landing from the left, and a second set of stairs led up to the same landing from the right. Jack stood there with a grin from ear to ear. I decided to take the stairs on the left.

We got the usual "hellos" and the "Boy, you don't look a day older" out of the way quickly. "I see you don't have an age limit on runners here. I almost got run over down there." I mentioned the man who had passed me in the church plaza.

Jack replied, "That was the boss. He turns in a few miles every morning. If you had shown up a month from now, he would have taken you up a mountain or two with him. The six mounds in his coat-of-arms depict the six peaks for which he holds the speed record in Italy.

"When he comes back, I'll introduce you. But, you won't see much of him until dinnertime. He goes to Venice today. Come, I'll show you his little corner of the world."

He opened the door. Its heavy opaque glass panels—protected by elaborate iron lattice work—required the strength of both arms.

We entered a large open space, the reception area of the house. Definitive paths had been worn into the ancient stone floor. One could make out where people had walked through the ages. There was nothing there. That is, not a single piece of furniture.

Today, this room is an impressive introduction to the house. Its walls are lined with ornately framed life sized oil portraits of the dozen or so bishops who have lived here in the twentieth century. At the far end of the room, the portrait of Albino Luciani—the only one to have risen to the papacy—is hidden behind a door that leads to a prayer station which fronts a window.

Like other images of Papa Luciani that have been planted by the Vatican across northern Italy—from the small village he grew up in Carnal de Argo to Venice—this portrait depicts a man of one-hundred-and-twenty who is in the final days of a long unsuccessful bout with pancreatic cancer—a part of the Vatican's ongoing deception to convince the public the 33-day Pope was at death's door when elected to the papacy.

The hand-painted arched ceiling in this grand vestibule boasts the coat-of-arms of the eighty or so bishops who served here in Vittorio Veneto since the castle was built in the eighth century.

Jack led me to a small alcove. The windowless area was as bare as it was small and clashed with its rich green, black and white marble terrazzo flooring which—instead of giving it the feeling of the wealth it reflected—gave it a feeling of coldness.

It was obvious, the floor here was not original; it had been added in recent times. Most of the opposite wall was made up by the room's centerpiece, a beautifully carved mahogany arched door.

The unbroken line of the yellowing wall was interrupted only by this door, a small dime store crucifix above it, and a cheaply framed photograph of Pope John XXIII off to one side.

A message was written on the photograph. Approaching it, I found it was written in Italian. I heard over my shoulder:

"'*Albino,*

Christ asked me to express His congratulations on this important day of your life.

His Servant John, 27 Dec 1958'

"It was given to the man who occupies the adjoining cell on the day he was made a bishop," nodding to the huge richly carved mahogany door. "Piccolo was the first bishop installed by John XXIII."

I was struck by his reference to the bishop as 'Piccolo' and, at the same time, struck by the yodeling of a little nun who ran out of an alpine clock on the opposite wall.

Mostly because of his toes

We chatted for awhile. He had just told me the bishop must have run off to Venice, "... but you will see him at dinner. He has been looking forward to meeting you," when suddenly appeared the man who had run past me in the plaza. Clad in shorts and sandals, his wet hair told me he had just come out of the shower.

Two things struck me—the countenance of his smile, and the perfection of his toes. I never thought of bishops as having toes, especially toes as flawlessly pedicured as these were. I wondered if the nearby convent provided this service for bishops, a service that, when I splurged for it, cost me fifty bucks a throw back in the states.

A third thing struck me—his voice.

The voice was a piping, rasping voice. Not as if he was talking through his nose, but one that would turn heads in a bar—a one-of-a-kind voice. It was this that made it relatively easy for me to follow what otherwise was heavily Italian-accented-broken-English.

I could not think of the bishop title. "I apologize. I forget what I'm supposed to call you?" He cut me off, "Just call me the same thing everyone else calls me, 'Piccolo.'"

"Yet, I must go. The thief of the ages is knocking at my door."

I turned toward Jack, "Did you hear someone knock?"

The bishop laughed:

"Time. Time is knocking. Time is a thief. It will rob one of one's childhood, deprive one of one's youth, and ultimately take one's life. But, it is a good thief. For it provides the span of wonderment for the child, the term of enlightenment while he grows, and the age of fulfillment as he gives...' [1]

...and my time to give is near." He was off.

"Piercing, huh?" Jack offered, noticing I had reacted to the bishop's voice. "When he was a teenager he had a tonsillectomy that went haywire and left him with a uniquely raspy voice.

"Anyway," getting up from his chair, "I will show you where he spends his time dreaming up the next chapter for this sprawling paradise here in the foothills of the Italian Alps." He moved toward the great mahogany door. Opening it, we proceeded in.

In the company of angels

The office could not have been more impressive. My heart sank a bit as I thought of my relatively modest surroundings back in the states. I thought of the tax-free exemption status of the Church. Yes, the rich marble terrazzo flooring continued into the room, but here it was not out of place. The walls were richly carved mahogany.

We were in the company of angels.

Each one in Byzantine fashion, each one in individual color, each one bearing a shield with coat-of-arms, each one armed with a weapon of medieval times, each one topped off with a golden halo, each one standing in a carved mahogany panel. Each one watching, each one waiting...

In addition to their protective presence, they seemed to be listening, as if all that would be said within these walls would be related to the one above. Two more, in three dimension and white marble, guarded a huge walk-in fireplace at the far end of the room.

Above the mantel was an aging oil painting of Christ driving the moneylenders out of the temple—its dark tones accented by the brilliance of golden coins cascading out of the painting beyond its heavily gold encrusted frame. I thought it could be a Rembrandt.

Jack corrected my misconception, "No, not Rembrandt. It's a Titian. This is Titian country. His best works are here in Vittorio Veneto. Piccolo put this one here to remind us that Christ, too, had to deal with the republicans." He laughed.

One side of the room was set up as a boardroom with a huge coffin-shaped mahogany table with gargoyles jetting out from its corners. Two Persian carpet runners lay along each side. So plush that if one didn't take notice, one would easily trip over them.

On them sat matching richly embroidered mahogany chairs—six on each side. There were no chairs at the table's ends. "Piccolo is an advocate of symbolism. We are all equal. No one is at the top."

On the other side of the immense room was a personal work and reception area. A sofa and armchairs in Italian provincial sat facing a huge kidney-shaped mahogany desk.

On the wall behind the desk—the only break in the perimeter of the room other than the door in which angels did not stand—was a framed document, this one in English:

Republic of Italy

For extraordinary heroism while engaged in military battle without regard to his own safety and risk of life, no matter how great, to the betterment of lives of others, no matter how small; the Republic of Italy is indebted to our eternal friend.

Aldo Moro, 21 September 1964

Murder by the Grace of God

Suddenly, the somber setting came to life with the chiming of the hour. To one side, a huge clock towered upward toward the ceiling.

"It's a great, great grandfather clock," Jack offered. "Valdini's clocks fetch upwards of a million dollars.

"The contents of this room, including its paneling, came out of a mountaintop monastery outside Naples. It was moved here as a protective measure during the war when the allies reached Sicily. Pius thought they might destroy it. He was right. They bombed the hell out of it, thinking it was used as an Axis headquarters.[2]

"Each of us sees in the clock a work of fine art and scientific achievement. Piccolo sees something else: the right of a good and healthy life for a thousand children. Within a week of his arrival, Piccolo started to sell much of this but the Vatican stopped him."

Jack walked to the mahogany table. Falling into a seat, he waved me into the opposite chair. He peered around the room suspiciously, examining the expressions of each of the angels which surrounded us. His action gave me the chance to count them, thirty-three in all.

I thought of the thirty-three centuries the Old Testament had wreaked bloodshed upon mankind, and of the thirty-three years Christ had lived, and of the thirty-three months of His ministry, and of the thirty-three months Anne Frank had hid in the attic.

In retrospect, I could add the thirty-three days of John Paul's papacy and the thirty-third day after his death when Roberto Calvi raised the first dollar that triggered *The Great Vatican Bank Scandal.*

But, I did not know it at the time. Or did I?

His eyes finally wandered back to me, "Let's go for a walk."

---

1 Luciani originally said this in eulogy to John XXIII in the Basilica di San Marco in Venice 4 Jun 63
2 The trappings of the room were returned to Naples in 1979. The space has since been divided into four separate rooms: two reception rooms lined with Italian provincial chairs and a secretary's office and the bishop's office. The author last visited the castle in January 2007. In the first reception room is a small glass case housing items of John Paul's ministry. Included is Aldo Moro's citation awarded the American soldier whose heroic action saved the lives of twenty-eight Italian school children

Chapter 18

Murder in the Veneto

"In revealing the deep dark secret that must have haunted him all his life, Gregoire forces the transformation of Christianity" [1]

Toby Johnson
White Crane Journal

A light mist was falling.

I followed Jack along a path edged in with lush underbrush that wound down around and then back up the mountainside.

We came into a grotto. Towering walls of darkened slate backed a waterfall plummeting down into a blue pond edged in greenery.

"Piccolo calls this his Garden of Eden." Glancing suspiciously about the cavern, "He meets with his best secrets here."

I repeated his confusing statement, "...his best secrets?"

"Yes, his best secrets." He paused.

Two large rocks sat at the pond's edge a conversation apart. He took one, and I, the other. He paused a moment to give me one last chance to take in all the wonderment that was about us.

He started, "The castle angels most likely do have ears and it is for this reason, I have brought you here. Though we have never been able to find them, we are certain the house is bugged.

"Yet, that is not why I brought you here." He waited for eye-to-eye contact.

"Earlier this year, Pasquale was found floating in the canal that runs behind your hotel. [2]

"Pasquale...?" A new name to me.

"Brother Pasquale. The inquest determined he had drowned. Piccolo had an autopsy performed. No water was found in the lungs; he was dead when thrown into the water. There was hemorrhaging in the brain; he had been clubbed. Piccolo's suspicions were sound."

He explained, "The protestors you passed on your way here are much more than union workers. They are trying to bring about a redistribution of wealth society here in Italy."

I agreed, "Yes, I saw their signs— 'Equal Pay for Equal work.'"

"A redistribution of wealth society is much more than equal pay," he corrected me. "It is communism. Today, Italy is on a fast track to becoming a communist nation sitting in the middle of Europe.

"Despite electoral progression is moving overwhelmingly toward communism, the work is going too slowly for much of Italy's impatient youth. They have taken to the streets."

"Why doesn't Piccolo stop them?" I challenged.

"Stop them? He and his priests have been leading them. So much so, the newspapers have tabbed the revolution '*the priest-worker movement.*' He's been encouraging them to stand up for their rights. The protestors are overwhelmingly street orphans who have survived to adulthood. Having been deprived of education, they are made to work virtually as slaves for a small pittance of their worth.

"Piccolo wants to bring an end to the Church's central dogma 'some children are born better than others and are entitled to more.' He wants to bring about a world in which every child has an equal opportunity to a good and healthy life.

"He believes the greatest advancement of mankind has not been the printing press or a myriad of other inventions as some might think…" He paused as if I might come up with the answer.

Instead, I shot him a look of apprehension.

"Contraception!" he exclaimed.

"Late in the nineteenth century, when contraception was first becoming a way of life, there were a billion people on the planet. Half of them were living in poverty and starving to death. Today, not a century later, there are over four billion, and a billion of those are living in dire poverty and starving to death. If not for contraception, there would be as many as 20 billion and 10 billion starving to death.

"The planet can sustain a limited population of humans because of the immense demand they place upon its very limited resources."

"Limited resources?" I gave him a dumbfounded glance.

"In two hundred years, man has exhausted half of the world's oil and coal deposits which took two hundred million years to create. We have exhausted all but a pittance of earth's natural forests. We have contaminated all of the world's rivers and are right now—as I speak—working on its oceans. We have polluted the air we breathe and have poked a hole in the ozone layer, God, Himself, cannot fix.

"Mankind is hell-bent on a fast track toward a day when the last light bulb will go out and it will gasp its last breath.

"Yet, unlike other species which through the process of evolution begin and ultimately cease to exist, mankind can manage its destiny and live forever. Its vehicle to eternal life is contraception.

"It follows, if we can only allow so many children to be born, it makes no sense to allow millions to be born of impairments and disease only to live unbearable lives and die unspeakable deaths.

"In addition to aborting fetuses known to be severely impaired, Piccolo is an avid supporter of genetic research. He is certain it will bring about a day when every child is born healthy.

"This makes him an enemy of the fixed-conservative." He waited.

"Why's that?"

"All Christian doctrine dictates the soul enters the body at birth. To the doctrinal conservative, it makes no difference how much pain and suffering an impaired child goes through after birth. All that counts is it goes to heaven. Unborn children go nowhere."

"Next, we have the difference between Christ and Piccolo."

I cast him a look of surprise, "The difference?"

"Like Piccolo, Christ wanted to bring about an end to poverty in the world. Yet, unlike Piccolo, He didn't know how to make it work.

"He didn't know how to make it work?" I repeated in a question.

He assured me, "Yes, he didn't know how to make it work.

"Christ never thought of socialism or communism—the burden of taking care of the poor could be shifted from the voluntary 'charity' of the individual, to the involuntary 'duty' of society.

"Actually, until the idea grew up out the French Revolution and was explicitly defined by Marx and Engels in their 'Communist Manifesto' in 1848, no one else had ever thought of it either.

"Marx and Engels defined a range of solutions to poverty, from 'socialism—a society providing every child an equal opportunity to make his or her contribution to society,' to 'pure communism—regardless of effort everyone gets an equal share of the pie.'[3]

"Christ was convinced that only a capitalistic society could work. After all, greed was a natural instinct of man. His only alternative was to trick the rich into helping the poor. Not with pennies, but with their entire fortunes. He made charity a prerequisite for heaven.

"He said it in so many different ways, if one could not get it in one way, one would be sure to get it in another way:

> 'Sell all that thou hast and give to the poor.' 'Lay not up for yourselves treasures upon this earth, where moth and rust doth corrupt. But lay up for yourselves treasures in heaven, where neither moth nor rust doth corrupt. For where your treasure is, will be your heart also...' 'It is easier for a camel to pass through the eye of a needle than it is for a rich man to enter the Kingdom of Heaven...'" [4]

He rambled on and on until my eyes told him to stop.

"Problem is no one believed Him. The rich continue to drop their pennies into the box while kids all over the world starve to death.

"Christ, Himself, knew His thesis would never work. In each of the gospels—lest one miss it in one gospel—He declares: 'You will not always have me. But, you will always have your poor.' [5]

"Though both of them have the same goal—a redistribution of wealth society—Christ placed the job with the individual—charity. Piccolo will place the job with society—taxation of the rich.

"Piccolo will make it the rule of the land. There is no room in his world for '...you will always have your poor.'" [5]

The politics of the day

"But, let's get back to Pasquale. Ten years ago when the Italian Communist Party reached double-digit electoral progression, Vice President Richard Nixon established NATO's Operation Gladio—a covert army of former Nazis—to keep communism out of Europe.

"Yet, in 1960, Nixon lost the presidency to John Kennedy and his successor Lyndon Johnson —advocates of a redistribution of wealth society. Gladio—unsupported by American presidents—remained dormant. During this time, the Communist Party of Italy has grown to very much more than simply double-digit progression in the polls.

"A Communist Italy is much more dangerous to the United States than the Soviet Union. Unlike Russia, Italy is a democratic society. Here in Italy communism is the will of the people.

"If it is successful in Italy, a redistribution of wealth society will spread rapidly throughout Europe and eventually to the Americas.

"But, today, Nixon is president. Someone who is convinced society can be driven only by greed. Nixon believes it is fair some children are born into vast wealth while others are born into poverty.

"He has beefed up the war against communism. We have learned he has ordered Gladio to carry out covert terrorist activities against the Italian population, to turn its mindset against communism."

"You're suggesting Nixon killed Pasquale?" I shivered.

Jack didn't bat an eye. "Operation Gladio did the job."

"But, why Pasquale …?" I started.

"Pasquale was one of Piccolo's 'secrets'—one of his lieutenants organizing youth in the Veneto—a threat to American interests here. He had to be taken out. Colombo has lost several others…"

"Colombo?" My ears perked up.

"Giovanni Colombo," troubled I'd never heard of him.

"When Paul—the Archbishop of Milan—became Pope in 1963, he replaced himself in the heart of industrialized Italy with Colombo together with the commission to lead Italy into a more just society.

"Paul's edict *Populorum Progressio* established basic rights of man including the right to a just wage and fair working conditions and the right of assembly. It ignited the *priest-worker movement.*

"It has been that priests have been preaching Paul's message, the Communist Party has been mounting in the polls.

"Piccolo is Colombo's partner. Together with Aldo Moro they are the driving force in Italy—in Europe—behind Paul's encyclical to bring about a day when every child has enough.

"Nevertheless, Piccolo called Paul and told him of the autopsy findings. Recognizing we are endangered Paul sent some guards up from the Vatican. One accompanied you on the train from Venice."

"Strange. I didn't notice…"

He cut me off, "Another was the gardener in the castle courtyard.

"Gladio is likely to continue picking off those in the ranks. If it were to take out Colombo or Piccolo, it would yield much more than a footnote in the world press. Yet, we are all in danger. Even Paul, himself, must taste his porridge suspiciously each day."

He paused briefly. Then he started up again, "Nevertheless, in case something happened to us, Piccolo feels someone should know. Someone, who it is reasonable to believe, will be around many years from now. Someone who could bring an end to this world of greed, as quickly as one turns off a faucet. That Piccolo, long after he is gone, perhaps, long after I am gone, will carry out his will.

Murder by the Grace of God

I stopped him, "But me? How could I possibly accomplish such a thing? I will probably be a 'nobody' at that time."

He didn't bat an eyelash, "You will do it in the same way every other 'nobody' has accomplished his or her objectives. The same way Mark and his contemporaries accomplished their objectives."

"Mark and his contemporaries?" I added a question mark.

"Yes, like the evangelists wrote of Christ generations after His time." He paused and raised his voice, "You, too, will write a book."

I would wiggle out of it, "But I don't know how to write a book."

The tone of his voice changed to that of an order, "You will write a book for each and every one of them!"

My mind drifted back to that time I had taken the pledge in the cemetery at Milan: "**To carry out that solemn promise, to answer that fervent prayer, to carry it out for each and every one of them, that what they fought for, those things they willed to be; will come to be, for each of them, and for me, and for you, and for all humanity.**"

There is a time in a man's life when the way he thinks, collides with the way he should think. For me, this was it.

Getting up, he patted me on the shoulder, "Enough said. Let's go to lunch. Vittorio Veneto is smack in the middle of Italian wine country. I will take you to a little sidewalk cafe where the food is terrible. Yet, what counts most, the wine is marvelous."

We wound down around the mountainside and strolled along the seminary. "This is Piccolo's crown jewel. It is what makes this such an important post. It was Piccolo who made it that way."

We passed one of those gelato stands one sees all over Europe. Jack boasted, "There are ten million of these in the world. This one is in first place. We will stop here on the way back."

"Not many people," I thought. "Each one—some walking, some running, and a few on bicycles—had obviously been there all his or her life; a hundred, perhaps two hundred Italians, and I."

As people looked at me, I relished my individuality.

Each one called out **"Ciao Giovanni!"** with an expression of great respect and admiration and awe, as if Jack were some kind of a God.

---

1 *White Crane Journal, winter issue 2006*, Toby Johnson Editor Emeritus
2 *Veneto Nostro* 21 Feb 69, Pasquale Cafaro
3 *'socialism' and 'communism' are defined as they are thought of today. There are infinite variations in a wide range of definitions, many of which are discussed in the works of Karl Marx and this book.*
4 *Mathew 19... Mathew 6... Mark 10...*
5 *Mark 14 Matthew 26 John 12 Luke 6 & 7 implies 'always have your poor' in other words*

Chapter 19

Albino Luciani and General Patton

"It is our differences that have built us into the great nation of one that we are. There is no room here for preachers and politicians who would choose to use them to divide us."[1]

General George Patton

We took a table at a sidewalk café where the street formed a wedge with its neighbor, one of those they try to duplicate in the big cities with very little success. Heeding Jack's advice, I decided on bread, cheese and fruit. He doubled the order.

Shortly, the waiter returned and spread an assortment of breads, cheeses and fruits. In the center, he placed a crystal clear bottle of wine set in chopped ice. I was about to get a taste of the afterlife.

Reaching for the bottle, Jack poured our glasses properly half full of this memory—this wine of the gods—which is still with me today. Like any other friends, who hadn't seen each other for years, we started out chatting about the good old times…

A thousand 'Ciao Giovanni's

I asked, "You sure are popular. Just being here gets you that?"

Jack brushed aside a bee that threatened to share his wine. "It has nothing to do with that. It is owed entirely to something else.

"My uncle was in the military during the world war. He held two *Purple Hearts* and a dozen other enviable decorations. He was hit in North Africa and hospitalized for six months. He was nominated for the *Medal of Honor*, but instead received a *Silver Star*.

"He was hit again, this time paralyzed from the waist down. He was taken down by friendly fire when he placed himself between his own men and twenty-eight Italian school children to alert them they were about to fire on the children.

"He was nominated for the nation's highest award. Because it had occurred toward war's end and helped to heal the wounds of war, and it had been witnessed by so many, we were certain this time he would reap the honor that had escaped him in North Africa."

"Wow. He won the *Medal of Honor!*" I beamed.

"Not quite," he was quick to correct my misconception. "This time, they gave him the *Distinguish Service Cross*." [2]

"But, I don't under…"

He cut me off, "The *Distinguished Service Cross* is awarded for risk of life 'not quite' justifying the *Medal of Honor*. The 'not quite' in my uncle's case was determined the same way as was the case of many other candidates who were passed up for the highest award."

"How's that?" I queried.

"During the world war, 'not quite' was most often defined as being soldiers of color and of certain ethnic backgrounds—Asians and Hispanics. In my uncle's case, it meant something else."

"Something else?" I repeated Jack's statement as a question.

"My uncle was gay. Because his life seemed wasted he felt he could be a martyr for the gay cause. Foolishly, he announced he was gay while the matter was still pending. He hoped he could attract national attention, but he didn't attract a fly. All he did do was to deprive himself of the nation's highest military award.

"He told my mother, his admission took more courage than when he placed himself before the firing squad to save the children.

"Nevertheless, this is why I am a celebrity in these parts. This is why wherever I go, I get a thousand 'hellos.' People believe some of my uncle's courage has rubbed off on me.

"Back then, homosexuality was not the type of thing his family wanted to talk about, much less see spread across the front page of the local newspaper. In fact, it still isn't today."

"So, the Army threw him out?" I presumed.

"No. Though those caught in homosexual acts were given a **'blue discharge'** there was no **'homosexual box'** to check barring one from serving simply because one was gay when my uncle had enlisted at the beginning of the war. Thousands of gay men and women served honorably through the years.

"When you have a war in which you are fighting for survival, one doesn't stop to sort out what the preacher thinks is morality.

"That he didn't attract a fly was not entirely true. He drew an official reprimand from Eisenhower; something General Patton, my uncle's commanding officer, tried to block.

"It was that Ike had added the 'gay box' to applications earlier that same year that prompted my uncle to take the action he did take. News of his heroism had spread. He intended to make a mockery of Ike's new policy to discharge gays as **'unfit for military service.'**

"So Eisenhower did throw him out?" I surmised.

"Not so." Jack's voice took on a bitter tone, "Before Ike could make his move, my uncle died; **'the war hero who had given his life to save the lives of twenty-eight school children'** who Ike intended to discharge as **'unfit for military service'** escaped the guillotine."[3]

"...a greater kind of courage..."

"Only his father flew to Italy. His mother was too distraught.

"The army provided full military honors. There was speculation that General Patton, who happened to be in the area, would attend.

"Although several hundred villagers attended, he didn't show up. In fact, not a single officer showed up, despite that my uncle was up for the nation's highest award. Yet, someone else did show up."

"Someone else?" I queried.

"Yes, Piccolo. It is not solely that I am fluent in Italian that I am here in the Veneto. Piccolo had officiated at my uncle's interment.

"At the time, Milan was conservative and no local priest could be found who was comfortable in officiating at the ceremony. The cardinal of Milan reached out into the Veneto country. The choice was the revolutionary and outspoken young priest from Belluno.

"A corporal showed up heading up a detail of four soldiers, three with rifles and one with a bugle. Piccolo doesn't remember too much of what he said, other than he had ended his string of prayers with an embittered comment: **'It is the soldier who shed his blood on the field of battle and not the preacher who cowers in his pulpit, who should determine who should or should not be free.'** [4]

"The detail fired off three volleys and the man with the bugle did the best he could with the taps.

"Three volleys for a man who gave his life to save twenty-eight school children. Yet, the rules call for nineteen volleys for political appointees of a president. It kind of tells one how America thinks.

"Anyway, as the crowd started to move away from the grave, a strange thing happened.

"A large olive green military sedan—one of those with the big bubble fenders one sees in the movies—entered the cemetery and moved along its outer perimeter. It came to rest in the road alongside my uncle's grave. A soldier got out of the front seat and opened the rear door. An army officer of about sixty stepped out.

"When Patton reached the gravesite he introduced himself to Piccolo and my uncle's father, as if the rows of stars on his shoulders could not have conveyed the message. A light rain was falling from darkened skies and one could imagine hearing the firing of artillery shells in the distance, though there was nothing there.

"Patton spoke decisively, pausing on each syllable, as if he were addressing Congress: 'At West Point, there are many courses. One learns many things. One learns the history of war, one learns the purpose of war, one learns the strategy of war, one learns the struggle of war, one learns the noise of war, one learns the horror of war, one learns the victory of war... one learns the hopelessness of war. Yet, the most important course one takes is taken on the great battlefield of war itself. That course is called 'courage.'

"'This is the difference between Ike and I. Ike has never taken this course. Not once in his lifetime, has he carried himself into battle, into the pit. Not once in his lifetime, has he pulled the boy out of the mud and searched for where the mud left off and the blood began. Not once, has he reached for the final pulse of this thing called life. Not once, has he given himself the opportunity to realize this great prize we know as 'courage.' His only experience in battle has been in his textbooks, and in his toy soldiers, and in his toy tanks, and in his toy ships that he moves about on his great table of war. Like the preacher in the pulpit whose only time in battle has been in the atrocities of the 'holy' ethnic wars in his scripture.'

"With a great tear forming in the corner of his eye, Patton placed his hand on my uncle's father's shoulder and told him: 'I apologize for Ike's action. It does not speak for me, it does not speak for those who fought alongside your son; it does not speak for America.

"'Your son has won for each of us this thing called courage. This thing called courage that I, too, have sought so many times.

"'As a commanding general, I have placed myself upon a tank at the forefront of battle in open line of enemy fire. With artillery shells bursting all about me, I have craved for the taste of this thing—courage. Yet, even I have yet to realize its dream.

"'Earlier this week, I assigned my most courageous and highest decorated officer to represent your son's fellow soldiers here today. Yet, early this morning, I learned that officer had failed in his duty by delegating his sacred responsibility to a subordinate.

"'Not because he had more important things to do, but because he didn't have the courage to be here—a different kind of courage—a greater kind of courage. He was afraid of what the press might think of him, of what his fellow soldiers might think of him, of what his family might think of him, of what America might think of him.

"'Your son had that kind of courage. He wasn't afraid of what the press might think of him. He wasn't afraid of what the army might think of him. He wasn't afraid of what his family might think of him. He didn't care what America might think of him.'

"The general then stepped a few paces to the left and placed his hand on the shoulder of the adjoining tombstone, the one marked: 'Anthony Jackson, *Bronze Star.*'

"'Today, the Christian-right persecutes blacks, many of whom have also shed their blood on the great battlefields of this war.'

"He then placed his hand on the shoulder of the next stone, the one marked: 'Patricia Wilde, *Bronze Star.*'

"'The world will never know of her valor, will never know of the things she did for its freedom. All that evidences she had ever been, is this small white granite stone and the marks upon it.'"

"Freedom without equality is not what it pretends to be..."

"The general then turned toward the crowd and raised his voice:

> 'After this war is won, after the final volleys are fired, after the smoke clears and the tears begin, America must fight a new kind of war, and that war will be fired by a new kind of courage.
>
> This war will win for America and all mankind this thing called freedom. But, that war, the war within, will someday win for America the great prize of equality for all men and women, something this war cannot do. For freedom without equality is not what it pretends to be. The diamond would be made of paste.
>
> It is our differences that have built us into the great nation of one that we are. There should be no room here for those preachers

and politicians who would choose to use them to divide us.

Today, men and women of courage are engaged in this great war which will soon crush the enemy from without, but it will take many more men and women of still another kind of courage—perhaps even a greater kind of courage—to rise up and crush the enemy from within.

Only then, would these brave men and women not have died in vain. Only then, will the diamond—this thing we call freedom—be real.'[5]

"As he climbed into the car, Patton turned to my uncle's father, 'I have been proud to have had your son serve in my army here;' and looking up, 'He is proud to have him in His army, today.' A tear dropped onto his cheek. He nodded to his driver. They were off.

"Yet, you're right. If my uncle were alive today he could do something. Actually, all other homosexuals who hold high military awards including the *Medal of Honor* could do something."

I interrupted him, "I thought you said they weeded out the gays in awarding the *Medal of Honor?*"

"Most gays remain in the closet today; even more so then. In the war, four hundred congressional medals were awarded. If one plays the percentages, this would mean a least three dozen are held by homosexual men. Of course, like my uncle most did not survive.

"Yet, if those who did survive were brave enough to come forward it would stop much of the preacher's bigotry in its tracks. But, as my uncle said, that would take a greater kind of courage than did his action when he stood before the children.

"Celebrities who make public their orientation make an immense contribution toward that day when the rights of all children and teens, no matter who they happen to be, will be protected equally under the laws of nations. In the nineteen-fifties, it was those in the public eye who owned up to having been born-out-of-wedlock that ended the horrific persecution of bastards in the United States."

With a gesture of reverent solemnity, he stretched out his arm and pulled back his sleeve. To one side of his watch-face was welded a *Silver Star*. On the opposite side was welded a *Purple Heart* with the image of George Washington in its center.

"The *Distinguished Service Cross* and the others are with him in the great cemetery at Milan. Yet, there is something more.

"A few years ago, Piccolo brought the matter to the attention of the Italian Prime Minister. On the twentieth anniversary of my uncle's death, at his gravesite with twenty-three of the surviving children looking on, Piccolo accepted the citation from Aldo Moro that is on his office wall on behalf of my uncle."

Leaving some of the wine in order that we would be able to find our way, I settled up with the waiter and we started back. Stopping at the gelato stand, I followed his lead, "One of these, one of these, one of these, and one of those." I wondered how the finest gelato in the world could have found its way so near to its finest wine.

At the end of the street, he went one way, and I the other. He called out after me, "Dinner is promptly at seven. Don't be late."

As I walked back to the hotel, it ran over and over again in my mind: "To carry out that solemn promise, to answer that fervent prayer, to carry it out for each and every one of them, that what they fought for, those things they willed to be, will come to be, for each of them, and for me, and for you, and for all humanity."

Author's note: Patton and Luciani shared an avid interest in the possibility of reincarnation. Patton was killed in an auto accident the following year. On Christmas day 1945, Luciani eulogized Patton in the Cathedral Duomo at Belluno:

"I remember them all
Many names, many faces
Many times, many places
Many ups, many downs
Many smiles, many frowns
Many struggles, many dreams
Yet always, me."

Albino Luciani [6]

---

1 *Affria Italiani* 28 Sep 44. Milan Italy 25 September 44. General George Patton.
2 the medal was awarded posthumously
3 Eisenhower banned homosexuals from serving in military service in April 1944.
4 Albino Luciani, Milan Italy 25 Sep 44. He repeated this at times during his ministry.
5 *Affria Italiani* 28 Sep 44 & *Corriere delle Alpi 17 Oct 73*. Albino Luciani quoted Patton's remarks in a homily in the Basilica San Marco in 1973. The original draft of this sermon is in the author's file. The balance of the story is to the best of Albino Luciani's recollection as he related them to the author.
6*Corriere delle Alpi* 26 Dec 45

Chapter 20

The Mud in the Street

'...A justified strike is in progress...to feel solidarity in progress of men fighting for their equal share is Christian charity...' [1]

Albino Luciani

I found myself in an ancient room of stone. Its focal point, a pair of bottle-bottom leaded glass windows peering out through iron grates. Though their opaqueness obscured the view, it was clear what they were looking at. The surviving ruins of the medieval castle walls.

The old stone floor, with its centuries of wear, was every bit as cold as it seemed to be. A beautiful antique sideboard of mellowed wood ran along the wall opposite the windows.

Just above it, an aging colorful tapestry of princes and paupers blanketed the wall. At the far end of the room, a giant oil painting in an overly encrusted golden frame depicted Christ's miracle of the loaves and fishes. I correctly assumed it was another Titian.

A huge iron cauldron hung in front of a huge fireplace cut into the ancient stone wall, as it was on the day it had been forced into retirement by the stove that now stood off to one side in the kitchen.

In the center of the room, lay a carpet of extraordinary value.

On it, stood four richly carved chairs that clashed with the table they surrounded—one of those cheap enameled tables of the forties. Four chairs, that would draw five thousand dollars each at auction, hemmed in a table that would go for five dollars in a yard sale.

Jack explained the strange gathering: "Bishop Caprio came up from the Vatican. When he saw the table was gone, he thrust his arms into the air like a man out of his mind. He ordered Piccolo to stop this madness, *'Sell all that thou hast and give to the poor.'*

"I have often wondered what would this first-century man who preached *'Sell all thou hast and give to the poor'* do if He were to stroll into the Vatican today. If He were to take a seat in St. Peter's Basilica and watch deranged madmen dressed up in women clothes of silk and satin prancing about an altar of marble and gold drinking His blood from a diamond studded chalice? What would Jesus think of a mob of ghoulish zombies lining up in a cannibalistic ritual to get a taste of His flesh? What would He think of this cult which drops its alms into a box intended for the poor which is used by prejudicial men to buy billions of dollars of expensive radio and television time to deprive certain kinds of God's children basic human rights and dignity under the laws of nations? What would He think...?"

Confused, I cut him off, "Piccolo built the orphanage that I passed at the foot of the mountain with money he got for a table?"

"No," he corrected me. "He built that one with money intended to build a church. The day he took up residence here, he received a letter from a terminally ill man. Lacking heirs, the man offered to leave his fortune to build a church dedicated to Christ the Savior.

"Piccolo went to visit the man the next day and asked him to leave the money to build an orphanage instead of a church. The man held his ground and demanded the great church be built.

"Piccolo reached into his hip pocket and played his trump card, one he often used to get his way:

> 'When I was a teenager, my father made me promise I would live my life in imitation of Christ. I have kept that solemn promise. Each time the fork in the road has come up—often only minutes apart—I have asked myself: Now, what would Jesus have done in this case? He then asked the man: Now, what do you think Jesus would do in this case?' [2]

"A week later, the man took up a shovel and broke ground for the orphanage, one designed for infants who otherwise would have been aborted because the girl was too young or too poor to afford them. He was buried a month later in a nearby cemetery. A granite marker was placed on his grave by the grateful bishop of Vittorio Veneto: *'Each day he breathes new life into the world.'*

"As long as a child lacks a roof over his or her head and has not enough to eat, not a block of stone will be laid to build a church. Not a stone has been laid to build a church in the diocese since he came here. Likewise, should he rise to the papacy, not a single stone will be laid to the honor and glorification of God in the Catholic world, until every child has a roof over his and her head and enough to eat.

"Before he arrived, it was commonplace on Sunday to see a hundred orphans gathering in the street in front of the church; out-of-wedlock bastards, retarded, crippled, deaf, blind...

"Their only possessions, the tattered and torn rags they wore, splattered with mud in the summer, spring and fall and frozen with flakes of snow in the wintertime. The wealthiest of parishioners would sneak around to the rear entrance of the church to avoid them.

"When Piccolo celebrated his first Mass here, an overflowing crowd came from miles around. When they showed up at the church on January 11, 1959, much to their surprise there wasn't an orphan to be seen. Some remarked: 'It is about time someone cleaned up this mess.' For the first time in years, they were able to ascend the grand staircase and enter through the main entrance of the church. Yet, when they entered they got the biggest surprise of all.

"There on the end of the first pews hung a small sign: 'Riservato ai bambini speciali di Dio'—'Reserved for God's special children.'

"Lined up, row after row, orphans gazed up at the magnificent altarpiece. His first words to his new congregation: 'Christ picked me up from the Mud in the Street and gave me to you' will someday be carved into the plain pine box that will one day entomb him.

"'Mud in the Street' was an expression used by churchgoers in referring to street orphans. That he had come from the 'Mud in the Street' fired rumors he had been born out of wedlock. Since bastards cannot be ordained, his enemies demanded he be defrocked.

"When the situation started to get out of hand, the Archbishop of Venice published a marriage certificate proving Luciani's parents Giovanni Paolo and Bartolomea had wed a year before his birth.[3]

"Nevertheless, this good man has picked thousands up out of the mud in the street and given them their rightful place in society."

"In the outside world when a child reaches their sixth birthday, he or she gets a party and everyone brings them gifts; conditioning the child how wonderful it is to get.

"Not here in Piccolo's world. In the months leading up to one's sixth birthday, the child is busy making small craft items.

"When the day arrives, everyone except the little boy or little girl gets a gift; conditioning the child how wonderful it is to give.

"Each time the fork in the road would come up for each of them in the past, they would ask themselves: 'Now, what is in this for me?' Now they ask themselves: 'Now, what is in this for others?'"

He tipped forward one of the chairs. "The chair you are about to occupy has held many others. On its back were aging brass plates:

Leo XIII 11 November 1879	Paul VI 23 December 1963
Pius X 2 January 1904	Paul VI 23 March 1964
Benedict XV 24 June 1904	Paul VI 22 July 1964
Pius X 23 September 1906	Paul VI 16 March 1966
Pius XI 22 September 1923	Paul VI 16 October 1966
Pius XII 2 February 1943	Paul VI 2 March 1967
John XXIII 22 January 1959	Paul VI 24 December 1967
John XXIII 14 July 1961	Paul VI 22 July 1968

Puzzled, I asked, "Why has Paul been here so often?"

Jack replied, "Here in the foothills of the Alps, is the only place Paul can get away from it all. Even at Castel Gandolfo, he is in the public eye. He holds his summits here—summits on poverty.

"He wants to rid the world of poverty. The only way to do that is Marxism—a redistribution of wealth society—an evil word in the west. Meetings must be kept secret. This is the perfect place.

"Most every cardinal of the pockets of world poverty has been here—Africa, China, India, Central America, you name it…

"In the minds of Paul and Piccolo, the union of capitalism and charity is not a sacred one. After centuries of trying it hasn't worked. Fifty thousand children starve to death each day while the rich drop pennies in the poor box as they exit magnificent palaces—basilicas and cathedrals—where they have visited their God for the day.

"But, Paul and Piccolo do know what will work—a society that affords each child an equal opportunity at education to enable each of them to make their optimum contribution back to society.

"In their world, charity would no longer be a voluntary function of the individual. It will be the involuntary function of society. The rich will be taxed to help the poor. Unlike the Soviet Union, their vision is for a democratic-Marxist society—the will of the people."

I winked a wink of doubt, "It is not realistic to think communism will ever be the 'will of the people.' Greed is something we are born with—the reason communism has always been an autocracy."

He could not have said it with greater certainty: "They will change 'the will of the people' when they are six years old!"

1 *Illustrissimi* Luciani commends the *priest-worker movement* in his letter to St Therese
2 *Veneto Nostro* 13 Jan 59
3 *Veneto Nostro* 12 Feb 59

Chapter 21

The Politics of Ghosts

"Theology is the study of tales told by ancient men to attain their political objectives which are exploited by modern men to attain their political objectives." [1]

Albino Luciani

Footsteps came down the stairs.

As if not a moment to lose, the bishop sat down. Rather than saying grace, he picked up his wine glass and offered a toast to Christ. He had barely finished, when he reached across for the rolls.

Jack followed with the fish and vegetables and started, "Lucien, here, wants to prove which faith is the true faith."

Piccolo didn't hesitate, "It can't be done. Yet, one can prove a particular faith is not the true one. Let me explain how this works."

The 'expert' said so—it must be true

"In Paris, where Modigliani had worked, a sculptured head was recovered by divers from the canal that ran behind the artist's house. On the assumption the work may have been executed by the master, it was brought to the attention of a local curator who thought it could be an original masterpiece. It was subsequently examined by experts recognized as the world's foremost authorities on Modigliani and it was determined, it had, indeed, been executed by the great artist.

"A local hippie challenged the find as being a hoax.

"Though the hippie had no credentials for making his claim, the experts saw it as an opportunity to gain publicity for their find. They arranged a live debate with the hippie on television. It was widely publicized and the press made the hippie out to be a fool.

"The hour-long debate allowed for a ten minute summary at its end for each of the parties. Although the hippie had disclosed serious flaws in the experts' analyses, their immense credibility in the field of art enabled them to seal their claim as being sound. It was clear to all viewers the hippie really didn't know what he was talking about.

"Finally the hippie got his ten minutes. He said something the art world has never forgotten: 'No one, not all the experts on this stage, nor all the experts in Europe nor, for that matter, all the experts in the world, can prove a particular work of art is an original executed by a particular artist. Yet, one can prove, a work is not authentic.'

"To the astonishment of all, he ran a film of he—himself—sculpting the head. He closed with: 'The only way one can tell one is truly in possession of an original work of art is to watch the artist create it, watch him complete it, watch him sign it, and take the work and place it in a safe to which only one knows the combination.'

"Religions are like fine works of art. When you believe one is the true one, you are relying entirely on the expert, the credibility of the preacher; someone who doesn't know anymore about it than you do. To put it bluntly, you are relying on your own gullibility.

"The only way you can know a particular religion is the true one is to have been there. In the case of the Jew, this means to have been there in the Sinai Desert when the Burning Bush—a Ghost—spoke to Moses. In the case of the Christian, it means to have been there when the Holy Ghost impregnated Mary. In the case of the Muslim, it means to have been there upon the winged-horse when the Angel Gabriel—another ghost—took Mohammed to meet the Supreme Ghost in the heavens. In the case of the Mormon, it means to have been there at the edge of the pond when two Ghosts—the Father and Jesus—appeared together to Joseph Smith on the edge of the pond.

"Otherwise, you are relying entirely on what someone said to someone else, who in turn passed it on to someone else, for all time. As my father told me, in those days, as in these days, men had great motive to lie in their ghost stories. If they convinced their fellowman they had talked directly with God, it would make one a great and wealthy man. Most of all, it would give one unyielding power over the minds of men. After all, one's words come directly from God.

"This includes Moses, Constantine, Mohammed and Smith and all the others who claimed to have visions of God. It also includes present day preachers who earn their livelihood this way, a few of which are trying to make this a better world to live in, but most of which get their kicks out of wielding power over the minds of men. So weakened is man by his mortality, he blindly pays the preacher for his salvation, despite the fact the preacher knows no more about the possibility of an afterlife than he does. He has never been there."

Other hippies run their films

"As with art, it is possible to tell a certain religion is not the true one. As more scientific facts become available, more and more do we question the prophet, and more and more is his credibility eroded.

"Today, no one doubts the hippie's testimony because we now have the facts. Yet, when he made his claim, no one believed him, not a soul. The credibility regarding the *Modigliani* sculpture was entirely with the so-called 'expert.'

"Likewise, when Darwin and Einstein first made their claims, no one believed them. The credibility was entirely with the expert—the preacher. Many thought Darwin and Einstein insane.

"Darwin claimed we had evolved from apes before the time excavations of prehistoric fossils and the development of modern genetics would prove his hypothesis.[2]

"Whereas Darwin spoke of things that could readily be seen—the resemblance of man to his fellow higher primates—Einstein spoke of things one could not see. He claimed everything from the air one breathes to the hardest substance known—diamond—is made up of moving particles—infinitesimal specs of energy which he claimed were the most powerful forces in nature; and from them had grown all living creatures and the world they lived in.

"The marble floor beneath us is bits of empty space—atoms—which are traveling at placements which give the illusion of solidity. Our bodies are made up of identical atoms, traveling at different placements, which give the illusion of more porous objects.

"What's more, Einstein found that infractions of space hold them together. Everything—not only earth—has a center of gravity.[3]

"When Darwin and Einstein proposed their theories as to how we all came about, few believed them. They obviously didn't know what they were talking about. What they claimed contradicted what the 'experts' were saying: God created Adam and Eve as adults.

"Like the hippie in the case of his make-believe *Modigliani*, both these men have now had the opportunity to have run their films.

"In Darwin's case, advances in archeology and genetics have proved his theory beyond a shadow of a doubt.

"In Einstein's case, photographs of an eclipse of the sun proved his theory to his fellow scientists. For the common man, today's microscopes are able to magnify millions of times—one can see this tiny bit of energy he spoke of—the atom—the most powerful force in nature. For those having no access to powerful microscopes, the splitting of a single atom at Hiroshima should have done the trick.

"So now, Darwin and Einstein, too, have had their time before the cameras. What they proposed as theory is now fact.

"Einstein's theory, as to the origin of man, is more devastating to Christianity's fundamental tale of creation—*Adam and Eve*—than is Darwin's theory of evolution. Einstein proved the egg came first; God did not create man and woman as adults. Einstein proved the fundamental unit of creation was an infinitesimal speck—the atom—which gave birth to all living things and the world they live in."

I agreed, "You're right. Darwin's theory of evolution is not quite as devastating as the preacher has the loophole of claiming God created Adam and Eve as caveman and cavewoman."

"Not so," he corrected me. "The Old Testament is an unbroken genealogy from Adam directly to Christ: 'Adam, Seth, Enos, Cainan, Mahalaleel, Jared, Enoch, Methuselah, Lamech, Noah, Shem, Arphaxad, Salah, Eber, Peleg, Reu, Serug, Terah, Abraham, Isaac, Jacob, Judas, Phares, Esrom, Aram, Aminadab, Naasson, Sakmon, Booz, Obed, Jesse, King Solomon, King David, Roboam, Abia, Josaphat, Joram, Ozias, Joatham, Achaz, Mahasses, Amon, Josias, Jechonias, Salathiel, Zorobable, Abiud, Eliakim, Azor, Sadoc, Achim, Eliud, Mattham, Jacob, Joseph, the father of Christ.'"

Startled, I shot him a questionable glance.

"I was a Straight-A seminarian," he explained. "Regardless, the chain is unbroken. The Bible gives the age at which all but three of them sired his firstborn. It also gives the age of death of each of them. One knows who was whose father, and who was whose son, all the way down from Adam to Christ. 'Adam begot Seth who begot Enos... who begot Jacob who begot Joseph—the father of Christ.'

"In ancient times, with no social practices restricting the age at which one could sire one's firstborn, the average generation length was about seventeen. The mathematical calculation 55 generations multiplied by 17 is 935 years or 929BC for Adam and Eve. [4]

"Biblical patriarchs, who lived from the time of the first pharaoh and Moses' time, lived to an average age of 273. Conversely, we have the archeological fact that the average lifespan of pharaohs excavated for the same period was 38 and the oldest lived to 81.

"Earlier patriarchs lived even longer. Adam lived 940 years.

"When the Bible was first put together in a single volume, [5] the authors realized if these patriarchs had lived normal life spans it would place the time of Adam and Eve sixteen hundred years after the pyramids had been built. Because the genealogy from Adam and Christ was unbroken, adding patriarchs was not an alternative. The only option was to add extraordinary lifetimes to the early patriarchs to push the date back to 4000BC—acceptable then, but not today—we all know mankind goes back countless millennia before that.

"There is no wiggle room here. The integrity of the Bible rests on the fact Adam and Eve were created around 4000BC—the reason no preacher will budge from that date—his credibility is at stake.

"Nevertheless, when these modern-day prophets—Darwin and Einstein—came along, the preacher would show up in the courtroom and—armed with his immense credibility—would win every time.

"But where is he today? He is not there. He is not there because he knows the 'hippie' now has his film. Darwin and Einstein now have the facts. They will make mincemeat of him.

"Religion is like a work of fine art. One might be an expert in fine art. Another might be an expert in religion.

"The art dealer is the expert in fine art. It is his job to win the credulity of his customers that they will respond with their awe and ultimately with their dollars. The product he sells is fine art.

"The preacher is the expert in religion. It is his job to win the credulity of his customers that they will respond with their awe and ultimately with their dollars. The product he sells is faith.

"It's the same game—just played with different cards.

"Yet, unlike the art dealer, the preacher has little 'faith' in the product he sells. He convinces his customers his saints cure cancer. Yet, when hit by an automobile, he goes to a hospital. He does not go to a church. His imagination—faith—cannot save him. He knows this because the 'hippy'—the medical community—has its film."

Political Science

"Yet, there is a more reliable way to determine a religion is not the true religion than scientific disclaimer." My ears perked up.

He answered my ears: "common sense!

"Consider the central core of the canon of Mother Church: 'Some children are born better than others and are entitled to more.'

"Without delving into the handicapped, the remarried, certain ethnic groups, transgenders, morphodites, homosexuals, born-out-of-wedlock children and others deprived of basic rights under the laws of nations by Mother Church, consider the plight of the little girl.

"Every pope and every priest conditions children from an early age 'little boys are better than little girls.' Only a little boy can grow up with the power to change a piece of bread into a God." He corrected himself: "Unless, of course, he was born-out-of-wedlock."

"After all, we all know God is a Man. How else could He have impregnated Mary and been the Father of Jesus?

"Yet, common sense tells us if we are all children of the same God, we are all created equal.

"We know this for a much more definitive reason. Christ defined His Church in the gospels. He could not have been more explicit:

'When thou prayest, thou shalt not be as Hypocrites are; for they love to pray standing in the synagogues and in public places that they may be seen and heard of men. They have their reward in this life. But when thou prayest, enter into thy closet, and when thou hast shut thy door, talk to me in secret. Ye will have ye reward in my Kingdom. When ye pray, use not vain repetitions as the heathen do; for they think they shall be heard for their speaking in public places...'"[6]

I had attended Mass every Sunday of my life. I wondered why no priest had ever mentioned Christ's definition of His Church?

He read my mind: "Regardless, Christ tells us our relationship is a direct and personal one and not the public display we make of it.

"All communist societies follow Christ's definition. Citizens are restricted to practice religions in homes or private chapels. They are not permitted to force their beliefs on others via political means.

"Faith is not God. It is what ancient men of motive defined as God in order to accomplish their political goals. Today it continues to be a business which entrepreneurs capitalize on man's tendency to believe in ghosts to accomplish political objectives.

"This is the difference between mythology and theology.

Murder by the Grace of God

"Though the Greeks and Romans had many gods, they were never perceived to be in all places at all times; they were never used for political purposes.

"The idea 'God is always watching us' was the brainstorm of modern men designed to accomplish their political objectives.

"Yet, it follows the definition of God—religion and atheism—is the same. Both religion and atheism agree: the ground beneath us and the air around us and the space beyond us—actually the composition of all atoms to the core of the earth to the infinity of the universe—is God. How else could He keep His eye on each of us at all times?

"Yet, religion claims the composition of these atoms—God—thinks like a man. The composition of all atoms is a Man.

"The 'expert' claims God made man to carry out God's political objectives. Yet, it is infinitely more reasonable to believe that man created God to carry out his own political objectives.

He said it with conviction: "Yes, according to all faiths, God is a Man." He paused to etch this truth into our minds for all time before knocking the ball out of the park: "All faiths were written by men!"

"The foundation of all modern religions is the tendency of the populace to believe in ghosts: saint ghosts, angel ghosts, holy ghosts, and so forth. People have a right to believe in ghosts. But, when one carries it beyond the world of 'Goldilocks and the Three Bears,' and claims this ghost, or that ghost, decreed some kinds of people are better than others and the others are to be subordinated or persecuted; it is not God. It is clearly the politics of men with hatred in their hearts.

"Believe me, God loves all of Her children.

"It is most likely, the true God is the God we know as a matter-of-fact gives us life—the God of Nature—the God of my atheist father. Studies have shown, children who grow up outside religion grow up free of prejudices instilled in children by faith, and are more likely to follow Christ's instruction: **'Love Thy Neighbor as Thyself.'**

"It was that my father saw Christ as a man, not as a ghost, that enabled him to see past the mythology of Christ, to the reality of Christ. Though he did not believe a man lived who had performed the miracles said of Christ, my father did believe that good men had written the gospels. My father's convictions are well founded.

"'**The Quest for the Historical Jesus,**' introduced by Reimarus in the eighteenth century—followed by long line of others—was finally put to rest by Nobel Laureate Albert Schweitzer in 1905, clearly established the gospels as theological and not historical documents.[7]

"The consensus of these scholars—among the most brilliant men who ever lived—clearly established Christ a theoretical figure, and not a historical figure. Christ was not a man, but an ideology.

"This is still true today. Despite centuries of investigations which have left no leaf left unturned, no one has ever found the slightest bit of evidence Jesus Christ ever lived. That is, a man who performed the thirty-five miracles Christ is said to have performed.

"Of course, a second quest for the historical Jesus continues to go on today in which the gullible grasp at the tiniest shred of hope such a man actually lived—the Shroud, the garden Jesus prayed in, the box containing the bones of His alleged brother James, His tomb…

"Yet, that there is no trace of Jesus, does not conflict with faith. There is no school of theology in the Catholic world that recognizes Christ as a historical figure. Schools of theology teach faith. They do not teach history. Christ is a matter-of-faith—not a matter-of-fact. The reason no pope has ever challenged Schweitzer's conclusions.

"Universities do teach history. If it was possible to attend in one's lifetime the history classes of all the universities in the world since the birth of mankind, one will never hear the words 'Jesus Christ.'

"One will learn of the Pharaoh Naumer followed by a long line of others all the way down to Cleopatra. People like Homer, Aristotle, Alexander, Confucius, Buddha, Caesar, Diocletian, Constantine, Mohammad, Kahn, Guttenberg, Galileo, Da Vinci, Michelangelo, Columbus, Napoleon, Fulton, Washington, Lincoln, Pasteur, Bell, Edison, Salk, Darwin, Einstein, Lenin, Tesla, Hitler, Churchill and millions of others—the overwhelming number of which were born as common men. Yet, one will never hear the words 'Jesus Christ.'

"There is no better demonstration of the imaginary boundaries of the human mind than the incredible phenomenon Christ is believed by more than half the western world to have been the most important historical figure who ever lived, whereas, in truth, He never lived.

"There is no better example of the confusion of faith and reality, than we think of Jesus Christ as a man who lived and think of Sherlock Holmes as a man who never lived. Just the reverse is true.[8]

"Still, it is reasonable to believe a man was crucified for radical ideas about the time claimed by the evangelists in the gospels.

"Like we do today, Christ lived in a capitalistic society—one driven by greed. In that, He threatened the rich and powerful at the top, by itself,—unless they shed their wealth in this life, they would not make it into the next life—may have ended in His demise."

I started in, "Yet, Jack tells me He left us with a hopeless quest, 'You will not always have me. But, you will always have your poor.'[9]

He didn't blink an eye, "Not if I have anything to do about it.

"Today four forces drive poverty and starvation in the world: overpopulation - the aged - the handicapped - lack of education

"The solution is obvious: contraception – social health and retirement programs – genetic research – education for all.

"Planned Parenthood will limit the number of children to one's means. Society will enact laws forcing citizens during their working years to contribute to retirement programs. Genetic research will eventually eliminate the chance of an impaired child being born. Redistribution of wealth in society will afford education for all.

"Christ's thesis—voluntary charity—will never work!"

He paused that we would remember it all the days of our lives. "On Napoleon's tomb is engraved, 'Man's only immortality is what he leaves behind in the minds of men.'

"True, not only of men; but, of Gods."

Both Jack and I gave him a questionable look of apprehension.

"It makes no difference whether or not Christ ever lived. What is important of any man—even one who claimed to be God—is not so much His life on earth, but rather what He left behind. Like Laozi, [10] like Buddha, like Lincoln, like Einstein and all the others.

"What is important of Christ's life is not His life on earth, not the miracles He is said to have performed, not His death on the cross, not His ascension into heaven. Like any God, or for that matter, like any man, all that counts is what He left behind: **'Love thy Neighbor as thyself.'** The truth Mark, Matthew, Luke and John left behind.

"These things we have talked of may seem devastating to religion as we know it today. Yet, from these few truths will one day emerge a new kind of religion, one no longer based on the hatred and greed of ancient men, but, one based on the fundamental truth all children are created equal and are entitled to their fair share of the pie."

He stopped. He asked, "Where do you go from here?"

"…to Rome and then back to the grind in the states."

He took out a card and scribbled on its back. "When you visit the Vatican, find the office of Paul Marcinkus in the Palace of the Holy Office opposite the Papal Palace on St. Peter's Square.

"He is one of my closest friends. I am sure he will be happy to give you a tour of the gardens—maybe even the Papal Palace, itself.

"Thank you," winking his perpetual smile. "You have given me good substance for my infallible sermon on the mount.'"

Glancing back, he answered my unasked question, "Shot for the cannon. See you on the battlefield." He headed for the stairs.

As the bishop's footsteps faded away, Jack explained, "Forgive him. He retires at precisely nine o'clock and is up at four. Even if the Pope was here, he would do the same thing."

"Wow, up at four. He must sleep all afternoon."

"He has no idea what a nap is. I will walk you to your hotel."

Note: For brevity, the author relates his time with Albino Luciani as if it was a single encounter, whereas there were about twenty sessions in all.

1 Albino Luciani's original uncensored thesis: *'The Origin of the Human Soul according to Rosmini'*
2 Darwin published *The Origin of Species* in 1859. The first Neanderthal fossil was discovered in 1856 but it was thought to be a modern man until thirty years later its origin and age was determined.
3 In 1919, observation of a solar eclipse proved Einstein's theory everything has a center of gravity
4 Herod died in 4BC. Allowing two years for the killing of the newborns, Christ was born in 6BC
5 the Bible—The Vulgate—was first put together by St. Jerome at the turn of the 5th century AD
6 *Matthew 6*. Christ's only definition of His Church could not be more explicit.
7 *'The Quest of the Historical Jesus'* Schweitzer Internet and libraries
8 Arthur Conan Doyle based his character *Sherlock Holmes* on Eugene Francois Vidocq—a French thief turned detective who first developed the analysis and deduction techniques exploited by Doyle. See the short story *'Sherlock Holmes'* in the author's book: *The Reincarnation of Albino Luciani*
9 Mark 14, Matthew 26, John 12. Christ's only phrase repeated intact in three gospels.
10 Laozi founded Taoism

Chapter 22

A Conspiracy of Popes

"I recommend the anovulant pill developed by Professor Pincus be adopted as the Catholic birth-control pill."[1]

Albino Luciani

It was sheer silence as we walked along the aging stone wall of the seminary and wiggled our way down through the village streets.

I broke the quiet of the night, "'Infallible!' Piccolo used the word 'infallible.' Does he really think he will succeed Paul?"

Jack could not have said it with greater certainty: "He is going to be the next pope." He studied my reaction before explaining himself.

"Paul visited here the week before he issued his decree banning contraception. The next week Piccolo questioned the edict publicly: "...some accommodations for birth control must be made within the confines of the Church."[2] His action had been part of Paul's scheme.

"Paul's ruling was inconsistent with what has been the mainstay of his papacy—to rid the world of poverty. The ban on contraception is the driving force behind poverty. Yet, Paul left the door open..."

I cut him off, "He left the door open?"

"Yes, he left the door open. He did not invoke infallibility. Paul made the most important decree of his papacy as a man, and not as a pope. He intended the ruling be changed by his successor. In the meantime, parishioners could make up their own minds..." He glanced sideways to me, "...as they have as you know."

This made no sense to me, "If Paul intended it be changed by his successor, why did he make the ruling to begin with? Most puzzling, why would he instruct Piccolo to challenge it?"

He didn't keep me waiting, "Paul did these things for a reason. In a single swoop he made contraception the number one issue of the election which will choose his successor. One-third of the voting cardinals are from third world countries where the contraception ban is the driving force behind poverty, starvation and disease—though conservatives, they will vote for the man most likely to repeal it.

"Call it a conspiracy of popes. Call it what you may. In instructing Piccolo to challenge his ruling, Paul made him that man."

The Vatican Treasures

I looked at him, "Do you really think, if Piccolo becomes pope, he will liquidate the treasures and give the proceeds to the poor?"

Jack explained, "If he gives the money to the poor, it would not curb poverty for a generation. Piccolo intends to get at the source of the problem—convert the world to a more compassionate society."

He froze the hairs on the back of my neck. "He will make his mark in Central America.

"Whereas the Vatican treasures cannot support a world war, they are more than enough to overthrow the juntas in this tiny isthmus of poverty. Marxism, as the will of the people, will spread rapidly through the Condor nations of Latin America annihilating greed in its wake. In the very same way the Marxist movement Piccolo leads today in the Veneto country will eventually reach all of Europe."

I countered, "You are forgetting it is in the best interests of the United States to maintain the stability inherent in a rich and poor society south of its borders just as it is in its best interests to maintain the stability inherent in a rich and poor society in Europe. Piccolo is up against the most powerful military force on the planet."

"You are overlooking a pope holds the trump card." He waited

"The trump card?" I waited.

"Infallibility!" He nailed his case shut: "In poverty stricken parts of the world, the faithful will do anything a pope tells them to do."

A week earlier, when I had called Jack and told him of my pending visit, I did it on the guise of holiday. I never told him I was on the other side of the fence. After all, it would defeat my purpose.

I was about to find out, the *priest-worker movement* of the Veneto country had its own intelligence operation.

We stood in front of the hotel—a southern hotel there in the most northern part of Italy. Spreading out his arms, he clasped them about me for the longest moment of my life, "Goodbye Lieutenant!"

He stepped back. That was the last time I saw him... alive.

And, Piccolo? That was the last time I saw him, too. Yet, I will always remember him. Yes, I will always remember him—partly because of his smile. But, mostly, because of his toes...

1 *Veneto Nostro* 21 Apr 68
2 *Messaggero Mestre* 28 Jul 68

Chapter 23

Scene of the Crime

"On nights Paul stays up late, his bedroom lights—by far the most visible from outside Vatican City—are routinely reported in the press the next day. No privacy at the top." Paul Marcinkus

The Bed & Breakfast Jack had recommended was near the Roman Forum, about a fifteen minute walk from the Vatican. I spent a couple of days enjoying the tourist rendition of Rome, before finding my way to the Palace of the Holy Office which houses 'The Institute of Religious Works' wrongly tabbed by history 'The Vatican Bank.'

I handed Piccolo's card to the guard at its grand entrance and he directed me to a corridor where I handed it again to a receptionist.

Marcinkus came out to greet me. Much to my surprise, instead of assigning a subordinate, he took me around the Vatican grounds himself. Best of all, he took me into the Papal Palace.

The Apostolic Palace includes dozens of buildings, thousands of rooms, hundreds of stairways and elevators. In the case of the Pope, one is talking about that building which houses the Papal Apartment.

As palaces go, it is not a particularly beautiful building. That is, from the outside. If located in the downtown section of a midsized city one could easily mistake it as an outdated department store.

It is a perfectly square freestanding sixteenth century building which facade faces St. Peter's Square. It is only four stories high but because of its ceiling height—thirty feet on each floor—it is as high as is a modern ten-story building.

The ground floor serves as the base of the building and houses 'The Patrimony of the Holy See' which is the Vatican bank.

The palace consists of the top three floors commonly referred to as the first, second and third loggias. Yet, they are the second, third and fourth floors of the building.

The papal bedroom occupies the upper right hand corner of the building. When its lights are on at night—the highest point on the outer edge of Vatican City—they can be seen for miles around.

Of all the places I had the opportunity to visit in Vatican City, I remember most vividly this important building. It is quite different from all the others. For the interior of all the others from St. Peter's, Basilica, to the Sistine Chapel, to the Apostolic Library, to the Gallery of Maps, to the Vatican Museum, were very much the same.

No matter where you went, you were roofed in by an endless array of frescos which, in turn, were hemmed in by encrusted frames of gilt and gold. If someone were not there to tell you where you were, you would never know where you were. But, the Papal Palace is much different. You knew where you were.

Swiss Guards flanked the great studded bronze door which marks the papal entrance to the building. They, like all Swiss Guards, are perpetual; they are always there.

One enters into a long white marble corridor running to the rear of the building. The floor is marble, the walls are marble, even the ceiling is marble. The ceiling is arched and the walls are lined with ancient sconces which at one time held gas lamps, candles and other primitive lighting, and are now outfitted with electric bulbs. Ashen remains darken the walls just above the sconces.

Although the Vatican contains the largest collection of ancient sculpture in the world, not a statue is to be seen. There is no carpeting here. One walks on the same white marble floor others have walked on for centuries through a beautiful white marble tunnel. A few hi-backed chairs ran along the wall and a mahogany desk greeted me as I entered the building. A guard sat there.

I was required to sign in and asked for my passport. Marcinkus was permitted to enter on sight. He told me persons of rank and those who cared for the papal household were not required to sign in; they were free to come and go as they pleased. This included maintenance workers who lived elsewhere in Vatican City.

Toward the far end of the corridor was the only hint of sculpture, an arched framework of cherubs which housed a grand white marble staircase leading straight up to an imposing door—this one more golden than bronze. Above the door was the papal coat of arms.

A Swiss Guard stood at the golden door.

He pressed a button and the door slid open. We followed him into what appeared to be a small vestibule. Yet, as we entered, I realized we were not in an apartment at all, but in an elevator. Here the stark white marble had come to an end and the gold and the frescos began.

Looking up toward the ceiling—if it were not for the size of the elevator—I would not know where I was. For there were the frescos of the heavens above which to the eye of the novice were every bit as magnificent as were those which looked down from the ceiling of the Sistine Chapel. I touched the shimmering white marble walls because they were so perfectly pristine, I thought them artificial.

I asked the bishop jokingly, if this elevator also went down. He was quick to respond that this particular elevator only goes up.

He told me there was another one at the other end of the building that went down. A matching golden elevator door was at the rear of the Vatican bank. It serviced the basement and the first, second and third floors of the building that housed some of the Curia cardinals, but did not extend to the fourth floor—the Papal Apartment.

It was a short ride. Exiting the elevator, I heard water gushing in the distance as if someone had left water running in a giant tub. Above our heads, a striking blue and golden leaded glass skylight peered down on the elevator which resembled an ornate golden birdcage sitting on the white marble floor—its golden dome cleverly concealing its mechanisms. Just to our left, a grand white marble staircase was crowned by a matching skylight of leaded glass.

Marcinkus told me the stairway was there to permit one to go from floor to floor without using the elevator. In the days before elevators it had been all that was there.

A guard sat at a desk—a match of the one that was on the first floor. I mentioned they must have gotten two for the price of one.

Marcinkus told me: "A changing of the palace guards takes place every three hours as the clock strikes twelve, three, six, nine and then twelve again. A guard has no authority to leave his post no matter what the needs. Not even a trip to the restroom is permitted.

"We are in the Papal Apartment. We call it the 'third loggia.' Its nineteen rooms occupy the entire top floor. Six people live here, the Pope, his valet and the four nuns who run the place."

He pointed to stairs just behind the guard. "These lead to the attic. The Pope's secretaries have their rooms there. There are two dozen other attic rooms, a few of which from time to time are occupied by nuns and the others are reserved for cardinals should the need for a conclave arise—those they paint horror pictures of in the press."

Turning from the guard, he opened a beautifully carved door with angels at its top poking spears down toward demons at its bottom.

As we entered, though there was no one there, he whispered: "This is the Pope's chapel. It is restricted to male members of the clergy living in the building." I later learned when Luciani arrived he extended this privilege to anyone who lived in the building including the nuns; a policy that was reversed when John Paul II took over.

Luciani never said Mass here. Rather he would assign the task to young priests who were studying in the seminary and serve as their acolyte. He would kneel before the priest, a practice which caused the priest to tremble. He would tell the young man: "You must not be afraid. In the eyes of Christ, all His children are equal."

The chapel ceiling boasted a magnificent blue, red and golden leaded glass rendering of *The Resurrection*. The room was entirely of marble as if we were enclosed in a giant sarcophagus. Running along the sides were wall sculptures—*The Stations of the Cross*.

Ten rows of four beautifully carved red velvet chairs with matching kneelers—two on each side of the aisle—ran the chapel's length. Up front, in the center facing the altar, was the papal throne—*The Lord's Prayer* carved in Latin on its black leather back.

A life-sized figure of Christ on a wooden cross set before a huge slab of copper colored marble served as a backdrop for the altar.

As we returned to the rear of the chapel, three beautiful arched stained glass windows rose up from the floor. I asked Marcinkus if they were by Chagall as they were predominately blue and reminded me of the ones at Chartres. He told me they were by someone else, someone whom I had never heard of and no longer recall.

He took me to a corner. A half-dozen or so golden chalices sat on a small table. "There are more than five thousand of these in Vatican City. Many are studded with diamonds, rubies, emeralds and pearls. Any one of them could buy the building we are standing in."

To one side of the windows was a small door. "The chapel is built here on the roof—an addition to the original building."

We walked through a tunnel of overhead latticework laced with vines set in a manicured roof garden. We continued along the St. Peter's Square side of the building and then turned toward the rear of the building where the tunnel took one last turn which dead-ended at the side wall of the chapel. A metal box was affixed to the wall.

"This is a part of a system that controls the roving night guard. He carries a key and must clock in at specific times and places or an alarm will go off in the control station. For security reasons, this guard has no regular schedule and might show up anytime.

"There are boxes located throughout Vatican City. In order to reach this one, the guard must pass by the guard at the apartment entrance and pass through the chapel onto the roof—places the apartment guard is not permitted to go lest he abandon his post."

As we retraced our way back to the door, it was clear the only access to the apartment from the roof was through the chapel door in full view of the perpetual guard at the entrance to Papal Apartment.

The Papal Apartment

Returning to the apartment, we passed by the guard and proceeded down a marble corridor. The sound of water gushing grew louder as we headed down its length. Like the corridor on the first floor, it was lined with bulb-outfitted ancient wall sconces. It was roofed in by an arched ceiling which rose at its pinnacle thirty feet above us.

Unlike the ground floor, it was a bit cooler. Marcinkus told me, that during the reign of John XXIII a service building was added along the rear of the palace building and the adjoining building of San Damasus together with units which cooled all three floors of the Papal Palace and the corresponding floors of San Damasus.

He was quick to add: "It never really worked in this old building. In summer months it gets unbearably hot here in the *third logia*."[1]

The addition housed a fire escape and elevator which entrances were concealed behind the altar in the chapel. It had a ground floor entrance which access was limited to Swiss Guards and maintenance workers. Yet, anyone coming from the service building would have to pass through the chapel and by the guard to access the apartment.

We proceeded past two sets of wide open baroque doors on our left—a vast room lined with provincial furniture—mostly hi-backed chairs arranged in a half-dozen sitting areas. "This is the salon—the papal living room—the reason the doors are always open."

Further down, we came to a set of richly carved doors on our left. "Here is the office of a pope's secretaries. Like those of the salon, its windows look out on the River Tiber. It includes a makeshift operating room where Paul had his prostate operation. It still serves that purpose for men-of-the-cloth living here. Or, God forbid, should any of them require embalming."

←   ←   ←   ←
Pope's bedroom & bathroom - secretaries' office - salon - guard
↓   River Tiber   ↓

We came to that point at which the corridor led to two beautifully carved mahogany doors as if they would open to a magnificent cathedral.

"Here are a pope's private rooms. If you were to turn the doorknob, it would open to a small study fronting the papal bedroom to off the left and the Pope's private library off to the right.

"There are no locks on any of the doors in the Papal Apartment. After all, everyone lives in the same house. A guard once stood to the right of this door just twenty feet from where the Pope sleeps. He became a cost reduction when modern technology moved in."

I repeated in a question: "Modern technology moved in?"

"Yes, in 1960, a communication system was installed in the Pope's private quarters. Until then, his only communication with the outside world was a phone and a bell-cord that hung over his bed."

←   ←   ←   ←   ⤶
mother nun - valet quarters - pope's library & study & bedroom
↓ St. Peter's Square ↓

We took a right-turn along the corridor which ran along the front of the building where we came to the valet's apartment and fitting rooms. Marcinkus told me: "By trade, he is a dress designer responsible for the creation and coordination of the Pope's wear.

"If we were to enter and pass through his reception room and open a door at its far end, we would find ourselves surrounded by silk and satin in a tailor shop. His windows look onto the square.

"His secretaries and valet have the most frequent interaction with the Pope—the reason they are located so close to him."

We reached the corner of the building. "Now we come to where the women of the house live. In Vatican City, men outnumber the women by twenty to one. Here at the top, they outnumber the men.

"This door opens to the rooms of the mother nun who runs the place. She looks out at St. Peter's and the San Damasus Courtyard."

There appeared a white marble life-sized statue of the Blessed Mother at the end of the corridor, set in a fountain which explained the running water I heard when the elevator door had first opened.

"Down here on the left, are the private rooms of three of the nuns who care for the residence. Each has a small sitting room, bedroom and bath. They do the cooking and housekeeping for the men of the cloth who live on the three floors of the Papal Palace."

```
_____↑ San Damasus Courtyard  ↑_____.
mother nun qtrs  -  three nuns qtrs - dining room - kitchen - statue
   ↱                      →                →                   →
```

He opened a set of doors. "This is the papal dining room."

An aging wooden table was surrounded by a dozen chairs. An old sideboard stood off to one side and a ragged rug hung on the wall at one end. At the far end was a door that led to the kitchen.

As we reached the statue at the corridor's end, he moved me to one side and pointed to a roving guard box on the wall behind it.

This remained precisely the layout and occupants of the Papal Apartment on the night of John Paul's death.

Marcinkus continued: "Directly under the quarters of the mother nun and those of the valet, is the apartment of the Secretary of State and the Pope's public office which overlook St. Peter's Square.

"Directly under the Pope's bedroom, is the apartment of the Dean of the College of Cardinals, and beneath the secretaries' office and the salon, are the apartments of the Undersecretary of State and the Foreign Minister who have the privilege of living here only because their offices—the Patrimony of the Holy See and the Council of Public Affairs—are on the lower floors.

"There is a boardroom on the first floor where they figure out how to avoid the problems of the Church," he laughed.

Later the bishop described the Pope's private rooms.

He looked up from St. Peter's Square and pointed to the top row of windows. "These windows, third, fourth and fifth from the right hand corner of the top floor are a pope's private library located directly above his office—the largest rooms in the building. Visitors who visit a pope often find themselves in this room. Its focal point is Da Vinci's *Ascension,* one of the most valuable paintings on earth.

"The window—second from the upper right hand corner—is a pope's private study. Had we opened the doors to his chambers, we would have entered into this room set up as a reception area with an antique desk and chairs. As I have said, this room serves as a vestibule to his library to one side and his bedroom to the other side.

"There is a sixteenth century bathroom here used by visitors. There is also a door to the secretaries' office which allows him direct access to his secretaries without passing through the main corridor.

Marcinkus told me: "As the study is used as a reception area for dignitaries visiting a pope's library, one room—and one room only—is the private domain of the leader of the largest church in the world." He described the bedroom in such great detail that if a roach had been sitting on a windowsill, he wouldn't have missed it.

The papal bedroom

"The window at the top right corner is the Pope's bedroom.

"Around the corner are two more windows which look out over Rome's baroque district. At night they resemble the glowing eyes of a huge pumpkin. When he stays up late Paul's bedroom windows—the highest in the Vatican—are the only lights on in the palace; always reported in the press the next day—no privacy at the top.

"As one enters the bedroom, one passes by a massive mahogany armoire which houses the Pope's everyday attire—his regal attire is stored in the valet's quarters down the hall. There are no closets in the Papal Apartment as it was built long before the time of closets.

"In the corner to the right of the window that looks out onto the square is a white marble statue of Christ by Bernini fronted by a red velvet kneeler. A perpetual red votive candle burns before the statue.

Murder by the Grace of God

"In the corner to the other side of the window, is a sitting area—a sixteenth century sofa and matching chairs share an overly ornate marble coffee table. On a side table is a white antique phone.

"Down a short corridor is a pope's private bath. As large as is a typical living room it is modern and has fittings of marble bathrooms found in presidential suites of five-star hotels. Until 1965, the space it now occupies was used as a private dining room."

Marcinkus hesitated... "That is, when they work. In addition to ongoing problems with its cooling system, the palace building is plagued by aging plumbing and wiring."

When John Paul I moved in, he had exercise equipment installed including a bench press and a treadmill in this bathroom.

"The papal bed is dominated by a bronze headboard.

"At its top center is a golden crucifix flanked on either side by threatening feline gargoyles which protect the Pope from evil spirits while he sleeps. The bed is outfitted with new mattresses with each changing of a pope, yet, the headboard has remained the focal point of the bedroom since the early twentieth century when elevators made possible the relocation of the papal residence to this building.

The strange set of circumstances that caused three men to sleep in the great bed in the Papal Apartment in the fall of 1978

"A red velvet bell cord hanging just above the pillows is wired to the guard's desk at the entrance to the corridor which leads to the chambers. If pulled, it would ring loud enough to wake the dead.

"At one time this was a pope's only contact with the outside world. But, as I have mentioned, modern technology stepped in.

"Nightstands flank either side of the bed.

"The one on the left serves as a communication center. There are buttons to the guard, to his secretary's offices and bedrooms, to the valet's rooms, to the kitchen, and to the mother nun's apartment. Another is wired to the secretary of state's office and bedroom.

"One more—a red button. The one reserved for emergencies. It activates a flashing red light in the corridor outside his quarters and buzzes the guard stationed at the entrance to the Papal Apartment."

This is the bedroom as it was the night of John Paul's death.

There was an electronic unit allowing him access to six people: his two secretaries, his valet, the nun who ran his household, his secretary of state and the guard who sat at a desk just sixty feet from where the Pope sat up in bed reading his papers.

Then there was the bell cord—rarely used. Yet, had he pulled it, everyone would have run out of the building.

Pope Villot

Marcinkus also took me on a tour of the second and third floors of the palace. As we passed Jean Villot's quarters, he told me at one time a proposal was made to move the secretary of state's quarters to a more remote part of Vatican City, particularly in that Jean Villot was both Secretary of State and the Cardinal Camerlengo.

The term of a Secretary of State comes to an end when a Pope dies. Yet, at that time the Secretary of State formed a commission with the Cardinal Camerlengo which acted as the Interim Pope.

During the interim period—though their primary duty is to guide the conclave—they had the full authority of a pope.

If an election were to stalemate for months, they had the power—should the need arise—to make changes to doctrine subject to confirmation by the College. This included the authority to change the rules of election. It also included unrestricted authority to order an autopsy of a pope's body if deemed necessary.

Jean Villot was only one of two cardinals to ever hold both the Secretary of State and Cardinal Camerlengo positions. He was one of only two cardinals to possess the sole powers of an Interim Pope in one man. Eugenio Pacelli (Pius XII) was the other.

Of the lower floors, I recall the restrooms most keenly. Bathe in gold and priceless works of art, the most striking was the famous *Raphael Bathroom* with trappings worth a king's ransom.

At lunch, I told Marcinkus of the great white wine Jack and I had enjoyed that afternoon at the village wedge café in Vittorio Veneto. He agreed, "As we priests change wine into the blood of Christ, so does the little wedge café turn wine into the blood of gods."

As we walked back to his office, he told me I now knew more about the Papal Palace than did the CIA and KGB combined. That was the last time I saw him.

It would not be the last I heard from him. Years later, he would to pick up a copy of my book in a Phoenix bookstore and call me.

Those inside the palace

On the night of John Paul's death, besides the Pope, there were six people in the Papal Apartment—the perpetual guard at its entrance, the mother nun together with the three nuns who slept along the San Damasus Courtyard side of the building, and the Pope's secretary Lorenzi who was sleeping in the secretaries' office while his attic rooms were being painted. The only private rooms unoccupied were those of the valet who was away on funeral leave.

Other than these, anyone gaining access to the Pope's bedroom, whether one came up the stairs or elevator or the fire escape through the chapel or down the attic stairs would have to pass by the guard.

On the floor below, were three Mafia family members: Carlo Confalonieri, Agostino Casaroli and Giuseppe Caprio. Confalonieri was of the Mafia family of the same name. Casaroli and Caprio were cousins in the Gambino family. In 1990, after Casaroli and Caprio retired, the Pope severed the Vatican's relationship with the Mafia; no cardinal has ever officiated at a Mafia family funeral since.

There was a fourth—the French cardinal Jean Villot.

John Magee was in his attic rooms up over the Pope's bedroom, accessible only by stairs in full view of the guard who sat at a desk at the entrance to the apartment. Three additional nuns were sleeping in rooms in the attic on the San Damasus side of the building.

This gives us another falsehood in the corrected Vatican release of October 10, 1978: **"We wish to correct our statement, it was the**

Pope's secretary Magee who discovered the Pope's body. The Pope was first discovered by the nun who delivered his coffee at the usual time. When she sensed something wrong she summoned Magee...'

In order for the nun to summon Magee—who she barely knew—she would have to pass by Lorenzi—who she had lived with for two years—who was sleeping twenty feet from where the Pope sat up in his bed, and pass by the guard in a time of emergency—a Swiss guard in addition to being a human fighting machine is a paramedic.

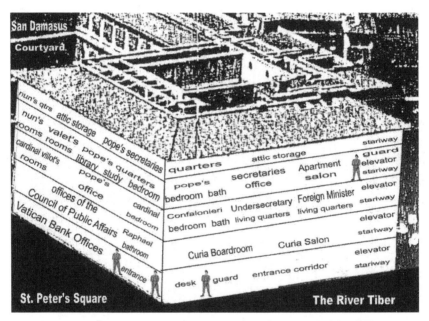

layout and occupants of the Papal Palace September 28, 1978

Those outside the palace

Could anyone outside the palace gain access to the bedroom?

For my knowledge of the interior of the palace, I must draw entirely upon my visit forty years ago, as they certainly wouldn't let me in there today. Yet, my recollection of its exterior is more recent.

I took one of those helicopter tours over Vatican City.

As the helicopter passed over the rear of the building, I struck on what I thought was much more than just a possibility. I slipped the pilot twenty bucks and asked him if he could make a closer pass. He told me he would not go closer, but that he would go around once again. He pointed to two guards who were stationed atop the roof of the service building that adjoined the rear of the palace.

He told me the tripods outside the shack were not telescopes. They could take down a helicopter in seconds. He was right. As we made the pass, both guards moved toward the tripods. He told me they were added after the assassination attempt on John Paul II.

When we came out over the side of the building, I noticed a row of iron fixtures running from the ground at the rear corner of the building to the top floor running all the way to the Pope's bedroom.

At one time, a catwalk extended from these windows to a fire escape which ran down the rear of the building. They had been painted to blend in with the building. Yet, they were there.

I had to be certain the fire escape was not there in 1978.

I toured the bookshops in Rome. In a little shop on the Via Pomezia, I found a 1963 picture of the palace—the year Paul was elected. The catwalk ran right up to the Pope's bedroom window.

They had been retained as a secondary means of escape when the service building had been added. This made sense as the corridor running through the apartment dead-ended at the statue; smoke coming from its entrance would block one from reaching the exit.

I had a momentary rush of adrenaline and despair. If the catwalk had been there the night John Paul died, anyone had the opportunity to commit the evil deed. Luckily, I found other pictures dated in the early seventies. The fire escape was gone. We can eliminate it as a means of access. Yet, one must still consider the roof.

The roof of the building adjoins the roof of San Damascus and its roof adjoins the roof of the next building and so forth. Yet, as we have said, anyone gaining access via the roof would have had to enter the Papal Apartment via the chapel door in full view of the guard at the entrance to the corridor leading to the pope's quarters.

We can conclude for now, only six people had direct access to John Paul the night he died—the mother nun Vincenza, the three nuns, the Pope's secretary Lorenzi and the apartment guard. Eight others living on the other floors would have to elude the guard.

We have described the private abode of popes of the past: a single room with sparse air conditioning with a single bathroom that does not always work and very little privacy—everyone in Rome knows when the lights go on and off. Just where does the pope live now?

The Sanctae Marthae Palace Hotel

The Vatican's five star hotel is the Sanctae Marthae Palace built at a cost of $20 million at a time a comparable hotel cost $10 million—the excessive cost owed to opulent marble bathrooms and exquisite mahogany floors—no synthetic materials.

In 1996, John Paul II—fed up with the air conditioning, wiring and plumbing problems of the Papal Palace—engaged his friend—Pittsburg gambling-boss John Connelly—to build Sanctae Marthae Palace on the guise it was being built for future conclaves.

Whereas, it did provide suites to accommodate conclaves, the plans included provisions for an apartment. Rumors surfaced he was building the opulent hotel for himself. As a result he never moved and was condemned to bear the mechanical problems and lack of privacy of the Papal Palace for the rest of his life.

Today, Francis occupies a three room suite formerly reserved for visiting heads of state and dignitaries. He chose the suite over the apartment for its palatial view of the Vatican Gardens and its bath includes an oversized whirlpool tub.

A marble staircase to the right leads to the papal suite

There is nothing wrong with a pope living in the lap of luxury. After all, he is a head of state. What is wrong is to deceive the public for political reasons he is living in poverty. He has, in fact, sacrificed gilt and gold for an abode of far greater comfort than enjoyed by his predecessors. An abode built with casino money. If one reasons the gambling industry preys on the poor—a palace built by the poor.

Its 106 suites are outfitted with furnishings characteristic of other five star hotels and royal palaces.

a sitting room in a standard suite

During conclaves widescreen televisions and all communication equipment are removed from the hotel.

As cameras are not permitted in the papal suite—other than the statue of Christ by Bernini relocated from the Papal Palace—its art collection and furnishings are unknown.

The polarization of popes

Francis' great political[1] acumen is vital to controlling the minds of his congregation. He bills himself as **'a pope for the poor,'** yet—for twenty years—he led the charge against countless social programs intended to help the poor. He believes charity is the option of the individual in a rich and poor society and encourages the rich man drop his wealth into the poor box. Though he has Christ's strategy on his side, one knows it has never worked. What's more, he is a bitter enemy of contraception—the driving force behind poverty.

He washes women's feet for photo-shoots,[2] yet he conditions children from an early age: **'little boys are better than little girls.'**

At the other extreme is John Paul: **"Charity is an excuse for individual compassion in a selfish world. It is the duty of society and should not be the option its citizens."** He would overrule man-made doctrine—'little boys are better than little girls'—and ordain a woman.[3]

---

1 'Political' = making things out to be the opposite of what they really are, to one's political advantage
2 The media has always been notified before each of these events, the reason they are widely televised

Chapter 24

Providential Coincidence

"Mother church will cease to be the cause of the world's problems and rather will begin to be the answer to them."

John Paul I

Nevertheless, before we go on. Let me tell you of what became of Jack; my friend Jack.

After Luciani became Patriarch of Venice, Jack was transferred from the Veneto country to Milan where he operated as a 'ghost' lieutenant in the *priest-worker movement* under Cardinal Colombo until 1977 when he was moved to Rome.

On the second day following John Paul's death, a small notice appeared in a Rome newspaper:

> "The body of a hit-run victim in a yellow shirt and tan shorts was found on the Viale Vaticano near the Vatican Museum entrance this morning. Police are looking for witnesses and someone to identify the man believed to be an American tourist in his thirties."[1]

...halfway between a *Silver Star* and a *Purple Heart*

As I drove into the funeral home parking lot I thought of my last visit with Jack—one of the few times I had seen him since the day he had stood at the pinnacle of secondary school life rendering the coveted address on graduation day. Perhaps, he should have used the words Lincoln had used so modestly at Gettysburg: ". . . the world will little note, nor long remember what is said here . . ."

Unlike Lincoln, Jack would have been telling the truth.

I thought of Jack's letter in which he had told me of John Paul's chat with the Curia cardinals a few weeks earlier: '...**Mother Church will cease to be the cause of many of the world's problems and rather will begin to be the answer to them.**'

As I stood before him, I couldn't see him, for the mutilation had been much too terrible to allow the remains to be viewed.

As I began to realize he was now still, I recalled what he once was, and I prayed he had had time to have completed his work. At the same time, I thought of Piccolo. I knew he had not had time to complete his work—which has caused me to write this book.

As I reached over and lay my hand on the lid of the coffin just above his heart, to confirm to myself this was forever goodbye, a tear came up out of my heart, and started from the crevice of my eye. As it crept toward the lid, I glanced, first, to the right, then to the left, and, again, to the right, and, finally, to the left, once more. I held it there, hovering on the edge of the cliff.

As I turned to the audience, waves of applause moved forward in muffled cries, sighs of desperation and hopeless sobs. I went to the one who sat in the front row and introduced myself. I shared with her a part of my life, which had been a part of her son's life.

She reached into her purse and brought forth a small package. Placing it in my hand, "Jack told me if anything was to happen to him, he wanted you to have this. We gave it to him for his ordination, the most important day of his life."

Later in the funeral home parking lot, I looked at the package.

It was postmarked '**Centrale Poste de Roma**' and dated a few days before the Pope's death. It had never been opened. Jack had called his mother sometime between then and now.

I was puzzled it was not postmarked '**Poste Citta Del Vaticano**' as had been true of his correspondence to me since he had been in the Vatican.

Nevertheless, I opened the box.

It was six o'clock...

...exactly halfway between a *Silver Star* and a *Purple Heart*.[2]

1 *Roma La Repubblica* 2 Oct 78
2 Jack's uncle's *Silver Star* and *Purple Heart* remain in the possession of the author today

Chapter 25

'Operation Pigeon' to the 'Grace of God'

John Paul I was found dead in his bed sitting up reading papers held upright in his hands shortly after 4:30AM September 29, 1978.[1]

In its official release, the Vatican claimed heart attack.[2]

The medical world responded: "the Pope could not have possibly died of a heart attack given his medical history, his family history and the position he was found holding papers upright in the hands."[3]

A few days later Vatican Radio explained the Vatican's position: "John Paul was able to retain the papers upright in his hands in the midst of a massive heart attack *by the grace of God...*"[4]

1978: On the heels of John Paul's death, Mario Zottola & Jesus Ramon Pena published *They Have Murdered the Pope: Operation Pigeon* driven by what were the most visible motives for murder at the time: John Paul's threat of economic movement toward Marxism in the west and liberal reformation within the Church. The book—a novel—came remarkably close to the truth in its fictional creation of 'Operation Pigeon'—a blend of curia cardinals and foreign powers and the disappearance of Vatican bank money in Central America.[5]

1984: David Yallop's *In God's Name* made the case for murder, employing witness and medical testimony to demonstrate the Pope could not have died of natural causes. He argued archbishops Marcinkus, Cody and Villot conspired in 'The Vatican Bank Scandal' to the financial gain of three Mafia types Calvi, Gelli and Sindona. John Paul was murdered because an audit he ordered of the Vatican Bank would have uncovered the 'scandal' transactions.[6]

1985: to discredit Yallop, the Vatican fabricated a biographical-brief creating a man who had been on the brink of death all of his life:

> "...When born the midwife baptized him because she thought he would die... as a child, malnourished... skin and bones as if he had survived Treblinka... always frail, confined in hospitals and in and out of sanatoriums over and over again all of his life..."

The fabrication continues into his papacy:

> "...Midway into his papacy he took possession of the Basilica St. John the Lateran. Attending bishops were intensely concerned of his deteriorating physical condition... he had noticeably suffered immense loss of weight... deep dark circles ran under his eyes. He did not stand in the car for the crowds on the way to the basilica because his legs had become so swollen he could not stand..." [7]

The truth—as we will establish—he was in impeccable health. When he became a cardinal in 1973, he was asked his secret of success:

> "Always on the job. From the time I entered grade school in 1917 until I graduated from seminary in 1935, I never missed a day. By divine providence tonsils and adenoids cropped up on holiday."[8]

The photo below 'right' was taken on September 23, 1978, the day John Paul took possession of the Basilica St. John the Lateran.

always a picture of good health

The Boy Luciani   The Priest Luciani   The Bishop Luciani   The Pope Luciani

Nevertheless, this fraud was published by various religious orders in Catholic countries under various titles by unnamed authors to mask its source: an anonymous priest in Italy, an anonymous monk in France, an anonymous Jesuit in Brazil, an anonymous missionary in India, an anonymous nun in the United States...

Most biographies, except for this book and Yallop's *In God's Name*, are sourced from this fraud. They annihilate the man he actually was to support his canonization in a conservative Church.

He was baptized in the church of San Giovanni Battista on October 19, 1917. Poorly-researched authors copy word-for-word: 'the midwife baptized him immediately because he was so frail she feared he would die. All his life he would suffer from poor health...'[9]

He did have four operations—today outpatient procedures but at the time requiring inpatient visits: tonsils at eleven and adenoids at fifteen—routine at the time for children; gallstones and hemorrhoids at fifty-two.[10] All in all, nothing unusual for a man of sixty-five.

> ne talked of love and hunger and of the sick to the audience of over 10,000. Conveying his love to the ailing, the 65-year-old healthy-looking pontiff said: "The pope has been hospitalized eight times and has had four operations."
>
> Washington Post, September 27, 1978

In 1936, he spent six weeks in a sanatorium/hospital for HAPE (High Altitude Pulmonary Edema) misdiagnosed as TB. *

In 1945, he spent a night in a Belluno hospital in connection with a broken nose suffered in a soccer game.

In 1947, he spent two nights in a Trento hospital for suspected HAPE in connection with an extended climb on Mount Pagenella.

In 1975, he spent a night in a Mestre clinic for a retina problem.

* This life threatening bout caused him to be overly concerned with his health. One might tab him a combination health nut and hypochondriac... insisting on tests well beyond those normally performed in twice-a-year physical exams. Going so far as to have hired a nurse—Vincenza—as his housekeeper. Yet, it never deterred his mountain climbing activities.

He died short of his genetic promise:

	age	per death certificate
Maternal grandmother	93	leukemia
Maternal grandfather	88	tuberculosis
Paternal grandmother	67	accident
Paternal grandfather	86	cirrhosis
Mother	72*	breast cancer
Father	80	prostate cancer
Brother**	91	pneumonia
Sister	89	inoperable tumor
Albino Luciani	65	unknown

* Birth on tombstone: 1879 vs. birth certificate: 1876. **a second brother died in infancy.

1987: John Paul II engaged John Cornwell to write *A Thief in the Night*. In exchange for access to Vatican witnesses, Cornwell agreed he would conclude death due to pulmonary embolism.

Cornwell proves the first bank scandal transactions took place under the reign of John Paul II thereby demolishing Yallop's motive the audit ordered by the 33-day Pope could have uncovered them.

Yet, in concluding the Pope died of an embolism, he ignores the testimony of his own expert witness—renowned cardiologist Francis C. Roe: "I've witnessed numerous embolism deaths and never known any of them to die unresponsive to what was happening to them."[11]

Whereas, it is possible for an embolus to pass through the lungs painlessly, in a massive pulmonary embolism that blocks the main artery of the lungs, one experiences acute pleuritic pain on a par with that of a massive heart attack. He would have dropped his papers.[12]

1990: Avro Manhattan reasoned the conspiracy involved much more than individuals; it involved nations. He concluded: 'the conspiracy that masterminded the Great Vatican Bank Scandal was the same conspiracy that plotted the murder of John Paul I.'[13]

Manhattan's thesis makes a lot of sense. History tells us clearly the bank scandal could not have happened had John Paul lived:

> In his papacy, he was on a fast track to rid the world of poverty. He would make his mark in Central America. He encouraged all Catholics to support the revolutionaries—to share in God's province is God's will. From there a redistribution of wealth society would spread to the Condor Nations of Latin America—those ruled by ruthless dictators—annihilating greed in its wake.

Just the opposite was true of John Paul II:

> The Opus Dei-backed Polish Pope rose up as the great ally of the coalition of the United States and ruthless dictators in their mission to crush the *revolution of the poor* in Central America.
>
> According to court records which tried the Great Vatican Bank Scandal, the first funds were raised from European investors on Nov 1, 1978—thirty-three days after John Paul I's death.
>
> In all, John Paul II sequestered $1.3 billion, ($12 billion today) funneling most of it to Central America where it disappeared.[14]

John Paul II toured every country in Central America, telling the people to stop supporting the revolutionaries. For the most part, the revolution of the poor failed, returning the isthmus to poverty.

Under Paul VI and John Paul I, *Liberation Theology* had thrived in Latin America. Under John Paul II, it died a natural death.

Under Paul VI and John Paul I, the *Communist Party* thrived in the polls in Italy. Under John Paul II, it died a natural death.

What's more, Avro Manhattan's premise is consistent with the first thing that came to mind when one first whispered the word 'murder' in the wake of the 33-day Pope's sudden death: John Paul's threat of economic movement toward Marxism in the western world which called the CIA to action, and his threat of liberal reformation within the Church which rallied Opus Dei and Curial cardinals to its side.

2013: *Murder by the Grace of God* proves Avro Manhattan's thesis:

The conspiracy that masterminded the Great Vatican Bank Scandal was the same conspiracy that plotted the murder of John Paul I.

Nevertheless, I owe a debt of gratitude to my predecessors. Had Pena and Zottola not set the stage, had Yallop not revived his legacy, had Cornwell not told the truth, and, most of all, had Manhattan not struck on the plot; I could have never written this book.

> Author's note: In 1973, he returned his 'attendance' certificates to the grade school in Carnal de Argo and to the Feltre and Belluno seminaries--on display until Yallop wrote his book in 1984. [15]

1 *ANSA News,* 29 Sep 78 Italy's most reliable news service
2 *Radio Vaticana* 29 Sep 78
3 *La Repubblica* 1 Oct 78
4 *Radio Vaticana* 10 Oct 78
5 *Han Asesinado Al Papa Operacion Paloma* Dec 78
6 *In God's Name,* David Yallop 1984
7 the document was prefaced by an imprimatur—the Vatican's seal the work has been censored of the truth. The 'imprimatur' is cleverly deleted by authors who copy the fabrication into their 'biographies.'
8 *Messaggero Mestre* 10 Mar 73 - *Nostro Veneto* 11 Mar 73
9 The certificate is dated Oct 19, 1912. Had the midwife baptized him the church would have dated it Oct 17, 1912. Per canon law, post-baptism by a priest is not baptism; one cannot be baptized twice.
10 These operations were performed in the Padua general hospital July '23 and July '27 and in the Pordenone Hospital April '64 and August '64
11 *A Thief in the Night,* John Cornwell 1989 pg 321
12 *Mosby's Medical Dictionary* or any other approved by the American Medical Association
13 *The Dollar and the Vatican* 1988 & *Murder in the Vatican* 1985 by Avro Manhattan
14 *Murder by the Grace of God* proves the money went to John Paul II's ally the Contras
15 *Messaggero Mestre* 28 Jul 73

Chapter 26

I have some cards for you...wanna play?

'In God's Name' David Yallop, 1984
'A Thief in the Night' John Cornwell, 1989

I have promised some scenarios as to what caused three men to sleep in the great bed in the papal apartment in the fall of nineteen hundred and seventy-eight. Here they are for you to choose from—all of the possible ways in which John Paul could have died.

Begin the investigation

In determining the true circumstances of the Pope's death, we must first separate the facts, from the probabilities, from the possibilities, from the rumors, from the myths. That we will do now.

There is only one absolute fact of his death agreed to by all witnesses including the Vatican release, the nun who found him, his secretaries, the embalmers and all others brought to his room:

The bed lamp was on and he was sitting up in his daytime clothes wearing his glasses reading papers held upright in his hands.

This is the starting point of any investigation. The position the body was found is the only known circumstance of his death.

There is no heart attack, no matter how sudden, that would not have allowed him time to pull the bell cord or press a service button to summon help. Or, for that matter, a heart attack so painless, it would have left him sitting up in his bed with his papers held upright in his hands. Unless, of course, one accepts the Vatican hypothesis, **"...he was able to retain papers upright in his hands in the midst of a massive heart attack by the grace of God."**[1]

It does not take a world-renowned cardiologist to tell one this. Anyone would know it. Yet, most Catholics believe the 33-day Pope died of a heart attack so sudden, he was unable to pull the cord which hung at his right shoulder or press an emergency button an arm's length to his left. So painless, he was able to retain the position he died in sitting up in bed with papers upright in his hands.

Analysis of death

How did John Paul die? There are only four ways anyone can die. One dies of natural causes. One commits suicide. One dies of accident. One is murdered. There are no other ways one can die.

Just what are the possibilities in John Paul's case?

Natural causes

That the Pope did not die of a heart attack does not necessarily mean he could not have died of some other natural cause.

Here we have powerful evidence that points to only one possible natural cause. The position which he was found points to a cause of death both instantaneous and painless—otherwise he would have reacted to the pain and dropped his papers. The only natural cause that can result in instant death without pain is stroke.

There are two kinds of fatal stroke—intra-cerebral and ischemic.

Intra-cerebral stroke or cerebral hemorrhage—bursting of blood vessels in the brain—can kill one instantly. Yet, it can be ruled out as it is accompanied by enormous throbbing head pain. He would have dropped his papers. We can eliminate this as a cause of death.[2]

Conversely, ischemic stroke—blockage of the carotid arteries in the neck carrying oxygen to the brain—is painless. Yet, an ischemic stroke is not instantaneous. It graduates through the body from top to bottom and takes several minutes—most often hours—to progress.[3]

Early warning signs are dizziness followed by numbness in the face, loss of speech, unable to grasp with either the left or right hand.

Even a massive bilateral stroke—infinitely rare—in the first few minutes affects only one hemisphere—one side of the body—which would have allowed him time to sound the alarm with the other extremity; unless, of course, he had been sleeping.[4] Yet, we know he was awake and reading. He would have had more than enough time to have acted; normally a three-hour window to seek help.

What makes stroke a long shot in the Pope's case is his relatively low blood pressure—as surefire a prevention of both heart attack and stroke that exists.[5] Blood viscosity and arterial passage instrumental to stroke are normally hereditary.[6] In his family tree, from his great grandparents to his siblings, to his cousins and nieces and nephews, not a single one has ever been known to have suffered a stroke.

Yet, what nails the lid shut on the supposition he may have died of stroke is the Vatican doctor who pronounced him dead.

Doctor Buzzonetti did not suggest stroke. Unlike heart attack, in the case of an unwitnessed death, a doctor can examine the condition a corpse is found and eliminate stroke as a possibility.

If John Paul had showed any signs symptomatic of stroke, the doctor certainly would have struck on it. Particularly, in that it would have headed off all of the rumors that have surfaced since. But, he did not. So one knows John Paul did not die of stroke.

Even without medical expertise, everyone who went to his room knew he had not died of stroke—the reason stroke has never been a consideration in all the investigations of his death which have been spent since: John Paul was awake and reading when he died.

Myocardial Infarction vs. Pulmonary Embolism

Here, again, one must dispel the myths.

At first, the Vatican claimed he died of **'myocardial infarction to the heart.'** After the Vatican's supposition was demolished by the medical world, the second Vatican release claimed John Paul had been suffering of 'low blood pressure and swollen legs' to plant the seed for what is its claim today: 'a massive embolism to the lungs.'

In 1984, David Yallop published *In God's Name,* and, in 1989, John Cornwell published *A Thief in the Night*. These bestsellers still reign, today, as the premier books concerning John Paul's death.

Both these men are reputable world-renowned journalists. One can trust what they reported was the truth. One knows this for a more definitive reason. Their witnesses were alive after their books were published and none of them challenged their witness. That is, except David Yallop's interviews with Roberto Calvi and Sister Vincenza—both in their graves when his book exploded in the press.

Yet, neither Yallop nor Cornwell subjected their witnesses to the scrutiny of a court of law. That we will do now.

For the most part, both interviewed the same witnesses of the Pope's death. Yet, they came up with entirely different conclusions.

In 1984, Yallop suggested murder. In 1989, Cornwell suggested pulmonary embolism. How is this possible? Conflicting testimony:

In 1987, nine years after his death, riled up and under pressure from Yallop in a television interview, an agitated Lorenzi blared out on the spur of the moment: 'John Paul had experienced chest pain.'[7]

In 1988, Cornwell probes Magee for confirmation of Lorenzi's claim. Magee—vague in his recollection—agrees the Pope might have had a 'choking pain.' What's more, he claims he brought it to the attention of Sister Vincenza.[8]

Yet, when questioned by Yallop a few years earlier, Vincenza was adamant there had not been the slightest semblance of pain—one reason her testimony in Yallop's book is the most damaging to the hypothesis the Pope died of natural causes. Of course, she had died in the meantime and Magee knew she was unavailable to Cornwell who discounts her Yallop-testimony as 'delusions of an old nun.'[9]

The embalmers told Italy's most reliable news service ANSA: 'they had been picked up at five-thirty that morning.' Because this caused a problem for their employer—the Vatican—they changed it for Cornwell ten years later '...it may have been closer to dawn.'[10]

Cornwell interviewed one additional witness, Lina Petri.

235

She told Cornwell: "My uncle suffered from low blood pressure. The manner of his death is consistent with pulmonary embolism. One is not aware of death in embolism..." [11]

Lina—John Paul's niece—was a medical intern at the Gemelli Hospital in Rome when the Pope died. One would wonder if she had missed class on the day pulmonary embolism was discussed.

To support her supposition, Lina claims the Pope's secretaries are making up stories that the pope experienced pain: 'It's odd it took them nine years to come up with this. Such a pain would be consistent with heart attack, but not embolism...' [12]

She is right about Lorenzi and Magee. Both men had been interviewed by dozens of journalists for the past decade and had never mentioned pain at all. This is particularly as strange chest pain would have supported the Vatican's initial claim of heart attack.

Nevertheless, she could not be more wrong about her supposition that her uncle died of embolism. One will not find a cardiologist in the world, today, who has known a patient to be unresponsive to the trauma of death in a massive pulmonary embolism.

This is consistent with the renowned cardiologist Dr. C. Francis Roe—the expert witness the Vatican made available to Cornwell: "I've witnessed many embolism deaths. Yet, I've never seen any of them die unresponsive to what was happening to them." [13]

In the case of a massive myocardial infarction that kills quickly, there is a strangulating pain—a 'Charley horse' to the heart. The heart is technically a muscle. Death can occur in minutes. [14]

In the case of a massive pulmonary embolism that kills quickly, a sharp stabbing pain to the lungs—pleuritic pain—is followed by a period of painful shortness of breath, followed by another period of palpitations, rapid beating of the heart ending in cardiac arrest. [15]

In a massive embolism, death normally occurs within an hour or two. There have been rare cases where death occurs in minutes, yet, these have been limited to patients being treated for the condition. [16]

In even the most instant death due to embolism, John Paul would have been afforded ample time to pull the bell cord or press a service button. He certainly would have dropped his papers. But, he did not.

Eye Embolism vs. Pulmonary Embolism

Lina based her theory on an eye embolism that had occurred a few years earlier.

Both Yallop and Cornwell interviewed Dr. Rama who had treated Luciani for a clot in the left retina. The condition was remedied with mild medication and he was released with no further concern.

Here again, we must apply what the world of medicine knows today. To think an eye embolism could develop into a pulmonary embolism would be as much as to say a man died of pneumonia because he sneezed on a single occasion a few years ago. Though both blood clots, one has absolutely nothing to do with the other.

A retina embolus originates in the throat and is microscopic in nature.[17] On the other hand. a pulmonary embolus originates in the lower extremities and is enormous in size. An embolism that blocks the pulmonary artery—an inch and a quarter in diameter—is as big around as a man's thumb and up to a foot long.[18]

It would not take a world-renowned cardiologist to tell one that a massive pulmonary embolus could not develop in the human body instantly when the patient has had no history of it. Also, that it could move from the legs through the heart to the lungs without the patient being aware of it. Again, one can draw on common sense.

This is precisely the position of the medical community today: though a retina embolus and pulmonary embolus are both clots, one has absolutely nothing to do with the other.[19]

Yes, had Luciani died of a clot to the brain—a microscopic clot that comes up from the throat—one might relate it to the retina problem. Yet, as we have just demonstrated, this was not the case.

This is consistent with a consensus of studies involving about three thousand patients who succumbed to pulmonary embolism; not a single one had a history of retina blockage. A separate study examining seven hundred patients who had succumbed to cerebral hemorrhage found fifteen (2%) had a history of retina blockage.[20]

The great preponderance of those who die of embolism suffer from an impaired gene rendering one a tendency to develop clots.[21] Just as the great preponderance of those who die of heart attack suffer from impaired genes which inhibit the body's capacity to rid the body of excess cholesterol—one-third of the human race.[22]

Too, some drugs—e.g. cancer drugs—can cause an embolus to form. Yet, most often embolism results from inactivity as when a patient is confined for a long time in bed.[23] John Paul was confined to the Vatican vs. being free to roam around Venice.

John Magee told Cornwell that John Paul not only walked on the afternoon before his death but: "...every day, through those thirty-three days, he walked on the roof for two hours."[24]

John Paul's personal physician Dr. Da Ros would confirm this in his interview with Andrea Tornelli in 2003: "Because the Vatican was more confined than Venice, I had advised him in addition to his daily exercises to walk a couple of hours at a brisk pace each day."[25]

Two hours at a normal walking pace—let alone a brisk pace—is six miles. How many people walk six miles a day and suddenly succumb instantly to a sudden circulatory blockage?

Low blood pressure

Yet, Lina is correct about her uncle's low blood pressure.

Luciani's medical records and the testimony of his doctors clearly tell us his blood pressure normally oscillated at about 100 over 60.

When Lina gave her testimony to Cornwell in 1988, low blood pressure was believed to be a contributing factor in heart attack and pulmonary embolism.[26]

Today, low blood pressure is known to be as surefire a prevention of heart attack and embolism that exists.[27]

I will leave it up to providence to decide whether Lina missed class when embolism was discussed or if she was making up stories.

Yet, of all the witnesses interviewed by the world's journalists through the years concerning John Paul's mysterious death, she knew, from her great grandparents to her present day siblings, not one had ever suffered stroke, heart attack or pulmonary embolism.

Anticoagulants

In John Cornwell's *A Thief in the Night,* Lina—to support her theory of embolism—plants the seed that her uncle may have been taking anti-coagulants.

To 'think' John Paul could have been on anticoagulants and no one known of it would boggle the imagination. After all, it would be no secret. Everyone in the Vatican would have known it.

Warfarin—the principal anticoagulant in 1978 as it is today—is a dangerous drug requiring weekly or biweekly viscosity testing lest one risk bleeding to death internally.

Today there are a few anticoagulants that do not require periodic visits to a lab—not available in 1978.

After Cornwell's book was published, the doctor who had treated Luciani for low blood pressure brought the rumor to an abrupt end. Dr. Rama told reporters: '...Luciani's viscosity ran on the thin side; the last thing one would do is prescribe a blood-thinner.'[28]

Dr. Da Ros—Luciani's personal physician for twenty years—confirmed this in his interview with Andrea Tornelli in 2003: 'Albino Luciani had never required anticoagulants anytime in his life.'[29]

'...papers upright in his hands.'

Nevertheless, concerning the most critical evidence determining the question of murder vs. natural causes, each of Cornwell's witnesses confirm the fundamental fact that had been published in the Vatican release '...the papers were held upright in his hands:'

> John Magee's testimony to Cornwell: "There he was, propped up with pillows, his papers still erect in his hands, his face turned to the right in a grin with his spectacles on; he looked intent on what he was reading."[30]

> Lorenzi Diego's testimony to Cornwell: "...He was sitting up in a position like this." Lorenzi imitated a typical reading position pushing his glasses slightly down on his nose. "The light by the bed was on. One would never guess he was dead. The sheets of paper were upright...That is, they had not fallen... I, myself, took the papers out of his hands..."[31]

Both these men confirm Sister Vincenza's description as released to French reporters and ANSA—Italy's most reputable wire service—the day the Pope was found dead:

> "The light was on. He was sitting up in his daytime clothes with his glasses on reading papers held upright in his hands. He

was looking at me. I greeted him, 'Good morning.' He held to a mime position deeply involved in his reading..."[32]

> Lina Petri spent a half-hour alone in the room with the body. Her description is consistent with the others:

"It was as if he was smiling at me. His face showed no sign of suffering... his hands rigid and upright ... there was something strange. He was wearing his daytime clothes...If in bed, why was he wearing his papal smock? ...His sleeves were all torn. Why should they be torn like that? I wondered..."[33]

Lina does not mention the glasses or the papers as she viewed the body four hours after it had been found and they had been removed.

Nevertheless, what is important here is that all parties agree:

...the papers were held upright in his hands

You will not find a cardiologist in the world, who would testify in a court of law today, John Paul could have died of heart attack or pulmonary embolism and not have dropped his papers.

John Cornwell's conclusion

One can speculate Magee—after nine years—added 'pain' to the soup as a condition of his being made a bishop as a prerequisite to the Cornwell interviews. John Magee was made a bishop on March 17, 1987, a short time before his interview with Cornwell.

One can speculate Lorenzi—after nine years—added 'pain' to the soup as a part of his special allegiance to a reigning pontiff required by his order of the Don Orione Brothers; as Lorenzi told Cornwell: "I have taken a vow of obedience. I do anything I am told."[34]

The Cornwell-testimony of these men is completely contradictory to what they had told Yallop a few years earlier, despite there is no record in the press they ever objected to what Yallop had published.

One can say Lina Petri told her stories to pave the way for her uncle's sainthood in a 'chauvinistic-prolife-homophobic' church.

This is not unusual, as there are websites and books published by relatives and others who knew him that annihilate the controversial man he really was for this same reason. One will not find 'God is the Mother' 'contraception' or 'homosexuality' in any of them.

One can trust all of these witnesses were at the mercy of John Paul II. Magee and Lorenzi were clergy and Lina depended on him for her uncle's sainthood. What's more, they were all alive after Cornwell published his book—with the exception noted below—they all verified in the press the witness they had given Cornwell.

Regardless, except for Lina Petri's whim of **'embolism'** and the Lorenzi-Magee tale of **'pain,'** the overwhelmingly weight of John Cornwell's investigation makes the case for murder. Much more so than does Yallop—the reason in my endeavor to arrive at the truth, I quote Cornwell much more than I do Yallop.

Yet, Cornwell ignores what his own expert witness told him at the time and concludes: **'John Paul almost certainly died of embolism.'**

Cornwell goes so far as to offer a hypothesis how the Pope could have suffered an embolism and still be in the position he was found:

> "Magee noticed light coming from beneath the bedroom door at about eleven o'clock at night and entered to investigate. He found the Pope dead on the floor. He roused Lorenzi and the two spent the night reminiscing about John Paul. They dressed him in his daytime clothes reading for the nun to find in the morning."[35]

After *A Thief in the Night* was published, both Lorenzi and Magee denied Cornwell's hypothesis. One knows what they told reporters was true—they would have never placed the spectacles on his nose. Like Vincenza, they knew he did not require them to read.

We know this for another reason. It is canon law that upon a pope's death the Camerlengo is to be summoned at once to tap on the forehead with a silver hammer and repeat three times: 'Are you sleeping Albino?' and destroy the papal seal (Fisherman's Ring).

The overwhelming weight of Cornwell's investigation suggests foul play. One might ask why he would set aside the compelling case he builds for murder and conclude pulmonary embolism.

One could say he did not know at his time, low blood pressure is as surefire prevention of heart attack and embolism that exists.

Yet, even at his time, the medical community told him clearly the Pope could not have possibly died of embolism and retained the papers upright in his hands; the reason he offered his 'hypothesis' Lorenzi and Magee found the Pope dead on his bedroom floor.

There is only one reason John Cornwell would ignore what the medical community was telling him and conclude embolism.

He was an honorable man who had given his word. It had been part of his arrangement with John Paul II—in exchange for access to witnesses he would conclude the 33-day Pope died of embolism.

In 1987, the Polish Pope had personally met with John Cornwell and approved those interviewed. If one gets one's fingers on the first edition of Cornwell's book, the English journalist was not happy he was permitted to interview select witnesses and not all witnesses.

Yet, in that meeting, John Paul II blessed Cornwell's work:

"I want you to know that you have my support and blessing in this work you about to undertake." [36]

John Cornwell's investigation told him the Pope could not have possibly died of embolism and retained his papers in his hands.

It could be he knew the press would follow up on his farfetched hypothesis: Lorenzi and Magee had found the Pope on the floor.

Though he had to conclude otherwise, it could be he wanted the world to know the truth. One will never know.

Yet, what one does know. Given the known circumstances of his death, it is the unconditional consensus of the medical community today John Paul did not die of pulmonary embolism or heart attack. As we shall see in what is yet to come, he died of a more deadly malady: the collaborating and politicking of men.

It is not important to know who took the papers from his hands. All that is important is who put the papers in his hands. Who put the papers in his hands is the same person who placed the glasses on his nose. Someone who did not know he did not require them to read.

Suicide

That he did not pull the bell cord or press a button could have been his intent. There is only one method of suicide that would have not left evidence of foul play for those who found him—poison.

Only two poisons when ingested result in close to instantaneous death: strychnine and cyanide—the reason they have found their way into so many mystery novels. Strychnine can be eliminated as it results in massive convulsions for a few minutes before death.

We have the possibility biting down on a cyanide capsule would have killed him instantly. Yet, none of these possibilities would have left him in the position he was found.

Yet, what closes the lid on suicide is motive.

It had been the coalition of his life-threatening bout with HAPE in 1936 and his driving ambition to live to accomplish his father's mission that had caused him to become the hypochondriac he was; requiring twice-a-year invasive physicals—unusual for a mid-aged man at the time—and engaging a doctor as his closest friend and a nurse as his housekeeper. Albino Luciani feared premature death.

Here was a very purposeful man who had worked all of his life to attain the position he now found himself in. Now he had the power to right the wrongs of the past, to bring an end to bigotry once and for all. Now he was in a position to bring an end to poverty and starvation in the world. That he would take his own life on the brink of the realization of his lifelong ambitions makes no sense at all.

Accident

Again, the position of the body is the clue.

If you can come up with an accident that could have left the body in the position in which it was found you are much more a Sherlock Holmes than I am. Surely, accident was not involved.

Unless, of course, he had been killed by an accident caused by someone's negligence who in covering up for their involvement, sat him up in the position he was found. This would be true if Lorenzi had accidentally killed his master.

Lorenzi? Why Lorenzi?

Of all the men in the world—other than the guard—he was the only one who had unlimited access to the Pope throughout the night.

In his case, he would not even have to pass through the main corridor as a door connected the office where he was sleeping to the Pope's private quarters. Let us consider the possibility.

Dr. Da Ros was emphatic that the only prescription he had issued Luciani still active at the time of the Pope's death was for treatment of the adrenal cortex as part of an energy metabolism program in connection with Luciani's strenuous mountain climbing activities. The injections—Cortiplex B—were given twice a year—toward the end of March and toward the end of September.[37]

Although not required for the medicine involved, one normally refrigerates injection vials. It is likely they were stored in the kitchen refrigerator with other medicine of members of the papal household. Cardinal Confalonieri stored his insulin in this refrigerator and one of the nuns who suffered from a thyroid condition also stored her medicine there. There may have been others.

One might assume Vincenza gave the injections. Yet, that they were given in the area of the buttocks, it is unlikely a nun would have had a pope drop his pants. They were most likely administered by his secretary Lorenzi, he had brought with him from Venice.

It is possible Lorenzi unknowingly injected the Pope with a lethal substance—he had mistakenly taken the wrong vial. If this had been the case, it would explain many circumstances.

It would explain why Lorenzi started the rumor of 'chest pain.'

It would explain why Lorenzi has repeatedly denied the Pope was murdered when he has no other way to know this.

It would explain why Lorenzi told Cornwell: **'John Paul was fed up with this world and he wanted only to die.'**[38]

It would explain the missing slipper socks which Lorenzi may have used to wipe the tinge of blood an injection would leave.

It would explain why the Pope was sitting up reading with his glasses on with papers held upright in his hands. It would make sense for Lorenzi to sit the Pope up reading papers to give the impression he died while reading the evening before.

It would explain why the Pope was dressed in his daytime clothes as the injection would have been given shortly after he retired at 9:30 the evening before. It would make no sense John Paul would awaken Lorenzi at four in the morning to give him an injection.

It would explain why the alarm clock did not go off. It had never been set to begin with.

Yet, this would be contradictory to Lina Petri's **torn sleeves:**

'...The sleeves were all torn. Why should they be torn like that? I wondered..."³⁹

Anyone who has ever dressed a dead body knows it is not an easy task—pulling, tugging, lifting this, pushing that. **'Torn sleeves'** would be consistent with the Pope was dressed in his daytime clothes after he was dead. **'Torn sleeves'** would be particularly consistent with the fragile laced fringed sleeves of a pope's smock.

Too, if he staged the body for the nun to find in the morning, why place the glasses on its nose? Of all the people in the Vatican, he and Vincenza would have known John Paul didn't need them to read. Yet, he may have been clever enough to have done this to place suspicions away from himself in the event foul play was suspected.

It may be the notes held in his hands were, indeed, listings of cardinals to be removed from office as the rumors had suggested—composed and staged by Lorenzi to cast suspicions toward others.

Yet, all of these suppositions contradict the embalmers' claim **'the body was still warm.'**

Then again, it may be the nun Vincenza did ask the Pope to drop his pants. She gave John Paul the injection. She accidentally killed the Pope. In her case, she could have given him the injection when she delivered the coffee—consistent with the embalmers' claim he had not been dead for more than an hour or two.

The argument against this is that—being a small woman—she would have had difficulty maneuvering the body into position. Also, in her subsequent actions, she never tried to cover up for murder. In fact, it was her unwavering witness through the years which supports much of the investigation that continues to go on today.

Regardless, this is all speculation. One will never really know.

One has to assume Lorenzi or someone else accidentally killed the Pope at the exact moment in history his enemies both inside the Vatican and across the pond wanted him dead. This is unfathomable chance of coincidence. Yet, it remains a possibility that someone accidentally killed the Pope and covered up their involvement. For this reason, though a long shot, one must keep accident on the table.

It is possible Lorenzi did not accidentally kill the Pope.

It is possible he was unknowingly an accomplice to murder. He thought he had accidentally killed the Pope and staged the cover up, whereas someone had tampered with the vials. One who knew the injections were given at the end of March and the end of September.

The hole in this theory is that anyone tampering with the vials would have no way of knowing Lorenzi would cover up the deed. Had he not covered up, there would surely have been an autopsy.

In conclusion, we have no chance of natural death or suicide. Though there remains a remote possibility of accident and cover up, we know, with a reasonable degree of certainty, John Paul was murdered. There are no other ways one can die.

Murder

Yet, just how was he murdered? How does one kill a pope?

To answer these questions, we must clear up some loose ends—the time of death for example. Let us close the door on that one.

All the witnesses agree he retired shortly after nine o'clock. He had a phone conversation with Cardinal Colombo of Milan which ended about nine-thirty. That was the last time anyone heard of him.

If one believes the doctor who declared him dead, the Pope died before midnight. If one believes the embalmers—'**the body was still warm**'—he died in the early morning hours.

Today, we know the time of death is quite material as it answers many questions including the most puzzling of all. How could he be dressed in daytime clothes and still be reading at midnight?

As we have said before, if one intends to read oneself to sleep, one will first don one's bedclothes and climb in between the sheets.

To fix the time of death, one must consider motive.

Would the embalmers have had any reason to lie? At least to this author, they would have had no reason to have lied. It is reasonable to believe, influenced by John Paul II nine years later, they modified their story for Cornwell that they may have arrived closer to dawn—a deception later exposed by Vatican motor pool records confirming a van had been dispatched to pick them up at 5:23AM.[40]

Yet, would the Vatican doctor have had motive to lie? Would Cardinal Villot, who issued the press release the Pope died before midnight, have motive to lie? The answer is a resounding "Yes."

There would be nothing unusual about embalming eight hours after death because Italian law which prohibited embalming earlier than twenty-four hours after death did not apply in the Vatican.

But, it would be highly unusual to have embalmed immediately after death—particularly, to have roused the embalmers at five in the morning, when the body would not lie in state until noon.

It makes all the sense in the world that Villot and the doctor lied about the time of death to place considerable time between death and the embalming to avoid suspicion of poisoning.

If the embalmers were right—embalmers have infinitely more experience than do doctors in examining recently expired corpses—this would mean the Pope died as late as four-thirty in the morning.

It would seem, the Pope had risen at his usual time of about four o'clock, turned off the alarm, completed his morning toilet, dressed for the day, and sat himself up in his bed reading while he waited for the 'coffee knock' on the door—just as the nun had assumed.

But, one knows he did not complete his morning toilet.

The embalmers prepared the body for the noon viewing. If he had shaved, they certainly would have reported it to the press as it would have confirmed their contention the body was warm. But, they did not. This means he died before he had the opportunity to shave. It also means he died before 4 o'clock in the morning.

This supports the Vatican's contention he died before midnight.

Light...*by the grace of God*

"...the light was on ..." allows us to narrow the time of death.

Paul weighed his privacy above the inept air conditioning system. He kept his windows closed with heavy drapes on them.

John Paul—like his successors—found it unbearable. He slept with the windows wide open.

Nevertheless, the police had a pool going—with the nights growing colder as to when he was going to close his windows. They were certain the Pope's light was not on at three in the morning as it was at that time the changing of police in the square took place and they would check the windows to see if anyone had won the pool.[41]

Murder by the Grace of God

Too, had the Pope's light been on all night it would have been reported in the news. There were times Paul's light had not gone off until after 2 o'clock in the morning—always reported in the press.

There was no notice in any newspaper the Pope's light was on all night. Conversely, a number of newspapers reported the Pope's light came on at about its usual time at 4 o'clock that morning. [42]

'Its usual time' had been so unusual it had become a topic of conversation. For the fifteen years of the reign of Paul VI, and for the five years of the reign of John XXIII, and for the nineteen years of the reign of Pius XII, the light would come on about six o'clock.

On the day following Luciani's election, the light came on at four o'clock. Even for a man-of-the-cloth, he was an early riser. That he was on-the-job at four o'clock was widely reported in newspapers.

That he left his windows open was capitalized on by the *left* as symbolic of his papacy: "He will open the windows of the Church and let in the free air."[43]

papal bedroom top-right

In the days following John Paul's death, the press reported early-rising Romans—who habitually checked his windows—testified his light came on at its usual time of about 4AM. Not a single person has ever come forward to contradict this testimony.

So we have another absolute fact on which to build our case:

The light was not on all night. Either John Paul or someone else turned it on at about 4 o'clock in the morning.

That the light was not on all night is consistent with the premise the Pope was killed before 4AM while sleeping—perpetrators would have turned it on at its usual time, just as they would have turned the alarm clock off at its usual time, as not to arouse suspicion. Light to commit the deed would have come through the undraped windows.

That the night had been chilly and the windows wide open would validate the embalmers' claim he had not been dead for more than an hour; environmental conditions accelerate the body's cooling.

The great weight of evidence, the testimony of the embalmers the body was still warm and that the light came on at 4 o'clock in the morning tells us John Paul was murdered sometime before 4 o'clock in the morning—with a reasonable degree of certainty between three and four o'clock on the morning of September 29, 1978.

To this day, the official position of the Vatican remains: the Pope died before midnight and the light was on all night—by chance the police and the crowds who roam the vicinity at night and those who lived in surrounding buildings had not noticed it had been on all night. The light had gone unnoticed all night ...*by the grace of God.*

Now, let us consider the possible instruments of murder.

Poison

There is the supposition John Paul was poisoned at dinner.

There are poisons one can conceal in food or drink that result in drowsiness and put one to sleep not inconsistent with the position the body was found. Yet, in the alphabet of poisons from A to Z, there is not one which allows the victim to go unscathed for hours and suddenly result in instant death.[44] This includes everything from the deadly plant *Omithogalum Umbellatum* to the *Barbados Nut*.

We can eliminate slow-arsenic poisoning as he would have been too ill to continue his office for weeks prior to death.

In Chapter 1, we put the *digitalis-Effortil* myth to sleep.

Yet, we must consider *Omithogalum Umbellatum* because it was cultivated in that section of the Castel Gandolfo gardens reserved for plants native to the Holy Land. Its butternut taste renders it easily concealed in foods with a butternut flavor.

When ingested it results in a sharp drop in pulse rate and severe respiratory convulsions that cumulate in death within a few hours. There is no known antidote. Though its symptoms are not consistent with how the body was found, we must keep this one on the table for this section of the gardens was cultivated by the amateur botanist Giuseppe Caprio—an archenemy of the 33-day Pope.

Creatures

A killer can kill in one of two ways. He either performs the deed himself or he employs another person or creature to carry out the deed. Let us first eliminate the possibility of a creature.

Other than venom, animals leave physical signs of destruction.

There are snakes which incisors are so fine they might not have been detected by the embalmers. The puff adder has incisors so fine that unless the victim actually sees the snake strike, he may not be aware he has been bitten. It has venom so powerful it results in near instant paralysis which could be consistent with how the body was found. Yet, being a large snake, it is easily detected under covers.

Yet, there exists no creature so poisonous it kills instantly. All of them allow, at the very least, a few minutes to seek help.

An exception is the giant golden scorpion.

The pale yellow scorpion, itself, kills more people on a per-capita basis than does any other creature on earth because it is indigenous to the desert where few people live. Yet, it injects very little venom which allows one considerable time to seek help.

On the other hand, a mutation of this species—the giant golden scorpion—injects enough venom to kill ten men on the spot.

In 1973, Bishop Casaroli was one of two dozen survivors on a French Caravelle jet which crashed in the Moroccan Mountains killing over a hundred passengers. While awaiting rescue crews, two of the survivors were killed by this predator.[45]

Because of this coincidence, earlier editions of my investigation examined the possibility John Paul may have been killed by a scorpion. Many came away with the conviction a scorpion had killed the Pope. So, I am guilty of creating a few myths myself.

My success in creating such a myth was made possible partially because scorpions kept by Casaroli in the miniature desert in the gardens at the Castle Gandolfo disappeared shortly after John Paul's death. Yet, it is likely the bishop removed them to avoid rumors arising, than it was they had actually been involved in the deed.

If one considers the possibility one slipped a creature under the Pope's door in the wee hours of the morning, a scorpion would make sense as scorpions are attracted to human body temperature—the reason desert campers are warned to never sleep on the ground.

Yet, there is a more compelling reason to exclude creatures.

It would be a poor choice of other available methods.

It involves chance and would require removal of the creature after the deed. If one was talking fiction, it would be a good choice. But, in the case of a real life murder, particularly one involving a head-of-state, it does not pass the test of common sense.

Yet, we must keep this one on the table because it involves Agostino Casaroli—another archenemy of the 33-day Pope.

Gas, guns, knives, smothering with pillows

One might imagine chloroform or other chemical-saturated gauze or sponge held over the face. Though these chemicals can be fatal, there is not one among them which does not leave a lingering odor for hours particularly in bedclothes.

One could imagine an odorless lethal gas seeping into the room. Yet, there is not one of these deadly chemicals that would not kill everything and everyone in the room not wearing a gasmask.

Two cockatiels he had brought from Venice were found to be very much alive in their cage in the corner of the bedroom.

In the covert murder of a pope, one does not resort to poisons, creatures, or, for that matter, knives, guns or blunt instruments. Since the eleventh century, all popes have laid in state on an open catafalque. One must take care not to damage the face or hands. If a pope lay in state in a closed casket, it would rile up more than rumor.

Lethal injection

How the Pope was killed tells us who killed the Pope. If poison was involved, one knows an amateur killed the Pope. If professional killers had been employed, it tells us how the Pope was killed.

It may seem more sinister and sell many more books to think of disgruntled old men of the Curia spiking the Pope's soup. Yet, this is not how popes are murdered in a modern world.

When one considers the murder of a head of state—in this case a controversial and dangerous man in the eyes of his enemies—there is no sensible alternative other than to engage professional killers.

Of *Operation Gladio, Operation Condor, Ordine Nuovo, Mafia, Red Brigades* and all other killer organizations operating in Italy at the time, only one had a physical presence in the Vatican in the fall of 1978: Licio Gelli's *Masonic Lodge P2*. There were about fifty Freemasons working as maintenance workers in the Vatican who had access to every nook and cranny in the Papal Apartment.

The courts that tried the wave of bombings and assassinations that terrorized the Italian people in the 1970s disclosed many cases in which Licio Gelli's P2 hit men had been paid to carry out the horror. In one case, Gelli, himself, was sentenced to eight years.

When 'no trace of foul play' is a necessary ingredient in the recipe for murder as in the case of an autocratic crime, there is only one choice of professional killers—lethal injection.

The perpetrators would have no room for error.

Lethal injection requires someone from the medical or scientific communities and/or professional killers.

One has to employ a toxin which will stop the heart instantly to avoid struggle. Such toxins are not readily available. One has to know how much of the toxin to inject. One has to know where to inject it. For example, 10ccs of potassium cyanide injected directly into the Vargas Nerve will result in instant paralysis and death.

One would avoid a toxin having the properties of an element—for example, digitalis or arsenic—which would assay of foul play as one could not guarantee autopsy would be performed. Unlike fiction writers pretend, there is no canon law prohibiting autopsy of a pope.

Insofar as elements can assay of foul play centuries after death, practiced killers would have surely avoided employing one. If John Paul's tomb was opened today it may not yield evidence of foul play. Yet, it would confirm what the medical community already knows today: he did not die of either heart attack of embolism.

On the other hand, as we shall demonstrate in what is to follow, if one were to exhume the tombs of Paul VI, Yu Pin, Villot and Nikodim today; it would wobble the Vatican Empire.

Lethal injection is the only method of murder consistent with the known facts of the case. A needle leaves a tiny mark. If wiped of the tinge of blood, it would not have been noticed by the embalmers.

The killer may have reached down by the side of the bed and picked up one of the white slipper-socks to clean the spot of blood; he would have been a fool to leave the other behind.

Lethal injection is consistent with a 'smiling' corpse.

There are toxins which give the victim an abrupt feeling of euphoria followed by instant death. 'Smiling' is not consistent with the enormous pain of heart attack or pulmonary embolism. It is also not consistent with the widely plagiarized digitalis-Effortil myth. Unless, of course, one can die vomiting with a grin on one's face.

Why dress him in his daytime clothes?

He would have been killed before 4 o'clock while sleeping. It would make no sense to attack him when he was awake. Though no Hercules, he was a mountaineer of very recent accomplishment.

Keep in mind there were no locks on any of the doors in the papal apartment as everyone lived in the same home.

Paid killers would have known the light always went on about 4 o'clock. They would have known he would normally have been dressed in his daytime clothes to greet the nun at four-thirty. The reason why Vincenza was not surprised the Pope was dressed for the day. He was always dressed for the day when she delivered coffee.

Why was Lina surprised he was dressed in his daytime clothes?

Vatican Radio had told her he had died the previous evening—if that were true he would have been dressed in his bedtime clothes.

Why did they place the glasses on his nose?

Like anyone else not close to him, they would have assumed he required them to read. He always wore them when reading in public.

The watch

We must not forget the watch he had been fumbling with at dinner. **"It was of such an unusual design, it looked like it had come out of 'Dr No."**[46] No one to this day knows where it came from.

There is the possibility it had been set for the time of death. A spring mechanism released a needle at the wrist—instant death.

The CIA has a department that develops contraptions of this sort. One does not have to depend on **'Dr No.'**

This may have left the body in the position it was found.

Yet, the watch at most could have rendered him immobile to facilitate the killer(s)' transgression. It could have never done the job by itself. For it could have never placed the glasses on his nose.

Unless, of course, it did come out of **'Dr No.'**

We know the position in which the body was found. We have examined every possible way he could have died. Not one of them would have left the body in the position it was found.

We have arrived at one more truth—one more absolute fact:

Someone sat him up in bed in his daytime clothes with his glasses on, reading papers held upright in his hands, with the light on.

We may never know who placed the spectacles on the man who did not need them to read? Who turned the light on which was not on all night? Who turned the alarm clock off which did not ring? Who dressed him in his daytime clothes? Who gave him the watch which ticked the time of death? Then again, was the watch set for the time of death? Who took the scorpions, the spectacles, the slipper socks and the watch? Who took the time to methodically destroy all nine copies of his Will?

Yet, one thing we do know. It was not John Paul.

He would have never placed the glasses on his nose.

Both David Yallop and I agree this good man was murdered. We differ in 'how' he was murdered: digitalis vs. lethal injection.

We also differ as to 'who' called the shot:

- his enemies within the Vatican?
- his enemies in the international banking world?
- his enemies across the pond?
- a combination of some or all of these?

We will answer this question in what is yet to come.

Vincenza Taffarel

Yet, we may never know who called the shot in Vincenza's case. Her witness in David Yallop's bestseller *In God's Name* is most critical to his conclusion the Pope was murdered.

David Yallop's book was published on June 1, 1984. Within a few days the world learned that John Paul I had been murdered.

Vincenza was the leading lady on Yallop's stage. Reporters were lining up to reap the scoop of the century. Yet, she was not there.

Sister Vincenza Taffarel was found dead in her bed as the cock crowed in the wee hours of the morning of June 17, 1984. [47]

One might speculate foul play in the providential coincidence of Vincenza's death. Had she died before Yallop published his book, the finger would point to Yallop. Yet, that she died after the book was published the finger points only to the Vatican. Her sudden and unexpected death robbed Yallop of confirmation of his work.

Yet, there is one other explanation.

Sister Vincenza took her final bow ...*by the grace of God!*

1 *Vatican Radio* 10 Oct 78
2 Mosby's or Medical dictionaries dated after 2000. Search: 'intra-cerebral stroke'
3 Medical dictionaries dated after 2000. Search: 'ischemic stroke'
4 Medical dictionaries dated after 2000. Search: 'watershed stroke'
5 Medical dictionaries dated after 2000. Search: 'low blood pressure stroke heart attack embolism'
6 Medical dictionaries dated after 2000. Search: 'blood viscosity arterial passage hereditary'
7 *Italia 1* 17 Oct 87. *Roma La Repubblica* 19 Oct 87
8 reprinted from *A Thief in the Night* John Cornwell
9 reprinted from *A Thief in the Night* John Cornwell
10 *ANSA* Mario di Francesco's interview with the embalmers—the Signoracci brothers 29 Sep 78
11 reprinted from *A Thief in the Night* John Cornwell
12 *reprinted from A Thief in the Night* John Cornwell
13 reprinted from *A Thief in the Night* John Cornwell
14 Medical dictionaries dated after 2000. Search: 'myocardial infarction pain'
15 Medical dictionaries dated after 2000. Search: 'pulmonary embolism pleuritic pain'
16 Medical dictionaries dated after 2000. Search: 'massive pulmonary embolism death'
17 Medical dictionaries dated after 2000. Search: 'retina embolus physical characteristics'
18 Medical dictionaries dated after 2000. Search: 'Pulmonary embolus physical characteristics'
19 Medical dictionaries dated after 2000. Search: 'retina embolus vs. pulmonary embolus'
20 *JAMA* Jul 94 *'Pulmonary Eyebolus?' 'British Medical Journal* Aug 99 *'Keep an Eye on the Brain.'*
21 Medical dictionaries dated after 2000. Search: 'embolism hereditary genes'
22 Medical dictionaries dated after 2000. Search: 'heart disease cholesterol genes'
23 Medical dictionaries dated after 2000. Search: 'causes embolus cancer inactivity'
24 reprinted from *A Thief in the Night* John Cornwell
25 *Il Giornale* 27 Sep 03 *'Andrea Tornelli interview of Dr. Da Ros'*
26 Medical dictionaries dated before 1985 *'heart attack stroke embolism low blood pressure"*
27 Medical dictionaries dated after 2000. *'heart attack stroke embolism low blood pressure"*
28 *La Repubblica* 3 Dec 89 *Dr. Rama*
29 *Il Giornale* 27 Sep 03 *'Andrea Tornelli interview of Dr. Da Ros'*
30 reprinted from *A Thief in the Night* John Cornwell
31 reprinted from *A Thief in the Night* John Cornwell
32 *ANSA News Service* 29 Sep 78 *Vincenza Taffarel*
33 reprinted from *A Thief in the Night* John Cornwell
34 reprinted from *A Thief in the Night* John Cornwell: Don Orione Brothers.
35 reprinted from *A Thief in the Night* John Cornwell
36 reprinted from *A Thief in the Night* John Cornwell
37 *Il Giornale* 27 Sep 03 *'Andrea Tornelli interview of Dr. Da Ros'*
38 reprinted from *A Thief in the Night* John Cornwell
39 reprinted from *A Thief in the Night* John Cornwell
40 *La Repubblica* 3 Nov 89   *ANSA News Service* 30 Oct 89   *La Stampa* 2 Nov 89
41 *Roma La Repubblica* 7 Oct 78
42 *Roma La Repubblica* 30 Sep 78
43 *Roma La Repubblica* 29 Aug 78
44 *Deadly Doses* Serita Stevens or search Internet or libraries: 'poisons'
45 *La Repubblica* 24 Dec 73 French jet crash Morocco Agostino Casaroli
46 *ANSA News Service* 29 Sep 78 *Vincenza Taffarel*
47 *La Osservatore* 17 Jun 84 *La Repubblica* 17 Jun 84

Chapter 27

Motive and Opportunity

"Some are like eagles soaring in masterly documents; others are like nightingales singing praises; I am a poor wren sitting on the lowest branch of the ecclesiastical tree saying it as it really is."

Albino Luciani, *Illustrissimi* letter to Chares Dickens

Luciani was not a great orator. Never did he speak in encyclicals deeply steeped in canon law and medieval theology to hypnotize his congregation. Never did he tap the scholarly voice of his intellect or academic acclaim to mesmerize his listeners. Never did he drive his spellbound audience to dictionaries. Never did he raise his voice in towering eloquence. Never did he rock the chandeliers.

Yet, what he did do—from the time he challenged his teacher at the seminary at Feltre, to the time he chatted with the boy Daniele in his last public audience—was reach the most brilliant scholar and the slowest child in the same sentence and be understood by both.

This is what made him so dangerous to his enemies.

Unlike his ecclesiastical counterparts who through intimidation and philosophical innuendos preyed on their gullible spectators; he spoke in conversation everyone could understand.

What's more, all he had to say made sense. It made sense because, unlike others who entranced their audiences with the make-believe world of yesterday, he spoke of the real world of today.

Italy

This past summer, as I had done so many times before, I traced my patron from the village of Canale d'Agordo to Belluno, then on to Vittorio Veneto, then on to Venice, and, finally, on to Rome.

I carried in my hand a copy of my book.

No matter where I was, in a park, in a pub, in a supermarket, in a coffeehouse, I was approached by Italians; each one with the same message: "You're not telling us anything we don't already know."

It is a rare Italian who doesn't know John Paul was murdered. What's more, they didn't have to wait six years for David Yallop's *In God's Name* to tell them that. The events of the time did it for them. Yet, their commonality ended there.

Those in the liberal north claimed he had been murdered for ecclesiastical reasons. He would fuel the emerging social evolution of contraception, feminism, genetic research, ecumenism, divorce and remarriage, single parenthood and even gay liberation.

Yet, in conservative Rome most were of another opinion.

They believed he was murdered to protect the regency of the papacy, something they agreed with and therefore looked the other way. The Roman prefers not to give up his king.

John Paul would not only shed his regal robes and the Vatican treasures but would annihilate much of the ritual of the Church.

He would pull them up off their knees chanting vain repetitions before plaster idols and put them to work helping others—a threat to those who really believed they could walk to heaven on their knees.

I found most Italians thought the perpetrators came from Italy.

Few Italians recognized the murders of Aldo Moro, Paul VI, Yu Pin, Metropolitan Nikodim and John Paul in rapid consecutive order had brought an abrupt end to rise of the Communist Party in Italy.

There is the old adage **'when one is in the forest one cannot see the forest for the trees.'** The people of Italy had been at the heart of the communist movement in Europe. A movement which threatened the stability—not only of Europe and Latin America—but the capitalistic world the United States thrived in. Could it be, few Italians considered the order may have come from the other side of the pond because one cannot see the forest for the trees?

Regardless, in investigating murder, one must first consider motive for it is the most basic requirement of murder. In fact, it is the only absolute requirement of murder. What's more, it is the most telltale evidence of murder. Once the super sleuth determines 'why' one was murdered, one has the murderer. Does one not?

So let us take these one by one. Let us give them each a chance.

Ecclesiastical motive

When one is dealing with men who would kill for doctrine, one is dealing with men of faith, not men of reality. They live and die for what they believe in, not for what they know. When Luciani was elected, much of what his ecclesiastical enemies stood for had come to an end and handwriting on the wall told them even the positions in the Church many of them held were also about to come to an end.

Yet, what gives ecclesiastical motive such great credence in this case is the Vatican's methodical destruction of the compassionate-progressive John Paul actually was and its creation of the heartless-conservative it has made him out to be.

That it has gone out of its way to destroy ecclesiastical motive for murder is compelling evidence at least a part of the conspiracy to murder John Paul came from right-wing factions within the Church.

Regardless, ecclesiastical motive to say the least would have been widespread. Any man-of-the-cloth who had an intense passion to resist change would be on the list.

Perhaps, most dangerous of all were those who feared he would destroy the idolatry of Christ and establish the ideology of Christ.

Like his father had done before him, he would rip the crucifixes down off of the walls and drag their spellbound spectators up onto their feet and put them to work helping others. He would change the Church—he would change the western world—back to what Christ had intended. This was made clear in his last public audience:

> "If Jesus wanted us to fall down and adore Him, He would be everything He told us not to be."

Then there was the threat he would expose the modern myths of Lourdes, Fatima and the Shroud and others like them.

Too, there would be those who enjoyed spending their Saturday afternoons listening to the sins of the flesh of eight, nine and ten year olds. These were also about to end. Particularly, high up on this list would be those Vatican cardinals who took pleasure in hearing the confessions of the beautiful Maltese altar boys.[1]

Most numerous of all would be those who didn't want to give up their pretty dresses and pompous ritual. These men in women's clothes would be threatened by his warning the day before he died:

> "...We, the clergy and our congregations who substitute regal attire and gold and pomp and ceremony in place of Christ's instruction, who judge our masquerade of singing His praises to be more precious than human life, will have the most to explain."[2]

There were those who feared the threat he was to the regency of Rome—the Vatican Museum, Castel Gandolfo and other royal assets of the Vatican Empire including possibly Vatican City itself—might be liquidated to help the poor. He would turn the property in the center of Rome—among the most valuable real estate in the world—over to developers and establish modest quarters in the countryside.

There were those who believed the Church could not survive without its monarchy, something John Paul was bent on destroying. Those who believed it is the regency of the papacy that controls the populace—in spiritual matters the people need a king who lives in a palace. There was concern among many that a pope with a Christ-like image would be unable to rule—the Church would fall to ruin.

Most of all, when one considers ecclesiastical motive, those who were in high positions and controlled the ecclesiastical destiny of the Church and were about to lose their jobs would top the list.

Men who were convinced immorality is synonymous with sex. Men who thought there was something wrong with sex—so much so, they believed it made them holier-than-thou to give it up.

As a seminarian, as a young priest, as a bishop and as a cardinal, he had many times told his audience:

> "We have made of sex the greatest of sins whereas in itself it is nothing more than human nature and not a sin at all."

Until now, he had been just another man-of-the-cloth talking through his hat. Yet, if he were to utter this same phrase as Supreme Pontiff of the Roman Catholic Empire, it would change the definition of morality in the Roman Catholic world—it would become canon law.

In a single swoop, he would destroy the ecclesiastical position of right-wing factions in the Church who waged an ongoing war against born-out-of-wedlock-children, women parity, contraception, genetic research, the sanctity of remarriage, homosexuality and a host of issues driven by the natural biological composition of man.

Murder by the Grace of God

The Last Supper [3]

So there were many inside the Vatican who may have had a motive to kill this pope and there were others outside the Vatican we will speak of. Yet, when one considers opportunity the list narrows; there were a very limited number of people who had access to John Paul's private quarters on the night he died.

In addition to those who were in the Papal Apartment—the four nuns and Lorenzi—we must consider those who lived on the other floors as they may have eluded the guard. There were eight in all.

Cardinal Villot, Cardinal Confalonieri, Bishop Casaroli and his cousin Bishop Caprio lived on the floors below the Papal Apartment; respectively Secretary of State, Dean of the College of Cardinals, the Vatican Foreign Minister[4] and the Substitute for General Affairs.[5]

Paul's secretary, John Magee, who had been retained by John Paul I as first secretary, had rooms in the attic just above the Pope's bedroom. Three of the nuns also had their rooms in the attic.

All except one of these arrived in the dining room at seven-thirty the evening of the Pope's death. Confalonieri didn't show up. He had left a message with the guard he wasn't feeling well and would be retiring early.

Other than the Pope, there were twelve at dinner: the secretaries Magee and Lorenzi, Villot, Casaroli, Caprio and seven nuns.

It was that the valet was away on funeral leave that made for the hallowed count. Also, Paul's second secretary Macchi—though he would show up to help out with the mail during the day—had been relocated elsewhere in the Vatican to make room for Lorenzi.

Again, we have to dispel rumors. Some authors imply Luciani brought the Guzzo brothers from the Veneto region to live with him in the Papal Apartment. Whereas these brothers were brought to work in the apartment, they lived elsewhere in Vatican City. They had their rooms in a small building near the Vatican supermarket.[6]

Regardless, with women among them, this gathering was a bit different than those who had gathered at another table two thousand kilometers away and two thousand years before, yet, nevertheless, every bit as clandestine; perhaps even a traitor or two among them.

John Paul arrived early. Concerned for the aging Confalonieri, he asked Sister Regina to bring the cardinal a bowl of soup.

He pointed to a chair as each of the others came into the room.

As the last one took a seat, Sister Regina came back into the room. John Paul asked her how the cardinal looked.

"He looked suspicious," she joked. "He made me taste the soup."

Everyone roared. The elder cardinal did not approve of Luciani. He also knew it was that he and seventeen others had been prevented from casting their votes by Paul who had excluded those over eighty from the voting conclave that had made Luciani's election possible.

The soup had been sent by the man the aging cardinal considered his greatest enemy—John Paul. Reared in a Mafia family he would have been a fool not to have required the nun to taste the soup.

Confalonieri had a long association with the press. It may be providential coincidence—more than he envisioned anything would happen to the new pope—that when Luciani was elected he referred to him as 'the **August Pope.**' When Luciani lived into September, he referred to him as 'the **September Pope.**' If he were to survive into October, he would have to rename him again, 'the **October Pope.**'

Regardless, it was an austere room to say the least. It had poverty written all over it. It was John Paul's favorite room in what was otherwise a lavish palace of golden chandeliers, feather pillows and priceless works of art. He felt most at home here. It reminded him of the impoverished village in the Italian Alps where he had grown up.

Its walls were graying and its unadorned windows looked out over the courtyard. There was an old table as one might find in a workshop. It was made of old planks of wood set upon two beat up wooden workhorses. It was the kind of thing that would be the first thing one would throw out once one would climb out of the cellar of poverty. Matching chairs surrounded it—to the extent it is possible to match a few old planks of wood. An old rug hung on one wall.

Everyone in the household had a secret, a secret they kept to themselves. John Paul did not know of this secret. If he knew of it, this room would suddenly become much less a home to him.

The table he was about to sit at was a first century piece of oak taken out of an eighth century monastery and would easily reap ten million dollars at auction. The old rug which hung on the wall could easily garnish a few million more. It was the carpet that had lain in the church which once stood where St. Peter's stood now. Any one of the chairs could easily be traded in for a Mercedes 550SL.

Murder by the Grace of God

John Paul and the twelve disciples

Sister Maria Elena sat at the head of the table. Who's she? She was the nun one would pass scrubbing the floors in the palace halls. At the other end sat the mother nun Vincenza. Most of the men present were not happy about it. Yet, they had to put up with it.

They did not understand this man who would have a simple maid at the head of his table. It was not necessary they understand him. All that was necessary was that he understood himself.

Magee and Lorenzi were bringing out the breads, the meats and the vegetables. The other men at the table cringed a bit, wondering when it would be their turn to take up the role of servant.

One of the nuns started to get up.

John Paul motioned her to sit down: "You have worked all day. I have not done much more than chatted all day." He disappeared into the kitchen and returned with a pitcher of water in one hand and a bottle of wine in the other and went around the table filling glasses.

The Pope gestured to Sister Maria Elena to begin grace.

In the fifteen years of Paul VI's reign, and in the five years of John XXIII's reign, and in the nineteen years of Pius XII's reign, and in the fifteen years of Pius XI's reign, and in the eight years of Benedict XV's reign, and in the eleven years of Pius X's reign, and in the twenty-five years of Leo XIII's reign, only two people had ever said grace in this room; the Pope, and in his absence, the Cardinal Secretary of State. What kind of pope was this who would have a mere woman, a scullery maid, lead the prayer?

The conversation was light. The Pope was laughing and joking.

He toyed with his new watch as does a boy with a gadget he found under a Christmas tree. Macchi had delivered the watch to the Pope—it had arrived by special post that afternoon.

At quarter to nine Casaroli said he had an appointment and left. It was likely he had no appointment at all; it was obvious he wanted to get out of helping with the dishes. He had done the same thing the evening before and the one before that and the one before that. He even carried a briefcase to cover for his leaving early. He just did not intend to yield to this latest rule of the house.

Concerned with Confalonieri's illness, John Paul asked Sister Genevieve to drop in on the cardinal and see if he needed anything. As she left the room he winked after her: "Tell him Sister Regina couldn't make it, she has been taken to the hospital..." He drew another round of laughter; this one followed by a bit of applause.

He vanished into the kitchen together with the nuns. The others lingered at the table chatting away. Just before nine Caprio claimed to have an appointment and left.

Villot joked with Magee and Lorenzi, "He must be training these nuns to be altar girls." He liked the idea a pope would do these things. What Villot didn't know was that John Paul was not training them to be altar girls. He was training them to be priests. It was likely Casaroli and Caprio had already guessed this.

Mother Vincenza and the other nuns remained finishing up in the dining room. The men followed the Pope down the corridor and stopped outside his door chatting a bit before retiring. A phone rang in the secretaries' office and Lorenzi left momentarily to answer it. Returning, he nodded to his boss, "It is Cardinal Colombo."

Villot went down the hall and past the guard and down the stairs. Magee and a trilogy of nuns went down the hall and bidding the guard goodnight disappeared up the stairs to the attic above.

John Paul disappeared into the office—for the last time.

The next day the cardinal of Milan would give the press the last words of his long time ally in the war on poverty:

"Sadly, Giovanni, when we have finished our work, and everyone has enough, there will always be those who want too much!"

When John Paul hung up it was 9:30PM September 28, 1978.

Those in the Papal Apartment

When one considers those who had unlimited access to the Pope's bedroom that night, one is narrowed to six people: Lorenzi who slept in the secretaries' office while his rooms in the attic were being painted, the four nuns who slept along the San Damascus side of the building, and the guard at the entrance to the apartment.

Anyone coming from the floors below or from the attic above would have to pass by the guard at the entrance to the apartment.

To seal our hypothesis—the Pope was murdered by professional killers by lethal injection—we must first eliminate these six who shared the rooms with John Paul. So let us look at these six who were in the Papal Apartment on the night of John Paul's death.

The guard

There was the guard who sat at the entrance to the apartment with an unobstructed view of the elevator, the staircase leading up from the lower floors, the chapel door leading to and from the roof terrace, and the stairs leading up to the attic. This could be either of two guards or both guards who rotated the post that night.

It is possible that either of these guards could have entered the Pope's bedroom during the night. If anyone chanced by, of course, the guard's absence would have been noticed. Too, there was always the chance the roving-guard might show up on his random rounds.

One has to consider the guards because according to reports the Vatican police assigned one of their men to the 3-6AM post in the papal apartment when the guard normally assigned the post fell ill. [7]

One has the providential coincidence, a human fighting machine of the Swiss Guard—in the optimum of good health—would fall ill, without foul play being involved in his illness, at the precise moment in history a Pope is murdered. Yet, there has survived no record to suggest foul play in the case of the displaced guard in the press.

The Swiss Guard is very limited in number—at the time one hundred and twenty. These are entirely committed to assigned posts. There are no spares. In those very rare instances a guard falls ill or for some other reason is unable to fill his post, the vacancy is filled by the Vatican police which supplement the Swiss Guard.

Vatican police recruits are often on loan from the Swiss Army—officers who aspire to the Guard serving an apprenticeship with the gendarme in the time preceding induction into the Swiss Guard.

The police, if called upon, fill off-hour spots that are away from the general public as they do not wear the attire of the Swiss Guard. If a vacancy occurs in a daytime shift, a guard is reassigned from a nighttime post which is away from the public eye and his nighttime post is filled, in turn, by one of the Vatican police.

It is not unusual for a rookie to be assigned the post closest to a pope in the wee hours of the morning because it is the furthest from the public eye. This does not endanger a pope, as there are three perpetual seasoned guards at the palace entrance on the ground floor.

In the case of guards, like any other suspect, one has to consider motive. The only motive a guard might have would be promise of rank or money. Though a long shot, it is one we must consider.

If the rookie guard who was assigned to the post closest the Pope had been part of a conspiracy, the deputy commander who assigned the guards would have had to have been involved.

It is possible any cardinal or bishop could have influenced this officer, particularly, one who might become Secretary of State—the position the Guard reported to—if anything happened to John Paul.

Though second in command, it is rare for a deputy commander to succeed to the top job—commander of the Swiss Guard. Yet, the promise may have been made in exchange for his cooperation.

Ronald Buchs—deputy commander at the time of John Paul's death—acceded to the commander post; but, not until 1982 when the incumbent commander fell ill and died.

Though a pope has unilateral authority to make any changes he sees fit, not being a political appointee, no pope has ever replaced the commander of the Swiss Guard upon taking office.

The promise could have been made the deputy commander would accede to the post when the incumbent commander died or retired.

We will leave this for the mystery buffs for now. Yet, we will come back to the rookie guard a bit later.

The nuns

Next, we have the nuns.

Vincenza certainly had the opportunity to have committed the crime at any time during the night. She, as we know, knocked on the door at four-thirty in the morning and discovered him dead. To wake the Pope she did not have to pass by the guard.

Could she have had a motive? One must assume most anyone could have a motive. Promise of rank or money is chagrin to a nun. Yet, one has the threat of harm to a loved one if she did not comply.

Vincenza had served Luciani for twenty years.

She was the closest person to him on earth. It is likely if anyone had threatened her he would have learned of it. Yet, it could be she gave him the shot in the rump. One will never know.

How about the other nuns? They must have fallen in love with this man. He was the first pope to demand they join him in the papal dining room. Until then, they had been confined to the kitchen.

What's more, they could for the first time pray to their God in the Pope's chapel rather than just scrub its floors for their masters to walk on. The nuns would be at the bottom of the motive list.

The valet

We know from the newspapers, the valet was on leave in connection with a death in his family.[8]

Nevertheless, if the valet had returned that evening he would have had to have passed by four guards. We know this did not happen as the palace guards were scrutinized by the press the next day in connection with rumors of foul play that had surfaced.

Today we know who was in the Papal Palace that night and who was not. For this we must give thanks to the rumors.

Just about every reporter in Italy was trying to land the scoop of the century. At first, because poison was thought to have been the culprit, they concentrated on who had access to the dining room and the kitchen and who did not. In that the Pope died so suddenly, they turned their attention to who had access to the Pope's bedroom and who did not. Unfortunately, reporters were unable to track down the rookie guard assigned to the post closest to the Pope.

The guards themselves believed the rumors to be true and were carrying on their own investigations. After all, they had experienced a laughing, joking, vibrant man one day, and a corpse the next.

Nevertheless, the record is there in the microfilm today. One knows who was at dinner that night and who was not, and when they arrived and when they left. One also knows who was sleeping in the Papal Palace and where they were sleeping the night the Pope died.

Though opportunity is not possible in the case of the valet, one has to consider motive. Was there a motive in his case? Perhaps, not enough to justify murder; but, it was definitely there.

It is not possible to replace a papal valet in the short term as he is the busiest man alive. A pope's vast wardrobe must resized.

Yet, in the longer term, this pope threatened the regency of the papacy upon which the valet's recognition in the world of fashion depended; it would destroy all he had lived and worked for.

In retrospect, the valet did not gain by the Pope's death as John Paul II replaced him with Opus Dei member Angelo Gugel who contracted leading fashion houses for the papal attire.

The Pope's Widow

Finally, one must consider the secretary Lorenzi. Other than the guard, he was the only man who had unlimited access to John Paul's bedroom that night; he slept in the secretaries' office twenty feet from John Paul's bed with only an unlocked door between them.

Motive in the case of Lorenzi could have only been personal. To see this one has to step back a few years.

At Vittorio Veneto, Vincenza, as head of his household, oversaw office duties assisted by nuns and students from the seminary.[9] Yet, he had a number of politically astute seminary instructors who could intelligently discuss the ongoing war between the right and the left.

In Venice, he had a new political soundboard Mario Senigaglia. Senigaglia was the man he used to get his most prolific message to his flock: "**We have made of sex the greatest of sins, whereas it is nothing more than human nature and not a sin at all.**"

Two years before Luciani's rise to the papacy, Diego Lorenzi came into his life. Lorenzi had no interest in politics.

It remains a mystery today as to why Luciani picked him. Lorenzi was an angelic looking young man to say the least. It may be that Luciani chose him for the innocence he projected.

When Luciani appointed Lorenzi as his secretary, the two moved into a small apartment on the fifth floor of the Patriarch's Palace in Venice on the guise of making rooms available for unwed mothers.

It was for this reason the press tabbed him *'The Pope's Widow'* after John Paul's death. Reporters have probed this possibility.

For example, John Cornwell in *A Thief in the Night* recounts Kay Withers (Chicago Tribune) interview with his Feltre seminary rector who was still alive in the Veneto: "**When Luciani was a student, how was he?**'The old man replied, 'Oh, just like all the rest.' So I said, 'I mean, was he interested in girls?' And he said, 'Oh dear, no, no, no, no, no, no...' as if it was the worst crime one could imagine—old fashioned seminary instructor and all. Then I asked, 'Well, was he interested in boys?' He nearly fell off his chair with fright."[10]

Unlike John Paul II, Benedict XVI and Francis I biographies which recount their brushes with the fair sex in their youth; there has survived no record of Albino Luciani ever having had an intimate relationship with a girl anytime in his life; also true of Paul VI.

Too, one has the Oraison incident in which he warned the priest to keep his sexual identity secret that had raised concerns of his own identity. One British journalist asserted he was an active sodomite. [11]

Regardless this possibility has nothing to do with this book other than the Catholic Church is the most homophobic force on earth. His family and others who seek his canonization deny anything he ever had to do with homosexuality. Here we depend entirely on the press.

Putting all this aside, the only possible motive in Lorenzi's case would have been personal. It might be he didn't like the way John Paul was eyeing the young guard. I leave this one for the dreamers.

Yet, that Lorenzi was the only man other than the guard with free access to the Pope that night and considering some actions he took on his own at the time and since, he must remain on the list.

He would have had the opportunity to commit the deed anytime during the night. He would have placed the glasses on John Paul's nose to cast suspicions away from himself.

Those in the attic

Magee and three of the nuns slept in the attic.

We have already eliminated the nuns. Yet, could Magee have eluded the guard? Could he have possibly had a motive?

Magee had served as first secretary under Paul VI and was retained as first secretary under John Paul. This is readily seen in that he served as spokesman for the papacy following the Pope's death. He also continued as first secretary under John Paul II.

Yet, it was expected he would eventually be replaced. Something he looked forward to. Magee wanted to return to pastoral work in his native Ireland. More so, he wanted to become a bishop.

If Magee was involved in John Paul's death, it has escaped this author. He did not gain in ecclesiastical rank as a result of the Pope's death. He remained in the same job for two years under John Paul II when he was transferred to pastoral work. It makes no sense it had been John Magee who had paved the way for Cardinal Wojtyla's rise to the world's stage. Not enough for this author to implicate him in the murder of a pope. Yes, if Magee had been named a cardinal, like others we will speak of, one might think otherwise.

Still one has to consider opportunity. Magee could have thrown something down into the Pope's bedroom which was directly below his rooms. Yet, the attic windows are small and open at an angle of three or four inches at the most. Also, a cornice jets out two feet over the Pope's windows. Not possible. Yet, he may have eluded the guard. If so, he would have had to elude him twice as he would have to return to the attic after committing the deed.

Although the events of 1978 don't seem to implicate him in the murder itself; the events of 1987 do implicate him in the cover-up.

Magee was obviously made a bishop in exchange for his testimony of 'pain' given Cornwell in *A Thief in the Night* in 1987 which contradicted the testimony he had given reporters for nine years.

The second logia

It is also possible John Paul may have been murdered by one of those who lived on the floor below who may have eluded the guard.

First, there was the secretary of state, Jean Villot.

John Paul's election had come as a blessing to him. Villot was a liberal particularly open to changing doctrine. As a result, during his tenure many of the Curia cardinals had not accepted him as their leader. He had no ecclesiastical motive to have killed the new pope.

When one considers succession as motive in a pope's death, the secretary of state would normally be at the top of the list as in modern history the incumbent has often succeeded to the top job. However, in the French cardinal's case, he was a liberal and unlike Luciani not a popular one. He would have never garnished the vote.

Although short of retirement age and in impeccable health, Villot was looking forward to shedding his robes and living in Rome. He planned to live out his years teaching in the Gregorian University. He had been a frequent guest lecturer at the college.

Although John Paul had reaffirmed his appointment as secretary of state immediately on taking office, it had been part of a blanket confirmation of all the cardinals as cardinals

It was no secret at the time Cardinal Benelli of Florence who had played a major role in Luciani's victory would get the job.

This was apparent, in that Benelli and not Villot had spent the thirty-three days of John Paul's papacy involved in the audit of the Vatican bank which would report to Benelli as secretary of state.

Yet, some suspicion does surround Villot, as he was responsible for much of the misleading information including both press releases which caused the rumors of foul play to flourish.

We will get to that soon. Yet, for now, concerning motive and opportunity, Villot ranks relatively low on the list. He had nothing to gain and much to lose. What's more, like Magee, he would have had to have eluded the guard, not once, but twice, as he would have had to have returned to his rooms after committing the deed.

Those of Mafia families

Cardinal Confalonieri occupied the rooms directly beneath the Pope except for the huge space beneath the Pope's library. He had a sitting room under the Pope's bathroom. He slept thirty feet below where the Pope sat up dead in his bed that fateful morning.

Everything John Paul stood for was Confalonieri's enemy. Yet, considering opportunity, he like the others who lived on this floor would have had to have passed by the guard twice.

It may be he feigned illness the night of the 'last supper' to avoid the finger pointing to him had he been in the Papal Apartment the night of the Pope's death. One will never know.

Next is Bishop Casaroli, also, high up on the motive list—a bit of his record, his aspirations, his ambitions, his hopes, his dreams...

It was not his objective to rise to the papacy. Yes, the desire was there, but he knew being the extreme ultraconservative he was he would never muster the vote of any of the moderates or liberals needed to win the papacy. His lifelong ambition lay in locking up the number two spot—secretary of state. Yet, in recent years his hopes had dwindled into sheer fantasy rather than ambition.

During the sixties, Casaroli's influence on Paul had made many men cardinals. So much so, it was expected his name would head the list in each succeeding consistory. His influence on Paul had been so great, it had driven doctrinal changes, some of which Paul would live to regret and never forgave him for. Midway through his reign, Paul started to ignore him. Casaroli knew as long as Paul lived, he would never be named a cardinal, much less secretary of state.

When Paul died his dream once again became an ambition: to be named a cardinal and succeed to the secretary of state position—the Vice President of the Roman Catholic Church.

Of course, in Casaroli's case, had advancement to the secretary of state position been the motive for murder, it would have had to involve three murders, as three men—known to be in good health at the time—had to die in rapid consecutive order to have allowed him to succeed to secretary of state: Paul VI, John Paul and Jean Villot.

In retrospect, today, one knows, this is exactly what happened.

Also, there was a nasty rumor Casaroli would be replaced as foreign minister with a moderate—someone who could better work with communists to work out solutions. If John Paul was to live another week, much less another month, Casaroli would not only be blocked from going up the ladder, he might go down the ladder.

An American bishop who had read my book called me and told me he had been a seminarian in the Gregorian University in Rome and was living in the Vatican the night the Pope died. He told me Casaroli treated everyone beneath him as if they were dirt under his feet; he considered himself to be a prince among princes of the Church and was always dressed in elaborate attire:

> "On that morning, we peons gathered in a cafeteria. There was no reason to believe anything had been involved other than murder. John Paul had been a raging locomotive just the day before on a rapid track to rid the world of poverty and now he was dead.
>
> The conversation quickly centered on Casaroli. If those present had been a jury, he would have been put away for life. Yet, this was probably because we hated him so much more than that we had any evidence which would stand up in court.
>
> His ambitions to be secretary of state were so intense they fit in with murder. Yet, what puzzled us most, the incumbent Jean Villot, like John Paul, was in enviable good health. Not one of us would have guessed he, too, would be dead in such a short time.
>
> On the other hand, we acquitted Casaroli on the grounds that in the second conclave Cardinal Benelli would certainly succeed to the papacy and that would mean curtains for Casaroli..."

Regardless, he was surprised I considered Casaroli a suspect. All others who had written about the Pope's death had ignored him. To be honest, I didn't consider him a viable candidate for the electric chair until I was years into my investigation.

Finally, we have Bishop Caprio. He would most likely move up in the Vatican bank structure if his cousin were to go up the ladder. Casaroli and Caprio were of the Gambino family, the most powerful Mafia family and the largest private contributor to the Church—the reason both men had risen to the Episcopate to begin with.

Caprio, having spent the past decade as secretary-treasurer of the Vatican's central bank, had the ambition to become chief financial officer of the Church—Prefect of Economic Affairs.

Yet, if one considers Caprio as a suspect, it would have required four murders, as four men—known to be in good health had to die in rapid consecutive order to have allowed him to realize his ambition: Paul VI, John Paul I, Jean Villot and the incumbent Prefect of Economic Affairs Egidio Vagnozzi.

In retrospect, today, one knows this is exactly what happened.

Like the others who lived on the second logia, both Casaroli and Caprio would have had to pass by the guard twice. Though low on the opportunity ladder they go high up on the motive list.

Let's rank these possibilities as to motive and opportunity:

	Motive	Opportunity
Absolute	Casaroli and Caprio Confalonieri	Guard(s) Lorenzi The four apartment nuns
Possible	Guard(s) Valet Lorenzi	Magee Casaroli and Caprio Confalonieri The three attic nuns Villot
Remote	The nuns Magee Villot	Valet

Approximate order of events:

Dinner	7:30PM
Pope ends his phone conversation with Cardinal Colombo	9:30PM
Pope dies of heart attack per the Vatican release	11:00PM
Police in the square check pope's windows and his light is not on	3:00AM
Pope dies according to embalmers	3:00AM-4:00AM
Pope's light comes on according to residents of neighboring buildings	4:00AM
The clock set for 4:20AM is turned off	4:00AM
Vincenza discovers John Paul dead	4:35 AM
Vincenza fetches Lorenzi sleeping twenty feet away	4:40 AM
Lorenzi sends Vincenza to fetch the doctor	4:50 AM
Lorenzi calls Villot and Magee on the Pope's intercom	4:50 AM
Magee who was sleeping in the attic arrives	5:10 AM
Villot arrives and performs the papal death ritual	5:20 AM
Motor pool dispatches van to pick up embalmers	5:23 AM
Confalonieri, Casaroli, Caprio arrive	5:25 AM
Doctor Buzzonetti arrives and pronounces him dead	5:30 AM
Embalmers arrive and examine the body	5:50 AM
Pope found dead by Magee per the Vatican release	6:30 AM
Official press release of the Pope's death Vatican Radio	7:30 AM
Lina Petri (John Paul's niece Pia Luciani) views the body	9:00 AM
Embalmers remove body to operating room in salon	9:30 AM
Villot seals the Pope's quarters	10:00 AM
Embalmers complete light embalming	10:30 AM
Embalmers interviewed by ANSA	11:30 AM
John Paul lies in state in St. Clementine Chapel	12 noon
Vincenza's comments reach the press	2:00 PM
The nuns, Lorenzi and Magee are sent on sabbatical	5:00 PM
Embalmers complete full embalming	9:00 PM

1 *Kullhadd* 13 Jul 93
2 John Paul I public audience 27 Sep 78
3 Details of his last dinner a composite of *La Repubblica* 3-5-16 Oct 78
4 The official title of Vatican Foreign Minster = *Secretary of the Council for Public Affairs*
5 The official title of the Under Secretary of State = *Substitute for General Affairs.*
6 *La Osservatore Romano* 8 Sep 78 *'Papa porte Guido Gian Paolo Guzzo dal paese del Veneto'*
7 *La Osservatore Romano* 30 Sep 78 *La Repubblica* 3 Oct 78 *La Stampa* 8 Oct 78
8 *La Nazione* Florence 28 Sep 78 *'Edoardo Calo'*
9 This is still true today; a nun serves as the bishop's secretary in Vittorio Veneto
10 *A Thief in the Night* pg 191.
11 *A Thief in the Night* pg 335.

Chapter 28

The Innocence of Autocratic Crimes

There is one last suspect we must consider in our investigation—the one who gained the most by John Paul's death.

Though an unpopular thing to say, to ignore Karol Wojtyla as a suspect in the murder of his predecessor is akin to eliminating the youthful husband of an aging wealthy heiress as a suspect when he is the beneficiary of a one-hundred-million-dollar policy.

For an unknown reason something goes astray in the intellect of the public when it comes to evaluating motive in the commission of a high profile crime. Any detective will tell you the person having the greatest motive—the one who gains the most—is found guilty of the crime of murder nineteen out of twenty times—the reason one concentrates one's investigation on those with the greatest motives.

Yet, when a crime is committed in the public forum not many consider motive in their speculations. Take JFK for instance.

The Kennedy Assassination

It was widely known Kennedy's vice president Lyndon Johnson had an intense craving to be president. He had prepared himself all of his life for the job only to have the prize taken from him at the wire by the upstart senator from Massachusetts.

Johnson knew he would never be president. He knew the more successful he was in his job, the more successful would Kennedy be in his job. If John Kennedy was successful, the nation was looking at a quarter-century of Kennedys, as his brothers the attorney general Bobby and a senator Teddy were coming up right behind him.

Yet, in Kennedy's murder, no one ever considered the man who had the most to gain to be suspect despite the fact that, out of fifty states, the murder happened to have occurred in Lyndon Johnson's home state where he knew everyone from government officials, to business magnates, to mob bosses to the shoeshine boy.

This included Jack Ruby, the man who silenced the man who killed Kennedy—Lee Harvey Oswald. With a simple phone call, Johnson could have set the whole thing up. The public ignored the rare coincidence the murder took place in the only state in which the vice president had any likelihood at all of pulling such a thing off.

In 1966, District Attorney Jim Garrison presented hard evidence linking Oswald—the man who pulled the trigger in the Kennedy assassination—to the CIA. Among other things, he proved the CIA paid for a trip Oswald had made to the Soviet Union.[1]

Then there is the strange bound between Johnson and Bush—Johnson a left-wing democrat and Bush a right-wing republican. One wonders how this polarized relationship ever came about.

For example, one has an incident that occurred in 1970 in which Congressman George Bush contemplated a run for the Senate.

He sought the counsel of President Johnson as to what is the difference between a congressman and a senator? Lyndon's famous reply: "**...the difference between chicken shit and chicken salad.**"[2]

In 1976, Bush's nomination for CIA-Director caused a furor in Congress. He was suspected to have been a CIA subversive agent in the early 1960s inferring a possible link to the Kennedy murder.

In Bush's CIA-Director confirmation process, Senator Byrd of Virginia asked him: "**Where were you on November 22, 1963?**"[3]

"**I don't remember,**" replied Bush. And he has never changed his story—he didn't remember where he was. Today, surviving photos demonstrate Bush was in Dallas on the day Kennedy was killed.

Whether or not the future president had been in Dallas that fateful day is immaterial. After all, he lived in Texas a few hundred miles away. What caused the problem: he couldn't recall being there.

Innocent until proven guilty

Karol Wojtyla also benefited by this phenomenon—the public's tendency not to consider the one who has the greatest motive. Unlike Johnson where motive would have been limited to one of personal gain, motive in Wojtyla's case would have been one of principle, that kind of motive which causes great men to kill great men.

There was no gain in principle in Johnson's case as he shared the same ideologies as Kennedy. He could have achieved his ideological goals even if Kennedy had lived. In retrospect, it was Johnson who eventually brought Kennedy's dreams and aspirations to fruition.

Murder by the Grace of God

Ecclesiastical motive for murder

When Hitler lost the war, Karol Wojtyla lost much of what he dreamed of, and now that Luciani had risen to power, the rest of his ambitions were about to come to an end. During the war Wojtyla and Hitler shared the same objectives: Pius XI had united the Vatican with the Nazi Party in the German Concordat. This does not mean Pius, Hitler and Wojtyla were bad men. At the time, this is the way most good Christians thought.

In the wake of Luciani's election, the Polish cardinal contemplates his future

Yet, there was a difference between these men. Hitler would achieve his ends through annihilation. Wojtyla would achieve his ends through political means. The results can be equally devastating. It makes no difference if a child dies in an extermination camp or whether he dies of starvation or AIDS in a third world country.

Regardless, if one considers the assassination of world leaders, the great weight of them have been ideologically motivated. Great men do not kill great men for personal gain. They kill them to permit the enactment of their own ideologies into society.

Notwithstanding their opposing positions on other aspects of the social revolution—feminism, remarriage, gay liberation and so forth, their disparity on contraception, by itself, could have done the trick.

One will never know what the 33-day Pope would have achieved concerning his ecclesiastical ambitions. Yet, only an imbecile could view his brief reign and not conclude he was on a fast track to rid the world of poverty—an objective he could have never attained without first removing the driving force behind it: the ban on contraception.

If one is a prolife extremist as Wojtyla was—believed God has preselected the sperm and egg that will eventually become a human being—the murder of John Paul I was not only a good thing to do, it was a holy thing to do. In Wojtyla's mind, Luciani was a baby killer.

That God has preselected the sperm and egg that will become a human being is clear in Jeremiah 1: "**I knew thou before thou wast in the belly and I sanctified thou when thou camest out of the womb.**"

Luciani threatened to make the 'pill' the mainstay of family life. Worse yet, he would make condoms available to teenagers to avoid untimely pregnancies and prevent the spread of disease.

To underline how ingrained this thinking is in men like Karol Wojtyla and Joseph Ratzinger. In March 2009, Benedict XVI visited countries so heavily infected with AIDS that pregnancy invariably produces an AIDS child born only to live an unspeakable life and die an unspeakable death. He told them to use a condom was mortal sin.

According to all Christian scripture ensoulment takes place at birth; no Christian church baptizes before birth.[4] That ensoulment takes place at birth is not limited to Jeremiah, it is explicit in the story of creation in Genesis and many other passages in the Bible.

In their minds, this life is as a grain of sand on the vast beach of eternity. To impede the union of a particular sperm and a particular egg which God has predetermined to be a human being from being born and achieving ensoulment is to deprive it of eternal life.

In the case of Luciani, the emphasis was on quality of life in this life—acceptance of what is given in this life and not lust for more.

According to Christian doctrine, Karol Wojtyla and Joseph Ratzinger are the 'good guys' and Albino Luciani is the 'bad guy.'

Regardless, in conspiring to murder John Paul, Karol Wojtyla would have a clear conscience as he went about his holy day-to-day business—he would have rid the world of a baby killer and not only preserved the ensoulment of billions of children, he would have saved countless others from eternal damnation—those adults who followed Luciani's rules for the pill would certainly lose their souls.

The Polish cardinal did have clear motive to have conspired to murder his predecessor since the latter threatened his ecclesiastical destiny. What's more, unlike Johnson, his motive would have been one of principle—that which causes great men to kill great men.

If one considers the history of the courts—99% of the time—the person having the greatest motive for a capital crime is found guilty.

Karol Wojtyla goes to the top of the list. The reader is reminded of the sacred code of the tribunal: **'Innocent until proven guilty.'**

1 *Washington Post* 17 Nov 66 Jim Garrison
2 *Houston Chronicle* 22 Jan 70
3 *Washington Post* 22 Jan 76
4 Late in the twentieth century *baptism by desire* canon was considered to include unborn children. Yet, it remains a matter of 'hope' and not a matter of 'faith' today

Chapter 29

A Conspiracy Buff's Delight

There is a much more concrete reason than ecclesiastical motive and personal ambition to include Karol Wojtyla among our suspects.

First, let us clear up the misconception concerning interim counts in a papal election, about which fiction writers make up stories.

Motion pictures, tabloids and books often sensationalize papal elections, reporting counts of the interim ballots in dramatic fashion.

Concerning the conclave which elected Luciani, one tabloid reported: "On the first ballot Pignedoli led with forty-one votes, Siri had nineteen, Suenens had thirteen...On the second ballot Luciani had come into the pack with fourteen, Suenens had advanced to twenty-seven..Pignedoli had all but dropped out of the race..."[1]

Another tabloid gave this account: "Suenens and Siri came out of the gate neck-and-neck with thirty votes each with Pignedoli close behind with twenty-two...Things remained relatively stable for the next two ballots and then on the fourth ballot Luciani suddenly made his move and came from behind to take the roses."[2]

Still a third tabloid captured the imagination of its readers: "A thirty-to-one shot Baggio came out of the gate with forty votes with the rest of the field scrambling behind him..."[3]

Even David Yallop dramatizes Luciani's election:

Ballot	1st	2nd	3rd	4th
Luciani	23	30	68	99
Siri	25	35	15	11
Pignedoli	18	15	10	
Spread among others	45	31	18	1

Dozens of others reported vastly different accounts. The reason for this disparity is because no one outside the conclave knows.

Yet, all these speculations are consistent in one respect: 'Luciani was elected on the 4th ballot on the first day.'

In Chapter 10—How a Pope is Elected—we established Luciani was elected on the 1st ballot and confirmed on 2nd ballot—consistent with the number of ballots possible under the 1978 conclave rules.

278

I have said this before—because it is paramount to what we are speaking of here—I will say it again. If a cardinal discloses anything relative to conclave voting, he excommunicates himself. No cardinal has ever whispered anything relative to a conclave voting process.

Yes, as we have said, after a cardinal dies, an author might claim the cardinal had confided with him before his death and write a book to capitalize on the suckers. Yet, no media has ever published what a cardinal might have said of a conclave while he was still alive.

What's more, you will not find a reputable news service in the world that has published the voting progression of any conclave.

For example, in John Paul II's election in October 1978, *The Washington Post, Associated Press, United Press International, The Times (London), The Wall Street Journal, La Repubblica (Italy), ANSA News, The New York Times* wire service, *Vatican Radio* and Vatican newspaper *L Osservatore* reported the identical wording:

"It is not known how many votes the new pontiff received as this information is restricted within the conclave." [4]

It is not only against conclave rules to announce interim counts to the public, but, prior to 1996 when John Paul II made changes to the rules, interim counts were not announced to conclave cardinals.

To the extent the seating arrangement discussed in Chapter 10 is true—the leading cardinal was placed in the center chair on the St. Peter's side of the chapel, the runner-up in the chair directly opposite him, the one receiving the next largest number of votes to his right, and so forth. So the cardinals knew who was running first, second, third, etc. Yet, as successive ballots were cast, none of the cardinals knew the number of votes cast for each of the candidates.

We do know Luciani garnished at least 75 votes—the two-thirds plus one vote required to elect him. That is all we do know.

The counters

Of course, someone had to know, because someone had to count the votes. When one considers Cardinal Wojtyla's involvement in a conspiracy involving the death of John Paul I, this is a critical point.

Murder by the Grace of God

In 1978, though the rules specified three counters, only two were chosen. Only these two and the Camerlengo were allowed at the table at the far end of the Chapel where the counting took place.

The counters—scrutineers as they were called—were selected by a vote of the cardinals. These were the most influential members of the conclave, as they were the only ones who—knowing how the interim voting was proceeding—could steer either side to victory. For this reason, they traditionally held extreme political positions—one coming from the far-left and the other coming from the far-right, to avoid giving one side an unfair advantage.

Leon Suenens—a liberal, and Karol Wojtyla—a conservative, were the two counters in the conclave that elected John Paul I.[5]

These were the only two who knew the results of each ballot as the election progressed. This included the Camerlengo Jean Villot—though present—was not permitted to know the results of interim ballots until the counters had come up with a winner. At that point, the Camerlengo would recount the ballots and a winner declared.

In 1975, because of rumors of conclave leaks—never proved—Paul VI tightened up the rules which made the 1978 conclaves the most guarded in history. For example, until then, others than voting cardinals were allowed in conclaves including pages and medical aides. In 1978, only voting cardinals were allowed in the conclave and guards were placed outside the doors of the Sistine Chapel. The reason, Cardinal Wright who required a nurse could not attend.[6]

In 1996, John Paul II made a change to the rules which greatly diminishing the influence of the counters. In future elections, the counter calls out to the electors the name of each cardinal voted for as he writes the vote on the tally sheet—not true in 1978.

Nevertheless, this is important if a conspiracy had been involved in the case of John Paul's death. Either of these two counters would have had to have knowingly or unknowingly participated in it.

These were the only two who could successfully strategize a successive election—the only two who knew those cardinals who had voted for Luciani and those who had not—the only two who knew who to go after to change their votes in a successive election.

The conspirators in John Paul's murder would have had to assure themselves another liberal would not win in a successive election. Otherwise they might be as well off with Luciani.

The only way they could be certain of this was to consult with Wojtyla, as Suenens was a liberal. What's more, they would have had to have consulted with him while John Paul was still alive.

There was virtually no change in the number of voting cardinals in the two elections of 1978. Luciani and one other cardinal had died in the meantime. However, the other cardinal—having fallen ill en route to the first election—had not voted in that election.

Cardinal Wright—who had not voted in the first election—showed up in a wheelchair for the second election. The number of cardinals remained the same—111—with Wright replacing Luciani.

Since a cardinal cannot vote for himself, this may have tilted the balance a bit to the left, yet, the political balance in the second conclave remained the same as it had been in the first conclave.

The cardinal who would have been elected in the second conclave would normally have been the same cardinal who would have been elected in the first conclave, had Luciani not been a factor in that election—someone fairly close to Luciani in ideology. One might put men like Benelli, Suenens, Colombo or Willebrands at the top—who like Luciani could attract those in the middle. Yet, this was not the case. Instead, a conservative won the second election.

In retrospect, the election that elected John Paul II was flawed. Suenens and Wojtyla should have been eliminated as candidates as they were in a position to have lobbied the second election in their favor as they knew how the voting had gone in the first election.

The counters in the first conclave should have been disqualified as candidates in the second conclave because one was dealing with the same constituency in both elections. John Paul II was elected in a tainted process; having been one of the counters in the previous election a month earlier, he had an unfair advantage over the other candidates. Yet, as one knows, it is too late to demand a recount.

Nevertheless, if John Paul had been murdered, either Wojtyla or Suenens had to have been consulted concerning the question: **Which cardinals does one go after to get them to change their votes?** Of all we know of these two men, the finger points only to Wojtyla.

This does not mean, the Polish cardinal would have necessarily been involved in a conspiracy as conspirators could have drawn this kind of information out of him without him being aware of just why they were asking questions. Yet, if a conspiracy had been involved in the murder of the 33-day Pope, this did take place. What's more, as we have said, it took place while John Paul was still alive.

'The Unknown Pope'

John Paul I, was billed in the world press as a 'moderate who had an open mind to changing canon in those cases where it imposed unfair restraint upon the everyday lives of innocent people.' [7]

Conversely, Wojtyla, when elected a few weeks later, was billed as a 'fixed doctrinal conservative;'[8] confirmed by his papacy. He changed doctrine only in those cases forced on him by society.

For example, because of confusion caused by his predecessor in the case of the first 'test tube' baby, immediately upon his election, John Paul II reconfirmed Pius XII's decree prohibiting genetic research and he did it in such a way that denied the ensoulment of artificially inseminated children in the same way doctrine denied the ensoulment of illegitimate children. In 1984, public pressure forced him to modify the doctrine to recognize all children have souls. [9]

How the game is played

Though a liberal can make headway in the moderate ranks, the middle is not fertile ground for a conservative. A conservative, by nature, does not believe in change.

A moderate has broken from his ecclesiastical past concerning one issue and remains firm on all other issues. A liberal is one who has broken from his ecclesiastical past on a number of issues.

The vote of a moderate can be gained by a liberal if the voting cardinal is willing to accept some of the other issues the liberal candidate stands for, in order to gain the change in the doctrine he wants repealed. But a moderate would never vote for a conservative because he would know, if a conservative were elected, the change in doctrine he, himself, sought would never come about.

A moderate—who wanted a repeal of the ban on contraception and stood steadfast on other issues—might vote for Luciani who also supported genetic research and women equality. The voting cardinal would accept the changes in what he felt were lesser issues in order to gain what he felt was the major issue.

Regardless, in 1978, which cardinals made up the moderates?

There were those who wanted the Church to loosen its ropes on celibacy, homosexuality, remarriage and women in the Church. Yet, none of these was the major issue in the first conclave of 1978.

The ban on contraception *Humanae Vitae* was this issue. This issue marked the difference between a moderate and a conservative; the moderate sought repeal of the ban, and the conservative did not.

Wojtyla's position concerning this issue had been made clear.

It had been spread across Europe when the proclamation was being drafted, **"No use of contraceptives regardless of spread of disease, poverty and starvation."**[10] He had been the loudest voice in the days leading up to the election against repeal of the doctrine.

This suggests it may have been Wojtyla, and not Siri, who had been the runner up in the Luciani election. After all, tabloids and books which have speculated through the years, the runner up was Siri, know no more about what goes on in a conclave than does the preacher about the afterlife—they have never been there.

The idea Siri was the runner up is inconsistent with the seating arrangement practice, **"...Cardinal Villot approached the cardinal in the center seat. Opposite him was Karol Wojtyla of Poland..."**[11]

If the supposition concerning the seating arrangement is valid, Cardinal Wojtyla was the runner-up in the first election of 1978.

Regardless, this is how Luciani had gained the moderate vote in the first election of 1978. Publicly, he had been the loudest voice concerning repealing the ban on contraception *Humane Vitae.*

As we have said, a few months before Paul issued the decree Luciani had sent a public letter to his boss Cardinal Urbani of Venice: **"I recommend the Anovulant Pill be adopted as the Catholic birth-control pill."**[12] A week after Pope Paul issued the doctrine, Luciani challenged it: **"...some accommodations for artificial birth control must be made within the confines of the Church."**[13]

Now we have come to a most remarkable conclusion.

Not only does a conservative win the successive election, but one who held stark ideological differences from those in the middle and those on the left concerning the most important campaign issue of the time. How is it possible the same cardinals elected the man most likely to repeal *Humanae Vitae* in August and turned around in October and elected the man most likely to hold the status quo?

Murder by the Grace of God

Circumstantial Evidence

Beyond motive and opportunity, one has another measure of who may have been involved in murder. I call it 'in retrospect.'

The astute detective concentrates his investigation on those who have the greatest motive because nineteen out of twenty times the one who has the greatest motive is found guilty of murder in a court of law. He does not ignore the youthful husband of the aging heiress who is beneficiary to the **one-hundred-million-dollar-policy**.

Yet, if one considers John Paul II having been involved in the murder of his predecessor one is dealing with scant evidence.

One is limited to the coincidence two men who shared the palace with John Paul the night he died were promoted by John Paul II after he became Pope. By another coincidence, he happened to have met with these two men in Genoa two weeks before John Paul's death:

> "13 September 1978, Cardinal Wojtyla of Krakow arrived last night at the airport. He will spend the week with Cardinal Siri. Bishops Casaroli and Caprio arrived by train this morning from Rome to visit with the Polish cardinal."[14]

When I first ran across this notice, I wondered what could be so important that would cause the Polish cardinal to journey hundreds of miles back to Italy when, just two weeks earlier, he had spent ten days with these men at the conclave that had elected John Paul?

There is no record Roberto Calvi or anyone else connected with the Ambrosiano/Vatican bank scandal attended this meeting. Yet, they may have attended as the press did not track the day-to-day movements of the general public as it did a visiting foreign cardinal.

One could assume they were meeting to plan the strategy as to how the conservative-right was to survive under the liberal papacy of John Paul. Or, perhaps, they were just planning the next conclave.

Usually, there is nothing wrong with right-wing leaders planning the strategy for the next conclave, just as there is nothing wrong with left-wing leaders planning the strategy for the next conclave.

What was unusual about this meeting—if indeed held to discuss the strategy of the next conclave—is the reigning pontiff was still alive. As a matter-of-fact, no one would have guessed—no, not in a million years—John Paul would be dead in two weeks time.

Nevertheless, there is nothing in the press to link this gathering to a conspiracy to murder the 33-day Pope. Also, the particulars of such a conspiracy can be handled by phone and other means; it is not necessary to meet face to face. Too, these men were friends and may have been doing not much more than vacationing together.

Regardless, by providential coincidence or plotted design, both these men were promoted shortly after John Paul II took office and neither of these promotions was an everyday occurrence.

Not long after Luciani's death, Agostino Casaroli was promoted past two hundred others who outranked him to *Secretary of State—Vice President of the Roman Catholic Church*.[15]

So as not to draw the wrath of those who were in line for the job, or, perhaps, not to avoid arousing suspicion, it was announced the appointment was temporary on guise to give the Polish Pope time to decide who was best qualified for the job. A few months later, John Paul II made the appointment permanent and, at the same time, he made both Agostino Casaroli and Giuseppe Caprio cardinals.

Soon afterwards—for reasons we will discuss in connection with the Vatican bank—he elevated Caprio to *Prefecture of Economic Affairs*—Chief Financial Officer of the Roman Catholic Church.[16]

Yet, it is the strange promotion of these three men to the three ranking positions in the Roman Catholic Church that could possibly link John Paul II to a conspiracy to murder his predecessor and, of course, the providential coincidence three other men—known to be in good health—died in rapid consecutive order to make it possible.

Regardless, it is an incredible coincidence, Karol Wojtyla picked up the proceeds of the 'one-hundred-million-dollar policy' and that Agostino Casaroli and Giuseppe Caprio got their share of the pie.

It is something more than a remarkable coincidence, one of two cardinals who had counted the votes in the previous election—of one hundred and eleven cardinals—won the next election. One of two cardinals in the first conclave—who could successfully strategize the second election in his own favor—won that election.

Still we have the astonishing phenomenon the same constituency of cardinals elected a liberal in one conclave and few weeks later made a complete about-face and awarded the prize to a conservative.

It had, in one month, elected a man who made it possible for homosexuals to adopt children, and, in another month, elected a man who warned of the intrinsic evils of homosexuality.

Murder by the Grace of God

It had, in one month, elected a man who was understanding of divorce and remarriage, and, in another month, elected a man who had condemned divorce and remarriage.

It had, in one month, elected a man who had taught: "We have made of sex the greatest of sins, whereas it is nothing more than human nature and not a sin at all," and, in another month, elected a man who thought there was something wrong with sex.

It had, in one month, elected a man who told the world: "I have sent my most heartfelt congratulations to the parents of the English girl whose birth took place artificially..." and, in another month, elected a man who had condemned the girl: "...a child of the Devil."[17]

It had, in one month, elected a man who declared: "...God is the Father, more so, the Mother,"[18] and, in another month, elected a man who required the solemn oath of his cardinals: "I promise to oppose the elevation of women in the Church for the rest of my days."[19]

Yet, most remarkable of all, it had, in one month, elected a man who had publicly objected to the ban on contraception—the predominate ecclesiastical issue of the time—and had, in another month, elected a man whose efforts had helped make it possible.

How did Karol Wojtyla possibly gain the votes in the middle?

We know he did not waiver on the issue of *Humanae Vitae* as the doctrine has never been changed or, for that matter, modified.

If he did not buy the votes of those in the middle with a tradeoff of ecclesiastical doctrine, how did he possibly gain them?

Could it be he bought them with the only other thing that buys votes? He bought them for cash?

Could it be Christ changed His mind? Could it be the greatest liberal the world has ever known appeared to the voting cardinals in the second conclave and told them to vote for a conservative?

Could it be they voted for the Polish cardinal because they thought he would look pretty in a white satin gown?

You've got it—none of these.

John Paul I drew a roar from the crowd in St. Peter's Square, in his first public words as Supreme Pontiff of the Roman Catholic Church: "A funny thing happened on the way to the conclave..."[20]

Consider the major issue in the first conclave.

Two-thirds of the cardinals were from first world countries which were ignoring *Humanae Vitae*—the ban on contraception—

and encouraging *Planned Parenthood.* If Wojtyla was elected, their congregations would be condemned to live out their mortal lives in a perpetual state of mortal sin. What's more, they would live out their supernatural lives burning in hell for all eternity.

One-third of the cardinals were from third world countries whose congregations adhered to *Humanae Vitae.* They would be looking at decades of poverty, disease, starvation and death.

One would wonder how Wojtyla could have possibly gained a single vote, let alone the overwhelming plurality he needed to win.

Something happened that caused these men to change their minds that made the Polish cardinal the overwhelming choice in the second election. Something that did not take place on the spur of the moment midway in the conclave as one might be led to believe.

As had occurred on the way to the first conclave, **a funny thing happened on the way to the second conclave of 1978.** We will get to that 'funny thing' before we turn the last page in this book.

Yet, for now, as we have proved in Chapter 10, the cardinals knew who they were going to vote for before they entered the second conclave of 1978. Just as they had known who they were going to vote for before they entered the first conclave of 1978.

John Paul II was not chosen by Christ.

Like John Paul I before him, he was chosen by the politicking and collaboration of men. Perhaps, the murdering of men...

1 *Fatti Duri* 29 Aug 78
2 *Nella Realta* 29 Aug 78
3 *Erba Italiana* 30 Aug 78
4 *Washington Post* 27 Aug 78. *New York Times,* on strike at the time was limited to wire service
5 *L Osservatore Romano* 27 Aug 78
6 *L Osservatore Romano* 25 Aug 78
7 *Philadelphia Inquirer* 27 Aug 78
8 *Washington Post* 18 Oct 78
9 *L Osservatore Romano* 19 Oct 78
10 *Dziennik Polski* 3 Jan 68
11 *The Times* London 29 Aug 78
12 *Veneto Nostro* 21 Apr 68
13 *Messaggero Mestre* 28 Jul 68
14 *Genova Secolo XIX* 13 Sep 78
15 *Agostino Casaroli* biographies
16 *Giuseppe Caprio* biographies
17 *Polityka* 26 Jul 78
18 *L Osservatore Romano* 11 Sep 78
19 *Washington Post* 22 Feb 01
20 *The Times* London 29 Aug 78

Chapter 30

The Murder of Paul Marcinkus

"You don't run money through war-ravaged parts of the world unless you intend it remain there."

Paul Marcinkus

Author's note: The great preponderance of authors—copying from one another—implicate Paul Marcinkus in the murder of John Paul I. This supposition is sound. For if Avro Manhattan's hypothesis is correct—the conspiracy that planned the Great Vatican Bank Scandal was the same conspiracy that plotted the murder of John Paul I—only the president and treasurer of the Vatican Bank could have possibly carried out such a scheme.

Yet, the fact is, Paul Marcinkus was not the president of the Vatican Bank.

As we will prove—before we get to the end of this book—those who were the officers of the Vatican Bank did carry out these clandestine dealings.

As for now, I give you a scene in the Papal Palace the night of John Paul's death:

He found himself sitting in a tailor shop, one of those reserved for kings.

There was a large sewing machine of the latest vintage. A ruffle of white satin flowed from its center as if a bell had rung and the seamstress had gone to lunch.

On a table, just off to one side, were a half dozen or so rolls of satin, each one of the very same shade of white.

Then, there was the gold. It was wound up on spindles lined up at one end of the sewing machine—a dozen or so golden sentinels watchfully guarded a grand catafalque of white.

To the other side of the sewing machine, rose a towering mirror with its edges encrusted in gold.

A platform stood before the mirror. There was a slight indentation at its center and a haze above it, as if a ghost were standing there.

It was flanked by a half dozen breast dummies, each wearing a part of some form of dress. One was all dressed up. All dressed up, just short of holding the Eucharist in its hands. It even wore the papal miter.

The breast dummies were all of the same size. Just a month earlier, they had been of another size. In just two weeks time, they would be of still another size.

Only he of all of mankind knew this.

Only he could make them change.

It would seem we have narrowed the suspects down to those from the lower floors who attended the last supper who may have hid in the valet's rooms. Both Casaroli and Caprio left dinner early.

The guard on the 6PM-9PM shift would have seen them arrive and assumed they had left during the 9PM-12PM shift and the guard on that shift would have never known they had been there.

The guard on the 6AM-9AM shift who would see them leave would assume they had arrived during the 3AM-6AM.

For the mystery enthusiast, Casaroli left dinner early carrying a briefcase in which he could have had most anything.

A conversation with Paul Marcinkus

In the summer of 2005, Paul Marcinkus, who had been living with another priest in a private home on a golf course in Sun City Arizona for fifteen years, picked up my book in a gay bookstore in Phoenix.[1]

It was that he recalled the young man he had once taken around the Vatican grounds, rather than anything in the book; he called me.

He began: "It makes sense members of P2 who were maintenance workers in the Vatican concealed themselves in the valet's quarters and waited for the early hours of the morning. The only other rooms not occupied at night were the dining room, kitchen and salon—often visited into the wee hours. Lorenzi happened to be sleeping in the secretaries' office which otherwise would have been vacant."

"Yes," I told him, "it was a godsend the valet's brother happened to have died a few days before John Paul's death."

"If P2 was involved," he corrected me, "it was no godsend.

"They would have had to vacate one of the quarters. The valet's rooms which annexed the Pope's rooms were best suited. This does not necessarily mean Casaroli and Caprio or other men-of-the-cloth could not have been sharing the valet's rooms that night; just that they would have been fools to have committed the deed itself."

Regardless, the day following Marcinkus' call, I searched the library microfilm for the obituary of the valet's brother.

The thirty-year-old had fallen from a sixth floor balcony in Arezzo south of Florence. Unwitnessed, police could not determine if it was accident or suicide. By providential coincidence, the Grandmaster of P2—Licio Gelli—had his villa in Arezzo.

Otherwise, Paul didn't tell me much more than I already knew.

Yet, opportunity knocks only once. I asked, "What happened to the $1.3 billion?"

A moment of silence persisted into minutes.

I followed, "Surely as president of the Vatican Bank ..."

Again, he didn't tell me anything I didn't already know. Yet, what Paul did do was connect a few dots for me. He told me:

> "As is still true today, all funds in and out of a country had to pass through its central bank; in the case of the United States—the Federal Reserve Bank, in the case of Italy—the Bank of Italy, in the case of the Vatican—the Patrimony of the Holy See.
>
> My bank, the Institute of Religious Works—wrongly called the Vatican Bank—was a depository of the Patrimony of the Holy See.
>
> As a depository of the Vatican's central bank, anyone could walk from the streets of Rome into my 'bank' and deposit money which could be wired anywhere in the world by the Patrimony of the Holy See without going through the Bank of Italy.
>
> This has been at the root of all the rumors through the years that implicate Vatican drug and other money laundering. During my watch, I will not say this did not go on. Not drug laundering but for legitimate transactions. The usual Vatican fee is 1/16th of 1%.
>
> The practice of controlling the flow of money through central banks was a means of stabilizing a nation's currency and it was often used to stabilize its economy as well. This brings us to the question you have raised: What happened to the $1.3 billon?
>
> At the time of John Paul's death, the Sandinistas' siege of the Somoza regime in Nicaragua had brought about an inflation rate so high that a dollar in a year's time was reduced in half.[2]
>
> To restrict the rate of inflation, the Nicaraguan central bank froze all money leaving the country for a year further aggravating its economy, as foreign companies shipping into Nicaragua would have to wait a year to get paid which payment risked being worth a fraction of the original invoice price. Foreign companies stopped shipping into Nicaragua further damaging its economy. Likewise, foreign investors stopped transferring funds into Nicaragua.
>
> It was under these conditions, shortly after John Paul I's death, Roberto Calvi began raising money from unsuspecting investors and depositing it the IOR. The Vatican bank—the Patrimony— wired the first $383 million of these deposits to an Ambrosiano branch in Nicaragua. After the Sandinistas seized the Nicaraguan

branch, most of the remaining deposits which disappeared were routed through Ambrosiano's Lima branch to Panama."

I cut him off. "But, surely you must know who got the money.

He hesitated as if he was about to confess to a murder he had committed years ago. He answered my question:

"You don't run money through war-ravaged parts of the world unless you intend it remain there."

A bell went off. John Paul II transferred hundreds of millions to Central America for an end use. He knew it would not come back.

One last question: "Did you ever visit Cardinal Siri in Genoa?"

Paul seemed annoyed: "Why would I ever do that? Everyone knows we hated each other."

This was paramount to me. It meant he had not been involved in the conspiracy that led to the bank scandal and John Paul's death.

I offered him my condolences for the recent loss of his partner. That was the last I heard from him.

Banca Cattolica Del Veneto

David Yallop and other authors claim an incident which occurred in 1972 motivated John Paul to order an audit of the Vatican bank: 'Marcinkus sold Banca Cattolica del Veneto to Banco Ambrosiano.'

Not true. Since the IOR acquired control of the Venice bank in 1946, it had operated under the auspices of the Patriarch of Venice. What's more, in 1960—as a depository of the Patrimony of the Holy See—it acquired *Banca Agente* status allowing it to operate in foreign markets without going through the Bank of Italy.

This is important, as it demonstrates Albino Luciani—the Venice bank's chair—had been engaged in the same offshore banking activities as Marcinkus of the IOR—taking in deposits of charitable orders—and God knows what else—and routing them through the Patrimony to offshore accounts thereby bypassing the Bank of Italy.

David Yallop—*In God's Name*—describes a fierce discussion between Albino Luciani and Cardinal Benelli when Benelli told Luciani, the IOR had sold the Banca Cattolica del Veneto to Banco Ambrosiano—so vivid one would think the English journalist was in the room when the conversation is said to have taken place in 1972.

So fierce, that Luciani threatened to pull his own money and that of his priests and parishioners out of the bank. As the rumor goes, this infuriated Luciani so much he would take his revenge by firing Marcinkus when he rose to the papacy; Yallop's alleged motive for Marcinkus to have murdered the new Pope He would retain his job.

This alleged conversation is at the heart of Yallop's thesis. If it did not take place, Marcinkus had no motive to murder John Paul.

I don't know if such a conversation ever took place. But, what I do know is one will not find it in the newspapers of the time. But, one will find this notice in the *Corriere Della Sera* April 17, 1972:

> "...The Patriarch has cautioned the rumor Banco Ambrosiano has acquired the Banca Cattolica del Veneto is unfounded. There is no change in ownership of the Banca Cattolica del Veneto. It continues to operate as 'Banca Agente' of the Institute of Religious Works in Rome. The transaction which took place in August of last year was an exchange of a minority interest in the Banca Cattolica del Veneto for shares in Banco Ambrosiano expanding Mother Church's control of the Milan based megabank to better allow it to serve its growing congregation in Latin American ... as one knows there has been no change in the Venice bank's name or its operations..."

One can best understand Luciani's comment in the word 'Banco.' 'Banc<u>o</u>' in Italian = 'Bench.' 'Banc<u>a</u>' in Italian = 'Bank'. 'Banc<u>o</u>' in Spanish/Portuguese = 'Bank.' Except for Banco Ambrosiano, all Italian banks are prefixed 'Banca.' Banco Ambrosiano was founded as an international bank to service the exploding Catholic Latin American population—a natural partner of the Vatican.

The Ambrosiano/IOR deal which took place in August 1971 was not made public until March of the following year. It involved an exchange of 36% of the shares in the Venice bank for a 15% interest in Banco Ambrosiano—the IOR share of Ambrosiano set by Italian law which limited Vatican ownership of private companies to 15%.

It was later alleged by the courts that tried the bank scandal that the Vatican actually held a controlling stake in Ambrosiano through its tributaries. For example, Opus Dei held another 15% and so forth.

Newspapers reported the par value of Ambrosiano shares Calvi traded was $46.5 million. Par value is used in such transactions so that investors maintain a constant portfolio; in this case 15% of Ambrosiano and 36% of the Venice bank. This led to a rumor that

Ambrosiano had acquired a controlling interest in the Venice bank which assets approached $420 million for only $46.5 million.

Ambrosiano had, in fact, traded a 15% interest in Ambrosiano with an asset base of $1 billon or roughly $150 million for 36% of the smaller bank or roughly $150 million—an even exchange.

The Ambrosiano/IOR deal was in many newspapers. You will not find one of them in which Albino Luciani voices disagreement.

What's more, Luciani continued to serve on the bank's board until 1975 when he turned the assignment over to his vicar general.

Yet, the rumor Marcinkus sold Luciani's Venice bank to Banco Ambrosiano for a song has been plagiarized by so many authors the only thing that can unravel its threads is common sense.

If Ambrosiano had acquired the Banca Cattolica del Veneto in 1971, the Venice bank would have lost its *Banca Agente* status which allowed it to operate in foreign markets without going through the Bank of Italy. The Ambrosiano-Vatican coalition would have no longer been able to by-pass the Bank of Italy in offshore transfers.[3]

Ambrosiano did acquire the Venice bank in 1989—changing its name to Nuovo Banco Ambrosiano—after changes in international monetary practices rendered its *Banca Agente* less relevant.

<small>Author's note: the reader is encouraged to search the Internet or library: 'Banca Cattolica del Veneto – Banca Agente' and 'Patrimony of the Holy See – Vatican central bank' IOR depository, etc.</small>

Why John Paul ordered the audit of the Vatican Bank

In 1984, David Yallop published *In God's Name* in which he incriminates Marcinkus in the murder of John Paul I: Marcinkus was part of a conspiracy to murder John Paul because the audit the Pope ordered would have uncovered transactions of what had exploded in the press in 1982 as *The Great Vatican Bank Scandal.*

For starters, Luciani had a background in finance and banking. Like Marcinkus, he knew you can't run the Church on Hail Marys.

His secondary field of study at the Gregorian University in Rome had been international finance, the reason his first administrative job was vicar general—chief financial officer—of the sprawling diocese of Belluno during which years he interfaced with dozens of banks.

In 1958, when he inherited the bankrupt diocese of Vittorio Veneto, he personally took control of its financial operations and brought the diocese to solvency and in time to prosperity. During his tenure there, he oversaw the operations of dozens of parish branches of the Banca Cattolica del Veneto, often riding to them on bicycles.

As archbishop of Venice, he chaired Banca Cattolica del Veneto.

When elected to the papacy John Paul took over the Vatican bank. In taking over a bank the first thing one does is order an audit.

Had John Paul not ordered an audit of the Vatican bank it would have been out of character for him, so I don't really have to answer the question: Why John Paul ordered the audit of the Vatican bank?

Yet, I will give you the results of the audit he did order.

The Vagnozzi Report disclosed the IOR was operating at a $40 million deficit and had been guaranteeing Ambrosiano contracts and clearing its funds into international markets by-passing the Bank of Italy in exchange for commissions; operations legal at the time.

More important, it demonstrated that no transaction relative to the Vatican Bank Scandal which would explode in the press in 1981-82 had been enacted either during or before the papacy of John Paul I.

The Vagnozzi dossier, the courts and all that history has recorded clearly established the bank scandal—the swindling of investors out of $1.3 billion—began and ended under the reign of John Paul II.

In retrospect, the results of the audit ordered by John Paul did not incriminate Marcinkus; it vindicated him. Up to the time of the audit, the 'shady deals' he had been involved in under Paul VI had been not much more than good business. What's more, Marcinkus knew the audit would vindicate him. He knew he was not about to lose his job. He had no motive to have murdered the new Pope.

What solidifies this thinking is the ecclesiastical fabric of Paul Marcinkus. Of the Vatican hierarchy John Paul inherited, Marcinkus most closely shared his embrace of the emerging social movements including contraception, Planned Parenthood, genetic research, feminism, state controlled abortions, divorce and remarriage, single parenthood, gay liberation and a general trend away from doctrine.

One thing more: In my time at Vittorio Veneto, Luciani had referred to Paul Marcinkus not only as one of his closest friends in the Vatican, but as one of his closest friends in the world.

The downfall of Paul Marcinkus

Regardless, it was the 'shady deals' he was about to be involved in under John Paul II which would bring him down.

Though Paul Marcinkus shared Luciani's ambitions in the social arena, he was an American capitalist and would have had serious concerns about the new Pope's war on poverty and how he was going about it; particularly as it involved Central America.

That he played a role in carrying out the bank scandal is a fact. Whether or not he was involved in the plot which led to the scandal is up for grabs. Yet, the events—which we are about to disclose—would acquit him on grounds of more than reasonable doubt in any court of law if charged with the bank scandal murders themselves.

It is my judgment he got caught up in the surreptitious dealings which led to the scandal because of the rising threat of communism in Central America and saw it as his duty to squelch the fire. It is reasonable to believe he knew the money was intended to head off the imminent fall of Somoza and the ensuing rise of the Contras.

Yet, as we will prove, the Vatican bank scandal did have much to do with the Pope's demise for it was the same conspiracy that planned the bank scandal that plotted the murder of John Paul I.

The murder of Paul Marcinkus

In June 2005, members of the Sicilian Mafia were brought to trial for the murder of Roberto Calvi.[4] On February 10, 2006, the Rome court filed papers in a Phoenix federal court to extradite Marcinkus.[5]

Marcinkus' testimony would be damaging to P2 and Opus Dei who many believe had lured Calvi to London on the guise of a loan to get him out of his predicament and murdered him.

On February 21, 2006, the Archdiocese of Phoenix reported Paul had been found dead on his kitchen floor. The viewing and funeral were of a closed casket in St. Clement of Rome Church in Sun City. Though pestered repeatedly by reporters, the archdiocese refused to disclose the nature of death. Cause of death remains unknown.[6]

---

1 *Root Seller Gallery*, Phoenix. Except for the time John Paul II sequestered him in the Vatican during the Vatican Bank Scandal trials, Marcinkus lived in Rome during his thirty years in the Vatican
2 *Cordoba* is the Nicaraguan currency; 'dollar' is used to simplify the illustration.
3 *Banca Agente* the ability to route offshore wires through the Patrimony of the Holy See
4 *La Repubblica* 6 Jun 05
5 *The Arizona Republic* 11 Feb 06
6 *Sun City Daily News* 22 Feb 06

Chapter 31

The Swiss Guard Murders

"The Pope's Conscience" — The Swiss Guard

Regardless, the Marcinkus encounter left me with two thoughts.

One that has much to do with what we are talking about here: Members of P2 concealed themselves in the valet's rooms the night of the murder. Tried criminal cases disclosed P2 had an arsenal of professionally trained hit men; some of them living in the Vatican.

This eliminates other groups, including the Mafia, that were not known to have had professional hit men in the Vatican at the time.

The other thought is no more than conjecture on my part and may or may not have had anything to do with what we are talking about here. Yet, no book—dealing with the murder of this Pope—would be complete without it: Could the rookie guard—assigned to protect John Paul at the moment of his death—have been Alois Estermann?

Who is Alois Estermann?

Alois Estermann was a young officer in the Swiss Army who served an apprenticeship with the Vatican police in the fall of 1978 and subsequently advanced to the Swiss Guard under the reign of John Paul II. He would rise rapidly through its ranks to the top.

In the mid-1970s, Alois had enlisted in the Swiss Army. At about the same time, he became a member of Opus Dei—the clandestine cult which was at the time financing Karol Wojtyla's rise to power.

Though officers in the Swiss Army are fluent in French, German and Italian; Estermann was also fluent in Scandinavian and Eastern European languages. It was that he was a linguist that made possible his rise to the pinnacle of his profession.

His ability to speak Polish led to assignments in both Warsaw and Krakow; he spent the last half of 1977 in Krakow. It was through his coincidental membership in Opus Dei, Estermann first made the acquaintance of the Archbishop of Krakow—Karol Wojtyla.

Alois was a twenty-three year old officer in the Swiss Army serving an apprenticeship with the Vatican police in September of 1978. There is no record the Archbishop of Krakow used his influence to get him this assignment at this relevant time.

It is not known if Estermann was the rookie guard assigned to the post closest to John Paul the night of his death. If he had been that guard, it does not necessarily mean he played a role in the murder.

From the time of Karol Wojtyla's election in 1978 through the end of 1979, Alois was involved in laundering drafts and documents through Scandinavian banks to Eastern European interests.

The next year, Alois was inducted into the Swiss Guard as the personal bodyguard of John Paul II. Estermann is the young man (arrow) cradling the wounded pontiff in the assassination attempt in the spring of 1981 in St. Peter's Square.

Alois quickly became the closest confidant in the Pope's life, so much so, he was nicknamed by the Swiss Guard: 'The Pope's Conscience.'

The personal relationship of Estermann and John Paul II was welded together during the years he served as the Pope's personal bodyguard, sharing rooms on trips to scores of countries and ski lodges. After the assassination attempt on the Pope's life, security measures required the Pope's bodyguard share his rooms whenever and wherever he traveled.

While in his twenties, Alois married **Gladys Romero** in her thirties also a member of Opus Dei. In fifteen years they had no children. It was that Gladys frequented a lesbian bar that gave rise to rumors of homosexuality; the marriage had been one of convenience.[1]

In 1989, Estermann was promoted to Deputy Commander and assumed operational command of the Swiss Guard. He was 34, the youngest to ever hold the position.[2]

Cedric Tornay

Murder by the Grace of God

In 1995, young attractive **Cedric Tornay** came into his life. Rumors of an affair surfaced when Tornay became a regular visitor at the Estermann apartment and Estermann made him a non-commissioned officer ahead of others in line, and appointed him officer-in-charge of the Papal Apartment itself. The embers of rumor were further stoked by an incident that took place in February 1998.

Swiss Guards, when not on duty, are permitted to go out on the town (Rome), but are required to return to the barracks by twelve midnight. Not to return by midnight, usually meant a guard met someone in a bar and slept over. Before Estermann took operational command, Swiss Guards were severely reprimanded for breaking curfew. Estermann did away with the practice and it is largely for this reason he was so well liked by the rank and file guards.

On the evening of February 25, 1998, Cedric Tornay broke curfew—slept over in Rome. Estermann issued an official reprimand.[3] The incident locked in rumors of an affair between the two. Estermann was in a jealous rage Cedric had cheated on him.

Other than this reprimand, which in the short term was withdrawn, there was no visible change in the relationship between them in the ensuing months; Tornay continued to be a regular visitor at the Estermann apartment.

Swiss Guards are recruited between the ages of 19 and 25. They must be Swiss citizens of the Aryan race and have completed basic training in the Swiss Army and cannot be born out-of-wedlock.

A few, like Estermann, aspire to be career Guards, while most, like Tornay, intend to complete a three-year tour and leave to seek other employment; the experience is attractive to employers.

In December 1997, the commander position in the Guard had opened up. According to Swiss Guard Code, an absolute prerequisite for the job is nobility and Estermann had been born into a working class family. Cardinal Secretary of State Sodano—to whom the Swiss Guard reported—conducted a five month search for a replacement finally narrowing his choice to a Swiss Army colonel.

Before Sodano could make his move, on May 4, 1998, John Paul II set aside the Code, and elevated Alois Estermann to Commander of the Swiss Guard. Sodano was infuriated with the Pope's action.

Yet, there was much greater alarm concerning Estermann than was merely his role in protecting the Pope.

Marcus Wolf, Deputy Commander of Stasi—the East Germany communist organization—attests Estermann had been a Stasi agent for years.[4] While a Stasi agent, Estermann had emerged much more than merely 'The Pope's Conscience.' Estermann had become the Pope's chief advisor, particularly concerning humane issues.

Curia cardinals viewed Estermann as taking advantage of the Polish Pope's growing senility, particularly as it concerned matters of the poor. There was a growing danger Stasi's communist ideology would find its way into canon law.

Estermann was not only a concern within the Vatican; he was equally a concern of the CIA across the pond. The anti-communist pro-capitalistic Pope—the CIA had put into the job twenty years before—was growing dangerously compassionate of the poor.

The Murders of Alois Estermann and Cedric Tornay

La Repubblica 5 May 98: "Estermann, who had been appointed yesterday as Commandant of the Swiss Guard, was found dead in his apartment after a neighbor investigated a loud dispute. The bodies of Mrs. Estermann and Cedric Tornay were found on the floor.

All three had died of gunshot wounds...According to Vatican sources Tornay's body was found sprawled atop his 9mm service pistol which was empty. No other weapon was found at the scene."[5]

On hearing the news, a nun who cared for the papal household told a reporter: "I can't imagine there was anyone in the Pope's life dearer than Alois; he looked at him as his own son. His Holiness had been a regular visitor to the Estermann apartment next to the Papal Palace and was devastated when he heard the news." [6]

John Paul II grieves over Estermann's coffin

A few years later upon John Paul II's death another nun told the press: "It was after Alois was murdered John Paul's health spiraled downward. Up until then, the Holy Father had shown some senility but was in excellent health. One of the most terrible things that can befall one is to lose one's offspring. It was solely the Holy Father's conviction of the afterlife that got him through that difficult time."[7]

The letter

Swiss Guards from the neighboring barracks were first on the scene followed by Navarro-Valls, Director of the Holy See Press Office.

The evening before the murders the Vatican claimed Tornay had given a friend a letter to be mailed to his mother. As the story goes, an unidentified Swiss Guard gave the 'letter' to Navarro-Valls who photocopied it and mailed the original to Tornay's mother.

One does not have to be an expert in criminology here.

Does it make sense Tornay would have given such an important task to a friend when he could have mailed the letter himself? Does it make sense his friend would hold onto the letter for a day?

In 2005, Tornay's mother in the interest of clearing her son's name brought the case to trial in a Swiss court. She presented the court with handwriting analysis and a mountain of other evidence proving the letter had not been written by her son.[8]

Motive

Nevertheless, in the letter, Tornay confesses of his plan to murder Estermann because the commander had left his name off the list of those who were to be awarded the Benemeriti Medal routinely given to Swiss Guards who complete three years of service.

When one evaluates motive for both murder of one's loved ones and suicide one must consider the worth of the Benemeriti Medal.

The Benemeriti Medal in the Swiss Guards has no distinction as to valor or gallantry or risk of life; all it means is one was there. It is the equivalent of the Good Conduct Medal awarded members of the United States armed forces on completion of their first tour of duty.

No listing of those who were to receive the Benemeriti Medal signed by Estermann has ever been found. Conversely, Tornay was included on a list of those to be honorably discharged that year. [9]

What's more, there is no record of a Swiss Guard having ever been denied the medal without a corresponding loss of rank.

Regardless, the neighbor found the Estermanns dripping with blood and checking for pulse found them warm to the touch.

She turned her attention to Tornay who lying face down with no blood visible thought he was still alive. Yet, when she turned him over, his mouth was caked with dried blood and the front of his clothes was covered with dirt. Having just felt the Estermanns pulse, she was surprised Tornay was cold to the touch.[10]

She was startled to find a gun lying under his body as his arms had been extended straight out before she turned him over. Had he fired the gun it would seem his hand would have fallen with the gun.

Her testimony together with photographs taken by Swiss Guards demonstrating the body had been moved led to speculation Tornay had been killed elsewhere and planted in the Estermann apartment to stage a murder-suicide. Navarro-Valls confiscated the photographs.

Regardless, the woman was devastated; just the evening before she had enjoyed a pleasant dinner with the three victims celebrating Alois' promotion to Commander of the Swiss Guard.

It was this woman's witness—dirt on the front of Tornay's shirt and that the bodies of the Estermanns were warm but that of Tornay was cold—that caused Swiss Guards to conclude there had been foul play in Tornay's death; one of their finest had been framed

Two days later at the annual assembly of the Swiss Guard, they demonstrated their conviction of Tornay's innocence. In his honor they left the place where Tornay would have stood vacant.[11]

The highest ranking Opus Dei member in the Vatican—Cardinal Secretary of State Angelo Sodano—took charge of the case.

He refused the offer of both the Italian police and Scotland Yard investigating teams and placed a gag order on Vatican personnel.

There was a stark difference between what the Rome newspapers reported and what the Vatican newspaper *L' Osservatore* had to say. Without either an investigation or an autopsy CASE SOLVED:

"At about 4pm last evening a triple murder was discovered in the flat of the commander of the Swiss Guard. Estermann's wife was the first to be discovered. Further inside, Estermann was found shot through the cheek and neck. Corporal Cedric Tornay was found slumped over the gun that had killed all three. After having killed the Estermanns, he had put the gun in his mouth and fired. Tornay was enraged over having been left off the list of those to receive the Benemeriti Medal. Cedric Tornay's revolver was empty. No other weapon was found."[12]

Murder by the Grace of God

Hickory Dickory Dock...

It is not unusual that Tornay's service weapon was found at the scene as all members of the Swiss Guard are required to keep their pistol fully loaded and on their person at all times.[13]

What was unusual is that Estermann's pistol was not found at the scene; he, too, was required to keep his pistol perpetually in his presence. Estermann had at least two pistols—the standard issue SIG Sauer 9mm pistol as did Tornay, and a ceremonial pistol, a Swiss Army SIG 49 6mm weapon, an auxiliary issue for ranking officers of the Swiss Guard. Neither weapon was found in the apartment.[14]

The magazine in a Sauer 9mm pistol holds nine 9mm shells. Nine shots had to have been fired or the gun could not have been empty.

Tornay's mother kidnapped her son's body and presented the court with autopsy results which proved among other things, the exit wound in the skull was 7mm; not consistent with a 9mm pistol.

In that an exit wound is slightly larger than an entrance wound, it was likely caused by a 6mm pistol. Also, Tornay's two front teeth had been knocked out, as if someone had shoved the gun into his mouth. He would not have broken his teeth if he had shot himself.

One does not normally shoot oneself in the mouth as the chance of survival is substantial. A Swiss Guard would know this. Scotland Yard statistics yield a 95.8% chance one will raise the gun horizontal to the temple. Firing a gun into the mouth originated in the Sicilian Mafia to terrorize the victim. One does not terrorize oneself.

The neighbor who reacted to a loud dispute said she did not hear gunfire. Had she heard shots she certainly would not have gone into the apartment. She would have summoned the Guard. The gun that killed the Estermanns was obviously equipped with a silencer.

Nevertheless, as we have said, when one investigates murder, one must consider the evidence which should be there and is not there.

In the case of Hercule Poirot's *Hickory Dickory Dock* we have the footprints which should have been there and were not there. In the case of Sherlock Holmes' *Silver Blaze* we have the dog which should have barked and did not bark. In the case of *the 33-day Pope* we have the alarm clock which should have rung and did not ring. In the case of the *Swiss Guard Murders* we have the commander's weapon which should have been there, and was not there. One thing more: shots that should have been heard, and were not heard.

In a fit of rage, Tornay was able to methodically count off exactly eight rounds and save the ninth round for himself? I don't think so.

In that Sodano and Valls refused to take Scotland Yard up on its offer, has left behind lingering rumors of homosexuality, Opus Dei, Freemasons and even CIA involvement in the Swiss Guard murders.

Yet, what counts here is: Was Alois Estermann the rookie guard assigned to the post closest to John Paul I the night of his death?

Lovers do share secrets. Did Estermann confide his involvement to Tornay which may have placed both their lives in danger?

Autopsy

The Vatican has a history of not ordering independent autopsy in the case of mysterious and/or unwitnessed deaths within its walls.

One might understand this in the case of John Paul where there were no physical signs of violence and one sought to avoid scandal.

Yet, it staggers the imagination one would not want to get at the truth in the case of the Swiss Guards which were obviously murder.

One might wonder why it follows this practice particularly in that it invariably leads to rumors which otherwise would never arise.

Autopsy was also not performed on Paul VI who had died in seclusion at the Castel Gandolfo, presumably of a 'heart attack.'

Although Paul, unlike John Paul, had had some health problems—including having had a prostate operation ten years earlier—he had no history of heart disease, none at all. One would wonder what were the circumstances of the mysterious death of Paul VI?

To best understand the mystery of Paul's death, one must first resolve the mystery of Paul's closest friend's death—Aldo Moro.

1 Alois Estermann biographies
2 Catholic Encyclopedia: Commanders of the Swiss Guard
3 *L'Osservatore* 28 Feb 98
4 *Poteri Forti* by Ferrucio Pinotti
5 *La Repubblica* 5 May 98
6 *La Repubblica* 5 May 98
7 *La Repubblica* 4 Apr 05
8 *Biel Bienne* 9 Jan 05
9 *La Stampa* 11 May 98
10 *Vatican Radio* 5 May 98
11 *L'Osservatore* 8 May 98
12 *L'Osservatore* 5 May 98
13 *Swiss Guard Code*
14 *Swiss Guard Code*

Chapter 32

The Murder of Aldo Moro

Author's note: The opening and closing bits of satire in the following chapter are used solely only to demonstrate how the CIA operates under its charter.

9:00AM January 30, 1976. McLean Virginia

It was his first day on the job. He swung around and looked up.

Mission

We are the nation's first line of defense.

We go where others cannot go and accomplish what others cannot accomplish.

We carry out our mission by conducting covert operations at the direction of the president to preempt threats against the United States of America.[1]

"There is something wrong here." He read it again. "Something wrong here." He scratched his forehead. "Something very wrong..."
"Yes..." his eyes caught the phrase: '...at the direction of the president...' He laughed.
Footsteps crept up behind him. He swiveled around.
Robin carried a small box. Placing it on the desk with one hand, she laid a small white card in front of him with the other. She gave him a smile and disappeared out of the room. He read the card:

George Herbert Walker Bush
Director of National Security
The United States of America

He swiveled back toward the wall: "...at the direction of the president..." He laughed again.

'Threats,' the word caught him.

There were hundreds of them.

What's more, there were hundreds of niches in the CIA scattered around the globe that took care of them. People who he—much less the president—would ever know who they were or where they were, let alone know what they were doing.

Each of them going about their sacred trust conducting ongoing covert operations to preempt threats against the United States; endless myriads of independent death squads commissioned by various presidents and directors all the way back to when Harry Truman had first established the CIA in 1947.

To some extent these are killer organizations. Yet, they rarely pull the trigger themselves. They have a bottomless barrel of money to pay others. The CIA has established links to scores of killer outfits in the world. In a split second, the top agent of any one of the subversive units of the CIA can dispatch a code and preempt most any threat to the United States. A sitting president rarely knows of their existence, let alone their activities. [2]

Except for the appointment of a few at the top, the CIA is not a partisan organization. When a new president takes office he usually appoints his choice to the director position. The director, in turn, might appoint a few to the top jobs. But, the buck stops there.

A newly appointed director does not clean house. As a matter-of-fact, according to its charter imposed upon it by Congress, a newly appointed director can't clean house lest he imperil the security of the nation. Actually, he wouldn't know where to begin.

No one, including its leader, has any idea how many employees are in the CIA. [3] This is the authority of Congress and a matter of national security. The number is usually placed between twenty and forty thousand, but, as a matter-of-fact, no one knows. One of a number of reasons the CIA is funded by a dozen other government organizations and lacks an identifiable budget.[4]

He looked back up at the wall once more: '... at the direction of the president...' and laughed again.

His eyes focused once more on the word 'threats.'

There were only two which he, himself, would ever have to deal with. There was the emerging threat of the Arab world, and then there was the ongoing threat of communism.

He had important partners in each of these jobs.

In the case of the Muslims, Israeli Intelligence headed the list, followed by French, British, German, Australian intelligence operations and dozens of others scattered around the globe.

When it came to communism the list was much shorter.

As long as he would sit at this desk he would have ongoing communications primarily with two people. There was the Director General of the United Kingdom's Secret Intelligence Service, Michael Hanley. More than any other nation, the United Kingdom most closely shares the capitalistic convictions of the United States.

More importantly, was the Vatican—the world's greatest enemy of communism and the redistribution of wealth society it demands. The Vatican is the most powerful force on earth driving a rich and poor society. The Roman Catholic Church thrives on poverty.

The common fundamental mission of communism, from Marx and Lenin to postwar Italy and Central America to modern day China has been to annihilate poverty in the world. If this were to happen the Church would lose most of its congregation.

The closer one is to the ground, the more vulnerable one is to vendors of the supernatural. The closer one is to starvation, the more vulnerable one is to vendors of the supernatural. The closer one is to death, the more vulnerable one is to vendors of the supernatural. The Catholic Church is the *King Kong of the Supernatural World.*

Poverty stricken people are uneducated and will believe most anything one tells them that gives them hope for better life in the next life. Prosperous people are educated and will not believe anything that does not make sense. As one knows, very little of what the Vatican has to say makes sense. That is, in first world countries.

Yet, in third world countries, all the Vatican has to say makes sense. In the most heavily AIDS infected areas of Africa, believers won't use a condom despite the inevitable risk of spreading AIDS and inviting pregnancies which will invariably yield AIDS children born only to suffer unbearable lives and die unspeakable deaths.

On this frigid January morning, as he gazed out across the frozen Potomac, George Bush's concern was not so much what was going on in Russia as what was going on in the Vatican, particularly as it concerned itself with America's neighbors to its immediate south.

Ever wonder why the poor in Central America—who outnumber their ruthless regimes ten-thousand-to-one—have never overthrown them to bring about a more equitable society. Why have they stood aside for years and allowed their children to literally starve to death?

The answer lies in Rome. Popes of the twentieth century have historically fed them faith rather than food. Pastors and bishops traditionally allied themselves with the rich, wining and dining in their mansions; in truth, they lived in mansions themselves.

Priests, monks and nuns if caught sympathizing with the poor were quickly defrocked by the ruling pontiff. The message from Rome: **'that your children starve to death is God's will.'**

However, the newly appointed CIA Director was confronted by a new kind of pope. From the start Paul had been sympathetic with the poor. His doctrine *Liberation Theology*—feed them food rather than faith—was beginning to take hold in Central America. His Marxist principles were threatening the stability of countries neighboring the United States, thereby endangering the security of the nation.

To make matters worse, Paul had made the renegade priest Oscar Romero bishop of Santiago de Maria. Rumors had it Paul would soon make him an archbishop and Primate of Central America. If that were to happen, only God knew what would follow.[5]

In Paul, the poor now had a pope who was telling them to share in God's wealth is God's will—an easy sell to the uneducated poor burrowing in the mud of the street. Something that made sense if one believes in God. As a matter-of-fact, if one believes in a good and just God it is the only thing that does make sense.

Embers of communism were glowing in America's backyard. As each day passed, Paul was becoming more and more dangerous to the security of the United States of America.

"My God," he dreaded the thought. "If the poor overthrow the rich in Central America it will spread to all of Latin America."

Bush was equally concerned with what was going on in Italy. The objective of the recent union of Moro's Christian Democratic Party and the Italian Communist Party was a society that affords every child an equal opportunity to make its contribution back to society.[6]

Moro would tax the rich to educate the poor through the college years. He would force the rich to help the poor. In Bush's mind, Moro, not the Soviet Union, was the world's greatest threat to the free capitalistic tenet on which the United States had been founded.

"Worst of all," he dreaded the thought, "Moro and the Italian Communist Party have a clear fidelity to free elections. Recent polls have them all but wiping out the opposition in the upcoming election. More dangerous, they embrace emerging social movements including contraception, Planned Parenthood, feminism, controlled abortions, divorce, remarriage, single parenthood, gay liberation and a general trend away from a Vatican controlled state."

His mind drifted back to the days that his father Prescott Bush as Managing Director of the Harriman Bank had financed Hitler's rise to power—going so far as to finance the German Army up to a year after the United States entered the war. George was eighteen when the feds seized his father's bank under the *Aiding the Enemy Act.*[7]

In order to avoid being drafted as a foot-soldier against his father's ally on the Western Front, through his father's influence George got into Naval Aviation School and served in the Eastern Theater. Two years later, he would ignore the sacred marine code—the captain is the last to leave the ship—and bail out of his TBM Avenger and leave his crew behind to perish in the sea.[8]

He thought of Hitler's *New World Order* declaration the day he became Chancellor of Germany: "**The National Government must preserve and defend those Christian principles upon which our nation has been built which define our morality and family values,**" which had been adopted as its primary mission by his Republican Party.[9]

"My God," he loathed the thought, "if the polls are right and the Communist Party achieves a majority in the Italian Parliament, it will spread rapidly through all of Europe. It will be the beginning of the end of all family values in the Western Hemisphere."

He knew how the success of the Communist Party in Italy had

come about.

Paul's edict *Populorum Progressio* had ignited the *priest-worker movement* led by men reared by atheist fathers—Luciani in Venice and Colombo in Milan. Together they had led the *priest-worker movement* which had given rise to the Communist Party in the polls.

To make matters even worse, in December 1973, the American Psychiatric Association declared homosexuality a matter of instinct and not a matter of mental illness.[10]

Paul not only failed to condemn the declaration, he accepted it. So much so, rumors flourished concerning his sexual orientation.[11]

"Yes," he gazed down at the tiny white card on his desk. "It will be the end of all family values in the Western Hemisphere. Paul is becoming more and more dangerous to the security of the United States of America. It is my duty—my sworn duty—to stop him!"

The equivalent of the CIA Director in the Vatican is the Vatican Foreign Minister. Like the CIA Director in the United States, he has a similar mission—stamp out communism at all costs.

At the time, Agostino Casaroli—Bishop Agostino Casaroli—was the Vatican Foreign Minister.

9:35AM Jan 30, 1976. Papal Palace, Rome

Casaroli swiveled around in his chair and looked up at the wall.

Mission

We are the Vatican's first line of defense.

> We go where others cannot go and accomplish what others cannot accomplish.
>
> We carry out our mission by conducting covert operations at the direction of the Pope to preempt threats against the Sovereign State of the Vatican.[12]

"A two-headed eagle," he thought. The one on the left keeping a watchful eye on the West. The one on the right keeping a watchful eye on the East—each one knowing exactly what it was looking for.

On that chilly morning in January 1976, the eagles didn't have to look far. The greatest threat of communism in the western world loomed just outside the Vatican walls. Italy was about to become a communist state; worst of all, by the will of the people.

Casaroli's eyes focused on the phrase: "**... at the direction of the Pope...**" He laughed.

He read it again: "**...at the direction of the Pope...**" He laughed again. His coffee spilled onto his lap.

The phone rang. He picked it up. It was George Bush...

Aldo Moro

A short time before the death of his lifelong friend Paul VI, former prime minister and leader of the Christian Democratic Party—Aldo Moro—turned up in the trunk of a car on Via Caetrina.[13]

Moro had emerged as the great enemy of the Vatican and the United States. He had been methodically going about changing the mindset of the Italian population—leading the people away from the Church and the rich and poor society its doctrines demanded.

Moro was encouraging the Italians to ignore the Vatican's ban on contraception and use their judgment as to how many children they can afford. He had become the leading proponent in encouraging the use of contraceptives, not only as a means of birth control but as a means of curbing disease; syphilis and gonorrhea had been running rampant among teenagers in Italy.[14]

It had been his lobbying much to the consternation of the Curia that had made contraceptives legal in Italy in the first place.

When the religious-right tried to push a bill through Parliament requiring a warning label on contraceptives: 'Use of this product will cost you your soul,' Moro not only killed the bill but pushed through another bill which—to the horror of fundamentalists in the Vatican and in Italy—made them available to teenagers.[15]

Moro was also lobbying abortion be made legal in order that it could be controlled by the state as it was resulting in unnecessary mutilation of women and often death; being illegal it resulted in countless abortions that otherwise might be prevented by the state. Implementation of *Roe vs. Wade* in 1973—which legalized abortions in the United States—had reduced abortions overnight from over three million to less than one million a year.[16]

In legalizing abortion the government sets the rules under which abortions can take place. For example, in the United States, third-term abortions are limited to those cases in which the mother's life is threatened or the child would be born severely impaired.

In 1978, driven by the Vatican's ban on contraception, abortions were exceeding a million a year in Italy—a country one-sixth the size of the United States.

Much to the chagrin of the Curia, Moro was embarrassing the Church by demanding it make sexual education more explicit and easier to understand in the curriculum of its schools. Worst of all, he was encouraging homosexuals, even transsexuals, to stand up for their rights. He was riling them up so to speak.[17]

Yet, most dangerous of all, on the heels of the 1976 election he had united his Christian Democratic Party (38.8% of the vote) with the Communist Party (34.4%) in the *Historic Compromise* which positioned communist ministers to take control of Parliament.[18]

The anti-communist archbishop of Krakow—Karol Wojtyla—called the new union: "An engine of destruction of all moral values in the western world."[19]

From the other end of Poland, Boleshaw Filipiak, pro-communist bishop of Gniezno and longstanding archenemy of Wojtyla, labeled the union: "The embryonic beginning of a more just world."[20]

Regardless, on March 10, 1978, Moro announced he would move communist members into control of Parliament on March 16th—an authority given him by the blend of his *Historic Compromise* and the results of the 1976 election. Italy was about to become a free communist nation sitting in the middle of Western Europe.[21]

Moro had not only emerged as the most influential man in Italy, he had emerged as the most influential man in Europe. The threat of communism loomed over all of Europe.

A Quiet Morning

Early on the morning of March 16, 1978, Eleonora Moro sat pensively at one end of the breakfast table while her husband scoured through a stack of newspapers at the other end.

She thought back a couple years to when she and her husband and four children had lived in freedom, back to those days when their lavish estate was a paradise with views as far as the eye could see.

Now, she lived in a fortress.

All she could see when she looked out of her windows were the blank stucco walls of the buildings that surrounded the modest fifth floor penthouse she now found herself living in. Moro had selected the building because those facing it had no windows.

On the floor beneath her, two dozen armed guards were either sleeping, readying themselves for the night shift, or getting up to the light of day. Two more on the roof above were armed with surface-to-air missiles should a low flying aircraft threaten the building.

It was as if she had moved into the Castel Gandolfo except the guards were not dressed in the elaborate garb of the Swiss Guard.

Outside the wall enclosing the building a line of cars was forming as if a funeral procession was about to begin.

Yet, these cars were not loaded with flowers and dressed-up mourners. They were loaded with more armed guards who would safeguard Aldo's way to his office and the safety of Giovanni—the last of their live-in children—as he made his way to school.

Speaking of the Castel Gandolfo, it was there it had all began two years before. When at the request of Paul VI, Aldo had spent a week at the papal residence within the ancient fortress.

She thought they would spend the time reminiscing about the good old days. Like the time she had told Aldo his first and only son was on his way. Of that time Aldo had suggested they surprise his 'uncle' and name the boy after him. So it was the infant was baptized Giovanni Moro by Paul who at the time was Giovanni Montini, Archbishop of Milan.

She knew something must have gone terribly wrong that week for shortly afterwards Aldo united his Christian Democratic Party with the Communist Party in his *Historic Compromise.*

Moro began to move the people away from much of the ideology of the Roman Catholic Church. After that, Aldo never met with Paul—at least as far as she or anyone else knew.

Paul's favorite son and chosen successor Cardinal Luciani and the man Paul had picked to succeed himself as Archbishop of Milan—Giovanni Colombo—had something to do with this strange turn of events. They had been involved in that clandestine meeting and she believed it had been their strategy to unite the two parties in the *Historic Compromise* to give them time to iron out their differences.

Nevertheless, it was then the threats began—the anonymous death threats to Aldo and his family. For the most part, Aldo ignored them.

Then one day, a threat came from across the pond—America.

The next day, Aldo hired an army of armed guards and moved his family out of the sprawling suburban estate she had once lived in happiness into the fortified prison which she now found herself.

Yet, on the other hand, she knew Paul and Aldo were constantly in touch with each other. It was she who approved the household phone bills for payment. Each week Aldo would make calls to Paul as if he were trying to reconcile himself with the Pope. She knew he must have been making some headway as the calls were lengthy. Paul had not been hanging up on her husband.

There was something strange about the order of the calls.

They followed a geometrical pattern on consecutive days of the week. If one week's call was at 8 o'clock on Monday, the next week's call was at 9 o'clock on Tuesday, and the following week's call would be made at 10 o'clock on Wednesday, and so forth.

It was as if Aldo knew at these particular times the calls would go directly to Paul without being routed through his secretaries as if to keep the matter of their possible reconciliation a private one between them. None of the calls were made by Paul as to leave no evidence of their communicating in the Vatican records.

Nevertheless, she missed Paul. It was a rare day in summer or winter the reigning pontiff would not show up at the Moro estate and spend the afternoon playing with the children and chatting with those who were lucky enough to get invited for the day. Yet, since she had moved her family here, Paul had never come to her 'prison.'

Yet, the void had been filled by Cardinal Giocomo Violardo, a frequent visitor to the guarded penthouse in the sky. Giocomo, who held a doctorate in civil law from a Rome university, was the vehicle Paul used to keep his fingers on what was going on in Parliament. The cardinal had powerful influence with devout Catholics in the House of Representatives—votes which Aldo often needed to lock up his agenda—the reason Aldo and Giocomo had grown so close.

Eleonora had no idea Giocomo's visits were about to come to an end. The next morning his body would be found under a staircase in a darkened corner of the Palace of the Holy Office (IOR).

Regardless, it was that morning she decided to ask Aldo just what was the story? She had noticed the phone calls and she wanted to know if he had made progress with Paul. She asked the question.

He took her by the hand and led her to an overly-stuffed wingback chair which looked out of an enormous picture window. One that, in her memory, at one time had enclosed a beautiful blue pond hedged in with the greenery of weeping willows which had served as a home for swans. But now, all she could see, on this magnificent spring day was the sun bouncing off a blank browning stucco wall.

> "Paul also has his walls. But, in his case the walls are built of flesh and bone and mostly of the minds of men. Unlike concrete, it will take much longer to tear them down. Only we here on the outside can help Paul tear down his walls. It is important his walls not know they are being taken down from the outside."

That is all he told her. He smiled and kissed her lightly on the cheek. He left her there in the chair and headed for the door. That was the last time she saw him.[22]

'A Quiet Morning' is a part of Eleonora Moro's court testimony in the Moro trial July 1982

The kidnapping of Aldo Moro

Moro set out from his self-made prison with a half-dozen security guards in two cars for the last time. The cars turned onto the busy Via Fani and moved at a whisker above medium speed.

Suddenly, the car directly in front of Moro's car slammed on its brakes. Moro's car crashed into its rear. The car with his bodyguards slammed into the rear of Moro's car, pinning it between the two.

The incident took place in front of the Café Randolfo on the south side of the avenue. Immediately on impact nine men and one woman dressed in the uniforms of the Italian airline Air Alitalia and armed with automatic weapons emerged from behind the bushes which hemmed in the sidewalk café. When all was said and done all Moro's bodyguards were dead or mortally wounded. Moro, himself, was whisked away in a three-car convoy escorted by motorcycles equipped with sirens. He was never seen alive again.[23]

An hour after the siege, Prime Minister Andreotti—expected to lose the upcoming election to Moro—addressed a shocked nation: **"This is obviously the responsibility of the Red Brigades. Under no circumstances will we negotiate with terrorists."**[24]

Andreotti's message confused the Italian people. Why would a left-wing terrorist group which up until that time had kidnapped thirty-two others all prominent right-wing leaders suddenly change direction and kidnap someone from their own side of the aisle?

Yet, Andreotti was right. A few hours later, the press received calls from people who claimed to be the Red Brigades. The ransom demands included three billion lire—five million dollars—and the release of sixteen Red Brigades' members being held by the state.[25]

Eyebrows were raised as to how Andreotti knew the kidnappers were the Red Brigades before they had identified themselves. That Moro was a prominent left-wing leader would point to a right-wing terrorist group like Ordine Nuovo or Avanguardia Nazionale.

That they identified themselves should have set off a bell by itself.

Though the Brigades had been brought to court and convicted of other kidnappings and murders they had never identified themselves as the perpetrators in order to protect themselves if brought to trial.

Though it had been involved in many kidnappings, the Brigades had never before committed a capital crime in the abduction itself. The gangland style of the attack was much more characteristic of right-wing terrorist groups than it was of the Red Brigades.

The abduction was witnessed by two hundred, several of whom knew members of the Brigades. Yet, no one recognized the attackers described as being in their forties and fifties. The Red Brigades was a youth organization, almost entirely in their teens and twenties.²⁶

There remained the question that of the rich and powerful Moro was by far the most heavily protected. Why take unnecessary risk in abducting him? Why not kidnap an easier target?

What's more, though involved in scores of kidnappings their demands had been limited to money; never release of prisoners.

It would seem if the Brigades desired release of prisoners they would have abducted children or other relatives of right-wing Prime Minister Andreotti who had little protection. Andreotti would have released the prisoners and paid the five million dollars on day one.

If the motive had been release of prisoners, why kidnap the greatest enemy of Prime Minister Andreotti who as head of state was the only person in Italy empowered to pardon prisoners.

All of Italy knew Moro was Andreotti's greatest adversary. The Brigades would have known their demands would never be met.

Despite these glaring inconsistencies, without other leads to go on, the police concentrated their search entirely on the Red Brigades.

The rise of communism in Western Europe

To determine who murdered Aldo Moro, as well as most of the others we have and will talk about in this book, one must understand what was going on in Europe and Central America regarding the rise of communism as a free democratic society in the western world.

We will get to Central America soon. Now we will cover Europe.

In the aftermath of the war, Italy and Spain emerged as sitting ducks for communism. The Italians had suffered under the *Hitler-Mussolini-Fascist* regime and were vulnerable to turn to the other extreme—communism. The Spanish had suffered under the *Franco-Escriva-Opus-Dei-P2-Fascist* regime and were more and more finding their salvation in communism. These were two of the most Catholic countries in Europe and their populations were fed up with the remnants of fascism the Vatican continued to impose on them.

Yet, the threat of communism in Western Europe was not taken seriously until 1958 when the Communist Party in Italy achieved a recognizable level of electoral progress. Immediately following the 1958 Italian election, the CIA and British Intelligence—through

NATO—established Operation Gladio—a right-wing terrorist militia with a mission to keep communism out of Western Europe.

Gladio remained relatively dormant until late in the 1960s when developments in northern Italy—*the priest-worker movement*—gave it the foe it had been established to defeat.[27]

The common objective of Aldo Moro, the Christian Democratic Party, the Italian Communist Party and the Red Brigades was to create a society that affords every child an equal opportunity to earn his/her share of the pie. The emphasis was on education to enable each of them to make their maximum contribution back to society.

Communism in Italy, at the time, was not in the pure Marxist sense of the word—all God's province is to be divided up equally. It intended only to impose heavy taxation on the rich to give equal opportunity to the poor. Its central objective was education for all.

The Italian Communist Party was not a pawn of the Soviet Union. Unlike Leninism/ Stalinism, it had a clear fidelity to democracy and free elections; how it had come to power in the first place.

The wave of terrorism in Italy

The wave of terrorism that would engulf Italy in the 1970s had its roots in the *priest-worker movement* of the late 1960s.

On March 26, 1967, in his encyclical—*Populorum Progressio,* Paul VI condemned private property: **'the distribution of the world's goods and resources should benefit all rather than a few.'**

He defined the inalienable economic rights of man.

Among these were: **'the right to a just wage and the right to fair working conditions and the right to join a union.'** He did not dance around the issue in vague innuendos. He was explicit in his intent:

> **'It is the inalienable right of no man to accumulate wealth beyond his needs while others starve to death because they have nothing.'**

The *priest-worker movement* in Italy—not to be confused with the *worker-priest movement* in postwar France—had begun.

The student movement took to the barricades and other social protagonists emerged to make their mark in the political arena. The factory worker class demanded fair wages for all.

Murder by the Grace of God

The revolution was concentrated in the northern industrial areas of Venice and Milan. The Archbishops of Venice and Milan—Luciani and Colombo—led the effort; their involvement kept largely under-the-table lest they be found in violation of the *Lateran Treaty*.

Paul had strategically placed these champions of human justice in Italy's major industrialized areas as a part of his plan.[28]

Luciani had a personal motive for leading the uprising as most of the workers were street orphans who had survived to adulthood.

Regardless, it was from this unrest in the northern factories emerged the left-wing terrorist group—the Red Brigades; for much of Italy's youth the progress was going too slowly.

Major players in terrorism in Italy

Red Brigades: a left-wing Marxist youth group which sought to accelerate the movement toward a more just society through terrorist activities. It actions were limited to high profile kidnappings of the rich and powerful who were using their influence to impede the progress toward communism in Italy.

Among those it kidnapped were magistrates including Genoa Judge Mario Sossi, industrialists including Vallarino Gancia, and a number of NATO officers. It financed itself with ransom money following a precise pattern: If the ransom was paid, the victim was returned. If it was not paid, the body of the victim was returned.[29]

While its members were repeatedly brought to trial in connection with the string of bombings that terrorized the Italian population in the 1970s, no Brigades' member was ever convicted of any of them.

An indisputable record of court decisions stand as historical proof the Red Brigades had no involvement in the wave of bombings that terrorized Italy in the 1970s.

The Brigades had no motive to terrorize the general public.

The population was very much on its side as demonstrated in the general elections. Its mission was solely to terrorize the rich and powerful who were restraining Italy's progress toward its mode of communism: **a society that affords each child an equal opportunity to make his or her maximum contribution back to society.**

Operation Gladio: right-wing covert military operation established by the CIA and Vice President Richard Nixon in Europe in 1958, with a primary presence in Italy and Spain, with a mission to stamp out communism—*revolution of the poor*—in NATO countries. It operated as a secret undercover branch of NATO armed forces. [30]

During the 1970s it formed a secret alliance between the CIA and Italian Intelligence—*The Parallel Sid*—in carrying out bombings of civilian targets and framing the communist youth organization—Red Brigades—to turn the mindset of the Italians against communism.

In tried criminal cases, its members were convicted of more than half of the bombings and assassinations that terrorized Italy in the 1970s. It was financed and armed by the CIA through NATO.[31]

Ordine Nuovo: Italian right-wing neo-fascist organization which carried out a series of bombings in the 1970s in protest of the communist movement in Italy. It financed itself by carrying out covert activities and providing expertise to Operation Gladio.[32]

Avanguardia Nazionale: Italian right-wing neo-fascist terrorist organization linked to Operation Condor and Operation Gladio. It financed itself by carrying out blackmailings and other undercover activities and providing expertise to both these organizations.[33]

Operation Condor: Chilean based right-wing covert operation organized by the secret service operations of the Condor nations of South America. The Condor nations were those ruled by right-wing military dictators which would fall to communism if the *revolution of the poor* were to take hold in Central America.

In 1976, CIA Director George Bush annexed Operation Condor into the CIA's family of undercover operations and extended its operations to Italy when convictions of Operation Gladio' members in connection with terrorist bombings of Italian civilian targets had weakened its effectiveness. [34]

Propaganda Due: commonly known as **P2**: right-wing clandestine Masonic Lodge operating in Italy. At the time of John Paul's death, it had professional hit-men working as maintenance workers in the Vatican. Several of its members were brought to trial and convicted of assassinations and bombings in Italy in the 1970s.

It financed itself by carrying out covert operations including capital crimes for anyone for cash which eventually made its leader, former Nazi Licio Gelli, one of the richest men in Europe. Much of its revenues came from the CIA. The courts established P2 as the No. 2 killer organization in Italy's wave of terror of the 1970s.[35]

Opus Dei: right-wing cult founded by Jose Maria Escriva which together with the Franco regime terrorized the Spanish people for decades. Its mission is to control the moral pulse of the world through control of the papacy and judicial branches of nations.[36]

These right-wing organizations and others like them shared the CIA-NATO-GLADIO anti-communist strategy which had been set into motion immediately after Richard Nixon took office in 1969.

The CIA-NATO-GLADIO strategy was to carry out a wave of bombings and assassinations in Italy designed to turn the mindset of the Italian people against communism. An instrumental part of the plot was to plant incriminating evidence to frame the Red Brigades and turn the mindset of the Italian people against communism. The mission was to halt the progression of communism in the polls which had reached the proportions of a snowball rolling down a hill.

There were other right-wing terrorist groups operating in Italy at the time, but the CIA's Operation Gladio allied itself with Ordine Nuovo and Avanguardia Nazionale because these organizations had recognized forensic and explosive experts who could be called upon to lock up convictions against the Red Brigades. Gladio allied itself with P2 insofar as covert executions were a part of its game.

The reign of terror in Italy

Nevertheless, the scheme started out with a bang in December 1969 with the bombing of Piazza Fontana—a Milan bank—leaving 17 dead and 90 wounded. This was followed by a wave of terrorist activities thru the 1970s cumulating with the August 1980 bombing of the Bologna train station leaving 92 dead 300 wounded.[37]

When the reign of American right-wing terrorism in Italy came to an end, 491 innocent civilians were dead including 97 children and more than 4,000 permanently maimed. The United States made the Italian people pay dearly for voicing their opinion in free elections.[38]

This CIA strategy—to terrorize the Italian population and frame the Red Brigades and turn its mindset against the youth group and communism—was exposed in the courts many times.

On May 31, 1972, a car-bomb in Peteano killed three policemen. A circled five pointed star—the symbol of the Brigades—had been scrawled on the hood of the demolished car. Several members of the Red Brigades were brought to trial.

A casual film taken by a tourist introduced by the defense showed Vincenzo Vinciguerra of Avanguardia Nazionale scratching the Red Brigades symbol on the hood of the car.

Court proceedings proved Marco Morin of Ordine Nuovo—an explosive expert in the Italian police—provided false expertise in testifying explosives used were the same as those used by the Brigades. Other expert testimony demonstrated the explosives were C4, a NATO explosive. The bomb material had, in fact, come from a CIA-Gladio arms dump in Verona.[39]

The court found that right-wing organizations Ordine Nuovo and Avanguardia Nazionale had collaborated with Operation Gladio and Italian Counter-Intelligence in the attack. Together they engineered the Peteano terror and wrongly framed the Red Brigades.

Although members of the Red Brigades were brought to trial on incriminating evidence found at the scenes—always accompanied by a circled five-pointed star—in every case the evidence was proved to have been planted and no member of the Red Brigades was ever convicted of a bombing of a public facility in the 1970s in Italy.

On the other hand, Brigades' members were convicted of capital crimes in connection with kidnappings of the rich and powerful. In all, at the time of the Aldo Moro kidnapping the Red Brigades' assassination toll had reached seventeen.

Those organizations convicted in tried criminal cases of the terrorist bombings of the 1970s in Italy: Operation Gladio 53%, Operation Condor 7%, Ordine Nuovo 13%, P2 Masonic Temple 19%, Avanguardia Nazionale 5%, others 3%.[40]

The Opus Dei-P2-Ambrosiano Coalition

How these right-wing organizations operated in harmony is best demonstrated by the interrelationships of some of the players.

Agostino Casaroli was a longtime friend of Licio Gelli, founder of the clandestine Masonic Lodge, Propaganda Due (P2), and Jose

Maria Escriva, founder of Opus Dei. An Opus Dei member since the world war, Agostino Casaroli was inducted into a Zurich branch of P2 Lodge No. 041-076 on September 28, 1957.[41]

As Foreign Minister with a focus on communism, Casaroli spent much time at the 'front' in Poland. It was he who served as the link between the Polish Cardinal of Krakow—Karol Wojtyla—and Opus Dei which eventually made possible Wojtyla's rise to the papacy.

He also introduced Karol Wojtyla to Licio Gelli. It was that Wojtyla and Gelli were avid skiers which molded their friendship. According to Wojtyla's secretary—Stanislaw Dziwisz—John Paul II took more than a hundred ski vacations during his papacy, most of them to a ski lodge in the Abruzzo region owned by Gelli.[42]

Opus Dei established a substantial treasury after the war when in its alliance with Franco it was paid handsomely for arranging the escape of Nazi war criminals through Madrid to Argentina. By 1950 it had emerged as a major investment house in Europe.[43]

The Opus Dei-P2 coalition went back to before the world war when Jose Maria Escriva—founder of Opus Dei—and Licio Gelli—founder of P2—were partners in the Franco regime cabinet.

In addition to the commonality of Escriva and Gelli, the key operating officers of Opus Dei held the corresponding jobs in P2. For example, Jose Mateos as treasurer of both organizations pulled the purse strings of the Opus Dei-P2 coalition; both organizations dealing with the same commodities in the same markets with the same bank—Ambrosiano; the reason the Opus Dei-P2-Ambrosiano coalition emerged as the largest foreign investor in Central America.

This clandestine union was defined by the courts that tried both the terrorist activities and the bank scandal many times.

For example, in connection with their convictions involving the Bologna bombing and other terrorist activities, in April 1998 Licio Gelli and Jose Mateos were brought to trial in connection with the Vatican bank scandal. The prosecution proved they had conspired with the Vatican and factions in the CIA in the scandal. Sentenced to twelve years, Gelli disappeared on the eve of his imprisonment.[44]

Yet, some officers of Opus Dei—believed to be—not proved to be—officers of P2 escaped trial; immunized from the Italian courts by John Paul II's authorization of the Prelature of Opus Dei retroactive to the day before Banco Ambrosiano went under.

The CIA and the Pope

Today, the CIA is positioned to assassinate many heads of state and others who might surface at any time as a threat to the security of the United States on a moment's notice. This includes a pope.

The CIA agent-unit commissioned to take out a pope, should a pope threaten the security of the United States, was established by George Bush in 1976 when Paul's pro-communist principles were driving the rise of communism in Europe and Central America.

Through Agostino Casaroli, Bush engaged Licio Gelli's Masonic Lodge P2 which had hit-men working as maintenance workers in the Vatican. This could have only intended to add the papacy to the CIA hit-list as CIA's Operation Gladio and Operation Condor already had Italy and all of Western Europe covered.

Illuminati News reports the Bush-Gelli deal involved a CIA payment of $10 million/month to P2 from mid-1976 until the pro-American anti-communist Pope John Paul II took office in October 1978. Subsequent events confirm this arrangement.[45]

Bush would eventually get some of the money back.

Gelli was the largest contributor to Bush's campaign for president in 1988. Gelli, when questioned concerning his trips to the Bush Kennebunkport estate, denied having a personal relationship with Bush. He explained his visits as being a matter of business.

Licio Gelli, Grandmaster of the Masonic Lodge killer organization Propaganda Due (P2) and major contributor to the Bush campaign, stands with Bush as he is sworn in as President of the United States in 1989. There are also pictures of Gelli standing with Reagan-Bush as they were sworn in as President-Vice President in 1981

The Bush family and the Vatican

Casaroli introduced CIA Director George Bush to Cardinal Karol Wojtyla of Poland and Curia Cardinal Joseph Ratzinger in 1976.

It may have been the coincidental relationships of their fathers with Hitler—Prescott Bush as Hitler's financier and the senior

Murder by the Grace of God

Ratzinger possibly as Hitler's bodyguard at Eagle's Nest—George Bush and Joseph Ratzinger struck up an endearing relationship.

In 1999, Bush's son Neil Bush and Joseph Ratzinger co-founded *The Foundation to Promote Ecumenical Understanding."*[46]

The president's other son Jeb Bush was the official representative of the United States at the coronation of Benedict XVI in 2005.

Father of George Bush, Prescott Bush, is shown here with his protégé, Richard Nixon. George Bush, in turn, would become Nixon's protégé. John and Robert Kennedy's murders made possible Nixon's return to the political arena. Neither Nixon nor Bush would have risen to the top had the Kennedy brothers lived as the nation was looking at a 24 years of Kennedys.

Casaroli and Caprio retired to a villa outside Naples on the same day in 1990. In his last act as Vatican Secretary of State Casaroli visited Bush in the Oval Office in October 1990 and had dinner with Bush and Gelli the following evening at the Vatican Embassy.

The Holy Alliance

The Holy Alliance is believed to have had its origin in a meeting between CIA Director George Bush and Cardinal Wojtyla during the latter's July through September 1976 tour of the United States. They met for three days Aug 26-28 at the Vatican Embassy in DC.[47]

No one knows what the future president and future pope talked about during the time they spent together. Yet, history tells us they most likely strategized their rise to the pinnacles of their respective worlds. CIA Director Bush would do everything in his power to move Wojtyla into the Papal Apartment. Wojtyla, in turn, would openly endorse Bush's rise to the Oval Office. As a sweetener, Bush would stack the U.S. Supreme Court with devout Catholics.

At the time not a single Catholic was on the Supreme Court as less than one-fifth of the American population was Catholic.

In retrospect, this is what happened. In the following election, for the first time in history a pope openly endorsed a presidential ticket by attacking the Reagan/Bush opponent Jimmy Carter.

The Reagan-Bush-Bush presidencies have met with the papacy sixteen times; more than all other presidents combined. What's more, they have appointed a wave of Catholics to the Court. In a nation overwhelmingly protestant and non-denominational, today, six devout Roman Catholics control the nine-judge court. Even those nominated by Reagan-Bush who failed to be endorsed by the Senate—e.g. the controversial nominee Robert Bork—were staunch Roman Catholics. The court is today entirely a Judeo-Catholic body which had its upbringing in the horrific rule of Mosaic Law.

United States Supreme Court Religious Affiliation

representing 20% of Americans		representing 80% of Americans
Catholic	Jewish	
Roberts	Breyer	none
Scalia	Ginsberg	
Thomas	Kagan	
Alito		
Kennedy		
Sotomayor		

Scalia and Thomas are openly members of Opus Dei. Roberts and Alito are believed to be members of the clandestine cult. I repeat, the mission of Opus Dei is to control the moral pulse of the world through control of the papacy and the judicial branches of nations. [48]

The Red Mass is held the Sunday before the United States Supreme Court convenes every October to ask the Holy Spirit's guidance. Cardinal Donald Wuerl and Chief Justice Roberts lead the justices at the Cathedral of St. Matthew in DC.

That George Bush was the principal in the Iran-Contra Affair and Karol Wojtyla was the principal in the Vatican-Contra Affair (Vatican Bank Scandal)—both having a common goal—should be more than enough to link George Bush to the Vatican Bank Scandal.

The courts that tried the scandal 1982-84 confirmed this. For example, from 1978 through 1980—the time of the scandal—George Bush chaired the First International Bank of Houston.

On October 16, 1979, John Paul II 'loaned' $134 million to a Panama City ghost affiliate of Bush's bank to the credit of United

Trading Company—also based in Houston. The money disappeared and was never recovered.[49]

Nevertheless, we have connected a few dots. Dots which make the world go round. We will connect many more as we go along.

The Historic Compromise

That the CIA strategy to terrorize the Italian people and turn them against communism had failed, was demonstrated by the results of the 1976 election: Christian Democrats 38.8%, Communists 34.4%, Socialists 15.8%, Proletarians (blue collar) 8.0%, Republicans 3.0%. Except for the tiny fraction garnished by the Republican Party, the vote was entirely on the *left*. Although each party had individual opinions as to how it would go about achieving its objectives, they all had one goal in common: a redistribution of wealth society: **a society that affords each and every child an equal opportunity to make his or her contribution to society.**[50]

When Aldo Moro enacted his *Historic Compromise* which united his Christian Democratic Party and the Communist Party giving the coalition an overwhelming plurality in Parliament, the CIA strategy shifted from terrorizing the rank-and-file population to eliminating the leaders of the pro-Marxist movement in Europe.[51]

The period 1976-78 witnessed a growing alliance of Moro's Christian Democratic Party and Berlinguer's Communist Party. It also witnessed a growing personal relationship between Moro and Berlinguer—their families pestered by reporters while vacationing together on the Aegean coast and the Island of Corfu.[52]

Aldo Moro's intent to bring communism into Europe was not a secret he shared only with Enrico Berlinguer. It was widely known throughout the world. This has been widely recorded in the world press in criticism levied at Moro from his right-wing enemies.

George Bush, a steadfast republican who spent a lifetime making the rich richer and the poor poorer, called the union: "**...a greater threat to the free world than is the Soviet Union.**"[53]

George Bush had been born into immense wealth. He knew what wealth could bring. He had been brought up in the lap of luxury, gone to the best schools, and had used his family's industrial and political power to rise to the top. Communism—a redistribution of wealth society—was his most bitter enemy.

Secretary of State Henry Kissinger reacted even more fiercely to Moro's action: "I believe the advent of communism in Italy and Spain is likely to result in a sequence of events in which other European countries will move in the same direction... the Communist Party has emerged as an effective vehicle for developing jobs and providing education for the common people and this endangers our free capitalistic society... If communism takes hold in Italy, NATO would collapse and the United States would be dangerously isolated..."[54]

In a follow-up, Kissinger pinpointed his position: "Domination by Moscow is not the issue. Communist control of Italy and Central America is the issue... It would have terrible consequences for the United States and it is today the number one threat to its national security and must be dealt with accordingly."[55]

Referring to Operation Gladio and other anti-communist terrorist organizations operating in Italy: "It is clear anti-communist forces within Italy are paralyzed by the success of the Communist Party in the polls and will be unable to stop it... A clean external amputation is preferable to internal paralysis..."[56]

One can only surmise 'external amputation' meant 'assassination of Aldo Moro by a foreign power.' What else could it have possibly meant? Aldo Moro, who had risen as the most influential man in Europe, was clearly the 'link' between communism and Europe. Remove the 'link' and communism in Europe would fail.

Two weeks before Moro's abduction, US Ambassador to Italy Richard Gardner released an official statement from the United States Embassy in Rome: "Moro is the most dangerous force in the history of the Italian political scene."[57]

A few days before the kidnapping—when it became known Moro would move communist members into control of the House of Representatives—British Ambassador John Killbrick warned: "The presence of communist ministers in the Italian Parliament is a serious threat to the security of the alliance of the free world."[58]

On the afternoon of the kidnapping from the other side of the aisle, reacting to Prime Minister Andreotti's claim the Red Brigades had abducted Moro, left-wing general and president of the Italian senate Benigno Zaccagnini pointed his finger directly at the United States and the CIA: "This kidnapping is clearly a part of a plan by foreign interests aimed at upsetting the new Italian majority. It has nothing to do with the Red Brigades." [59]

The Bush-Casaroli-Kissinger-Gardner fears were well founded. Unlike all other countries communism had invaded in the past where it was faced with the insurmountable hurdles of immense poverty, poor education and relentless revolution, Italy was a thriving stable democracy. As a matter-of-fact, it was free elections that had moved the country toward communism to begin with.

Bush, Casaroli, Kissinger and Gardner were terrified communism would succeed in Italy for it would certainly follow quickly in Spain where it had already reached double digit electoral progress. It would eventually spread to all of Europe.

It was the *Historic Compromise* of 1976, more than anything else, that caused Moro's name to move up to the top of the CIA hit-list.

It was his impending threat to move communist members into control of the House of Representatives that pulled the trigger.

The plot to assassinate Aldo Moro

To understand who murdered Aldo Moro one must first consider motive. The greatest motive to have carried out the murders of Moro and others on our list was shared by a coalition of three states: the Vatican, the United States and Great Britain. These three shared a common motive: Stamp out a common enemy—communism.

In this context, the key players in a conspiracy involving an assassination of a foreign leader embracing communism would be the CIA, British Intelligence and the Office of the Vatican Foreign Minister—the Vatican's counterpart of the CIA and the SIS.

In the case of a NATO nation, a conspiracy to assassinate a citizen would be most effective if it included the Intelligence operation of the targeted state—in Italy, at the time, Italian Counter-Intelligence.

This was particularly true in Moro's case, as Italian Counter-Intelligence had raided dozens of Red Brigades' hideouts through the years and had storerooms full of items seized in the raids which could be planted to frame the Red Brigades. It also had several buildings in Rome where Moro could be retained which would escape a controlled search for the former prime minister.

The coalition of these foreign states had a more than willing partner in the incumbent Italian prime minister—Giulio Andreotti.

Andreotti had spent a lifetime fighting communism and condemned the *Historic Compromise* from the day Moro made it public.

In addition to his hatred of communism, he had a personal motive for wanting Moro out of the way. The *Historic Compromise* had given Moro an overwhelming plurality in the upcoming election; Andreotti was about to lose his job.

Italian Counter-Intelligence reported directly to Andreotti and the extent of its search for Moro could be restricted by him. The prime minister took a hardline approach and not only refused to pay the ransom money but refused to enter into dialogue with those who held Moro. Dialogue alone can often lead to where the victim is held whether or not the calls are made from the site. Perhaps, Andreotti didn't want anyone to know where Moro was being held particularly if it was within the Italian Counter-Intelligence network. Perhaps, he knew dialogue would be a monologue with himself.

Why Andreotti refused dialogue with the terrorists in Moro's case is no mystery today. Three years later when his friend Ciro Cirillo was kidnapped he took no hardline approach at all; he paid ransom on demand. In Moro's case, he would not even engage in dialogue.[60]

The murder of Carmine Pecorelli

To give some credence that leaders of free nations—let alone CIA directors—have the capacity to kill. In November 2002, former Prime Minister Andreotti was convicted in a Perugia court of having ordered the assassination of Carmine Pecorelli through the CIA and Italian Intelligence and was sentenced to 24 years; later pardoned by the Supreme Court of Cassation because of his public service.[61]

Pecorelli was a reputable journalist and editor of *Osservatore Politico*. In a cryptic article a week after the Moro murder in May 1978 he established a credible connection between Operation Gladio and the CIA and Andreotti and the Moro murder.[62]

Early in 1979, Pecorelli gained important contacts within Italian Counter-Intelligence. His colleagues testified in the Andreotti trial Pecorelli had been working on an article which would expose **'The Role of the United States and Italian Intelligence in the Moro Murder.'** He was murdered on March 20, 1979; his house ransacked, the manuscript destroyed and the office of *Osservatore Politico* destroyed by fire. What Pecorelli knew about American and Italian Intelligence involvement in the Aldo Moro murder, died with him.[63]

'A clean external amputation...'

In CIA headquarters in Virginia, the strategy of framing the Red Brigades for the bombings—having been exposed many times in the courts—had not only failed, it had moved the populace further to the left. In 1976, as we have said, the vote all but annihilated the right.

Moro had emerged as a monumental progressive threatening to weld communist ideology into Italy's ruling coalition. It was the sworn duty of the CIA to stop him.

Yet, the rapid succession of court proceedings in Italy had not only cleared the Red Brigades of involvement in the bombings; it had clearly established right-wing terrorist groups had repeatedly tried to frame them. This tied the hands of the CIA and Gladio.

An assassination of Moro could not be blamed on the Brigades as the populace would know the true perpetrators. If a car bomb was used to assassinate Moro and a circled-star scratched on its hood, it would point to the CIA and Operation Gladio and not the Brigades.

Hence, in planning a Moro assassination—'a clean amputation'—the possibility of framing the Red Brigades was out of the question.

Or was it?

A change in strategy

The Red Brigades did have a long record of kidnapping the rich and powerful and holding them for ransom. Moro certainly fit that mode for he was both rich and powerful. Yet, there was the problem he was on the wrong side of the fence. The others victimized by the Red Brigades were right-wing enemies of the socialist-communist movement. Moro was its greatest ally.

Court trials had clearly defined the pattern of the Red Brigades: Kidnapping of high profile figures. If the ransom was paid the victim was returned, if not paid the body was returned. Regardless of the victim's wealth, the ransom was always set at about $5 million.

Operation Gladio and its allies in the underground terrorist world of Italy had no record in the courts of ever having kidnapped their victims. In retrospect today, it would seem the CIA struck on the idea of following the pattern of the Red Brigades. It would kidnap Moro and hold him for ransom of $5 million and plant incriminating evidence sufficient to indict and convict the Red Brigades.

It would include in the ransom demands, the release of Brigades' members to seal the case against them. Too—as only Prime Minister Andreotti could pardon prisoners—this would preclude a third party from meeting the monetary demands.

As we have said this condition should have raised eyebrows as in the long string of Red Brigades' kidnappings they had never before demanded release of prisoners; demands had been limited to cash.

The CIA would instruct Andreotti not to engage in dialogue with the kidnappers lest it accidentally lead to where Moro was held—most likely in either a NATO or Italian Counter-Intelligence unit.

Yet, the CIA had the problem Moro and the Brigades shared the same ideology. Whereas his *Historic Compromise* in 1976 may have been met with some apprehension in the Brigades, when it became known prior to his kidnapping, in the spring of 1978, Moro would move communist ministers into control of Parliament, it was met by much celebration within the ranks of the Brigades. It would make no sense a left-wing communist terrorist organization would murder the man who was about to make Italy a communist nation.

For this reason—most critical to the operation—Moro was not to be harmed in the abduction. Had he been killed in the abduction, the finger would have pointed directly to Gladio and the CIA.

That his driver sitting next to him and six armed bodyguards were killed and Moro untouched points to a highly precisioned SWAT team—characteristic of NATO precision trained Gladio hit men.

When Moro was abducted he was not on his way to his office. He was on his way to the Italian House of Representatives to start the ball rolling to move the Communist Party into control of Parliament. He had the authority to do this vested in him by the 1976 election which he had put on hold with the *Historic Compromise.* [64]

If Moro had completed his journey to Parliament that day, Prime Minster Andreotti would have lost his authority, as Moro's coalition of the Christian Democratic Party and the Communist Party would have not only controlled three-quarters of Parliament, it would have controlled Andreotti's cabinet as well. The timing of the Moro

Murder by the Grace of God

kidnapping to the exact point in time the Communist Party would enter into controlling majority in Italy was no coincidence.

The motive in the Moro murder pointed clearly toward enemies of the growing threat of communism in Europe; the Vatican and the CIA and their allies in the capitalistic world would top the list.

Yet, as we have demonstrated, in the case of an autocratic crime the public ignores motive in its perception of guilt. So do the courts.

The Moro trial

Four years later, Mario Moretti and the Red Brigades were brought to trial for the kidnapping and murder of Aldo Moro.

In its judgment the court relied entirely on the testimony of ten Red Brigades members who turned state's evidence in exchange for lighter sentences. Not the slightest link of Moretti and his followers was made to the Aldo Moro murder despite that the trial spanned a year-and-a-half.

A mountain of conflicting evidence was presented by the defense.

The Brigades' members who testified against Moretti claimed Moro had been held outside the city although they did not know where. Yet, the red Renault Moro's body was delivered in had been stolen from a building only six miles from where it had been found.

The car had been serviced the day before and the speedometer reading noted by the garage showed the car had moved only fourteen miles. If it had gone outside the city it would have traveled a minimum of thirty-two miles at the nearest point. The police determined Moro had been shot after he was placed in the trunk as several bullets passing through the body had lodged in the trunk's walls; he could not have been transferred from another vehicle.[65]

Had the car traveled directly from the point of theft to the United States Embassy and then to the Via Caetani where it was found, it would have moved twelve miles. Yet, avoidance of roadblocks set up by police could have caused it to detour. Of course, there were hundreds of other buildings in the same area this would be true of.

In fact, had Moro been held by Italian Intelligence, the agency had two buildings within these limits—one a high security retention center. The court did conclude Moro had been held inside the city.

The defense introduced court transcripts of a mall-bombing that had occurred a year after the Moro murder. Two Alitalia Airline pilots—members of Operation Gladio—had been convicted in the case. The two, serving five year sentences, were questioned about the theft of the Alitalia uniforms used in the Moro kidnapping. Both prisoners denied involvement. Of course, if they had been involved in the Moro murder, they would be looking at life sentences.[66]

A *Brigate Rosse* backdrop in a photo of Moro released by his captors was questioned. Comparison of the photo with a banner seized in a raid of a Brigades' Bologna flat two years before the kidnapping proved they were the same banner. It was found to be missing from the Italian Counter-Intelligence criminal evidence inventory in Rome. It would have had to have been obtained by someone in the Italian Counter-Intelligence network.[67]

Although not one of the two hundred witnesses of his kidnapping identified any of the defendants, bullets extracted from Moro's bodyguards and found at the kidnapping scene—NATO 5.56 mm—proved M-16 semi-automatic weapons—available only to U.S. armed forces—had been used in the abduction. It should be noted, the 9mm pistol later used to execute Aldo Moro was a commercial weapon available to most anyone.

On July 19, 1982, Moro's wife Eleonora testified in open court:

> "In recent years, Aldo had been threatened dozens of times. Yet, it was on the morning after Kissinger's threat that Aldo took security measures. We moved from our estate into the fortified building on the Via Forte Trionfale; bodyguards occupying the floor directly beneath us. The windows were sealed in with bulletproof glass and wire mesh. It was like being locked up in a high security prison. It was terrible," she told the court. "I couldn't even open a window. Nevertheless, after that, Aldo, I and Giovanni never left the apartment without a half-dozen heavily armed guards."[68]

Asked what the American diplomat had told Moro:

> "It is one of the few times Aldo told me exactly what had been said to him. So I have always remembered it. I will repeat it now: 'You must abandon your policy of bringing these (communist) political forces in your country into coalition, or you will pay dearly for it.'"[69]

As a precaution, she and her son Giovanni were shown dozens of photos by Aldo's guards. The pictures were mostly members of Operation Gladio, Ordine Nuovo and Avanguardia Nazionale.

When shown a photo of Licio Gelli of P2, the guards told her: "'We have reason to believe not only Aldo's life is in danger but that of Pope Paul as well. This man has people living in the Vatican.'" She told the court: "We had no fear of the Red Brigades. Although we did not agree with their activities, they were very much on our side."[70]

Although she did not name a name, Eleonora testified in her opinion she was certain that Aldo's kidnapping and murder had been ordered by "a high ranking United States official."[71]

In the Moretti trial the prosecution presented no forensic evidence linking Moretti to the crime and the weapon was never found. In that the court could not determine where Moro had been held, it had no hard evidence connecting Moretti and the Brigades to the crime. All it had was the questionable testimony of ten turned-state's witnesses who had no idea where Moro had been held.

Despite the lack of evidence and Eleonora's testimony and the Kissinger and other American statesmen' threats in the world press, Moretti and twenty-two others were found guilty on all counts.[72]

Eleonora's testimony and the lack of evidence and the fact that Moro and the Brigades were on the same side of the political arena caused many Italians to view the conviction with the same sort of skepticism as was the 'Warren Commission Report' viewed in the John Kennedy assassination in the United States. To these less than gullible citizens it made no sense the Red Brigades would murder the man who was about to bring its dreams to fruition.

Most of those who have written of the Moro murder explain this conflict of interest by suggesting Mario Moretti was actually an Operation Gladio (NATO) officer who had infiltrated the ranks of the Red Brigades. This allegation has never been proved. If true, of course, the Moro murder would point directly at the CIA.

A year-and-a-half and a hundred thousand pages of testimony failed to determine where Moro was held captive. The prosecution went so far as to offer immunity to any Brigades' member charged in the crime who could disclose the location of the 'People's Prison.'

The hunt

To understand this more clearly one must consider the extent of the search for Moro. The entire Italian army reserve was activated. Every house and building in Rome was searched. Roadblocks were set up throughout the city. Every vehicle entering or leaving the city and many moving within the city were searched.

Prime Minister Andreotti labeled the place where Moro was held as the **'People's Prison,'** despite that the people overwhelmingly supported Moro. In all, the search spanned fifty-four days. Not a trace of Moro could be found.

There were few places that were immune to search: the Vatican, embassies, building(s) the Italian Counter-Intelligence designated as off-limits and a NATO complex on the edge of Rome.

Several embassies waived immunity and invited police to search their facilities; the United States and British embassies were not among them. Even Paul VI waived immunity, yet, he could not get Andreotti to search the Vatican grounds.[73]

The Parallel Sid

Eight years later, in court actions led by Judge Casson in 1990, General Giandelio Maletti—Chief of Italy's Intelligence—testified he had collaborated with the CIA and Operation Gladio in ordering most of the terrorist activities in the 1970s. Maletti told the court:

> "The CIA wanted to create an Italian nationalism capable of halting what it saw as a dangerous slide to the left and for this purpose it employed right-wing terrorism to change the mindset of the Italian population. American taxpayers paid the salaries of thousands of Gladio members and other right-wing terrorists and provided them with what was at one time 139 caches of weapons and explosives strategically placed throughout Italy."[74]

Maletti was among dozens of Italian Intelligence officers found on a list of 962 members of P2 seized in the 1981 raid of Gelli's villa. Examination of the list by Judge Casson's court determined that Richard Nixon's National Security Advisor Henry Kissinger had **'authorized (paid) Licio Gelli to add 400 high ranking Italian and NATO officers into his Lodge in 1969.'**[75]

In addition to Maletti, the Chief of the Italian Military Secret Service and the Chief of Italian Counter-Intelligence were also on the list. All three were double agents drawing salaries from both Italian and American taxpayers. The latter were also subpoenaed by Judge Casson and they confirmed Maletti's testimony.

Three of the magistrates who had presided over the Moro trial were found to have been on the list. To make matters worse, the list had been discovered before the Moro trial and this information had been withheld by Italian Intelligence from the Moro trial of 1982.

Vincenzo Vinciguerra of Avanguardia Nazionale, who was serving a life sentence for the Peteano bombing, testified: "**Ordine Nuovo, Avanguardia Nazionale and other prominent right-wing terrorist organizations had cooperated with Operation Gladio and the Italian military secret service to terrorize the general population and frame the Red Brigades to destroy the political left in Italy.**"[76]

By midsummer 1990, Judge Casson's findings flooded the press. Confronted by the scandal, former Prime Minister Giulio Andreotti addressed Parliament on August 3, 1990 and owned up to his involvement with the CIA and Operation Gladio in the terrorism of the 1970s. He provided a document to the Italian Senate on October 24, 1990 formally recognizing the existence of Gladio. He testified that the United States and other capitalistic countries including Great Britain had been behind the bombings of the 1970s.

He quoted and agreed with General Zaccagnini President of the Italian Senate's remark the day of Moro's abduction: "**This is clearly a part of a plan by foreign interests aimed at upsetting the new Italian majority. It has nothing to do with the Red Brigades.**"

Andreotti's document detailing CIA and Gladio involvement in the terror of the 1970s—*The Parallel SID*—was published by the Italian magazine *Panorama* it in its entirety.[77]

On Casson's findings and other revelations in the 1990s, despite serving six consecutive life sentences, Moretti was freed in 1998.

If one ignores motive, it could have been Mario Moretti who pumped ten bullets into the blanket covered body of Aldo Moro in the trunk of a car on the morning of May 9, 1978. If one considers motive, the CIA pulled the trigger; at the very least gave the order.

That it was Aldo Moro's *Historic Compromise* that led to his demise is demonstrated by the final act of his kidnappers.

The body of Aldo Moro was found in the trunk of a car on the Via Caetani precisely 1,757 meters from the Christian Democratic Party headquarters in one direction and precisely 1,757 meters from the Communist Party headquarters in the other direction.[78]

It was on the heels of Judge Casson's findings and Andreotti's disclosure of *The Parallel Sid* a leak in November 1990 revealed Avro Manhattan was writing a book linking the CIA and right-wing factions in the Vatican to the murders of Aldo Moro, Metropolitan Nikodim, John Paul I and other Marxist leaders in the Church.[79]

As we have said, *Murder by the Grace of God* is that book.

Representatives of nations from around the globe poured into Rome for Aldo Moro's funeral.

Strong and unyielding through his hour-long eulogy, the eyes of the pro-communist pontiff Paul VI came to rest in a threatening stare on Giulio Andreotti and Henry Kissinger who sat in the first row:

> "...The extremist believes he can halt the carriage of change. But, there are too many wheels. Take one away and another will rise up to take its place. His is a futile struggle. He has no place in time. No place in humanity. No place beyond humanity..."[80]

9:00AM May 14, 1978. McLean Virginia[81]

On the other side of the pond in CIA headquarters in McLean Virginia, a bushy eyebrowed man took up the morning edition of *The Washington Post* and read: "...Take one away and another will rise up to take its place."

He mumbled to himself, "Henry was wrong: 'Amputate the link and communism will fail."

He turned and looked up at the wall, '...threats ...'

He turned back to the desk. "The ball has shifted from the most influential man in Europe, to the most influential man in the world."

He opened a book. There was a list of names.

At the top of the list he struck out the name ~~Aldo Moro~~.

Beside it, he wrote the name *Paul VI*.

Murder by the Grace of God

1 *CIA Charter -mission*
2 *CIA Charter - subversive agents*
3 *CIA Charter - employees*
4 *CIA Charter - budget*
5 *Oscar Romero* biographies
6 Combined platform, Italian Communist Party & Italian Christian Democratic Party, 1976
7 *Prescott Bush* biographies; the Feds seized the bank October 29, 1942
8 In the inquest, Bush testified he thought his crew was dead. Other members of Bush's squadron saw his radioman bail out as the plane crashed into the sea. Through his father's influence George Bush was awarded *The Distinguished Flying Cross*.
9 *New World Order*, '*Adolph Hitler Installed German Chancellor*' 1 Feb 33
10 *New York Times* 16 Dec 73, 'APA removes homosexuality from list of mental disorders'
11 *L'Espresso* Mar 74
12 Mission of the Vatican Foreign Minister rephrased to mirror that of the CIA. The eagle is satire.
13 *La Repubblica* 11 May 78
14 *Corriere Della Sera* 27 Sep 76
15 *Affari Italiani* 22 Aug 76
16 *Statistical Abstracts of the United States* 1970-75
17 *La Repubblica* 10 May 77
18 *La Repubblica* 24 Jul 78
19 *Malopolska Silesia* 25 Jul 76
20 *Tygodnik Zamojsk* 26 Jul 76
21 *La Repubblica* 11 Mar 78
22 *La Repubblica* 22 Jul 82; Eleonora Moro's testimony of July 19, 1982 in the Aldo Moro trial
23 *The Times* London 18 Mar 78
24 *La Repubblica* 18 Mar 78
25 *The Times* London 19 Mar 78
26 *The Times* London 20 Mar 78
27 search *Operation Gladio* Italian history
28 *IL Messaggero* 12 Feb 69
29 search *Red Brigades* Italian history
30 search *Operation Gladio* Italian history
31 *La Repubblica* 24 Oct 90 - *La Stampa* 24 Oct 90   Article: *Prime Minister Andreotti—Gladio*
32 search *Ordine Nuovo* Italian history
33 search *Avanguardia Nazionale* Italian history
34 search *Operation Condor* Chile history
35 *search Propaganda Due P2* Italian history
36 search *Opus Dei* Catholic history
37 *La Repubblica Piazza Fontana* 13 Dec 69 - *Bologna Railway Bombing* 3Aug 80
38 *La Repubblica* 24 Oct 90 -*La Stampa* 24 Oct 90   Article: *Prime Minister Andreotti—Gladio*
39 *La Repubblica* 1 Jun 74 *Vincenzo Vinciguerra Peteano Bombing* Italian history books
40 *La Repubblica* 12 Sep 81 *Italy Reign of Terror*
41 *Neue Zurcher Zeitung* 10 Oct 57
42 *A Life with Karol* Stanislaw Dziwisz
43 see Chapter '*How a Pope is Elected'*
44 *La Repubblica* 22 Jul 88 *Tuscany - La Repubblica* 29 Apr 98 *Ambrosiano*
45 *Illuminati News* Jul 79
46 *St. Petersburg Times* 23 Apr 05
47 *Malopolska – Silesia* 27 Aug 76 Le cardinal Wojtyla se rencontre avec le Directeur de CIA Bush.
48 United States Supreme Court Justices as of January 2013, the time of publication of this book
49 *Wall Street Journal* 27 Apr 87 *'The Vatican's Role in the Fall of Ambrosiano'*
50 1976 Election results Italy
51 search: *Historic Compromise* in any library
52 *Telegrafos Corfu* 23 Jul 77
53 *Washington Post* 16 Aug 76.
54 *Covet Action Quarterly* Washington DC No. 49 Summer 94
55 *TIME What if Communists Win a Role?* 26 Apr 76
56 *TIME What if Communists Win a Role?* 26 Apr 76

57 *L'Europeo* 1 Mar 78
58 *La Repubblica* 12 Mar 78.
59 *La Repubblica* 18 Mar 78
60 search: *Aldo Moro* see also *NATO's Secret Armies* Ganser pg 79
61 *La Repubblica* 18 Nov 02 *Giulio Andreotti*
62 *La Repubblica* 21 Mar 79 *Carmine Pecorelli*
63 *La Repubblica* 21 Mar 79 *Carmine Pecorelli*
64 search any Italian history journal: *Historic Compromise Aldo Moro*
65 *La Repubblica* 18 May 78
66 *La Repubblica* 12 Jul 82
67 *La Repubblica* 16 Jul 82
68 *La Repubblica* 20 Jul 82 and 21 Jul 82 ([1])
69 *La Repubblica* 20 Jul 82 and 21 Jul 82 ([1])
70 *La Repubblica* 22 Jul 82 and 21 Jul 82 ([1])
71 *La Repubblica* 23 Jul 82 and 21 Jul 82 ([1])
72 search *Mario Moretti* Italian history
73 *La Repubblica* 22 Apr 78
74 *The Guardian* 26 Mar 2001 '*Giandelio Maletti Gladio*'
75 *La Repubblica* 5 Apr 1981 also NATO's Secret Armies p 74 Ganser
76 *La Repubblica* 14 May 84 '*Vincenzo Vinciguerra*'
77 *Panorama* December 1990
78 *La Repubblica* 10 May 78
79 *BBC News* 7 Nov 90
80 *La Repubblica* 14 May 78
81 closing satire

([1]) In addition to being in the court's transcripts, Kissinger's threats have been widely published in books about the Moro murder including the bestsellers, *The Aldo Moro Murder Case* by Richard Drake 1995 pg 85 and *Days of Wrath* by Robert Kat pg xxiv. NATO's Secret Armies by Ganser pg79

Chapter 33

The Murder of Paul VI

"We have fought the good battle. Let us finish the run!" Paul VI

In July of 1978, from the tower of strength he had been at Moro's funeral, Paul was worn out. He was pale and lacked any semblance of energy. He had been taking uncharacteristic naps. They had begun shortly after Moro's funeral. It seemed the strain of losing his friend was too much for him. He agreed to take a rest at Castel Gandolfo.

There are five magnificent palaces including the papal residence within the retreat. Yet, the Castel, itself, is a part of the ruins of an embattlement built by Urban VIII in the seventeenth century to protect the city of Rome and St. Peter's—Castel Franco to the north, Castel Sant'Angelo to the east, and Castel Gandolfo to the west.

Sitting high on a hill it keeps a watchful eye over St. Peter's. The basilica's immense dome can be viewed from its northern turrets.

To the west are the glistening waters of the Mediterranean, and to the east, is a perfectly oval shaped blue lake set in a field of green trees. Off in another direction, one can view wooded slopes falling swiftly down to the gray murky waters of an ancient volcanic crater.

If one is privileged to witness the view from the papal rooms themselves, one can see the Apian Way lined with towering trees on either side—soldiers standing at attention awaiting their emperor to proceed down between them. On a perfectly clear day, one can follow them along the ancient viaduct all the way down to the Adriatic Sea.

Off in one direction, one can see the low rolling Alban Hills. Off in another direction, one can see still another blue lake edged in by the ruins of the palace of Diocletian, where Constantine—founder of the Roman Catholic Church—had played as a boy.

The world's most beautiful gardens are here too.

The architecture of the gardens is a composition of Italian, French, German, Russian, Chinese, Japanese, Indian, African, Australian and even American. Not even the Eskimo and Arab have been left out.

In one corner, Arctic roses peek up from a carpet of tundra, and just a few feet away, flowering cactus bloom in a miniature desert of sand; one must watch for polar bears and scorpions at the same time.

The gardens are edged in by palm trees at one end and evergreens at the other. Even Christ would be at home here. There is patch of ground taken out of His hometown of Nazareth—this one fenced in to keep small children and stray animals out.

Its crown jewel is the striking plant *Ornithogalum Umbellatum.* Because of its white star design, its flower is commonly referred to as the *Star of Bethlehem.* Every bit as dangerous as it is beautiful it has found its way into mystery novels. Its nut flavored bulb, if concealed in nutty flavored foods, results in respiratory convulsions culminating in death within hours.

It seems the only thing one cannot see, is snow.

The Godfather's last ride

In the still of the darkness of the evening of July fourteenth nineteen hundred seventy-eight, Paul left the Vatican for the last time. He warded off his secretary Macchi's offer of assistance as he climbed into the limousine that would take him to the papal retreat. Carlo Confalonieri—the aging dean of the College of Cardinals—did take Macchi up on his offer as he struggled into the car next to the Pope.

The car was a black Mercedes from the pool of vehicles reserved for use by Vatican cardinals. He had chosen not to use the helicopter which usually took him to the castle. He would go incognito this time by ground as if he knew of his impeding fate; he wanted to be witness to the streets and the people of his beloved Rome for this last time.

Although decidedly slower than he had been at the time of Moro's funeral there was little outward change in his appearance other than a mustard-like tinge to his skin. His face looked like it was hewn out of yellow pine. It was flaking, as if God had used a chisel on him.

Jean Villot—Paul's longtime friend and confidant—had decided at the last minute to go along for a few days. He climbed into the car from the other side so as to wedge Paul in between the two of them.

That Villot chose to go along was a break in protocol as the secretary of state remains in the Vatican when the Pope is away. Macchi took the jump seat in the rear compartment and Magee—Paul's other secretary—slid silently into the seat next to the driver.

Though one was a priest, one a monsignor, one a cardinal, one a dean and the other a pope; all five were dressed in black, entirely in black. Five men—six with the chauffeur—dressed in black suits with a half-dozen black boleros topping them off.

Except for the presence of Swiss Guards in their elaborate attire to either side of the palace doors, one would assume the Mafia was taking the Godfather for his last ride. As if a gangland episode was about to occur along the way; somewhere between here and there, his body would be thrown from the car, perhaps beneath a viaduct.

Particularly, if one were to notice a second black Mercedes follow the first one out of the gates. Four more men in black suits topped off with matching boleros—Swiss Guards—so as not to attract notice.

Yet, nothing happened along the way. Except for Paul's offer to share his cough drops, his only words during the short ride were: "Why do I tire so?" No one offered an answer. No one took him up on the cough drops either. After all, it was midsummer.

He wiped his lips. A tinge of red spotted a white handkerchief.

"...to die like a cat or a dog."

Indeed, it was his last ride. Three weeks later spiraling steadily downward he was dead. The daily naps progressing to all day sleeps, to near coma, to the morning of the final day when he showed signs of recovery. Then early that same afternoon, he developed an acute respiratory problem and his blood pressure dropped dramatically.

'Heart attack' was announced to the press. His brother Senator Luigi Montini who had learned of his condition on the news was en route to Castel Gandolfo when Paul's pontificate came to its end.

Popes are not normally hospitalized—the privilege of royalty in Europe where the hospital packs up its bags and comes to them. This had been true when Paul had his prostate surgery ten years earlier; a small room in the secretaries' office was converted into a makeshift operating theater which remains today. Yet, in cases of serious illness, an intensive care mobile unit is usually summoned from Rome.

For some reason Paul's physician never called for a unit. Not even after he had suffered the 'heart attack' with which he lingered for almost a day. This, despite that when the news reached Rome an intensive care unit was offered by a hospital ten minutes away.

Actually, except for a consultation with an urologist in Rome, Dr. Fontana made no attempt to seek outside help although the Pope was critically ill. Also, no notice of his illness was released to the press or even his family until after he had suffered the presumed heart attack.

Members of the medical profession criticized this inaction.

They questioned why Paul was not returned to the safety of the Vatican once it was known he was seriously ill as it had both the equipment and personnel to have saved his life.

When members of the press questioned the doctor as to why this was not done, he told them the heart attack was sudden and it was obvious Paul was dying; until the last day—though very tired—Paul had not shown signs of serious illness.

Unbeknown to him, however, another member of the press was interviewing another witness at the same time. The mother nun told the reporter: "The Pope had been bedridden for the past two weeks suffering from a high fever and had been slipping in and out of a coma since Tuesday night,"—five days prior to the 'heart attack.'[1]

A second nun said she was with him when the attack occurred:

"He had eaten his cereal and juice that morning and it seemed he was getting better. Toward noon Cardinal Confalonieri began to say Mass by his bedside and Paul interrupted him and completed the Mass himself. We were delighted he was getting better.

In the early afternoon, we loaded his soup with vegetables. When I brought it to him he gobbled it up like he had been starving to death. He picked up the bowl of butternut pudding and was midway through it when he suddenly dropped the bowl onto the sheets and started choking and gasping for breath.

At first, I thought it was that he had been eating too quickly. Then I realized I was witnessing convulsions. I ran out of the room and fetched Doctor Fontana. He examined Paul and told us it was just a matter of time. From that time on Paul gasped for breath as if each was his last; his chest rising and falling with each gasp."

The press asked the nun if Paul had experienced pain: "He did not complain of any and his expression did not reflect pain. It was that he couldn't breathe. He was gasping for breath."[2]

This led the profession to conclude Fontana had misdiagnosed the Pope's condition; respiratory failure without pain is not symptomatic of heart attack. This criticism by the medical profession was well founded as a common physician would have known this, much less a pope's physician. In fact, most laymen would have known it.

The nun who had the scullery duty of emptying the bedpan told a third reporter: "There had been nothing but blood in the pan for a week."[3] Although bloody discharge from the bladder is a sign of serious illness it has nothing to do with a heart attack

An urologist in Rome confirmed the nun's story, telling still another reporter, he had been consulted by Paul's physician earlier in the week concerning a bladder infection.[4]

When these conflicting testimonies were released the next day, editorials in Italian, French, UK and even American newspapers criticized this inaction on the part of the Pope's physician. Neither the doctor nor the Vatican ever responded to the criticism.

Dr. Sebastiano Caffaro, President of the Italian Medical Society, was particularly harsh: "It is unbelievable a pope could be left to die without the care one would afford a cat or a dog."[5]

The South African heart specialist Christian Barnard condemned Dr. Fontana's failure to call for an intensive care unit: "If that had happened anywhere else in the world, the doctor would have been denounced by his medical association and found himself in court."[6]

The Montini family—pestered as to why they were not kept informed of Paul's deteriorating condition—issued a press release: "Whereas errors in judgment may have been made in connection with Paul's illness, we take no issue with the will of God."[7]

The final vigil

At the time of Paul's death there were two dozen people at Castel Gandolfo. At his bedside were his secretary Magee, Dr. Fontana, Cardinal Confalonieri and two bishops—Caprio and Casaroli.

Outside in the hall was the Castel Director Emilio Bonomelli together with four nuns who cared for the papal residence and two monks who cared for the gardens. A ceremonial guard stood outside Paul's bedroom door. Elsewhere within the fortress were a half-dozen Swiss Guards and a couple maintenance workers who had been repairing the kitchen exhaust system that day.[8]

Caprio had arrived a few hours prior to the presumed heart attack. An amateur botanist, he cultivated the desert section of the gardens.

Cardinal Villot was not present. Yet, he had been summoned to the Castel the day before to witness the elevation of Cardinal Yu Pin to Grand Chancellor of Eastern Affairs. Contemplating death, Paul told him: "We have fought the good battle. Let us finish the run."[9]

With the time between the rising and falling of his chest growing more and more apart, Paul died as if falling asleep—the slowing of his breathing broken only by the murmuring of prayers.

Arsenic poisoning

Commonly available in household chemicals, tasteless and odorless, arsenic is easily concealed in food or drink.

It results in symptoms characteristic of natural illnesses and unless a doctor specifically suspects foul play it will go undetected.

Initially there is jaundice, flaking skin, esophagus soreness and a bit of coughing up of bloody mucosa. It progresses slowly to a deteriorating condition accompanied by severe dehydration, swollen extremities most often culminating in pulmonary oedema.

Toward the end, there is a bloody discharge from the bladder—the most telltale sign of arsenic poisoning in a living person. In the end are convulsions and respiratory collapse. There is a pungent odor in the corpse not easily erased by conventional embalming.[10]

The elderly are particularly vulnerable to slow-arsenic poisoning as many of its symptoms are compatible with advanced aging and death will come within a month or so whereas a younger person might survive six months or even years with the same undetectable dosage.

Paul, at eighty, was a sitting duck for murder.

All of the conditions of Paul's death were symptoms of slow-arsenic poisoning, precisely the symptoms of arsenic poisoning, from the uncharacteristic naps, to swollen legs, to the flaky skin, to the sore throat, to the bloody discharge, to the obnoxious odor his body gave off which delayed its viewing in St. Peter's by a day.

Paul lay in state for a day at the Castel Gandolfo where fans were installed to disperse the odor. After a second embalming—injected with perfume—he smelled like a flower and moved to St. Peter's.[11]

That he developed a severe pulmonary condition when it seemed his body was fighting off the poisoning, something more lethal may have been added to quicken the process.

In that no autopsy was performed, no one knows what killed Paul. Yet, the medical community established it was not a heart attack.

Much has been said to exhume the body of John Paul I. Yet, the

Murder by the Grace of God

circumstances of his death suggest professional killers and lethal injection. Yet, in the case of Paul's corpse, arsenic—an element—traces would survive in Paul's hair and fingernails today.

It may be that it was so widely known Paul suffered from swollen legs and died that prompted the Vatican to claim John Paul had complained of swollen legs, something we know today was not true.

A few weeks later [12]

A few weeks later, in CIA headquarters in Mclean Virginia, a bushy eyebrowed man read the featured story in The Washington Post: "At an audience today, John Paul told a worldwide television audience: '...It is the inalienable right of man to own property. Yet, it is the right of no man to accumulate wealth beyond the necessary while other men starve to death because they have nothing...'"

He recalled Paul's last words at the Moro funeral: "...Take one away and another will rise up to take its place..."

He thought back to Kissinger's instruction: "Amputate the link and communism will fail."

He turned and looked up at the wall, '...threats ...'

He turned back to the desk. "The ball has shifted, again; this time, from the frying pan, into the fire."

He opened a book. There was a list of names.

At the top of the list was written ~~Aldo Moro~~ *Paul VI*.

He took his pen and struck out the name ~~Paul VI~~.

Beside it, he wrote *John Paul I*.

Author's note: Paul most likely elevated Yu Pin to Grand Chancellor of Eastern Affairs to gain eastern cardinal votes to replace votes of those cardinals who had been upstaged by Luciani's defense of the first artificially inseminated child.

1 *IL Messaggero* 7 Aug 78
2 *IL Messaggero* 7 Aug 78
3 *La Stampa* 8 Aug 78
4 *La Repubblica* 8 Aug 78
5 *Rinascita* 8 Aug 78
6 *Cape Times* 12 Aug '78
7 *Leggo* 28 Aug 78
8 *L'Osservatore Romano* 8 Aug 78
9 *L'Osservatore Romano* 9 Aug 78 - Paul's last words to Cardinal Villot
10 *Mosby's Dictionary of Medicine* or other medical dictionary approved by the AMA
11 *L'Osservatore Romano* 8 Aug 78. Also: embalming Paul VI
12 Closing satire

Chapter 34

The Murder of Cardinal Villot

According to canon law the term of a secretary of state ends when the Pope who appointed him dies.

When John Paul I appointed Villot as secretary of state it was known the choice was transitional. At the time of his untimely death, the newly elected pope was in the process of replacing Villot with Benelli; something both men were looking forward to—Benelli looking forward to taking over management of the Church and Villot looking forward to teaching in the Gregorian University in Rome.

This is one reason John Paul placed Benelli in charge of the audit of the Vatican's central bank—it would soon report to him as secretary of state. So there was no secret or surprise when John Paul retained the French cardinal in this transitional role.

The surprise came when John Paul II rose to power. Instead of replacing Villot—who stood for everything he was against—he retained him in the most powerful administrative position in the Church. Villot was in excellent health and short of retirement age and Benelli was no longer a part of the equation. Why did John Paul II install this liberal cog in the conservative wheel of his papacy?

Could it be if he replaced Jean Villot with Agostino Casaroli on day one it would have caused a furor among the two hundred cardinals and archbishops who outranked Casaroli?

Could it be if he replaced Villot with Casaroli on day one—one of three bishops of Mafia families who shared the palace with John Paul the night he died—it would have raised suspicions of murder?

Could it be he needed time—not a lot of time, but some time—to ease his friend Casaroli into the job?

Could it be like Aldo Moro, Paul VI, Yu Pin, Gracias, Filipiak, Nikodim, John Paul I and a long line of others before and after them we will talk about, Jean Villot, too, fell victim to foul play?

In the dead of the night

A few months after the deaths of Paul VI and John Paul I, Jean

Murder by the Grace of God

Villot was found in a dark alley in the wee hours of the morning just outside the Vatican walls. An ambulance took him to Gemelli Hospital where he was pronounced dead on arrival.[1]

Agostino Casaroli ordered the body snatched from the hospital and returned to the Vatican before a hospital doctor could execute a death certificate.

Villot's death certificate is signed by the same doctor—Renato Buzzonetti—who had executed that of John Paul I. According to the Catholic Encyclopedia Villot died of **'acute bronchial pneumonia.'**

His sudden and unexpected death came as a surprise to students at the Gregorian University in Rome where earlier that day he had given a lecture on the worker-priest movement in postwar France in which he had played such an important role.

In John Cornwell's *A Thief in the Night* Monsignor Sottovoce gives the English journalist the following account:

> **"Poor Villot died not long after John Paul. Very ironic, of course. He collapsed near the Vatican wall and got taken to Gemelli. The Vatican people rushed around and snatched the body...I kid you not! They pretended the corpse was still alive, took it back to the Vatican, and said he died in bed! Don't for God's sake ask me why, and don't say I said so..."**

'Ironic?' Does this mean anything to you?

In his time, Cornwell was in a much better position than I am today in determining what happened to Jean Villot.

When Cornwell interrogates Lorenzi about John Paul's death, the frustrated priest, too, suggests foul play in Villot's death: "Why not ask me about Villot's death? He died suddenly and unexplained?"

Yet, Cornwell leaves the reader with an unanswered suspicion: "Villot's mysterious death." Unfortunately, he does not pursue it.

Yallop missed the boat entirely; does not connect the dots at all.

Nevertheless, I don't think in this case I have to quote medical dictionaries. Everyone knows one does not teach class one day and drop dead of pneumonia a few hours later.

Needless to say no autopsy was ever performed.

Villot did not lie in state—no viewing of the body—unusual for a cardinal much less a cardinal secretary of state. A funeral mass was offered by John Paul II in St. Peter's Basilica. The Pope's homily beside the sealed coffin: "We are gathered here around the coffin of our brother..." can be found in library microfilm and the Internet.

<small>Author's note: the reader is reminded that John Cornwell's *A Thief in the Night*—unlike other books written about the 33-day Pope's death—had the cooperation and approval of John Paul II and the Vatican. In addition, controversial testimony given him by witnesses such as that reprinted here was confirmed by reporters after Cornwell published his book.</small>

The strategy of Jean Villot

When one considers foul play in the death of Jean Villot, one is limited to his role in the events surrounding John Paul's death.

It was he, as interim pope, who released the statement John Paul died before midnight and had been found dead by his secretary Magee at six-thirty in the morning. Also, John Paul held a book—*The Imitation of Christ*—upright in his hands.

Whereas, the Pope had undoubtedly died in the early morning hours and a nun had found him at four-thirty holding notes written on the stationary of Vittorio Veneto upright in his hands.

It had been Villot who summoned the embalmers at five in the morning. One might think he lied about the time of death in order to place time between John Paul's death and the embalming so as not to arouse suspicions of poisoning. Yet, today, one knows from the embalmers the embalming did not take place until after ten o'clock.

Jean Villot lied about the time of death and roused the embalmers at such an early hour to arouse suspicion of poisoning.

Villot was one of the most brilliant men in the Church. Six out of six mistakes in a brief release is not characteristic of a brilliant man.

He made these 'mistakes' intentionally. He knew the press would interview those witnesses of John Paul's death, just as they had interviewed those witnesses of Paul's death. He knew the embalmers would tell the press they had been picked up at five-thirty which would conflict with the Vatican release the Pope had been found at six-thirty. He knew the mother nun would confirm the discrepancy in time and tell the press she had discovered the Pope at four-thirty.

If Villot had not created all the confusion that surrounded John Paul's death, there would have been no investigation by reporters and all of the books investigating his death that have been written since would have never been written.

Murder by the Grace of God

This is particularly the case when one considers Villot continued to rile up the press by placing Vincenza, Magee and Lorenzi on sabbatical to unknown destinations—why remove the only witnesses to the discovery of the dead Pope if the Vatican had nothing to hide?

What's more, he issued a corrective release more confusing than the original release causing the press to expand its investigation.

Yet, one can claim this is all speculation.

Yet, speculation turns to fact when one considers the papers. What Villot did with the papers John Paul held in his hands.

Villot destroyed them and their content has never been released. Content, which if made public would have brought an end to the most prolific rumor—John Paul held in his hands lists of cardinals to be replaced. Had their content been released it would have brought an end to the rumors and the case would have been closed.

According to the embalmers, John Paul held stationary of Vittorio Veneto in his hands; likely notes of controversial issues he had taken daring stands on. Would it make any sense he would have brought blank diocese stationary to the Vatican? Would it make any sense he would write down a list of a dozen or so names?

Villot knew they were notes written while the Pope had been bishop of Vittorio Veneto. Not a roster of cardinals to be replaced, Villot knew if he were to release them it would have brought an end to the rumors. He destroyed them. He wanted the rumors to persist.

Villot acted in the way he did, not so much to protect Mother Church, but to create rumors that would trigger an investigation into the Pope's death—an investigation that was conducted by just about every reporter in Italy now being brought to fruition in this book.

Again, if one considers Karol Wojtyla and Agostino Casaroli as coconspirators in John Paul's murder, it would have required three murders as three men—known to have been in good health—had to die in rapid consecutive order to have allowed Casaroli to succeed to the secretary of state position: Paul VI, John Paul I and Jean Villot.

In retrospect, one knows, this is exactly what happened.

---

1 *Gemelli Hospital* 9 Mar 79

Author's comment: Catholic Encyclopedia, Wikipedia and all other Vatican controlled sources emphasize Villot 'died in his bed in the Vatican' despite the Gemelli Hospital record

Chapter 35

The Great Vatican Bank Scandal

"The conspiracy that planned the Vatican Bank Scandal was the same conspiracy that plotted the murder of John Paul I."

Avro Manhattan

Books and articles written about the 'Vatican Bank' have left the reader engulfed in mystery as to what it was all about and the writer the expert as to what it was all about. The details of the bank scandal presented in banker-mumbo-jumbo fashion all mixed up. Like a thousand peanuts roaming around under three thousand shells.

Yet, one doesn't have to be a world-class banker to understand *The Great Vatican Bank Scandal*. One has to do not much more than view the events in laymen's terms anyone can understand:

> The fraudulent activities that exploded in the press as 'The Great Vatican Bank Scandal' in 1982, began 33 days after the death of John Paul I, when the president of Banco Ambrosiano—Robert Calvi—collected the first dollar from an unsuspecting investor.
>
> The money was deposited by Banco Ambrosiano to the account of the IOR in the Patrimony of the Holy See (the Vatican's central bank) which, in turn, transferred it under the guise of loans to shell companies in Central America, Luxembourg and Lichtenstein.
>
> The money transferred to Nicaragua and Panama—the bulk of swindle—disappeared and no one ever found out what happened to it. Some of the money loaned to the European shells was recovered by the courts that tried the case 1982 through 1984.
>
> The scheme culminated in a $1.285 billion shortfall (about $12 billion today) part of a much larger $3.5 billion shortfall which brought down one of Europe's biggest banks—Ambrosiano.[1]
>
> Except for the $1.3 billion, most of the $3.5 billion shortfall had been built up in the 1970s when Roberto Calvi over-valued shares in his banks and acquired unsecured investments.

Murder by the Grace of God

Again, central banks controlled the flow of money in and out of countries to regulate exchange rates and protect national interests.

Italy's national interests at the time of John Paul's death are best demonstrated by the most recent election in which the communist-democratic-socialist parties gained 97% of the vote vs. 3 % for the republican minority. The Italian people were very much on the side the Sandinistas in their struggle to overthrow Somoza and other dictators in Central America to bring about a more equitable society.

Again, the loophole that led to the bank scandal, as well as shady deals under Paul VI we will talk about, was the Vatican's ability to get money out of Italy without passing it through the Bank of Italy.

One could walk into the IOR depository from the streets of Rome and deposit cash which could be wired through the Vatican's central bank anywhere in the world including enemies of Italy.

If the hundreds of millions Ambrosiano raised from unsuspecting investors been routed through the Bank of Italy to shell companies in war-torn Central America not a dollar would have ever left Italy:

Actual flow of funds in the bank scandal:

Shady deals under Paul VI

One could write a book about the shady banking deals under Paul VI—many have—but, they have very little to do with what exploded in the press as *The Great Vatican Bank Scandal* in 1982.

Though the banking activities under Paul involved some of the same people and established the international monetary mechanisms involved in the rip off of European investors which took place under John Paul II, they had nothing to do with the scandal per se.

To believe any of the transactions involved in the bank scandal which broke in 1982 occurred under Paul VI (1963-78) is to believe it took four years for highly competent investment houses to realize they had been ripped off. This is just not how the real world works.

There were one hundred and forty plaintiffs representing tens of thousands of investors involved in the courts that tried the scandal. To believe not one of them sensed something was wrong for more than four years does not pass the lowest hurdle of common sense.

Nevertheless, there were events under Paul VI that set the stage for *The Great Vatican Bank Scandal.*

In 1969, Michele Sindona was introduced by the Gambino family to a family member Giuseppe Caprio who was Secretary/Treasurer of the Patrimony of the Holy See—the Vatican's central bank.[2]

Caprio hired Sindona to school the Vatican in offshore banking. This gave birth to rumors the Vatican was laundering drug money. Dirty money would flow from eastern sources to the Vatican and then to offshore shell companies and be returned as clean money. It was then deposited in the account of the Gambino family in Banco Ambrosiano; the transactions having bypassed the Bank of Italy.

In 1975, Paul Marcinkus became a board member of Ambrosiano Overseas Limited—a Nassau branch of Ambrosiano which began to route transactions through the Patrimony (IOR) to get them in and out of Italy without passing through the Bank of Italy.[3]

Courts determined—in one transaction in 1978—Ambrosiano transferred $184 million from Licio Gelli's account through Panama based Bellatrix earmarked for political purposes in Central America.[4]

In another transaction, Ambrosiano transferred funds from an Opus Dei account which bought shares in a Rothschild bank. Calvi manipulated the value of the shares which resulted in a $142 million swell in Ambrosiano and an offsetting deflation in Rothschild.[5]

Courts determined Calvi/Opus Dei siphoned off the Ambrosiano 'swell' to the dictator Somoza in Nicaragua and ruling regimes in El Salvador/Guatemala to suppress the *revolution of the poor*. It was this deal that caused some to believe Rothschild directors had been involved in the Roberto Calvi murder—never proved in the courts.[6]

Murder by the Grace of God

Courts many times demonstrated that Opus Dei members Roberto Calvi, Michele Sindona and Licio Gelli poured tens of millions of their own money through shrouded activities into suppression of the *revolution of the poor* in Central America in the 1970s. Being among its largest investors, stability of the region was vital to their interests.

Shady deals of the CIA

Nothing better demonstrates how the CIA functions independent of the president and congress than was its role in the Contra war.

An Italian court investigating the Vatican bank scandal linked CIA agents to the Vatican-Ambrosiano scheme to raise money from unsuspecting investors and funnel it through the Vatican bank to Somoza and the Contras after Carter cut off military assistance to these right-wing opponents of free elections and human rights.[7]

Another Italian court investigating the Vatican bank scandal disclosed the CIA circumvented presidential order when it funneled tens of millions of its own funds through Banco Ambrosiano to the Contras in the fall of 1980 while Carter's order was still in effect.[8]

Another tribunal investigating the bank scandal disclosed the CIA circumvented presidential order when it moved arms and money through Banco Ambrosiano to Romeo Garcia in Guatemala and Paz Garcia in Honduras after Carter had cut off support to both these dictators for violations of human rights.[9]

Conversely, presidents have used the CIA to bypass congressional denial of funding of causes a president sees fit.

In 1972, the democratic congress had cut off funds for President Nixon's war in Central America. Nixon engaged Sindona to acquire control of the Franklin National Bank. Two years later it collapsed.

The courts determined Sindona and Nixon had siphoned off large sums of the bank's money to Somoza and other dictators in Central America to suppress the *revolution of the poor* there. The Patrimony of the Holy See took a $40 million hit when the Franklin Bank went under to the extent the IOR had guaranteed the transactions.[10]

Then one has the more celebrated case of the Iran-Contra Affair. As world opinion turned against American intervention in Central America in the eighties, congress began to limit aid to the Contras in the war-torn countries of Nicaragua, Honduras, El Salvador and Guatemala. In December 1982 congress cut it off completely.

This set the stage for the Iran-Contra Affair in which Reagan bypassed the congressional freeze on aid to the Contras and directed the CIA to sell arms to Iran and transfer proceeds to the Contras to suppress the *revolution of the poor* in Central America. Reagan's popularity and advancing age saved him from impeachment. When questioned about the affair he told Congress: "I don't remember."[11]

It was reasonable to believe if the Sandinistas defeated Somoza in Nicaragua, a redistribution of wealth society as the will of the people would spread through Central America and the Condor nations of South America like a row of dominos crumbling to a single tap.

➢ It was the common interest of Calvi, Sindona and Gelli to head off the fall of Somoza in Nicaragua to the Sandinistas. This is seen clearly in that after Somoza did fall the Sandinistas seized companies/banks in which they had fortunes invested.
➢ It was the sacred duty of right-wing factions in the CIA to head off the fall of Somoza to preserve the basic capitalistic tenets upon which the United States had been founded.
➢ It was the sacred duty of right-wing factions in the Vatican to head off the fall of Somoza. Children grumbling in the mud are more vulnerable to the supernatural than those growing up in a world of opportunity. As we have said, the Roman Catholic Church is the King Kong of the Supernatural World.

These forces conspired to carry out dealings so fragmented that all the king's men and all the king's horses since have not been able to put them back together again. One man stood in their way.

John Paul I.

1 *TIME Europe* 82-84
2 *L'Osservatore* 19 Oct 69   *La Stampa* 23 Dec 69
3 *L'Osservatore* 22 Jul 75
4 *Washington Post* 15 Sep 78
5 *TIME-EUROPE* Oct 83
6 *TIME Europe* Oct 83
7 *La Repubblica* 12 Feb 83 *Ambrosiano* Italia
8 *La Repubblica* 12 Feb 83 *Ambrosiano Roma*
9 *Latour vs. Ambrosiano* Paris 1985
10 *La Repubblica* 17 Oct 75
11 *Washington Post* 3 Dec 86

Chapter 36

The Vatican-Contra Affair

In the 1970-80s there were two fronts on which the CIA and the Vatican were confronted by communism as a free democratic society: Italy and Central America. If Italy fell to communism—a redistribution of wealth society—all of Europe would surely follow. If Central America fell to communism—a redistribution of wealth society—all of Latin America would surely follow.

One is not speaking here of the Soviet Union.

The Soviet Union was never a free democratic society.

The Soviet Union was an autocracy. More so, it was never a communist society in the true 'Marx' sense of the word. It remained, from beginning to end, a rich and poor society.

The communist movements in Italy and Central America for the most part rejected Soviet intervention. Although the Soviets courted revolutionaries in Central America with offers of arms, the insurgents had no intent of getting out from living under one regime to end up living under another. The political ideology of the Soviet Union was never a formidable threat to the United States. Being a tyranny, it had the entire free world against it.

It was in those parts of the world communism was raising its ugly head as the will of the people which was so dangerous to the United States. As Kissinger had warned: "Domination by Moscow is not the issue. Communist control of Italy and Central America is the issue. It would have terrible consequences for the United States and it is the number one threat to its national security..."[1]

The two fronts in the movement toward a free democratic-communist society

When John Paul I came to power in the fall of 1978, communism as the will of the people had already achieved electoral success in Italy. In Central America, the American President Jimmy Carter, who believed in free elections and a redistribution of wealth society, cut off financial and arms assistance to the Somoza regime which had ruled poverty-stricken Nicaragua with an iron fist for decades.

To make matters worse the reigning pontiff John Paul I—the youngest pope in four hundred years—was in impeccable health and seemed good for at least a quarter century. More lethal than money and bullets, here was a pope who was telling the poor to stand up for their providential share of God's wealth was God's will.

There was a growing inevitability the Somoza regime that had ruled Nicaragua ruthlessly for decades would fall to the Sandinista revolutionaries who would install free elections and a redistribution of wealth society as the will of the people. Communism as the will of the people would spread rapidly through Central America and the Condor nations of South America—those ruled by military dictators.

As Avro Manhattan had so prudently voiced: 'the United States was looking at a swarm of mini-Cubas in its backyard.'

It was the combination of a democrat in the White House and a democrat in the Vatican that triggered the Vatican Bank Scandal.

Somoza

It is the thesis of Avro Manhattan: the bank scandal transactions which occurred before the fall of Somoza (July 1979) were funneled to Somoza to halt the Sandinistas' impending takeover of Nicaragua.

Manhattan was on firm ground in thinking this way.

From March 14, 1979 through July 14, 1979, the Patrimony—the Vatican's central bank—transferred $383 million under the guise of 'loans' to shell companies in the Ambrosiano branch in Managua Nicaragua. The related notes were in the name if the IOR.

On July 19, 1979, the Sandinista Liberation Front took the capital city of Nicaragua overthrowing the Somoza regime.[2]

By mid-August the Sandinistas had seized manufacturing plants, banks and other facilities that had supported Somoza. Among these was the Ambrosiano branch in Managua. The balance in the shell company accounts the Vatican had loaned $383 million was 'zero.'[3]

Murder by the Grace of God

The flow of money to Somoza:

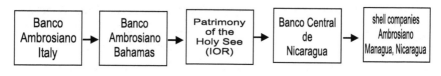

The Contras

After the Sandinistas seized the Nicaraguan branch, Ambrosiano opened a branch in Peru. From this point on the scandal money—$907 million—was deposited in the IOR by the Lima bank and then 'loaned' to Panamanian and European offshore shell companies.[4]

Of this, $444 million was transferred to a Panamanian affiliate of the First International Bank of Houston. The related IOR notes were issued to shell companies operating throughout Central America.

The flow of money to the Contras:

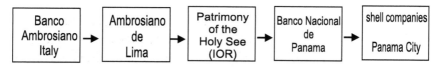

Let us step back a bit. On the eve of the Sandinistas' takeover, a plane disguised with Red Cross markings flew into Managua and rescued two hundred of Somoza's National Guardsmen and flew them to a CIA compound in Miami. On October 16, 1979, they were flown to a CIA training camp in Honduras bordering Nicaragua.

There are other Contra groups operating in Central America. Yet, these are what we are speaking of when we say 'Contras'—remnants of Somoza's army trained by the CIA with a mission to contain the Sandinistas within Nicaragua and possibly destroy them altogether.

It is the thesis of Avro Manhattan: **the money routed through Lima to Panama after the fall of Somoza was funneled to the Contras during the time Jimmy Carter would not support them.**

Manhattan was on firm ground in thinking this way.

On October 16, 1979—a year to the day John Paul II took office and the same day on which the Contras were flown to Honduras by the CIA—the Lima branch made a deposit of $134 million in the IOR which 'loaned' it through the Patrimony of the Holy See to a Panamanian shell company United Trading Corporation.[5] It was followed by another $330 million to other Panamanian shells. It disappeared and no one has ever found out what happened to it.

European shell companies

The Lima branch deposited another $463 million in the account of the IOR in the Patrimony which 'loaned' it to shell companies in Liechtenstein and Luxembourg. This money was partially recovered by the courts that tried the case in the 1980s:

It is the thesis of Avro Manhattan: the bank scandal money transferred to these European 'offshore' accounts was intended to buy arms for the Contras from foreign markets. Cash drawn down in Panamanian currency would have been readily available only in Central American markets which had very limited arms production.

> Author's note: No European central bank would have been involved in the transfers to the Liechtenstein-Luxembourg banks because they were technically 'offshore' banks operating within Europe. It was to bypass charges and delays inherent in routing funds through central banks that 'offshore' banks like those in Luxembourg and the Cayman Islands were first established.

It is the thesis of Avro Manhattan: it was in anticipation of the inevitable fall of Somoza and the looming rise of communism as the will of the people in Central America that the Vatican Bank Scandal was conceived during the papacy of John Paul I in the fall of 1978.

The courts

The courts determined the money that disappeared in Nicaragua and Panama was drawn down in cash—not wired to banks or investment houses; they were not able to determine what happened to it.

One could speculate private men—Calvi, Gelli and Sindona—drew the money in Nicaraguan currency—*Cordoba*—and laundered it through the local black market for a fraction of its face value. This makes no sense when they could have run all the money through the Ambrosiano Nassau or other 'offshore' branches. It would have been readily available in European currencies with no risk at all.

Of the $463 million wired to Liechtenstein and Luxembourg $215 million was recovered. $248 million had been drawn down in cash and the courts were unable to determine what happened to it.

The courts charged that the shell companies the Vatican 'loaned' the $1.3 billion were actually owned by the Vatican.

Generally, this could not be proved because of immunity of the Holy See from Italian courts provided under the *Lateran Treaty*. Yet, the courts did prove Ambrosiano created the shell 'United Trading Company' in 1970 and the IOR had acquired all its shares in 1974.

On the other hand, the same courts determined that a half-dozen of the Panamanian shells, including Astolfine, Erin and Fisalma, had been created by the CIA for espionage activities in connection with the Cold War. This may have been linked to—reasonable but not proved—CIA Director George Bush who was chairman of the First International Bank of Houston at the time of the bank scandal.

Yet, like all the others, all we really have is circumstantial evidence.

> It is the thesis of most other authors led by David Yallop: **the $879 million that was never recovered was drawn down by private interests: three men-of the cloth—Marcinkus, Cody and Villot—conspired in a scheme to the financial benefit of three Mafia types—Calvi, Gelli and Sindona—in swindling European investors of hundreds of millions of dollars and routing it through the Vatican central bank to Central America where it disappeared.**

In April of 1987, Laura Colby of the Wall Street Journal wrote an article based on Yallop's idea—'**The Case against Paul Marcinkus**'—implying the Vatican had reaped huge sums for its part in the fraud.[6]

Marcinkus retaliated with a rebuttal:

> "The commissions the Vatican received in these transactions—1/16th of one percent (.0625)—was modest relative to charges levied by most national banks for similar transactions. This has been substantiated by the joint commission. An amount so small it could not possibly justify the enormous risk in routing funds through unstable parts of the world..."[7]

At the time, central banks imposed tariffs of 1/32 of one percent up to one percent for funds flowing out of a country. The United States Federal Reserve Bank, e.g., skimmed off ½ of one percent.

The 'joint commission' Marcinkus refers to is the consensus of the great multitude of courts that tried the bank scandal. One might question—in that Vatican banking records were not available to the courts via protection afforded under the *Lateran Treaty*—how the courts knew how much the Vatican profited on the transactions.

The courts did have the record of Banco Ambrosiano Italy and had extradited the records of the Lima and Managua Ambrosiano branches and those of the Liechtenstein and Luxembourg 'offshore' banks. The differences between that deposited in the Vatican Bank and that received by these banks was $1/16^{th}$ of one percent.[8]

As we have said, all one has is circumstantial evidence.
Yet, we do have something else.

Common sense:

Is it more reasonable to believe: three men-of the cloth conspired to the financial benefit of three Mafia types in swindling European investors of hundreds of millions of dollars and routed it through the Vatican central bank to Central America at great risk when they could have routed it directly to 'offshore banks' like the Cayman Islands or the Bahamas with no risk at all?

Is it more reasonable to believe: "You don't run money through war-ravaged parts of the world unless you intend it remain there."

It is the thesis of both Avro Manhattan and this author:

The conspiracy that planned the Vatican Bank Scandal was the same conspiracy that plotted the murder of John Paul I. The intent of the bank scandal transactions was to finance the Contras during the time an American president would not support them.

The Great Vatican Bank Scandal could have never taken place had John Paul I lived. One more bit of circumstantial evidence:
The Great Vatican Bank Scandal began thirty-three days after John Paul I sat up dead in his bed.

Murder by the Grace of God
The Vatican Bank Scandal Flow of funds 1979-1981[9]

Source: the courts that tried the Ambrosiano/Vatican case 1982-1984

Ambrosiano Italy (investors)	$1,285 million ($15 billion in today's $)
	↓
Ambrosiano Nicaragua	$378
Ambrosiano Lima	$907
	↓
Vatican bank – APSA/IOR	$1,285
	↓
Astolfine S.A. Panama	70
United Trading Company Panama	217
Erin S.A Panama	104
Bellatrix S.A. Panama	117
Belrose S.A. Panama	64
Starfield S.A. Panama	92
Fisalma S.A. Panama	61
Other Panamanian ghost companies (8)	97
Sub-total Panama	$822 million Somoza and the Contras
Manic S.A. Luxembourg	92
Nordeurop S.A. Liechtenstein	371
Sub-total Europe	$463 million for arms for the Contras

Deposits from the IOR/APSA to ghost affiliates
Total 1.285 million

Year	1979				1980				1981	
Quarter	1st	2nd	3rd	4th	1st	2nd	3rd	4th	1st	2nd
	$227	$156	$192	$198	$117	$78	$89	$98	$93	$37

In the end, investors recovered sixty percent of their investments without interest. $215 million was recovered from Manic and Nordeurop, $241 million from the Vatican, and the balance from liquidation of unrelated Ambrosiano assets.

---

1 *TIME* '*What if Communists Win a Role?*' 26 Apr 76
2 *NY Times* 20 Jul 79
3 *NY Times* 9 Sep 79
4 *La Repubblica* 29 Sep 79
5 *Wall Street Journal* 27 Apr 87
6 *Wall Street Journal* 27 Apr 87
7 *Wall Street Journal* 22 May 87
8 *La Repubblica* 2 Jan 84 *Ambrosiano Italia*
9 *TIME-EUROPE* Oct 84 *La Stampa* 6 Sep 85 *Ambrosiano Italia, Ansbacher vs. Ambrosiano* Irish Supreme Court 1987, *Latour vs. Ambrosiano* Paris 1985 and other courts that tried the scandal

Chapter 37

The Vatican Bank Murders

On the heels of court proceedings in July 1984, John Paul II paid European investors $241 million through the Italian courts.[1]

The involvement of John Paul II in *The Vatican Bank Scandal* had evidently been much deeper than the 1/16th of one percent it had earned on the transactions—less than $1 million—when the Polish Pope made the settlement. He knew what he was doing all along.

This at least partially satisfied the Vatican's role in violating the seventh commandment: **'Thou shalt not steal.'** It did not satisfy its role in violating the fifth commandment: **'Thou shalt not kill.'**

To determine who carried out the Vatican bank scandal murders, we must determine who carried out the bank scandal transactions. To do this we must first identify the organizations involved in the bank scandal and the men who plucked these strange strings of fate.

The playing field

The Patrimony of the Holy See (APSA): as it still is today, was recognized by the **'International Monetary Fund'** as the **'Central Bank of the Vatican.'**[2] All monies passing in and out of the Vatican had to pass through APSA. **The Patrimony of the Holy See**—not the IOR—was the **'Vatican Bank'** that handled the bank scandal transactions.

The Patrimony and some of its representative accounts in 1978:

The Patrimony of the Holy See (Vatican's central bank)
Giuseppe Caprio, Secretary/Treasurer
↓ ↓ ↓ ↓ ↓ ↓ ↓
SGI IRI COC SA ITA MED IOR ← Venice Bank

SGI - Society General Immobiliare – controlled Vatican real property including properties outside the Vatican: Castle Gandolfo, Gregorian University, seventy embassies and other property. Value considered upwards of $5.4 billion in 1978. The Church's field assets are owed by dioceses and are not owned by the Vatican.

IRI - Institute of Industrial Reconstruction - controlled Vatican interests in private companies reported to be upwards of $3.2 billion in 1978. For example, the Vatican was the largest shareholder in Alfa Romeo and Italian utilities.

Murder by the Grace of God

COC (Vatican Museum) – control of inventory/acquisition of Vatican treasures.

SA – Special Administration - controlled Vatican interests in public companies through stock exchanges, reported to be upwards of $2.4 billion in 1978.

ITA - Italmobilaire – controlled its interests in banks. In addition to its substantial interest in Ambrosiano and 'Catholic' banks, the Vatican had controlling interest in Provinciale Lombarda, Piccolo Credito Bergamasco, Credito Romagnolo, San Germiniano, San Prospero and San Paolo. 1978 value estimated at $3.8 billion.

MED – radio/television/newspapers. Controlling interest in *Il Gazzettino, Corriere delle Alpi* & a score of other right-wing papers and media. Value: $1.9 billion.

IOR – Institute of Religious Works – a depository for funds collected by religious orders, 'Peter's Pence' and tourist revenues to support the lifestyle of the papacy. Its residue—usually a deficit—was its deposits vs. the cost of maintaining Vatican City and its properties. It was also a holding company having controlling interest (64%) in its northern branch Banca Cattolica del Veneto and other Catholic banks in Italy and a 15% interest in Banco Ambrosiano. Total estimate $900 million.[3]

The Institute of Religious Works (IOR): funds would be deposited in foreign currencies and converted to Vatican lira which traded at par with the Italian lira. Yet, as a depository—not a bank per se—it could not function as a bank outside the Vatican. It was that the IOR was the 'business' involved in the Vatican bank scandal that it has been wrongly tabbed the 'Vatican Bank.'

Bank of Italy: the central bank of Italy. With the exception of transfers in and out of the Vatican which was within Italy, all funds flowing into or out of Italy had to pass through this bank. It was this loophole in Italian monetary law which led to the bank scandal—the APSA/IOR functioning as an offshore bank in the center of Rome.

The Vatican Bank: in this book 'Vatican Bank' refers to the joint activities of IOR and APSA. The IOR was the 'business' and the APSA—the Patrimony—was the 'bank' involved in the scandal.

- Paul Marcinkus as president of the IOR—a depository in the Patrimony—accepted the deposits in the IOR and executed the notes in the name of the IOR to the shell companies.

- Giuseppe Caprio as Treasurer of the Patrimony—the Vatican's central bank—transferred the money to the shell companies in Nicaragua, Panama, Luxembourg and Lichtenstein.

Banco Ambrosiano: one of Europe's largest banks and Central America's largest foreign bank. It was founded as an international bank to service the exploding Catholic Latin American population.

Ambrosiano Group Banco Comercial: the Banco Ambrosiano branch bank in the capitol city of Nicaragua. From March 1979 through the fall of Somoza in July 1979, $383 million was deposited by Ambrosiano to the account of the IOR in the Patrimony of the Holy See which, in turn, wired it under guise of loans to accounts of shell companies in this Ambrosiano branch. It disappeared.

Banco Ambrosiano Andino: in August 1979, Sandinistas seized the Ambrosiano branch bank in Nicaragua forcing it to establish this branch bank in Lima to handle the future bank scandal transactions.

Players inside the Vatican

Author's note: Incumbents, descriptions and interrelationships of Vatican positions in this book are taken from the *Catholic Encyclopedia*. *Wikipedia* and other Internet indexes are reliable only insofar as they are sourced from the *Encyclopedia*.

Giovanni Benelli: Florence Archbishop, As Nunciature Auditor to Latin America (1960-64) and as Undersecretary of State (1960-77) under Paul VI he had supervised offshore banking activities for two decades. Together with Cardinal Vagnozzi he headed up the audit of the Vatican bank ordered by John Paul I in 1978.

Giuseppe Caprio: as Secretary/Treasurer of the Patrimony of the Holy See (APSA) he handled the technicalities of the transfers from the IOR account to the shell companies where it disappeared.

Agostino Casaroli: Vatican Foreign Minister. He was elevated to Secretary of State by John Paul II. During the period of the bank scandal transactions both the IOR and APSA operated under the office of the Secretary of State. After the scandal broke in the courts in 1981 the status of the IOR was changed directly to the Pope.[4]

Pericle Felici: Prefect of the Tribunal of the Apostolic Signatura and legal counsel to the papacy. That he had served as legal counsel for banking activities under Paul VI and had been removed as legal counsel for banking activities under John Paul II made this astute lawyer suspicious which caused him to launch his own investigation of goings on in the Patrimony—the central bank of the Vatican.

Paul Marcinkus: President of the Institute of Religious Works.

Jean Villot: He held the dual positions of Secretary of State and President of the Patrimony of the Holy See under Paul VI.

Players outside the Vatican

Roberto Calvi: President of Banco Ambrosiano—largest investor in Central America—which had in the 1970s funneled huge amounts to its dictators to suppress the *revolution of the poor* there.

Graziella Corrocher: private secretary and bookkeeper of the scandal transactions and closest confidant of Roberto Calvi.

Giuseppe Dellacha: Banco Ambrosiano Treasurer who handled the technicalities of the transactions from Ambrosiano through its Nicaraguan and Lima Ambrosiano branches to the IOR/APSA.

Licio Gelli: Grand Master of P2 and a major investor in Central America. He had funneled tens of millions to its dictators to suppress the *revolution of the poor* to protect his interests there.

Michele Sindona: In his alliance with Ambrosiano, he was a major investor in Central America. In the 1970s he funneled tens of millions to Somoza and other Central American dictators to suppress the *revolution of the poor* to protect his interests there.

The Vatican Banking Organization

Positions, incumbents and interrelationships of those involved in Vatican banking activities when the game began in the fall of 1978:

← = reporting status when John Paul II was elected

John Paul II ←Prefect Tribunal of the Apostolic Signatura   Cardinal Pericle Felici
↑
Secretary of State   Cardinal Jean Villot
↑
Prefect of Economic Affairs   Cardinal Egidio Vagnozzi
↑
President of the Patrimony of the Holy See Cardinal Jean Villot
↑
Secretary/Treasurer of the Patrimony   Bishop Giuseppe Caprio
↑
President Institute of Religious Works - IOR   Bishop Paul Marcinkus

Concerning the mechanics of the bank scandal transactions two of these officers would have been directly involved—Paul Marcinkus and Giuseppe Caprio. Though it was possible for Marcinkus to deposit money in the IOR account, only Caprio could get it into the international market through the Patrimony—the central bank of the Vatican. None of the transactions could have taken place without the joint concurrence of Marcinkus—the man who ran the business—and Caprio—the man who ran the bank. When we speak of the bank scandal transactions we are speaking of the actions of these two men and, of course, Roberto Calvi and Giuseppe Dellacha who handled the technicalities of the related transactions within Ambrosiano.

Chronology of events

On **October 17, 1978**, John Paul II rose to the papacy. In his first public statement he condemned *Liberation Theology*. He warned radical priests and nuns—the principal inspirers of revolutionary guerillas in Central America—to cease supporting the revolution.[5]

On **October 30, 1978**, the Pope removed Pericle Felici as legal counsel to the Patrimony restricting the scope of the Tribunal of the Apostolic Signatura to canon law—a confusing move as Felici was a brilliant lawyer well versed in international monetary law.

<small>Author's note: It is not unusual for a pope to change the authority of a Curia post. E.g. in 2002 Joseph Ratzinger became Dean of the College of Cardinals and elevated above the Secretary of State. The Dean of the College under Paul VI had been an honorary position of the oldest cardinal.</small>

Calvi began raising money from investors. The Italian courts that investigated the Vatican bank scandal determined the first 'scandal' investment claimed by a plaintiff took place on **November 2, 1978**.[6]

Early on the morning of **March 9, 1979**, the body of Cardinal Jean Villot was found in a darkened alley outside the Vatican walls.[7]

Casaroli ordered the body snatched from a Rome hospital and returned to the Vatican. Giuseppe Caprio told reporters Villot was still alive and he was at his bedside when he died in the Vatican.[8]

The transfers to Central America could not have taken place as long as Villot remained President of the Patrimony of the Holy See. Casaroli replaced Villot as Secretary of State and Caprio replaced Villot as President of the Patrimony—the Vatican's central bank.[9]

At this early stage as the bank scandal transactions started to get underway John Paul II had revamped his banking organization:

Murder by the Grace of God

John Paul II
↑
Secretary of State   Bishop Agostino Casaroli
↑
Prefect of Economic Affairs of the Holy See   Cardinal Egidio Vagnozzi
↑
President/Treasurer of the Patrimony – APSA   Bishop Giuseppe Caprio
↑
President of the Institute of Religious Works   Bishop Paul Marcinkus

The courts that tried the bank scandal determined the first transfer to Nicaragua (2.3 billion lire—about $3 million) took place the day following Cardinal Jean Villot's funeral—**February 14, 1979**. [10]

The mysterious death of Cardinal Vagnozzi

Although the Prefect of Economic Affairs does not normally get involved in the day-to-day goings on in the dozen or so departments that report to his office, it became obvious Cardinal Vagnozzi was becoming aware of the surreptitious happenings going on around him when on **June 16, 1979** he jokingly told a reporter: "**If one were to engage the entire armies of the CIA, the KGB and Interpol combined they would never be able to figure out how much money is involved here and where it is coming from and where it is going.**"[11]

On **June 30, 1979,** Vagnozzi was made Chamberlain (Treasurer) of the College of Cardinals—a confusing move as the incumbent Gabriel-Marie Garrone had not been in the job a year.

Vagnozzi's office was moved from the Patrimony on the ground floor of the Papal Palace to the Government Palace where he became engulfed in managing the properties of a hundred plus cardinals.[12]

Though he continued to retain his title as Prefect of Economic Affairs, he was rarely seen in the Patrimony again until late in 1980 in connection with an audit of the bank's records. Though the bank traditionally closed its books at the end of each calendar year, since the time of Paul VI the Prefect personally conducted an audit every fourth year; audits had been performed in 1968, 1972 and 1976.

In mid-December, Cardinal Vagnozzi returned to the Patrimony on the ground floor of the Papal Palace to conduct the audit required every fourth year of APSA which included its IOR depository.

On the morning of **December 26, 1980**, Vagnozzi was found dead on the floor of his Vatican apartment.

It is not unusual for the Vatican not to disclose cause of death at the time of death. Yet, normally a few months afterwards for official reasons it proclaims the deceased died of a 'heart attack' or 'cancer' or...? In Vagnozzi's case cause of death has never been disclosed.[13]

On **January 30, 1981**, Giuseppe Caprio was promoted to Prefect of Economic Affairs—Chief Financial Officer of the Church.[14]

On the same day, Secretary of State Casaroli replaced Caprio as President of the Patrimony of the Holy See. One can only surmise this was to avoid anyone else learning of the scandal transactions.[15]

At this point, the transactions which would eventually culminate in the bank scandal were privy to only four men in the Vatican: John Paul II, Agostino Casaroli, Giuseppe Caprio and Paul Marcinkus.

Ambrosiano would deposit cash in Marcinkus' IOR depository. Casaroli and Caprio would 'loan' it to offshore shell companies.

The updated Vatican banking organization:

Pope   John Paul II
↑
Secretary of State   Cardinal Agostino Casaroli
↑
Prefect of Economic Affairs of the Holy See   Cardinal Giuseppe Caprio
↑
President/Treasurer of the Patrimony - APSA   Cardinal Agostino Casaroli
↑
President of the Institute of Religious Works - IOR   Bishop Paul Marcinkus

Threads begin to unravel

On March 17, 1981, police raided Licio Gelli's villa at Arezzo.

They found a list of 962 members of Masonic Lodge P2 which included Roberto Calvi, Michele Sindona, Jose Mateos Giuseppe Caprio, Agostino Casaroli and Alvaro Portillo—Primate of Opus Dei—and other prominent members of the right-wing cult.

They uncovered evidence Roberto Calvi had transferred hundreds of millions of dollars extracted from unsuspecting investors through the Vatican to shell companies in Central America.[16]

Murder by the Grace of God

A month later, the scandal transactions as determined by the courts which tried the Ambrosiano downfall had come to an end.

After a lengthy trial which persisted into the following year, Calvi was convicted of bank fraud and given four years and released on appeal. During the trial he was distraught and made no effort to defend himself. Asked by a reporter why he didn't defend himself, Calvi answered: **"I am in the service of someone on the other side of the wall."**[17] In Rome 'the other side of the wall' is the Vatican.

On September 26, 1981, in the midst of the Calvi trial, John Paul made Marcinkus President of the Sovereign State of the Vatican.

This changed IOR's reporting status directly to the Pope. It also changed it from a depository in the Patrimony of the Holy See to an independent bank. More pointedly, in that it is the Pope's civil title, it gave Marcinkus diplomatic immunity from Italian courts.[18]

The role of Joseph Ratzinger in Central America

On November 25, 1981, Joseph Ratzinger was moved to the Vatican as Prefect of the Congregation of the Faith.[19] His office and that of Marcinkus—IOR—shared the Palace of the Holy Office.

Back in 1978, when the CIA and Opus Dei had wiggled their candidate into the top job, they felt secure for twenty-five years as the Polish Cardinal was only fifty-eight when elected.

In 1981, with the attempt on the Pope's life, assassination or even accident became a possibility. The CIA/Opus Dei coalition needed a backup on board should anything happen to the Polish Pope.

As the most powerful ecclesiastical voice in the Catholic world, Ratzinger masterminded the *anti-Liberation Theology* crusade and removed it from everyday life in Latin America to the history books.

Being a master of deceit, Ratzinger put together a razzle-dazzle platform designed to convince the poor of Latin America the concept of *Liberation Theology* was not only in conflict with the teachings of the Church—some children are entitled to more—but its promise of redemption was actually a restriction of opportunity for the poor.

By the end of the twentieth century he had silenced Leonardo Buff and other champions of *Liberation Theology* often referring to them as 'communists.' In 2005, he added it to the vow required of candidates for the 'red hat,' 'I pledge to suppress the role of women in the Church, homosexuals, contraception, Liberation Theology...'

Ratzinger took on the job of chief of propaganda in the Vatican not only in its war against *revolution of the poor* in Central America, but against *revolution of the poor* in Italy and Europe and anywhere else communism happened to raise its ugly head.

'Twin-engine bomber headed for Monti Parioli'

Vagnozzi's death had left only two men in the Church who had sufficient banking expertise to have been aware of the surreptitious goings on in the Vatican bank—Cardinal Felici and his closest friend Cardinal Benelli of Florence.

Felici had been removed from the Vatican banking organization when John Paul II rose to power leaving it without legal counsel. Benelli, as undersecretary of state, had overseen all Vatican banking operations for ten years before being moved to Florence.

A blend of newspaper reportings took care of both of them:

"Cardinal Giovanni Benelli—once a leading candidate for the papacy—died an hour after he was removed from the hospital to his home yesterday afternoon. His death comes as a surprise a day after his doctor told reporters: '...the cardinal is making good progress for recovery and should be released in a day or two.'

When criticized for having moved the cardinal, sources in the Vatican said Benelli requested he be removed from life support and returned to his residence. Yet, when questioned, ambulance attendants said the cardinal was unconscious when moved.

Cardinal Secretary of State Agostino Casaroli—who happened to be in Florence at the time—took immediate charge of the body and said there would be a three hour viewing of the coffin this morning in the Basilica di Santa Maria del Fiore. Following a funeral mass, Benelli—one of the youngest cardinals ever to die—will be interred beneath the floor of the cathedral this afternoon.

Factions in the Vatican complained as to why Benelli would not lie in state in the Vatican where he had served for ten years and was close to many Curia cardinals. Local sources complained of the brevity of the viewing—it was customary bishops be viewed for three to five days to allow the congregation to pay respects.

The sixty year old Benelli had been in the process of lining up votes against the ratification the Prelature of Opus Dei. He told reporters just yesterday: 'I am anxious to get back to work.'

Following the death of John Paul I in 1978, Benelli and Felici rose up as enemies of Opus Dei, so much so, they were labeled by the press: 'A twin-engine bomber headed for Monti Parioli.' Opus Dei headquarters is in the posh Monti Parioli district of Rome.

This past March, the bomber lost its other engine when Felici—having just returned from Panama—presided over the Marian Congress. The cardinal had finished the consecration of the Mass and was in the midst of his sermon when he suddenly grasped his head with both hands and fell dead onto the podium.

At the time of his death, the Vatican's chief legal counsel Felici was involved in investigating allegations that the coalition of Opus Dei and the Masonic lodge P2 had been involved in what has since exploded in the press as the Great Vatican Bank Scandal.

The twin-engine bomber headed for Monti Parioli is down. There are no survivors..."[20]

Author's note: Concerning Benelli's untimely death, there are many toxins which concealed in food or drink can induce 'heart attack' in a healthy person. Concerning Felici's untimely death, Methothianate mixed with alcohol results in a fatal brain hemorrhage about a half-hour after ingested—the time that had elapsed after drinking the wine in the consecration of the Mass. Canon law decrees sacramental wine must be alcoholic; one cannot substitute grape juice. The *Catholic Encyclopedia*—official record of the Church—records Felici's death as 'sudden and unexplained.'

If Opus Dei had been brought to trial for the murder of these two men, any court would acquit the cult on the grounds of self-defense.

Threads continue to unravel

It was on **March 22, 1982**, Pericle Felici dropped dead after sipping wine. On the heels of his death the scandal exploded in the press.

Marcinkus was harassed by reporters as to how this could happen. On **April 29, 1982** he slipped: "I have told John Paul II, if we continue to sweep things under the rug we will eventually trip over it."[21]

Marcinkus became a prisoner in the Vatican. He was moved from his Rome apartment to the Vatican and was not allowed to go out of its gates until after the scandal was resolved in 1984. This not only cut him off from reporters, it protected him from Italian authorities should they circumvent the immunity of his 'papal' title.

On June 5, 1982, Roberto Calvi wrote a letter to John Paul II warning him of the imminent collapse of Banco Ambrosiano. Calvi threatened, the Pope would have to resign unless the Vatican stepped up and satisfied the demands of the investors.

A copy of the letter submitted as evidence in Italian court trials and widely published survives as compelling evidence John Paul II, Casaroli and Caprio had involved Calvi in the conspiracy which led to the Vatican bank scandal; Calvi had been assured if the 'deal' was uncovered prematurely he would be made whole.[22]

Events which followed on the heels of Calvi's letter demonstrate right-wing forces in the CIA had been involved in the scheme from the start: **The 'deal' had been a stop-gap tactic in which the Vatican would finance the Contras through the Carter years.** The CIA would step in and satisfy the debt before it went sour.

This is consistent with the CIA's role in having joined right-wing factions in the Church in electing John Paul II. Reagan was now president and had taken up the cause for the Contras. It makes sense the Pope would have his hand out for the $1.3 billion.

This is also consistent with a remarkable world event that occurred just two days after the Polish Pope received Calvi's letter.

Threads come undone

On **June 7, 1982**, *Air Force One* touched down in Rome.

For security reasons, the president's visit had been unannounced. President Reagan had been critically wounded in an attempt on his life the previous year and John Paul II had survived an attempt on his life at about the same time.

John Paul and Ronald Reagan were sequestered behind closed doors on the guise they were discussing Polish Solidarity. [23]

A president cannot pick up a phone and talk to a pope privately. There is no assurance phones cannot be tapped on either end. The only way they can be guaranteed privacy is in person.

Polish Solidarity could have been discussed before television cameras. It was no secret where the pope and the president stood.

Murder by the Grace of God

Some claim it was in this meeting *The Holy Alliance* was formed. The Pope controlled twenty percent of the votes in the United States where presidential elections are decided by one or two percentage points. John Paul II would support the Reagan-Bush campaigns by attacking their opponents. In exchange, Reagan/Bush would appoint a wave of practicing Roman Catholics to the Supreme Court. [24]

Yet, the timing of Reagan's visit to the precise moment in history the collapse of Ambrosiano became imminent and investigations by the courts were looming on the horizon is compelling—if not absolute proof—it had to do with the Vatican bank scandal.

No one knows what this president and pope talked about that day. Yet, what was taking place on the floor below tells one that.

Casaroli, Caprio and Marcinkus were meeting with United States Secretary of State Alexander Haig, CIA Director William J. Casey and National Security Advisor and his Deputy Robert McFarlane.[25]

Let us connect some dots here.

Alexander Haig had been NATO Commander (1974-79) during which time Giulio Andreotti's document *The Parallel SID* disclosed the CIA, NATO (Gladio) and Italian Intelligence had conspired in the terrorist activities in the 1970s in Italy intended to turn the mindset of the Italian people against communism.

To the extent the CIA had been involved in the murders of Aldo Moro, Paul VI, John Paul and some others we have talked of, Haig would have been the United States official intervening between the CIA who called the shots and P2 who carried out the deeds.[26]

Before being named to the NATO post, Haig, as Nixon's Chief of Staff, had met with Licio Gelli of the fascist P2 lodge conveying American funds to Gelli's plans for a new Italy. Gelli had the unique distinction of having served under all three fascist dictators. He had served as an Intelligence officer in Hitler's SS Guard, as a blackshirt under Mussolini and had served in Franco's cabinet in Spain.[27]

William J. Casey was the CIA Director who would be caught up in the Iran-Contra Affair just a few years later. Under President Reagan the CIA directed the Contra-war in Central America[28]

In 1985, Robert McFarlane would resign as National Security Advisor in the wake of the Iran-Contra affair. Oliver North—top operations officer in the scandal—reported directly to his office. [29]

Nevertheless, this meeting—its participants widely named in the press—involved the **'three Vatican principals in the bank scandal'** and the 'three United States principals involved in the Contra war' is much more than compelling evidence the president's trip had to do with the bank scandal and the Contras in Central America. Reagan did not want the scandal to break in the press as 'The Vatican-Contra Affair.'

If this is true—and the events of the time certainly demonstrate it is true—the money which disappeared in Central America had—in fact—gone to Somoza and the Contras during the time (1979-1981) the American President Carter would not support them.

It makes sense right-wing forces in the CIA had been involved in the scheme to begin with. This would be consistent with the CIA's role in Karol Wojtyla's rise to the top. This would also be consistent with: **The conspiracy that planned the Vatican Bank Scandal was the same conspiracy that plotted the murder of John Paul I.** It makes all the sense in the world the Pope had his hand out for the $1.3 billion.

Reagan was now president and had already enticed congress to support the Contras. Though he did not give him the $1.3 billion, it may have been prearranged he would funnel through the CIA the $241 million which John Paul II would eventually satisfy his 'moral' obligation in connection with the Vatican bank scandal in 1984.

Regardless, a few days later, **June 18, 1982**, is the scene alleged by the film *Godfather III* to have occurred on the night John Paul I died four years earlier. Calvi had broken bail and left Italy. He was found hanging from a scaffold under Blackfriars Bridge in London.[30]

On the same morning, **June 18, 1982**, pedestrians found the body of Calvi's secretary and closest confidant—whatever he knew, she knew—Graziella Corrocher splattered on the sidewalk beneath the fourth floor window of her office in Milan. Corrocher left a note in her typewriter, **"...Calvi should be twice cursed for the damage he did to the bank and its employees."** Although police were unable to determine who typed the note, they did determine it had been typed on another typewriter and then placed in her typewriter.[31]

The scandal broke on **August 6, 1982** when Banco Ambrosiano filed bankruptcy.[32] Of its $3.5 billion 'black hole,' $1.285 billion was traced to money raised by Calvi from European investors which was funneled by Ambrosiano's Nicaraguan and Lima branches through IOR/APSA to shell companies where most of it disappeared.[33]

On **August 23, 1982**, the Vatican announced John Paul II had 'authorized Opus Dei a Prelature of the Holy See' effective **August 5, 1982** immunizing its officers from Italian courts. The timing of the Prelature retroactive to the precise day before the bank's collapse is compelling evidence the Pope knew officers of Opus Dei had been involved in the fraudulent deception of European investors—*The Great Vatican Bank Scandal*—and the murders surrounding it.[34]

The Pope was attempting to immunize those outside the Vatican namely Opus Dei Primate Alvaro Portillo and its Treasurer Jose Mateos and its wealthiest member Licio Gelli. He was not trying to protect those inside the Vatican including himself, Casaroli, Caprio or Marcinkus as they were already immunized by the sovereignty of the Vatican afforded under the *Lateran Treaty*.

On **October 2, 1982**, Giuseppe Dellacha, the Ambrosiano officer who handled the technicalities of the transactions from Ambrosiano to IOR/APSA was found sprawled across the sidewalk beneath his fifth floor window of Banco Ambrosiano in Milan.[35]

On **October 12, 1982**, capitalizing on the fact few cardinals spoke out in favor of the Opus Dei Prelature, Cardinal Benelli of Florence called for its ratification by the College of Cardinals setting the date for November 1, 1982.[36] As already pointed out, the sixty year old was in the midst of lining up votes against its ratification when he succumbed to an alleged 'heart attack' on **October 26, 1982**.[37] Opus Dei Prelature was ratified by the College on **November 26, 1982**.[38]

By a most remarkable coincidence, by the time the courts had undertaken the investigation of the Vatican bank scandal, the only people still alive who had been involved in the scandal transactions occupied the most powerful positions in the Roman Catholic world.

By providence of even a more remarkable coincidence, three of these men had met in Genoa midway through John Paul I's papacy.

By providence of even a more far reaching coincidence, two of these were 'sound asleep' in the Papal Palace the night of September 28, 1978 when John Paul I left this earth to meet his Maker.

By the grace of God all others who could bear witness to the Vatican bank scandal transactions were dead.

The Great Vatican Bank Scandal organization—living and dead—as it stood when the bank scandal went to trial in 1982:

John Paul II ←Paul Marcinkus   President of the Sovereign State of the Vatican
↑
Agostino Casaroli   Secretary of State & President of the Vatican bank
↑
Giuseppe Caprio   Prefect of Economic Affairs &Treasurer of the Vatican bank

~~Jean Villot~~   dead   found in alley in Rome; body snatched from hospital
~~Egidio Vagnozzi~~   dead   cause of death never disclosed
~~Pericle Felici~~   dead   drank wine in consecration of the mass
~~Giovanni Benelli~~   dead   many toxins precipitate heart attack I healthy persons
~~Roberto Calvi~~   dead   hung under bridge
~~Graziella Corrocher~~   dead   fell from high floor
~~Giuseppe Dellacha~~   dead   fell from high floor

1 *TIME-EUROPE* Oct 84
2 Search: International Monetary Fund Vatican central bank: *The Patrimony of the Holy See*
3 *Catholic Encyclopedia – Instituto per le Opere di Religione*
4 *L'Osservatore* 27Oct 81
5 *L Osservatore Romano* 19 Oct 78
6*TIME-EUROPE* 82-84
7 *NY Times* 10 Mar 79 *'Jean Villot'*
8 *La Repubblica* 12 Mar 79
9 *L Osservatore Romano* 29 Apr 79 - *La Repubblica* 1 May 79
10 *TIME-EUROPE* Jan-Jun 83
11 *La Repubblica* 17 Jun 79
12 *L Osservatore Romano* 1 Jul 79 *La Repubblica* 3 Jul 79 *Catholic Encyclopedia*
13*NY Times* 30 Dec 80 See *Catholic Encyclopedia Second Edition* for cause of death
14 *L Osservatore Romano* 31 Jan 81
15 *L Osservatore Romano* 31 Jan 81
16 *La Repubblica* 18 Mar 81
17 *La Repubblica* 25 May 82
18 *L Osservatore Romano*27 Sep 81 Marcinkus lived outside the Vatican in Rome at the time
19 *L Osservatore Romano*26 Nov 81
20 Composite of *NY Times, Washington Post, The Times- London, La Repubblica* 27 Oct 82
21 *La Repubblica* 30 Apr 82
22*TIME-EUROPE* Nov 82 *Ambrosiano Italia*
23 *L Osservatore Romano La Repubblica NY Times Washington Post The Times* 8 Jun 82
24 United States Supreme Court incumbents – see chapter *The Murder of Aldo Moro*
25 *L Osservatore Romano La Repubblica NY Times Washington Post The Times* 8 Jun 82
26Search: Alexander Haig biography search: NATO generals
27Search: Licio Gelli biographies
28*TIME* 12 Oct 87. Search: William J. Casey biographies & Iran-Contra Affair
29 *Washington Post* 5 Dec 85. Search: Robert C. McFarlane biographies
30 *The Times* London 19 Jun 82
31 *La Repubblica* 19 Jun 82
32 *La Repubblica* 7 Aug 82
33 *TIME-EUROPE* 82-84
34 *L Osservatore Romano* 24 Aug 82
35 *La Repubblica* 3 Oct 82
36 *La Repubblica* 13 Oct 82
37 *NY Times* 27 Oct 82
38 *NY Times* 29 Nov 82

Chapter 38

Tittle-Tattle of the Ages

What happened to the $1.3 billion?

A rash of confusing investigations has left us with rumors as to what happened to the money that disappeared. Did it go to:

- Somoza and the Contras?
- Solidarity?
- Private interests?

By a considerable margin the strongest of these rumors is the first one—the money went to suppress the *revolution of the poor* in Central America. It is the strongest of the rumors because it is the only one that passes the test of common sense.

Though the courts that tried the bank scandal were unable to resolve what happened to the money, they did determine 'where' and 'when' it disappeared. We also know 'where' and 'when' Somoza ruled Nicaragua and the Contras emerged. We know one thing more: these where(s) and when(s) match.

Yet, let us consider the others to see if any of them make sense.

Solidarity

The theory the money went to Solidarity is perpetuated by the same people who claim the bank scandal took place under Paul VI. As if to say Paul ripped off the investors, put it in the bank for a few years, and the Polish Pope spent it when he came along.

These people do not know their history—the time events took place. Solidarity was conceived in the fall of 1980 two years after the Vatican bank scandal began. By the time Solidarity became a viable movement, the Vatican bank scandal was history.

Though unable to determine what happened to the money, the Italian courts did determine 'when' and 'where' it disappeared. Routing money through war-torn parts of the world and then to Poland makes no sense at all. One could argue some funds routed to the European shell companies could have ended up in Poland.

Yet, what nails the lid on this theory, more than anything else, was the fact that the Polish Pope was an open ally of Solidarity. He did not have to get involved in surreptitious illegal operations to finance the cause. He could have done this openly and directly.

Personal motive: Calvi-Gelli-Sindona-Portillo

One might conclude Calvi, Gelli, Sindona and Portillo were in it for the money. Their P2-Opus Dei-Ambrosiano coalition was not only a wealthy financial organization, it was a powerful political force suppressing *revolution of the workers*—communism—in Italy and *revolution of the poor*—communism—in Central America.

To the extent these men had been footing the bill to suppress the *revolution of the poor* in Central America in the past, it makes sense they would benefit if the tab were to be picked up by investors.

What's more, if Somoza and other ruling juntas were to fall in Central America, they stood to suffer immense financial losses as they had enormous interests in banks and companies operating there.

One could speculate these men drew down the money in Central American currencies and laundered it through the local black market for a fraction of its face value. Yet, does this make sense when they could have run it through the Bahamas where it would have been available in European currencies with no risk at all?

Regardless, one must keep in mind these were not necessarily bad men. It depends on which side of the aisle one is on. Like their allies in the Vatican they were champions on their side of the aisle.

They were champions in protecting the sacred canon upon which their Church had been founded: **some children are born better than others and are entitled to more.** They were champions in preserving the secular canon upon which the United States had been founded: **accumulation of vast wealth by some while others starve to death because they have nothing.** They had dedicated their lives to

Murder by the Grace of God

destroying the quest of Marxism: a society in which every child has an equal chance to make his or her contribution back to society.

An American caught up in a revolution

I know, because, at the time, I was one of them.

At the time of the bank scandal and the *revolution of the poor* in Central America, I was a financial officer of the world's largest packaging corporation which had vast amounts of money tied up in the war-ravaged countries of Central America. Though a devoted admirer of this man I had met in Vittorio Veneto and of Paul VI, for at least this time in my life I was on the other side of the fence.

Paul's *Liberation Theology* had ignited the *revolution of the poor* in these tiny countries which had all but destroyed their economies.

Yet, Central America remained an important market for my company's products. Whereas one had no problem getting one's goods into these countries, the problem came when one tried to get one's money out of these countries. I was faced by the same banking restrictions which had been faced by those involved in the Vatican bank scandal and dealing with the same banks at the same time.

In one instance, I had tens of millions of dollars tied up in a Rothschild bank in Panama. Restricted by its central bank, I was looking at upwards of a year of unprecedented inflation before I would get my fingers on it. By that time it would be half its worth.

I came up with the idea of executing a guarantee in the name of my 'Fortune 50' giant to Rothschild: if the debt went sour it would hold Rothschild harmless. Rothschild paid me the cash up front.

My parent company's treasurer motioned for my dismissal—I had usurped what he considered his unique authority. My secretary saved me. She researched the company's charter which held any corporate officer could execute a guarantee. I was off the hook

Regardless, as the *revolution of the poor* began to take hold in Central America after Jimmy Carter became president and cut off aid to the incumbent juntas, members of the ruling families in the war-torn zone of Honduras, Nicaragua, Guatemala and El Salvador sought refuge in Costa Rica, Panama and the United States.

I recall meeting with the owner of a huge paper converting complex in El Salvador. Guards with automatic weapons flanked the entrance of the Miami Beach hi-rise. Another accompanied me on the elevator which opened directly into a penthouse apartment. The man was on life support transferred along with him from a hospital the day before where bullets had been extracted from his stomach.

Too, I recall my morning joggings on the grounds of my San Jose hotel accompanied by an armed guard. I had chosen Costa Rica as a base of operations because it bordered the war-torn countries, yet, had a mystique of relative safety about it.

Regardless, it was this experience—when the **'Great Vatican Bank Scandal'** broke in the press—I questioned why Ambrosiano would have deposited the money in banks of shell companies in Panama City if it had intended it to ever leave Central America.

It made sense that it established a branch in Lima after its assets had been frozen in Nicaragua upon the overthrow of Somoza. Yet, it made no sense when its Lima branch deposited the money in the Vatican bank which, in turn, transferred it back to Panama.

From Lima, it could have transferred the money to any bank in the world. If it sought a safe haven from foreign interests the Nassau Ambrosiano branch would have been the perfect haven.

Why transfer it back to Central America where central banks would freeze or delay the flow of funds out of the region for periods up to a year. The only thing that makes any kind of sense at all, the money was never intended to leave Central America.

This is consistent with Marcinkus' reply to my question where the money had disappeared: **"You don't run money through war-ravaged parts of the world unless you intend it remain there."**

Peaceful demonstrations

Though relatively safe in Costa Rica, I was reminded there was no such thing as safety in Central America when three bullets took down my business partner in a drive-by shooting as we strolled up the walkway into the Playboy Club one evening in San Jose. Then there was the time I ignored warnings not to go into El Salvador.

The Lear Jet taxied onto the runway to security rarely afforded presidents—two dozen guards in full military gear with automatic weapons. The trip to the plant—the road lined with armed guards I could see, and many more I guess I could not see—the driver on the radio in ongoing dialogue with roadside guards making a half-dozen detours en route to avoid ambush.

The giant complex loomed up out of the forest much more like an ancient fortress rather than the state-of-the-art manufacturing facility it was. Yet, its turrets did not hold medieval men with bows and arrows, but many more guards, these with machine guns.

I wondered why Paul and John Paul had not followed the model of Gandhi's peaceful demonstrations which had been so successful in India. Demonstrations had also worked for them in Italy where free elections had given rise to communism in the polls.

I was puzzled why they would cast these defenseless countries into havoc and revolution which over the years would cost thousands of lives when one had the option of peaceful protest.

I got the answer on that first evening in El Salvador when I enjoyed a hundred-dollar-a-plate dinner in an upscale restaurant as the guest of my Salvadorian hosts. When we were about to leave, the waiter showed up with bags containing what we had left on our plates. I motioned him, 'No.' He tucked one into my hand anyway.

We came down the steps from the restaurant to be greeted by a dozen or so half-naked children. I don't recall if any one of them had all his or her limbs. At least one of them could not see.

We threw the bags into the mud in the midst of them.

They went at it like vultures tearing the bags apart and clawing at rice and beans mixed with the mud in the street with bare hands— those who had hands. I recalled Luciani's words: **"Christ picked me up from the mud in the street and gave me to you."**

It was then I realized that decades of peaceful demonstrations had brought nothing but an occasional burst of gunfire from the roadside and starving children in the mud of the streets.

It was then I realized where Paul and John Paul were coming from. In a land ruled by self-serving juntas—backed by the power of the United States—demonstrations was not a viable alternative.

Paul and John Paul knew their actions would cost lives—lots of lives. The thousand children who starved to death each day in this tiny isthmus caught up between the world's great oceans gnawed at their conscience each moment they delayed.

Each night as they lay their head on the pillow they relived:

...a thousand miniature caskets lowered into the ground.

Chapter 39

The War in Central America

"The young are stepping up to stop man's exploration of man. Some in docile garb rush into the squares. Others in more gallant dress see violence justified... all guerillas needed to social justice revolution."

Albino Luciani, letter to Figaro Illustrissimi[1]

democrats: a redistribution of wealth society	republicans: a rich and poor society
John XXIII	President Eisenhower
Paul VI	President Nixon
President Kennedy	President Reagan
President Carter	President Bush
John Paul I	John Paul II

Let us step back a bit in time for those readers who may not be familiar with what was going on in Central America in the 1970s and 1980s which provoked the Vatican bank scandal.

It is no secret the union of the United States and the Vatican has controlled the political destiny of Central America in modern times.

The United States supplying money and arms through the years to ruthless dictators to maintain a rich and poor society consistent with the capitalistic tenets of the United States and the papal guideline for the poor: 'it is God's will your children waddle in the mud.'

Liberation Theology

On January 1 1969, in a private audience of priests and nuns from Central America, Paul VI first spoke of *"Liberation Theology."*[2]

For the first time, priests and nuns—driven by Paul's encyclical and their own compassion for children starving to death while the rich dined on fine cuisine and exceptional wines—began to lead the poor of Central America upwards into a better world.

In the late twentieth century—when the war in Central America ended—though few had reached notoriety, nine hundred priests and nuns had died carrying out Paul's edict, many of them bearing arms and leading militias to bring about a more just society.

Yet, in that same year—as the poor in Central America took up rifles against their ruthless dictators—Richard Nixon was elected president. He sent hundreds of millions of dollars and planes and tanks and guns and bullets to mow the insurgents down.

The United States took on the role of supporting ruthless dictators against the poor who were struggling to achieve free elections and a more equitable society. America, which prides itself as the epitome of democracy, allied itself against those struggling for democracy.

Yet, Paul would live to see another event across the pond that would give his cause renewed hope. A few years later, Jimmy Carter was elected president of the United States.

The playing field

Nicaragua: A week after taking office in January 1977, Carter cut off aid to the Somoza regime for human rights violations.

In 1979, the Sandinista Liberation Front, a socialist/communist party which had grown up out of Paul's *Liberation Theology,* overthrew the Somoza dictatorship. Under Carter, the United States was the first nation to recognize the new government.

El Salvador: The Sandinistas' success in Nicaragua had given the people of El Salvador renewed hope. The revolutionaries began to tip the scales against the regime which had ruled for centuries.

On March 29, 1980, Oscar Romero was gunned down with an American made bullet as he spoke a sermon calling for the CIA's death squads to cease terrorizing the Salvadorian people.

On the heels of Romero's assassination, the FMLN emerged—an umbrella group sheltering five militant-socialist-communist groups struggling for human rights. All-out civil war broke out.

Guatemala: in 1951, Juan Jose Arbenz—redistribution of wealth society—was elected by the will of the people. In 1954, under Eisenhower, the CIA implemented Operation WASHTUB.

It planted a Soviet arms cache in Nicaragua to falsely link Guatemalan ties to the Soviets Union. Arbenz was replaced by the United States with a military junta which it suffered under for years.

In 1978, in a fraudulent election, General Romeo Garcia assumed power giving birth to two parallel guerrilla groups, the Organization of the People in Arms and the Guerrilla Army of the Poor. In 1979,

Carter cut off financial and military assistance to the Garcia regime. The revolutionaries moved toward democracy.

Honduras: the military dictator Policarpo Paz Garcia provided safe haven to the Contras which together with the CIA set up the terrorist group *Battalion 3-16*. Honduras remains in poverty today owed primarily to United States dominance there.

Panama: except for economic impact causing its central bank to slow monies flowing out of the country for periods of up to a year, Panama was insulated from the revolution by the American presence of nineteen military bases. The courts determined the lion's share of the Vatican bank scandal money was routed to Panama; taken down in cash, it could have ended up most anywhere in Central America.

Costa Rica: enjoyed relative economic and political stability as compared to its neighbors. Yet, like neighboring Panama, during the period of the bank scandal transactions 1979-1981, its central bank froze monies flowing out of the country for periods of up to a year.

Lillian Carter, the American president's mother visited Paul in his last days at Castel Gandolfo. I can't help but think he asked her to convey his appreciation for what her son was doing to bring an end to an everyday event in this tiny isthmus caught up between great oceans—a thousand miniature caskets lowered into the ground.

The Reagan-Bush Contra War

As 1981 dawned, the region was on a path to free elections and a more equitable society. Contras' funds had been cut off by Carter in

Murder by the Grace of God

the United States and Italian court proceedings of the Vatican bank scandal were about to cut off their flow of funds from the Vatican.

An event occurred that would be the Contras' salvation. Ronald Reagan and George Bush took over the White House.

Reagan and Bush chose Honduras as a base for their Contra war. They established an air base at Soto Cano equipping it with a vast battery of military power including planes, helicopters, tanks, jeeps, automatic weapons and ammunition. What's more, it was turned into a state-of-the-art training base for the Contras' death squads.

In identical fashion, as had the Nixon administration employed CIA's *Operation Gladio* to carry out terrorist activities in Italy and frame the *Red Brigades* to turn the mindset of the Italian people against communism in the 1970s, the Reagan-Bush administration commissioned CIA's *Battalion 3-16* to carry out terrorist activities in Guatemala, El Salvador, Nicaragua and even Honduras cleverly plotted to frame the Sandinistas and turn the mindset of the people against the Sandinistas and communism in the 1980s.

CIA's *Battalion 3-16,* in conjunction with the Contras, carried on widespread bombings, kidnappings, rape and murder of civilians.

In 1982, the Guatemalan guerrilla groups joined in coalition with Salvadoran guerrillas (FMLN) and Nicaraguan guerrillas (FSLN) in a war against the United States. Reagan-Bush escalated the war raising their requests in Congress from millions to tens of billions.

Though there were thousands of kidnappings, rapes and murders of innocent civilians including children, few reached notoriety.

In 1980, four nuns flew from Nicaragua to El Salvador to help guerillas. They were brutally raped and murdered.

As it had in hundreds of other cases the Reagan administration framed the guerillas. This deception drew a flood of congressional support for Reagan-Bush's Contra war until late in 1982 when five Salvadorian soldiers in *Battalion 3-16* were convicted of the crime.

Though a tiny part of the atrocities, the incident caught fire in the press and turned world opinion against United States intervention.

At about the same time, Reagan-Bush began to lose their voice in congress. Though they continued to hold an edge in the senate, the house drifted overwhelmingly toward the democrats. In December 1982, congress cut off funds for the Reagan-Bush Contra war.

Reagan appealed to the Pope who, as the most influential man in Catholicism, could do what bullets and bombs could not do.

Early in 1983, John Paul II toured all of Central America.

He told the people to stop supporting the revolutionaries. The revolution came to a halt as if one had turned off a water faucet.

Perhaps, nothing demonstrates more clearly what the CIA-Opus Dei-P2-Ambrosiano coalition was looking at when John Paul I made overtures that he did not oppose the revolutionaries, but rather he would encourage them to bring about a more equitable society. Had he lived ten more days to address the Puebla Conference, the United States would have been dealing with a half-dozen mini-Cubas in its backyard. The reason slow poisoning was not an option in his case.

Regardless, on returning to Rome, John Paul II defrocked dozens of priests and nuns who had supported the revolutionaries. Although his visit brought a temporary lull to the revolution, within a year the people woke up and the revolution began to take hold once more.

Yet, communism had already taken hold in Nicaragua where the Sandinistas had come to power. Reagan and Bush, terrified it would spread to other countries and bring an end to poverty in Central America, took drastic measures to fund their Contra war.

In 1985, in a CIA covert operation, they secretly sold arms to Iran and diverted the proceeds to the Contras—the Iran-Contra Affair.

Contras' financing during the reign of terror in Central America:

1979-1981	1981-1982	1983-1984	1985-1986
Vatican Bank $	United States $	Papal Influence	Iran-Contra Affair $

It was the providential coincidence of a democrat in the White House and a democrat in the Vatican—the powers of money and influence required to enact *a* redistribution of wealth society in Central America—that cost John Paul—the easier target—his life.

Yet, one is smoking funny cigarettes when one thinks John Paul was murdered because the audit he ordered threatened to uncover a bank scandal which transactions had not yet occurred.

I say, the proceeds of *The Great Vatican Bank Scandal* went to Somoza and the Contras. The disappearance of the money in Nicaragua is consistent with the fall of Somoza in 1979 and the subsequent routing of the money to Panama and its disappearance in Central America match the rise of the Contras to a tee.

Murder by the Grace of God

Is it mere coincidence all these champions of a redistribution of wealth society—Aldo Moro, Paul VI, John Paul and scores of others we have talked of—died of natural causes at the precise moment in world history communism happened to have been taking hold in Europe and Latin America as the will of the people? I don't think so.

I say this with much more than mere supposition.

All of the known facts point to this conclusion. One does not have to be an expert in international banking and finance to know this. One has only to use the intelligence one has been gifted with and apply a bit of common sense: "One does not run one's money through war ravaged regions of the world unless one intends it remain there." Paul Marcinkus first said it. We have proved it.

What's more, in my case, I know because I was there.

I woke up in my hotel room to the shouting in the streets in Guatemala City on the morning Jimmy Carter became President of the United States. I was standing in the boss's office on Shippan Point on Long Island Sound being charged with the task to figure out a way to get my company's money out of Central American banks on the day John Paul I lay on a catafalque in the Clementine Chapel. I was enjoying lunch in San Jose when word came Oscar Romero's blood had been splattered on the altar in neighboring El Salvador. I was sound asleep in my bed in Panama City the night four nuns of the Maryknoll order were raped and murdered returning from Nicaragua. I was there in the lamplight of the evening in San Salvador when a dozen half-naked, half-limbed, starving children scrambled at the rice and beans mixed with the mud of the street.

Where was the rest of the world when this horror I have spoken of here was tucked stealthily into the inner pages of newspapers?

On their terraces sipping coffee reading the comics and sports sections of the morning edition? In church listening to their emissary from Rome campaign for Reagan and Bush?

Yes, dropping their five-dollar bills into the poor box to support heartless men of a Vatican regime with their bellies filled and nestled comfy in their feather beds with pillows of down each night. While, on the other side of the world, a thousand miniature caskets waited silently in the dark, for the coming of the dawn.

1 *Messaggero di S Antonio* Apr 72; justifies the war in Central America and the Red Brigades
2 *L Osservatore* 2 Jan 69

Chapter 40

Baby Pigeons

How is it possible the same constituency of cardinals elected a liberal in one election and just a few weeks later elected a conservative?

Well, it is time to hang this one out to dry.

It would seem easier to solve the mystery as to why there are no baby pigeons while ducklings follow their mother in and out of the water in the park than to explain this strange occurrence.

There are no baby pigeons in the park because pigeons nest in high places and a pigeon nears adulthood before it is able to fly.[1]

Like the baby pigeons our malady, too, has a sound reply.

The money bought the conclave votes

In the search as to how the same constituency of cardinals elected a liberal in one election and a few weeks later elected a conservative, we came to the conclusion Karol Wojtyla could not have possibly traded off ecclesiastical concessions for them. We know this because the contraception doctrine from which the cardinals in third world countries sought relief has never been repealed or even modified. This gives us the supposition he could have bought the votes with the only other thing that buys votes—money—the $1.3 billion.

This is consistent with the money disappearing in Latin America where most of them lived. It is also consistent with the timetable of the transactions which began shortly after John Paul II was elected.

These were mostly conservative third world cardinals who held the doctrine banning contraception to be philosophically sound, yet, objected to it because of the poverty and starvation it was generating among their congregations. They had voted for Luciani in the first election because he was the most likely to repeal it.

If they were offered huge sums of money to annihilate much of the poverty the ban on contraception caused, they could hold to their conviction the ban on contraception was sound and yet minimize its downside—starvation. They would have their cake and eat it too.

Giuseppe Caprio as Secretary/Treasurer of the Patrimony of the Holy See controlled the purse strings of the papacy. From a banking perspective he was the only person in the Vatican who could make it work. Caprio's relationship with Calvi—the only person outside the Vatican who could make it work—went back a decade to the time Caprio had brought Calvi's associate Sindona into the Vatican fold.

From this prospective that the bank scandal had been a part of the Genoa meeting makes sense. Yet, it makes no sense forty cardinals could have been approached to sell their votes for cash, without one of them raising the alarm. We will leave this one for the dreamers.

"A funny thing happened on the way to the 1st conclave..."

In our analysis of the conclaves of 1978, in the second conclave Wojtyla would have had to gain a minimum of 40 votes which had been cast for Luciani in the first conclave because Luciani was the most likely to repeal *Humane Vitae*—the ban on contraception.

Why did they vote for Wojtyla in the second conclave when they knew he would never repeal the doctrine?

Thirty-eight third world cardinals were in the 1978 conclaves. Why would twenty Latin American cardinals and eighteen from other third world countries vote for a liberal in one election and just a few weeks later vote for a conservative?

In our chapter '**How a Pope is Elected**' we determined Karol Wojtyla—like Albino Luciani before him and Joseph Ratzinger after him—won the election on the first day of his conclave. The election had actually taken place before the conclave opened.

To obscure the lobbying, nominating, politicking and tallying of votes that goes on before the conclaves, Wojtyla's election—like that of his successor—was announced on the second day.

Yet, with one hundred and eleven cardinals to choose from, what made Wojtyla the overwhelming choice of the second conclave? What was it about this man that made him so attractive to these forty cardinals that they would suddenly change their political position on what was the most important ecclesiastical issue of the day?

"A funny thing happened on the way to the 2nd conclave..."

Under Paul VI, *Liberation Theology* had been merely a matter of principle. To the cardinals in the first election it was not much more than talk and wishful thinking. In his short reign, John Paul I had made it much more than just talk and wishful thinking.

Whereas Paul had waged his war on poverty from the pulpit, John Paul had made it clear he would wage it on the battlefield. Whereas Paul had fed them faith, John Paul would feed them arms.

To the voting cardinals in third world countries, Paul's encyclical had suddenly changed from being merely wishful thinking to being a matter of their own survival.

Consider the events which followed the 2nd conclave of 1978.

Although hundreds of priests and nuns and even a few bishops supported and fought for and even gave their lives for *Liberation Theology* in the war-ravaged countries of Central America, after John Paul II's election—with the exception of Lorscheider of Brazil—none of the Latin American cardinals or African cardinals ever spoke out in favor of it. In fact, most of them spoke out strongly against *Liberation Theology*. There is a reason for this.

They lived in mansions and were a part of the elite themselves. They dined on fine cuts of meat and caviar and wine together with the wealthy whose influence had made them bishops and ultimately cardinals—the wealthy families of Latin America were by far the largest contributors to the Church. They did not want war.

If revolutionaries were successful in overthrowing their ruthless dictators in Central America, it would drive a wave of uncontrollable uprisings in the Condor countries of South America—Argentina, Brazil, Chile, Uruguay, Paraguay, Bolivia, Ecuador and Peru—all ruled by extreme right-wing military dictators.

In the second conclave, these cardinals were offered candidates like Benelli, Colombo and Suenens. Like Luciani, these would go after the dictators of Latin America. Like Luciani, they would dig up the *Historic Compromise* which had been buried with Aldo Moro. They would turn Italy and perhaps all of Europe into turmoil.

They could not take another chance on another liberal who might threaten the capitalistic foundations their world was based on. They could not take another chance with another liberal who thought the movement toward the *left* was going too slowly.

Murder by the Grace of God

In the first conclave **Humane Vitae**—the ban on contraception—had been the pivotal issue. In the second conclave another of Paul's doctrines had suddenly risen to the top:

Liberation Theology – feed them food rather than faith – Communism

This is what made a man, who may not have been a factor in the first conclave, the overwhelming choice in the second conclave.

The word 'Communism' struck fear into the hearts of the voting cardinals, just as it struck fear into the hearts of Americans who had supported the Nixon/Kissinger terrorization of the Italian people and the Reagan/Bush terrorization of the poor in Central America. They didn't care if it was the will of the people. To them, confused by what was going on in the Soviet Union, all 'communism' was bad.

What's more, communism both in Russia and China had risen as the great ally of atheism. The Vietnam War between Catholicism and Atheism had rendered 'Communism' synonymous with 'Atheism.' It meant the end of their world. They were about to lose their jobs.

Karol Wojtyla had spent his life fighting communism. Poland was at the frontline of the cold war—capitalism vs. communism. Of all the cardinals, he was the overwhelming choice to defeat this demon which had raised its ugly head under John Paul I—feed them food rather than faith—communism. No one else came close.

They voted for the man most likely to respond to Kissinger's alarm: **"Domination by Moscow is not the issue. Communist control of Italy and Central America is the issue... It would have terrible consequences for the United States and it is today the number one threat to its national security and must be dealt with accordingly."**

They voted for the man most likely to maintain the status quo—pheasant under glass and swirls of *Latour* at their dinner tables while a thousand miniature caskets were lowered into the ground each day.

Nevertheless, we have answered the question:

How is it possible the same cardinals elected a liberal in one election and just a few weeks later elected a conservative?

Communism had raised its ugly head.

---

1 pigeons near adult size and can fly in about 45-60 days. Smaller birds fly as early as two weeks.

Chapter 41

Ides of March

1978 Poverty Summit, Vittorio Veneto

It was the middle of March nineteen hundred and seventy-eight.

Halfway up the mountainside the ancient castle loomed out over the sprawling village of Vittorio Veneto.

Ghostly clouds swirled about its surviving towers forming a silent marquis hinting of the shrouded happenings going on beneath them. Yet, they could not foretell the horror of what was about to come.

Thirty-three men surrounded by thirty-three angels. Each one in Byzantine fashion, each one in individual color, each one bearing a shield with coat-of-arms, each one armed with a weapon of medieval times, each one topped off with a golden halo, each one standing in a carved mahogany panel. Each one watching, each one listening...

The enormous clock ticked so loudly it bellowed each passing moment in time. Each of the room's occupants answered in unison with a twitch each time it marked a spot in time.

The Poverty Summit

Here in the foothills of the great Dolomite Mountains for three days and for three nights had been clustered together the leaders of the Marxist movement in a heartless world.

There were those whose congregations were literally starving to death in the wake of the rich and poor society imposed upon them, and there were others who just wanted to help.

A bit of what had happened in the Russia Revolution.

In 1918, Lenin's Bolshevik Party was defeated by the Peasant Party in a free election—the will of the people. Unfortunately, it was the will of uneducated people. Lenin's objective was to achieve an equitable society in an organized manner by progressively increased taxation of the rich; he would force the rich to give the poor equal opportunity, not only in food and shelter, but in education, to enable each of them to make his or her utmost contribution back to society.

However, the opposition Peasant Party offered a much better deal to the poverty stricken masses at the bottom: a turnkey Marxist society in which the government seized all property and divided it equally among the poor—a free ride. Thus, motion pictures of war-torn Russia—e.g. *Doctor Zhivago*—depict mansions being divided up into apartments for the poor. Having lost the election, Lenin took control via military force; we all know what happened after that.

Yet, we are speaking here of another kind of communism. One which had already captured the vote in Italy and was poking its nose into the impoverished nations of Central America and other parts of the world as the clouds swirled about the towers of Vittorio Veneto.

One is speaking of a free democratic communist society driven by the will of the people—one that forces the rich to help the poor.

One is not speaking here of a society which foregoes a free enterprise system and simply divides up the pie equally. One is speaking of a society which affords each child an equal opportunity to make his or her maximum contribution back to society.

The primates of world poverty

There were thirty-three in all scattered about the immense room.

There was Valerian Gracias, Archbishop of Bombay and Primate of India. Gracias—the 'Reincarnation of Gandhi' as he was often called—was determined to succeed where his namesake had failed.

In recent years, Gracias had risen as an enemy of the capitalistic world imposed upon him. Although he had reservations concerning contraception, he was the great ally of Luciani concerning the pill.

"It would be a godsend to the teeming masses of our country"[1] he once reasoned with Mother Teresa who opposed contraception—she didn't care how much starvation overpopulation wrought despite she spent her life trying to minimize the damage it brought.

Cardinal Yu Pin—Primate of China and protectorate of five hundred million peasants who were literally starving to death—sat in front of a huge fireplace trying to keep warm.

He peered up at an aging oil painting of Christ throwing the money makers out of the Temple—golden coins splashing down out of its ornate frame. Its artist, centuries removed from the room, depicting the goings on within it to a tee—rid the world of greed.

Chatting with him was Cardinal Delargey.

As archbishop of the stately province of Wellington Delargey oversaw the impoverished islands of the South Pacific. It was no surprise the two were together here at Vittorio Veneto as they were often seen together in the public eye. They were the best of friends.

With them was Cardinal Trinh Nhu Khue, Primate of Eastern Asia—overseer of Korea, Vietnam, Cambodia and other countries which had borne the brunt of the Vatican's war against atheism. Buddhist countries cast into decades of suffering and death by Pius XII and just now emerging from the horrors of the Vietnam War.

Off to one side, the Polish Cardinal Boleshaw Filipiak of Gniezno sat pensively gazing out of the only window in the room. He peered across the seemingly endless span of Vittorio Veneto.

During World War I it had been the site of the bloodiest struggle of all. Near the Austrian border, the village to the north was in the German ranks and the one to the south in the Allied ranks. Brother fought against brother. In the end one in ten was alive. To symbolize peace, the villages were united—Vittorio Veneto—Veneto Victory.

Though he had no official title to say so, the Primate of Poverty in Eastern Europe thought back three-and-a-half decades before.

During the war Filipiak had been leader of the **Polish Resistance.** When Karol Wojtyla had risen in the Nazi ranks to quartermaster of the Solvay Chemical plant in Krakow, he approached Wojtyla to divert supplies to the **Resistance.** Karol refused. Filipiak was arrested and spent the rest of the war in a Nazi prison camp. Though he had no proof, it was his conviction, Wojtyla had turned him in.[2]

In the eastern bloc of European nations, millions of born-out-of-wedlock children remained confined to streets and sewers. Filipiak would bring about a society that affords each of them an equal opportunity to earn his or her fair share of the pie.

So severe was the rivalry between Wojtyla and Filipiak, John Paul II struck Filipiak's record from the Catholic Encyclopedia, the official record of the Roman Catholic Church. Filipiak is the only twentieth century cardinal not mentioned in the huge volume.

At the far end of the vast room, Metropolitan Nikodim and Oscar Romero sat at a massive desk. Off by themselves, they were deeply immersed in their own bit of intrigue.

What is known today—not known at the time—the youthful leader of the Marxist movement within the Orthodox Church was a

Murder by the Grace of God

secret agent for the KGB—the Soviet Union's counterpart of the CIA. So much so, his every move was tracked by the CIA. He had spent much of the trip from Leningrad looking over his shoulder.

Though the effort to bring about a Christ/Marx-like society had met with autocracy in the Soviet Union, Nikodim was convinced it could succeed as a free democratic society.

Oscar Romero was witness to the epitome of a rich and poor society; his people were literally dying in poverty. At first, he thought he could bring an end to oppression via peaceful protest.

It had been a year since he found out it didn't work. After Paul had made him Archbishop of San Salvador, a long line of priest and nun assassinations followed. Within a few months, among dozens of others, his dear friends Fathers Rutilio Grande Garcia and Alfonso Grande Oviedo had been cut down by death squad bullets.

Shortly after Oviedo's death, he abandoned peaceful protests and spoke out in support of the guerillas and, many times, pointed his finger directly at the CIA for assassinations of priests and nuns.

One might suspect Romero sought Nikodim's intercession with the Soviets for arms assistance for revolutionaries operating in El Salvador and neighboring Nicaragua. One will never know.

Nevertheless, the primates of the world's pockets of poverty were gathered together. Not for the first time, for they had been here before, and would be here again. At least, that is what they thought.

What's that? Africa? We all know what goes on there or maybe we don't want to know what goes on there. Regardless, you're right, Cardinal Bernardin Gantin—Primate of Africa—was not there.

There was a reason he was not there. He was an enemy of Paul's *Liberation Theology*. He did not believe in revolution. He did not believe society could be driven by people helping other people.

Gantin believed society could only be driven by greed. He did not believe Christ is 'What is in this for others.' He was convinced Christ was 'a piece of bread in a cup and a golden idol on a wall.'

Yet, it could be he didn't want to give up his palace in Benin or his posh apartments in Paris and Rome. One will never know.

The politicians

Enrico Berlinguer, leader of the Italian Communist Party was gathered together with the communist mayors of Italy's largest metropolises, Giulio Argan of Rome and Vittorio Korach of Milan. With them—sharing a white marble coffee table—was Aldo Moro.

Cardinal Giocomo Violardo knelt at a prayer station in a dark corner of the huge room brightened only by the flickering of candles.

He thought back a few years to the time he had caused an uproar when he had been caught distributing Holy Communion to a group of Protestants and Communists. He explained to his adversaries, "This is what Communion is all about—Communism—Christ."[3]

Regardless, Paul answered the demands of Curia cardinals for his excommunication by making Giocomo Secretary for the Discipline of the Sacraments and at the same time made him a cardinal.[4]

One would wonder what the Secretary for the Discipline of the Sacraments does. Not much. Paul filled in his time as the Vatican's chief lobbyist in the Italian Parliament.

Other than Paul, the astute lawyer was the closest person in the room to Aldo Moro. He was looking forward to the upcoming Thursday morning when Moro would move communist ministers into control of Italian Parliament.

Giocomo was not a lobbyist in the common sense of the term. He didn't wine and dine politicians in classy restaurants or spend his time working hotel lobbies. He lobbied them the same way all preachers lobby their prey—from the pulpit.

When a particular bill was on the table, Moro would furnish Giocomo with a list of Parliamentary members together with where they lived. The local parish would be privileged to have a Vatican cardinal give the Sunday sermon— Giocomo would cleverly lean his message toward the issue at hand and win over the votes.

It was fortunate he was praying to his God. He was about to meet Him. His body would be found beneath a marble stairway in a dark corner of the Palace of the Holy Office on that coming Friday morning. The Vatican paper reported: "...the cardinal undoubtedly stumbled and slipped over the balustrade late last evening."[5]

Moro would never learn of the loss of his dear friend. He would never be privileged to give the eulogy at the funeral of Cardinal Giocomo Violardo. By the time Giocomo lay in his coffin, Moro, himself, had already been kidnapped and readied for his own coffin.

The ringleaders

Eight men were gathered on the other side of the room.

As leader of its largest church, Paul was the most influential man on the planet. Yet, he sat at the head of the table nervously wiggling his toes in his shoes. He seemed more immersed in himself than what was going on around him. Yet, he was much more concerned with the order of the day than he was with his impending doom.

Cardinal Egidio Vagnozzi sat next to Paul as he held the purse strings of Paul's war on poverty. As Prefect of Economic Affairs he oversaw the Vatican's central bank. One cannot fight a war—particularly a war on poverty—without money.

To Paul's other side sat his legal counsel Cardinal Pericle Felici, Prefect of the Tribunal of the Holy See. Next to Felici was the man who was always next to Felici—Cardinal Giovanni Benelli. The two were bounded together in a driving cause to destroy Opus Dei—the clandestine cult which ruled the opposing force in the Church.

Albino Luciani sat chatting away in French, so fluent one would never believe he had rarely traveled outside of Italy. His audience was Leon Joseph Suenens. Cardinal Suenens? Who's he?

Suenens was the leader of human fairness in the Church.

When John XXIII had created the liberal party in the College of Cardinals, which for a thousand years had known only one party, he gave it a leader. He explained when he named Suenens a cardinal: **"He will open the windows and let in the fresh air."**[6]

John XXIII, Paul VI and John Paul I had been fluent in French.

It was no mystery in John's case as he had spent much of his ministry in France. It was no mystery in Paul's case either as he had the French cardinal Jean Villot at his side. But, how did Luciani, who rarely traveled outside Italy, become so fluent in French?

The reason was Cardinal Suenens. Scarcely a day would go by in his twenty years as a bishop and as a cardinal Luciani would not pick up the phone and run an issue or two by the Belgian cardinal. This was also true of both John and Paul. Scarcely a day would go by they would not pick up the phone and ask Suenens' advice.

When Luciani rose to the papacy he was fluent in Italian, English, French and Spanish and could converse with limitation in Russian, German, Chinese, Portuguese and a number of African dialects.

Pericle Felici had served as apostolic nuncio to Africa and Giovanni Benelli had served as apostolic nuncio to western Africa and Albino Luciani had run missionary operations in Africa for many years. Even though its primate was not one of those scattered about the room, Africa was well represented here at the summit.

Cardinal Colombo of Milan and Cardinal Villot who had set up the summit rounded out those at the top.

Finally, there was the host, the presiding bishop of Vittorio Veneto—Antonia Cunial—and a dozen or so interpreters and aides strategically placed here and there throughout the great room.

There were thirty-three in all.

Thirty-three men surrounded by thirty-three angels. Each one in Byzantine fashion, each one in individual color, each one bearing a shield with coat-of-arms, each one armed with a weapon of medieval times, each one topped off with a golden halo, each one standing in a carved mahogany panel. Each one watching, each one listening...

Early the next morning, a few ran off to Belluno and Venice to catch planes, while the others stayed on for the day.

Wine at the corner-wedge café

On the afternoon of March 13, 1978, fourteen men sat around a table in a sidewalk café in a mountain village in northern Italy. In casual clothes they went unnoticed though one was the reigning Pontiff and another was the Marxist leader of the Russian Orthodox Church. Included were Italian cardinals who had been behind the rise of the Communist Party in the polls in Italy and the principal cardinals of impoverished parts of the world including the primates of China, India, Latin America, South Pacific and the papal nuncio to Africa.

It was the composition of these men that was the great enemy of Opus Dei, the clandestine cult which sought to control the papacy and the moral pulse of the world. More so, it was the great enemy of the capitalistic world led by the United States. They left at four o'clock and Aldo Moro reserved the table "for this time next year."

On the morning of March 13, 1979, Benelli and Felici awoke. They had decided not to travel to Vittorio Veneto that day. After all, all the others were dead. Unaware of their impending doom, they, too, were as good as dead.

So what do we have?

Murder by the Grace of God

We have the providential coincidence the boy Luciani and the boy Rotov had a common rearing by atheist fathers and a common mission to bring about a redistribution of wealth society; Luciani working the western front and Rotov working the eastern front.

We have the providential coincidence the youthful leader of the Russian Orthodox Church—Metropolitan Rotov Nikodim—was the first foreign VIP granted an audience with John Paul I and dropped dead at the Pope's feet immediately after sniffing steaming coffee.

We have the providential coincidence Yu Pin—who would have locked up the election for Luciani—dropped dead at Paul VI' funeral

We have the providential coincidence the unexplained deaths of Paul VI, John Paul I and Jean Villot in rapid consecutive order made possible the rise of John Paul II, Agostino Casaroli and Giuseppe Caprio to the most powerful positions in the Roman Catholic world.

We have the providential coincidence two of these three had free access to each of these victims the night they died.

We have the providential coincidence Karol Wojtyla's long time adversary Cardinal Boleslaw Filipiak died of undisclosed causes the day before the conclave that elected the Polish Pope opened.

We have the providential coincidence Aldo Moro was abducted and subsequently murdered on the very morning he was scheduled to move communist ministers into control of Italian Parliament.

We have the providential coincidence Paul's 'voice' in the Italian Parliament—Giocomo Violardo—was murdered on the same day.

We have the providential coincidence Egidio Vagnozzi dropped dead while in the midst of his audit of the Vatican bank.

We have the providential coincidence John Paul's proclamation **"It is the inalienable right of no man to accumulate wealth beyond the necessary while other men starve to death because they have nothing"** was followed the next day by his unwitnessed death.

We have the providential coincidence that of eleven people who could have known of the Vatican bank scandal transactions, only four were alive when the case came to trial in the Italian courts.

We have the providential coincidence the disappearance of the 'Vatican bank' money in Central America coincided with the fall of Somoza and the rise of the Contras during the Carter administration.

We have the providential coincidence the same cardinals elected a liberal in one election and elected a conservative a few weeks later.

We have

Murder '...by the grace of God'

April 4, 1919	Francisco Marto	arsenic ([1&2])
February 20, 1920	Jacinta Marto	arsenic ([1&2])
September 5, 1968	Brother Pasquale	blunt object
March 16, 1978	Aldo Moro	kidnapped/shot
March 16, 1978	Cardinal Violardo	fell over banister
May 9, 1978	Aldo Moro	shot to death
August 6, 1978	Paul VI	arsenic ([2])
August 11, 1978	Cardinal Yu Pin	lethal poison
August, 17, 1978	Cardinal Suenens	attempt on life
August 17, 1978	Cardinal Benelli	attempt on life
September 5, 1978	Archbishop Nikodim	cyanide powder
September 11, 1978	Cardinal Gracias	arsenic ([2])
September 21, 1978	Cardinal Suenens	attempt on life
September 27, 1978	Edoardo Calo (valet)	fell off terrace
September 29, 1978	John Paul I	lethal injection
September 30, 1978	John Amedore	hit-and-run
October 14, 1978	Cardinal Filipiak	arsenic ([2])
November 27, 1978	Cardinal Trinh-Khue	arsenic ([2])
January 29, 1979	Cardinal Delargey	arsenic ([2&4])
March 13, 1979	Cardinal Jean Villot	unknown
March 29, 1979	Carmine Pecorelli	shot to death
March 24, 1980	Archbishop Romero	shot to death
December 26, 1980	Cardinal Vagnozzi	never disclosed
March 22, 1982	Cardinal Felici	Methothianate ([2])
June 17, 1982	Roberto Calvi	hanging
June 17, 1982	Teresa Corrocher	fell out window
September 12, 1982	Giuseppe Dellacha	fell out window
June 9, 1983	Michel Sindona	poison
October 26, 1982	Cardinal Benelli	Vatican order
June 17, 1984	Sister Vincenza Taffarel	unknown
November 26, 1990	Avro Manhattan	unknown ([3])
March 18, 1996	Cardinal Suenens	lethal injection
May 4, 1998	Alois Estermann	shot to death
May 4, 1998	Gladys Meza Romero	shot to death
May 4, 1998	Cedric Tornay	shot to death
February 20, 2005	Archbishop Marcinkus	not disclosed

Murder by the Grace of God

(1) On Feb 13, 2008, Benedict XVI opened Lucia Santos' beautification process.
(2) Death consistent with-not proved. Four cardinals, not mentioned in this book, also died in 1978-1979. To the best of the author's knowledge they died of natural causes. Their average age—77 compared with the average of those above—56.
(3) Body found by his wife Nov 26, 1990 on her return from a week in London. Cause and date of death unknown—remains under investigation by the author.
(4) Perhaps the most puzzling death was that of the youngest cardinal in the 1978 conclaves Reginald Delargey of Wellington. Many books have been written trying to explain it, "...whispers in the 1978 conclaves...He looked dreadful...wasted away skin and bones... final stages of cancer in the first conclave were obvious...most surprised when he showed up at the second conclave..."* Photo (right) taken during the second conclave of 1978 does not substantiate this. Yet, he was hospitalized.

After the second conclave he fell ill and was confined in the diocese controlled Sisters of Mercy Mater Misericordiae Hospital in Auckland. Doctors were unable to diagnose his condition. It was that severe restrictions were placed on visitors and the diocese refused to disclose the nature of his illness which triggered widespread rumors. Those closest to him who felt they had the right to visit him were turned away.

Cause of death **'inoperable adenocarcinoma of stomach'** on his death certificate also appears on the death certificates of Valerian Gracias and Trinh Nhu Khue other eastern cardinals stricken at the same time. Gracias died in a Vatican controlled Catholic hospital in Bombay and Khue died in a Vatican controlled Catholic hospital in Hanoi.

The Church has many times influenced what goes on a death certificate—a practice facilitated in Catholic hospitals. John Paul I and Villot are not exceptions.

Delargey had been the closest confidant of Cardinal Yu Pin and the loudest voice calling for an autopsy when the Grand Chancellor of Eastern Affairs keeled over at Paul's funeral. He insisted with reporters Yu Pin had no heart problems. He had occupied the cell next to Yu Pin the night before Yu Pin dropped dead.

The story is told of the progressive Delargey's visit to the Papal Palace after Luciani was elected. He asked the Pope, **"We are good men. Why is it we have so many enemies?"** John Paul didn't hesitate, **"We were born before our time."**

* *Life and Work of Reginald Delargey: The Untimely Death of Cardinal Delargey* Nicholas Reid 2008

We have one more for the road →

Author note: the general scope of this chapter is dramatized by the author as related to him by Antonio Cunial bishop of Vittorio Veneto after John Paul's death in November 1978.

1 *Maharashtra Times* 22 Apr 78 or search Internet 'Valerian Gracias contraception'
2 The scene of Filipiak pleading with Wojtyla quartermaster of a German supply depot to divert supplies to the Resistance is depicted in the 2005 CBS film starring Jon Voight, *Pope John Paul II*.
3 *L'Osservatore Romano* 5 Jan 65
4 Cardinal Giocomo Violardo *Catholic Encyclopedia*
5 *L Osservatore Romano* 18 Mar 78
6 *La Repubblica* 20 Mar 62

Chapter 42

The Murder of Cardinal Suenens

When John Paul II rose to power he ordered a costly renovation of the papal retreat at Castel Gandolfo, going so far as to add a majestic swimming pool for his personal enjoyment—an about-face from his predecessor who had threatened to sell off the opulent estate.

When he was elected the IOR had a deficit of forty million dollars. Had it had a surplus instead of a deficit, his spending would have gone unchallenged. Because the 'bank' operated at a deficit, it brought harsh criticism of the new Pope's irresponsible spending.

Among the critics was Cardinal Suenens:

"In order for one to see what has happened here, one must first understand the function of the IOR. It is not a bank at all in the common sense of the word. One can see this clearly in its title: 'The Institute for Religious Works.'

It is a clearing house for funds that have been raised for the poor by charitable orders. By quite a margin its largest client is Mother Teresa whose order ministers to the poor and dying in the slums of Calcutta and other impoverished cities of the world.

It also serves as a clearing house for 'Peter's Pence'—funds raised from rich parishes to support the lavish lifestyle of the papal household. From a banking perspective, it is a depository in The Patrimony of the Holy See—the Vatican's central bank.

Because 'Peter's Pence' was insufficient to support the Pope's extravagant spending, the money for his swimming pool and other improvements to the Papal Palace and the Castel Gandolfo came from funds raised by Mother Teresa and others like her intended to help children suffering from starvation and illness in the world.

Also, it is not pastorally correct of His Holiness to use these funds to pay for expensive vacations at luxurious resorts reserved for the very rich. Also, it is morally wrong to pay Vatican cardinals huge salaries out of these same funds intended for the poor."[1]

Suenens is referring to an eighteen percent pay raise for Vatican cardinals the Polish Pope had granted immediately after his election.

"It is almost as if it had been a part of the deal" was whispered in pubs by disgruntled Romans an Italian was not chosen.[2]

Suenens was wrong about the vacations. Mother Teresa didn't pay for them. They were paid for by Karol Wojtyla's friend Licio Gelli. Most of them took place at the opulent Ovindoli Ski Lodge in the Italian Abruzzi region. Gelli owned the resort.[3]

Bodyguards

A few weeks after a section of a frieze fell and killed a visiting French bishop in Brussels and Cardinals Suenens and Benelli had narrowly escaped death when a chip of a frieze fell from a Vatican building, there was third incident. Suenens' secretary threw him to the ground to avoid an onrushing car in Brussels. The hospital reported the cardinal suffered a mild concussion in the mishap.[4]

There is nothing in the record to prove any of these incidents were indeed attempts on his life. Yet, it was obvious the cardinal, himself, sensed he was in danger as he was never seen again in public without two young priests who—if not for their garb—could be mistaken for soccer players—clearly serving as bodyguards.

As a precaution, he moved his office from the first floor of his residence in Brussels to the third floor. A move unnecessary, as a few weeks after the last failed attempt on his life, the Polish Pope removed Suenens as Primate of Belgium. No longer with pastoral influence Leon Joseph Suenens seemed as good as dead.

Yet, he was not quite dead. He continued an assault from the *left*. Yet, with some minor exceptions concerning the rights of women in the Church, he had little success. Every now and then he would gain notoriety at times in Europe and at other times in the United States.

In his bid for reelection Ronald Reagan made a commitment to the Christian-right leader Jerry Falwell that he would use his veto power to ban funding of AIDS research; something he did do three times during his presidency. On the campaign trail with Falwell—citing the homosexual link to AIDS—a heartless remark slipped out in a television interview: "They live like that, let them die like that."[5]

From Brussels, Suenens lashed out at the American President.[6]

1986, Elizabeth Taylor led celebrities in an event raising millions to establish AIDS research.[7]

Suenens spoke of the Hollywood Bowl event: "When the Gods of Washington fail us," he told a reporter, "we can always count on the Gods of Hollywood to bail us out."[8]

On the tenth anniversary of his friend's death, Suenens spoke of Albino Luciani: "Heroes are those who dream dreams and are willing to pay the price to make them come true, for you and for me."[9]

The following year, Bernardin Gantin reprimanded the bishop Jacques Gaillot for having sanctioned the union of two homosexuals who were facing imminent death from AIDS: "The French bishop will cease advancing repulsive practices in society."[10]

Suenens criticized Gantin's action: "I feel it my duty to remind the African cardinal when Jesus said 'Love thy neighbor as thyself,' He meant all thy neighbors."[11]

A few years later, Gantin removed Gaillot from his bishopric for preaching *Liberation Theology*. Suenens quoted Gaillot's demise: "'He had a dream to be able to accompany the poor, the excluded, the distressed...to be able to show his indignation at destitution, injustice and famine...without fear of the guillotine...'"[12]

Regardless, Suenens' vision for the Church, his vision for the world, was so vast it would have required Vatican III to bring it about. Vatican II—the equivalent of World War II in the Church—opened the door to change. Vatican III—the equivalent of World War III in the Church—would have been required to bring it about.

Suenens was the force behind John XXIII, Paul VI and John Paul I, three popes of the twentieth century who allowed their conscience to overrule their scripture—three popes of the twentieth century who had brought the elevator of human justice to the fiftieth floor of the one hundred story building of righteousness. But, it has remained there since—their successors choosing to lock it there forevermore.

Cardinal Leon Joseph Suenens was scheduled to speak at John Carroll University in Cleveland. Disturbed that John Paul II was loading the College of Cardinals with conservatives, Suenens, who had once—together with Luciani—championed the ill-fated cause to remove the election of the Pope from the College of Cardinals to the Synod of Bishops, was about to call on the Vatican to remove the authority to appoint bishops from the Pope to the Synod of Bishops.

A draft of the speech he never made was found in his typewriter. A housemaid innocently released it to a *Sun Times* reporter:

Murder by the Grace of God

"...One can see what I say here, very vividly. If, in the case of the United States, the President were allowed to appoint the members of Congress, he would then have the power of a dictator. He could load the Congress entirely with those who share his own convictions—democrats or republicans, and thereby muster the vote to render his own appointment invincible. Believe me, in what I have to say here today, a plane with only one wing can fly in only one direction. That direction is very decidedly down!"[13]

American newspapers reported: "Vibrant and on the job to the end...Suenens...the Architect of Twentieth Century Catholicism...the chief negotiator of Vatican II...was found sitting up in bed wearing his reading glasses...Upright in his hands was clutched a book... The bed lamp was on and the window next to his bed was wide open.

The book was his own book, one he had written years before. The book was 'Day by Day.' It was opened to page fifty-six.

His eyes were open and they seemed to be fixed on a phrase at the bottom of the page: 'Let us all look around us with new eyes. A whole world of discovery will open up before us.'

It seemed Suenens was editing his bestseller for republishing.

In the margin of the opposite page were scribbled the words: 'Always look forward, never look back!'"[14]

The great man had left his mark in time. John XXIII, Paul VI and the little boy Albino Luciani had left their mark in time. Disciples of Lacordaire: "Have an opinion and do something about it!"[15]

The record is there for all time. It is there for men and women of good conscience to soak up.

1 *Le Soir Brussels* 2 May 79
2 *La Stampa* 2 Nov 78
3 *A Life with Karol* Cardinal Stanislaw Dziwisz - *IL Messaggero* 23 Jan 07.
4 *La Tribune de Bruxelles* 12 Dec 83
5 CBS News 12 Sep 83. In 2003, a documentary including this clip was censored by television channels
6 *La Tribune de Bruxelles* 17 Sep 83
7 'The Queen of Theology' in the author's book '*The Reincarnation of Albino Luciani*'
8 *Los Angeles Times* 26 Mar 86
9 *Philadelphia Inquirer* 29 Sep 88
10 *La Repubblica* 22 Nov 88
11 *Philadelphia Inquirer* 25 Nov 88
12 *Voice of the Desert* Feb 95
13 *Sun Times* 21 Mar 96
14 composite of *New York Times/ Boston Globe/ Cleveland Sun Times/ Washington Post* 19 Mar 96.
    Five months after his death the Vatican declared Suenens died of thrombosis – embolism
15 Reprinted from Albino Luciani's book *Illustrissimi* 1976

Chapter 43

"...by the grace of God."

"Charity is an excuse for compassion in a selfish society... it will never stem the tide."
Albino Luciani[1]

In its corrected release Vatican Radio explained: "...John Paul was able to retain his papers upright in his hands *by the grace of God.*"

Bullshit!

There are one hundred and sixty thousand words in *Murder by the Grace of God*. Whereas, alone, any single one of them might lose its voice in court, I am reasonably certain if taken en masse to the tribunal they would withstand the test of time.

    As we have demonstrated, the press is immensely more reliable than witnesses of motive who want to make him out to be whatever serves one's political purpose. Yet, insofar as it comes from different arenas, even the press can be less than reliable in determining the true cloth of a man, particularly one as controversial as this one.

    Though not possible to reconstruct precisely the man he actually was, hopefully, we have come close to what a pope should be.

    Then again, the press is particularly reliable in the case of murder. That is, the reports as they first appear immediately following events before the clergy and fiction writers get their fingers on them. The reason references herein are from early reportings of events. One will not find Effortil, digitalis or anticoagulants in any of them.

    What we have set forth does not necessarily in every case prove murder. Yet, the great preponderance of evidence suggests murder. These people—known to be of good health—died suddenly of strange circumstances at a time others had great motive to kill them. Their deaths remain unexplained because the Vatican repeatedly refused to take actions normally prudent under the laws of nations.

Canon Law prohibits autopsy on the body of a pope

You will hear this from poorly researched 'scholars.'

Traditionally autopsies have not been performed on popes.

Autopsy to effectively determine foul play is limited to modern times. Autopsy before the twentieth century was usually performed for research purposes. Just consider what is known of DNA now and not known in 1978. Autopsy today would require far less intrusion and yield vastly more accurate evidence than if performed in 1978.

As I have said before, though there is no canon requiring autopsy in circumstances normally required by the laws of nations, there exists no canon that prohibits autopsy of a pope.[2]

In those cases where murder was suspect, the Vatican repeatedly denied independent autopsy which could have prevented rumors.

In those cases where murder was apparent, the Vatican denied independent investigation which could have solved the crimes.

In the case of the Swiss Guard murders, the Vatican had nothing to lose and everything to gain by taking Scotland Yard up on its offer to investigate the murders. Why would one not want to know who killed these three, one of which was the closest person to the sitting Pontiff. Why didn't John Paul II overrule Cardinal Sodano and take Scotland Yard up on its offer? Why would he have not wanted to know who had murdered the most precious person to have ever come into his life? Could it be an investigation would have traced Alois Estermann to have been the rookie guard assigned to the palace the night of John Paul's death? One will never know.

What we do know is John Paul died suddenly at the age of 65 when he appeared to be—and medical records proved him to be—in exceptional health. We also know many people wanted him dead.

There are those who rumor the weight of the papacy killed him.

There have survived scores of pictures and films of his papacy. It is a rare spot in time to find a glimpse of him not smiling, laughing and joking—the reason he is remembered as the smiling pope.

Albino Luciani was having the time of his life. One does not die of stress when one is having a good time.

The medical world

As we have said Albino Luciani died short of his genetic promise.

His mother died of cancer at 72 at a time life expectancy was twenty years short of what it is today. He lost a grandmother in an accident. His other grandparents and father lived into their eighties and nineties. Both his full-blood siblings outlived him by a quarter century; his sister dying in her 90th year and his brother living to 91. Heart disease, embolism or stroke not a factor in any of their deaths.[3]

His last physical exam witnessed a man of impeccable health.

It is the unwavering consensus of the medical community—given the known circumstances of both his life and death—John Paul did not die of heart attack, pulmonary embolism or stroke.

'Luciani was a doctrinal conservative. He didn't care how much suffering doctrine imposed on the everyday lives of innocent people.'

You will hear this from those who want to destroy ecclesiastical motive for murder. You will hear this from those who think there is something holy about depriving others of equal rights under the laws of nations. You will hear this from those who seek his canonization in a conservative church. For this reason his family and some others who knew him will deny anything of a controversial nature he may have said or done; particularly his compassion for homosexuals in a homophobic church. Unreliable witnesses to his true testament.[4]

Nothing strikes closer to the true doctrinal composition of Albino Luciani than were his first words to his newly acquired congregation in the Basilica di San Marco February 8, 1970:

> "Today science has developed tremendously and purified our knowledge of thousands of defects in our religious knowledge of the past. Our religious knowledge must cleanse itself of these falsehoods which are not a part of the true Christian revelation... The glory of the Church will not be judged in its worship of mythical specters of the past, nor in its magnificent buildings and ritual of the present, but in its efforts to realize fraternal union among all people no matter who those people happen to be..."[5]

Unlike self-anointed 'scholars' on the life of Albino Luciani who never knew him—eagles soaring in tea-aged documents, pheasants deceived by Curia decoys, vultures tugging at his mortal remains as if he is somewhere up there—I am that poor wren on the lowest branch of the biographical tree saying it as it really is:

"He is not up there. He is still here!"

What is important of this man is not his life on earth, not the things that are said of him, not even the lingering mystery of his death. Like any God—or for that matter—like any man, all that counts is what he left behind:

> "Never be afraid to stand up for what is right, whether your adversary be your parent, your peer, your teacher, your politician, your preacher, your constitution, or even your God." [6]

A man on a mission

Nothing better demonstrates what he was all about than something he said two days before he was found dead. Lifting a chalice to worldwide television cameras, he asked his congregation:

"This chalice contains one hundred and twenty-two of the world's most pristine diamonds while children all over the world starve to death. Do you really think this is what Christ meant by His Church?" [7]

Pope Francis I   Castel Gandolfo

Notices in newspapers around the globe the day he was elected seemed uncoordinated. They said all kinds of things.

Because it was part of the Associated Press release, there was a tiny clipping which appeared in all of the world's newspapers: [8]

> He once said: "The true treasures of the church are the poor, the little ones to be helped not merely with occasional alms but in a way they can be promoted."

Slipped into inner pages it went mostly unnoticed. It had been extracted from something he had said as a cardinal two years earlier:

> "The Church's real treasurers are the poor, the little ones not to be helped by means of mere occasional alms but by a society which affords each little one the opportunity to contribute to society. Charity is an excuse for compassion in a selfish society; sandbags placed against onrushing waters will never stem the tide..."[9]

Albino Luciani was convinced the coalition of capitalism and charity could not work. The world had poverty written all over it.

He would force the rich to help the poor. He once told the nun Vincenza: "When I preach compassion for the poor, they call me a saint. When I do something about it, they call me a communist."[10]

Abhorred by what was taking place in the Soviet Union, he was encouraged by the success of what had already taken place in Italy which had drawn the wrath of Henry Kissinger: "... the Communist Party has emerged as an effective vehicle for developing jobs and providing education for common people. This endangers our free capitalistic society... If communism takes hold in Italy, NATO would collapse and the United States would be dangerously isolated..."[11]

Luciani would demolish the driving force behind poverty with the 'pill.' He would create a society based on the principle, his principle:

> "What is important is not how many children are born, but that every child that is born has an opportunity at a good and healthy life."[12]

Reprise

Whereas they do not all support my case, I have presented all the events of the time—thousands of them in chronological order.

It is the strategy of writers to leave most of them out and present only those that support one's suppositions and even those out of order. It puts the reader at a disadvantage to the writer's conclusions.

Murder by the Grace of God

Like a shell game with a thousand shells and a half-dozen peanuts, mesmerize the reader and he'll believe most anything you tell him.

I have taken the time to put them in historical order for a reason. Though I am reasonably certain the conclusions I have set forth are sound, I am only one mind. Yet, it may be it will take many minds, many investigations, to carry this game to its end.

Perhaps, the day is not far off when someone with great analytical skills—a real life *Hercule Poirot*—will drive the ball into the net.

Aside from stories of his young life which are my direct witness, I have said nothing here that has not been said before me either in the press or in the writings of this good man. All that is to my credit is that for the first time the full record has been brought together in one place: "**Twentieth century capitalism as it was jointly embraced by the Vatican and the United States and those caught up in it.**"[13]

So we have walked with him, and we have talked with him, in the woods, together with Pinocchio and the Cat and the Fox and the Poodle Medoro. Yet, I feel I have said poorly what Albino Luciani could have said so much better. Still, the important thing is not that I have written, but that you have listened.

Now, take it with you. Carry it with you to the ends of the earth. That what they dreamed of, those things they fought for, those things they willed to be; will come to be, for each of them, and for me, and for you, and for all humanity.

Author's note: there is a misconception the Vatican's vast wine collection is financed with money collected for the poor. Not true. It is the product of French, Italian and other wineries presenting popes and cardinals with cases of their finest vintage through the years. Most modern popes—including John Paul I and his successors—have been wine connoisseurs. John Paul II was a champagne connoisseur.

1 *Messaggero Mestre* 22 Jan 76
2 Catholic Encyclopedia; a partial autopsy was performed on Leo XIII in 1903
3 Birth, baptismal and death certificates
4 See chapter 'Operation Pigeon to the Grace of God' 1985 Vatican fabricated biography
5 *Messaggero Mestre* 9 Feb 74. The quote subsequently published *The Times*
6 *Messaggero Mestre* 7 Mar 73 speaking to a youth group in Venice the day he became a cardinal
7 *La Stampa* 28 Sep 78
8 Clipping is from *The Evening Bulletin* 29 Sep 78. The phrase appears in all newspapers of the time
9 *Messaggero Mestre* 22 Jan 76
10 *Veneto Nostro* 17 Sep 67
11 *Covet Action Quarterly* Washington DC No. 49, summer '94. *Washington Post* 28 Jun 76
121 *La Repubblica* 2 Aug 78 Luciani on artificial insemination
13 T. Frances Elliott's review of 'Murder by the Grace of God' *The Times,* London

Appendix A - Image Bibliography

Page   Shutterstock license ID 4EF4DD3C16029726C712D6106F2EB514393D541F 12/23/11
4   John Paul I Memorial – *author photo*   page 6:   John Paul I – *Associated Press*
7   Paul VI – *Associated Press*   page 8:   Avro Manhattan – *United Press International*
11   Jack's letter - *author property*
14   Caricature 'three popes in bed' by *Ben Vogelsang* – *author's property protected by copyright*
19   John Paul I - *Associated Press*
22   Papal Palace at night - *author photo reprinted on page 248*
27   Giorgione Altar – *author photo*
37   Anthony – *author photo*
38   Fatima crown - *shutterstock.com/Micael Antonio Maria*
40   Daniele – *author photo*
45   Funeral – *author photo*
50   Feltre tower – *author photo.* Cart - *shutterstock.com/Yannahlit*
52   Albino Luciani - *Angenzia Ansa 1923*
56   Boy reading Bible - *shutterstock.com/Mikale Damkier*
62   Battlefield graves & Hitler/soldiers attending mass - *German propaganda photos*
65   Neukolln Stadium - *Berliner Kurier 1934*
66   Bishops at Dachau/ Orsenigo-Hitler-Ribbentrop - *German propaganda photos*
67   Orsenigo-Hitler - *German propaganda photo*
73   Vittorio Veneto castle – *author photo, reprinted on page 173*
98   Benedict XVI - *Associated Press*
107   Angouleme Cathedral – *author photo*
113   Lucia Santos - *Verdade das Pessoas Oct 17, 1917*
119   Worship - *shutterstock.com/Stravinsky*   Child - *shutterstock.com/Meuniero*
126   Cardinals Krol and Wojtyla - *Philadelphia Inquirer* 29 Sep 69
137   John Paul II - *Associated Press*
141   8 year old Karol Wojtyla - *Laski Italfoto 1928*
142   Actor Karol Wojtyla - *Malopolska Silesia 1943*
144   Hitler Youth poster & scouts – *Yank magazine Nov 44*
146   Albino Luciani - *Italian Resistance photo 1942*
171   Sculpture female and two males – *author photo*
174   Photo of author – *author's property*
175   Ancient wall & bishop's mansion - *author photos*
176   Coat-of-arms & castle ceiling – *author photos*
204   God is always watching, *Shutterstock.com/Bruce Rolff*   'Matthew in Hell' *author photo*
210   Papal Palace – *author photo*
215   Papal Apartment - *Shutterstock.com/Xufang*
218   Caricature 'three popes in bed' by *Ben Vogelsang* – *author's property protected by copyright*
221   Diagram of the Papal Palace – *created by and property of the author*
223 & 224 Sanctae Marthae Palace corridor & sitting room *Associated Press*
228   Albino Luciani collage – *created by and property of the author*
232   Cards - *shutterstock.com/Argus*
276   Karol Wojtyla - *Malopolska Silesia* 7 Sep 78
288   Tomb of John Paul I - *author photo*
297   John Paul assassination attempt - *Associated Press*
298   Cedric Tornay - *Shutterstock.com/Jensen*
299   John Paul prays over coffin - *Associated Press1998*
321   Peteano Terror – *author photo*
323   Bush Inauguration – *author photo*
324   Nixon & Prescott Bush – *United Press International*
325   Red Mass – *author photo*
333   Moro Banner – *La Repubblica 1982*
356   Central America and Italy and Central America page 385 – *author maps*
402   Reginald Delargey – *author photo*
410   Pope and wine cellar – *author collage*   Front cover background - *shutterstock.com/Andriano*

Murder by the Grace of God

"Murder by the Grace of God" is the complete edition of 'Murder in the Vatican'

sequel to 'Murder by the Grace of God'

old partial edition

new complete edition

preview on: www.johnpaul1.org

The Reincarnation of Albino Luciani: In Search of the Human Soul

Important note: see page 75 in 'Murder by the Grace of God'

In 1947, Albino Luciani defended his doctoral thesis 'The Origin of the Human Soul...' in which he defined the human soul—just what is it one is trying to save? What's more, he stumbled upon the secret to eternal life.

Luciani's thesis is presented in a series of fun and entertaining conversations with a ten year old boy. As Dante once took the reader through the levels of hell, the reincarnated Luciani takes the reader through the heavens of the Christian, the Jew, the Muslim, the Hindu, the Buddhist, the Tao and one more—a long lost religion holding the secret to eternal life. One no longer has to guess. One can know in this life, one will live forever. Listen as he tells you what he meant, when he told us:

"Don't knock yourself out over smart monkeys and Adam and Eve. Each of us is responsible for our own evolution. We can either choose to remain as mortal men, or we can evolve as Gods."   Albino Luciani, February 26, 1947

'The Reincarnation of Albino Luciani' includes many stories of Albino Luciani's seminary days and young priesthood not included in 'Murder by the Grace of God.'

Author's books in paperback, hardcover and e-book are available on all Internet sites.

Signed & discounted on author's listing '**vaticandirect**' under '**new**' on Amazon.com

Booksellers: 48% discount UK and USA: bkorders@authorhouse.com 888 280 7715

Author's books are previewed on: **www.johnpaul1.org**

The newspaper plagiarizer

The reason most Albino Luciani biographies read the same is that they can be traced back to a 'biography' fabricated by the Vatican to destroy the liberal identity of the 33-day pope which David Yallop had so responsibly revived in 1984. Each 'biographer' plagiarizing those before them.

It has also been said, this book is not really my book. As one critic put it: "A greater newspaper plagiarizer has never come down the pipe." [1]

It is a composite of the work of a long line of reporters who recorded his every move from the time he became a bishop in 1958, to that time he woke up dead in his bed in the fall of 1978, and well beyond his death.

This book is about connecting dots that make the world go round.

Friend and foe have contributed to the accuracy of these dots.

Usually a reference date missed by a day or two, to a few who have found conflicting testimony in the press—the reason I often include more than one reference for an event to give both sides of the story so to speak.

I want to thank those of the medical and criminology world who have contributed to the proof of what at one time was little more than Avro Manhattan's suspicions: the conspiracy that planned the Great Vatican Bank Scandal was the same conspiracy that plotted the murder of John Paul I.

I want to thank those who have taken the time to review my work on the Internet and in journals and those I have met along the way—including Albino Luciani and Paul Marcinkus—that made it possible.

I want to thank those who recommend it to others.

Lucien Gregoire

Contact:

George Lucien Gregoire
University of Maryland
38 South Paca Street, # 403
Baltimore Maryland 21201
Email: vatican@att.net   voice: (1) 410 625 9741   author's books: www.johnpaul1.org

1 *ALR* Johnathan Steele, 22 Jan 2011; *Murder by the Grace of God* sources over 500 press reports

Made in the USA
Middletown, DE
31 January 2017